REMEMBER ARNHEM

Remember Arnhem

JOHN FAIRLEY

To Harry,
Best wishes
John Fairley

The Story of the 1st Airborne Reconnaissance Squadron at Arnhem

PEATON PRESS

Peaton Press
Bearsden

First published 1978
Reprinted 1979
Second edition 1990

ISBN 0 9515509 0 X

Printed in Great Britain by
Bell and Bain Ltd.
Thornliebank, Glasgow
for Peaton Press,
12 Birkhall Drive,
Bearsden, Glasgow
G61 1DB

For Freddie

The greatness of the Reconnaissance Corps lay in the distinctness and brilliance of its regimental identity, its style, smartness and flawless sense of standards . . . A regiment is an institution, not merely for achieving material ends, but for evoking the human virtues necessary for their achievement. When it succeeds in doing so, it has created something that cannot die and becomes itself undying.

SIR ARTHUR BRYANT

FOREWORD

Major-General R. E. Urquhart, C.B., D.S.O.
One time commander 1st Airborne Division

The 1st Airborne Reconnaissance Squadron was a unique small unit with a tremendous spirit. Its story during a comparatively short existence, but which took it from North Africa into Europe and then to Norway, and of the individuals who served in its ranks, is graphically described in this book; and few books of this kind have been so thoroughly researched. John Fairley had no connection with the unit during the war, and is therefore without the prejudice or loyalty which sometimes tends to influence such accounts, but there is no doubt as to his interest in the facts.

The greater part of the story deals with the experiences of the unit in Holland in September 1944. In telling this, the author, who has physically covered every yard of the ground over which it operated, gives as a background an accurate and well-balanced report of the 1st Airborne Division, during the Battle of Arnhem and Oosterbeek.

Future historians may well be grateful to John Fairley for this excellent result of persistent work.

Port of Menteith
1978

If in the years to come, you meet a man who says, "I was at Arnhem", raise your hat to him and buy him a drink.

Daily Express War Correspondent,
Alan Wood, reporting from the slit
trenches at Divisional Headquarters,
towards the end of the Battle.

PREFACE

From 17th to 26th September 1944, the 1st British Airborne Division fought at Arnhem and Oosterbeek in the Netherlands in a battle destined to be regarded as one of the most harrowing engagements of the Second World War. One of the units involved in the struggle was the highly specialized 1st Airborne Reconnaissance Squadron. This book is an attempt to tell the story of the Battle of Arnhem through the activities and involvement of the officers and men of that unit.

The research began from the simple beginnings of a personal enquiry into the circumstances surrounding the death of a friend, who was probably amongst the first half-dozen British soldiers to be killed. The interest generated as a result of that then led to a more extended investigation into the part played by the entire Squadron. At an operational strength of not more than 250 all ranks, the 1st Airborne Reconnaissance Squadron was only a small part of the total Divisional force. In no way was it comparable in size to any of the established parachute battalions, but its unique contribution stemmed from the fact that its representatives saw action in almost all the main sectors into which the battle fragmented. This was due, in part, to accidental circumstances, but, in the main, to the nature of the reconnaissance role itself.

Accounts of Arnhem have usually tended to concentrate either upon the broad strategy, with little of first hand reminiscence, or else to offer personal accounts, with only passing reference to the general stages of development through which the battle moved. The present book is an attempt to combine both approaches, by relating the documentary material of the official reports to individual recollection, in order to try to deepen and enrich the perspective.

What follows is the result of five years of research and investigation, which began with the major task of finding the men some thirty years after the event. The existence of an old comrades association – principally London-based – was an initial help but, for the rest, it was a matter of placing enquiry letters in numerous newspapers throughout the country. Thanks to the co-operation of the Press and an overwhelming response from the reading public, many more former members of the Squadron were then found, so that the final total of those traced came close to one hundred.

Most of the survivors are today living in Britain, but others are in Australia, Canada, Africa and mainland Europe. In nearly all cases, tape-recorded accounts have provided stories which have never before been included in any history of the Battle. Travelling the many miles, both at home and abroad, in order to interview people or visit archive deposits has been fruitful and rewarding, but it has also taken a great deal of time, which is why it has only now been possible to put the story together. The nature of the research has also been such that thanks are due to many people for help readily given. This has been done elsewhere in these pages, but I would also wish to express here a special word of thanks to Major-General Roy Urquhart and to the late Freddie Gough for all the interest shown and for the consideration and encouragement which they accorded me in the course of my work.

Despite all efforts, there remain a number of former members of the unit who have not been contacted. For the most part, any such deficiency has been largely redeemed through the generous co-operation and help provided by those who were traced. Consequently, as far as I am able to tell, and on the basis of the evidence that was available to me, what follows is an accurate account of the events which overtook the officers and men of the 1st Airborne Reconnaissance Squadron during the course of those memorable nine days. In some ways, the story may also be regarded as providing historical revision that is, perhaps, overdue. A great deal of mythology and over-hasty judgment has found its way into accounts of the Battle of Arnhem, and much of it has been perpetuated from one text to the next. The repeated assertion, for example, that the Reconnaissance Squadron lost nearly all its vehicles at the outset, due to glider mishap, has been generally accepted without question, yet it is wholly untrue.

In the narrative which follows, it is intended that the general reader should be able to follow the principal developments of the Battle, since the main outline of events runs as a thread throughout the account. Indeed, from the viewpoint of the military historian, it is possible to tell the story solely in terms of those events, and, in doing so, to examine the strategies, the tactics, and the battle orders of a great military force striving to attain an objective designed to bring about the speedy end of the war. Yet, there was more to it than that – something far and away beyond what is provided by the bare, impersonal narrative reports – for the fundamental substance of it all was human conduct and activity, the predictable and the unpredictable alike. Those who took part were perceptive, feeling individuals, with the virtues and vices, the strengths and weaknesses of everyday mortals. At none of the levels of operation was there anything of the super-heroic, which is why the account set down in the following pages is, above all else, a tale of ordinary men. Nevertheless, from the totality of it all, there emerges something that is truly extraordinary, for the sum of their collective experiences is unquestionably one in which the qualities of loyalty, endurance, comradeship and humour are mystically combined and interwoven so as to illuminate the unique human story and the unsurpassed epic of courage that will forever be immortalized in the name of Arnhem.

JOHN FAIRLEY
September 1978

PREFACE TO THE SECOND EDITION

Since the issue of the first edition in 1978, interest in the Battle of Arnhem and Oosterbeek has grown steadily and there has been a growing demand for opportunities to visit the battlefield. I should like, therefore, to thank my colleague, Barry Matthews of Galina International Battlefield Tours, Hull, for having responded to this, with tours of such high quality. I am also particularly grateful to my good friend, Henk Duinhoven of Oosterbeek for his encouragement and practical help to me.

JOHN FAIRLEY
February 1990

CONTENTS

ILLUSTRATIONS

Thanks are due to the following for permission to print illustrations:

Imperial War Museum, R. Guthrie, Mrs D. Barlow, D. van Woerkom, *Daily Mail*, Bundesarchiv Koblenz, Director of Ordnance Survey, J. Watson, H. A. Duinhoven, Associated Newspapers Ltd., Rank Organisation.

MAPS

PROLOGUE

It is the badge which makes it easy to pick them out – an upward-thrusting spearhead flanked by lightning bolts, forming an outline rather like that of a fir tree. The base is a scroll, upon which *Reconnaissance Corps* has been flawlessly chiselled into the stone. Most are found singly or in pairs, flanked by the badges of other regiments, but in one row there is a group of five, identical but for the names, the last of which is that of a young Scot from Motherwell – Tom McGregor – who came here to die.

Reading the inscriptions on adjacent stones . . . Bucknall – Goulding – Brumwell . . . one is vaguely conscious of the familiar ethnic amalgam that seemed to characterize army nominal rolls or duty rosters . . . Stacey – Irala – McSkimmings . . . until suddenly, like a camera lens sharpening into focus, the eye is arrested by Brawn, a name long forgotten but that instantly reawakens dormant memories of times long past. So, with a growing clarity, images and recollections of dreary rain-washed Lochmaben are resurrected into consciousness and one remembers how it was in that winter of 1942 . . .

Dominated by the red sandstone grace of Halleaths Hall, the sprawling complex of green-painted Nissen spread itself out over what had once been the woods and pasture land of a sizeable estate. Gone was the copse of evergreen that had screened the house from the south-westerlies that blew from the Solway. In its place was a waste land of tree stumps, bracken, scrub and a man-made assault course of formidable proportions. Flanking the desolation were the garages, vehicle parks, stores and offices. Beyond, stretched the grey concrete desert of the barrack square, from which the voice of RSM Harrison would daily rise in stentorian admonition, matching its strength to the challenging clatter of the passing Bren gun carriers.

The interminable tramp of marching feet, the torchlight squads searching for litter in the post-reveille darkness, the repetitive bugle calls that marked the phases of the day, Crosby's latest hit – "White Christmas" – harshly discordant on the NAAFI radio, recruits intoning their liturgical ONE-two-three-ONE, frost crackling under the tyres of the armoured cars, swishing wireless antennae, smoking coke stoves, spicy-smelling "blanco", green webbing, khaki berets, white stripes, stewed tea – each is a separate memory, yet all are recalled as kaleidoscopic elements in a pattern of movement, sound and scent that permeated the routine days and into which there was little intrusion by the outside world.

Into sharper focus comes the sloping meadow and the mud-churned path that linked the half-laid concrete road with the cluster of draughty tin huts at the bottom of the field. Names and faces flicker into consciousness – Evans, Watson, Brawn and all the others, each of whom, in his own way contributed towards the warmth and friendship of the group. Yet, what comradely unity there was could be very much a transitory thing, for change was an accepted condition of life in war time and each coming and going was always an occasion for readjustment.

It was no less so when, with training completed, the time came for section DO 5 to leave. Unlike the departure of previous drafts, theirs was a unique posting, for each was to join the airborne unit of the Corps. Worger and Turner were to remain behind as instructors for succeeding intakes, but Oakley, Evans and Brawn were to go and already, almost before the "goodbyes" were said, the select band seemed to have gathered around itself something of the mystical aura of "airborne". There were no passing-out parades in those early days, but just a handshake or two and some simple exchanges: "All the best – perhaps we'll meet again sometime – good luck." Then they were off, jolting down the pot-holed road, the exhaust from the "3 tonner" lingering on the damp Dumfriesshire air, long after we had waved them out of sight, already conscious that, as the new senior "class of '42", it would soon be our turn to be transferred to an active service unit.

Now the imagery of those far-off Lochmaben days surrenders to the quiet sanctity of this still place and to the reality of the inscriptions laid upon the light grey stone. It is here that the mute granite perpetuates the memories of the two with whom comradeship was once shared – Brawn, the friend who looked to a reunion, yet waved what was to be a last goodbye, and apprentice architect McGregor who, had he been given the chance might have helped build the brave new world for which he had fought. But for them, as for the others buried here in the Airborne Cemetery at Oosterbeek, there was to be no future – in September 1944, it suddenly ran out.

Chapter 1 JANUARY 1941–SEPTEMBER 1944

"Where have you been all the day, Billy boy?"

In its early stages, the struggle upon which Britain entered in 1939 was distinctly anticlimactic in any military sense. The euphoric optimism that marked the end of the "phoney" war was short lived, and the ultimate collapse of France in June 1940 a disaster which the "miracle" of Dunkirk did nothing to ameliorate. From the beaches of north-west Europe a demoralized British army was hastily shuttled back to England, leaving behind much of its arms and equipment as spoils for the victorious forces of the German Reich. That the anticipated invasion of England did not follow as a natural sequel was almost entirely due to the quality of resistance put up by Fighter Command of the Royal Air Force in the unforgettable struggle for air supremacy. Not until the woodland greenery of Kent had taken on the tints of autumn was the point of critical resolution reached. Only then was the Luftwaffe forced to concede defeat. For Britain, the long agony of the "Blitz" was still to come, but for the immediate and foreseeable future, she was to be spared the intolerable oppression that was already characterizing German conquest on mainland Europe.

Nevertheless, it appeared that, on land at least, the enemy was having it very much his own way, and so, in an attempt to counter the condition of virtual stalemate that had arisen, the decision was made to create a number of new and specialized units within the army. In part, the object was to support and, where possible, extend the type of harassment operation already developed by the commando units – what Churchill had referred to as "butcher and bolt" raids. Such a strategy was considered to be desirable, as much for its morale-boosting value as for the collection of military information or the destruction of enemy coastal defences. More than that, however, it was the response of a dynamic war leader whose plans for a more sophisticated military strategy included developments in everything from amphibious warfare, "striking companies", glider-borne forces and parachute units, to intelligence arms and espionage services that would be more skilled and daring than anything that had gone before. As a result, there emerged, amongst other new formations, the Parachute Regiment, the Glider Pilot Regiment, the Special Air Service and the Reconnaissance Corps.

At the time of its formation on 1st January 1941, the specific role of the Reconnaissance Corps was defined as that of obtaining "vital tactical information in battle for infantry divisions." Under conditions of wartime censorship, this strategic function was not publicized. Instead, bizarre alternatives were offered on press hand-outs and these found their way into print with additional colourful embellishments. As a result, there followed numerous articles about a new race of supermen who were capable of endless feats of physical endurance but who, at the end of it all, would still be capable of taking on any force that the Germans might put up against them. "They have to be tough," said the *Daily Mail*, "with cold, scientific brains behind their brawn." Nor was the British Broadcasting Corporation far behind the popular press in comparable and misguided comment. It was announced one morning on the eight o'clock news bulletin that, as the result of a Cabinet decision, the purpose of a newly formed unit – to be designated the Reconnaissance Corps – would be to provide a force of men who would throw themselves across barbed wire entanglements in order to form human bridges for the remainder of the division to use in carrying out a rapid advance upon the enemy. Thought up in terms of strategies more appropriate to the static warfare of the Somme, it was an odd piece of publicized nonsense that revealed nothing of the true function of what was to become one of the most diversified regiments in the British Army.

In truth, the proper function of the Reconnaissance Corps was to obtain and pass back information about the enemy's movements in the field. Out ahead of the division, the reconnoitrer's task of swift, penetrative probing was a skilled and dangerous one. With something like twice the fire power of the average infantry battalion, a reconnaissance regiment usually moved to the task in fast armoured cars and Bren gun carriers, with its own back-up assault troops and supplies carried in trucks or jeeps. Effective wireless communication was set up mainly through 19 or 22 sets, both of which had a normal operating range of ten miles on speech and further on morse. Since their task was as gatherers of information, this facility was essential to the proper functioning of a reconnaissance formation. Furthermore, as so-called "divisional" troops, their intelligence was not fed through normal brigade channels, but directly back to divisional headquarters.* "Their role," wrote Arthur Bryant, "was that of the cat's whiskers – armoured, mechanized transmitting whiskers. Those who served had to be intelligent, enterprizing, brave, enduring and highly skilled."

The men selected for the Reconnaissance Corps were privileged to wear its distinctive badge of a golden spearhead flanked by two lightning flashes. All derived pride from their unique role, so often undertaken behind enemy lines and never more appropriately epitomized than in the opening line of their own regimental march – "Where have you been all the day, Billy boy, Billy boy?" But the information obtained under battle conditions was often dearly bought, for, out of all who served throughout the five brief years of the Corps' existence, more than one in ten of them died in action. Regiments of the Reconnaissance Corps gained their battle honours in every theatre of operation, each one building up and cherishing its particular traditions and its unique corporate ethos. In this respect, none achieved greater distinction than the smallest of them all, the 1st Airborne Reconnaissance Squadron, spearhead of the 1st British Airborne Division.

The fact that it was considerably smaller in size than the average unit of the Reconnaissance Corps was entirely in keeping with its specialist role as part of an airborne division. Ordinarily, a regiment was made up of four squadrons, with each in turn divided into four troops. As a much smaller force of only single squadron strength, the airborne unit was well below the standard complement. Formed originally from the 31st Independent Brigade Anti-Tank Company, it emerged in January 1941 with its new title of 31st Independent Reconnaissance Company. In

* Out of this notion of communication by-pass, there emerged the GHQ Liaison Regiment, more colloquially known as "Phantom Recce". Recruited to a great extent, although not exclusively so, from the Reconnaissance Corps, its wireless links went straight from the front line to the War Office in London.

November of that same year, it became a glider-borne force and was once again renamed, this time as the 1st Air Landing Reconnaissance Squadron.* The first commanding officer was Major T. B. H. Otway, the man who was later to lead the memorable D-day attack on the Merville battery. Soon, however, he was succeeded by Major C. F. H. Gough, with whose name the unit became synonymous. It was Gough who built it up into the fighting force of distinction and quality which it subsequently became.

Freddie Gough's prime concern was to recruit officers who had those particular gifts of personal initiative and imagination that he considered most appropriate for the specialized reconnaissance role. As a consequence, all applicants were carefully vetted and scrutinized by the commanding officer, whose criteria of judgment were very much his own, and who knew exactly what he wanted. Not a few were returned to their original units, carrying neither stigma nor disgrace, but with their services regretfully declined, simply because they did not meet the Squadron commander's precise requirements. As for the other ranks, most of the senior NCO's were regular soldiers, drawn in originally by the prospect of a new and imaginative aspect of soldiering. Nevertheless, the bulk of the force was made up of men from Britain's wartime army; those who came at first, transferred from a diverse range of established units but, from 1942 onwards, the newly-established Reconnaissance Training Centre increasingly provided men for this, as for all other branches of the Reconnaissance Corps.

In April 1943, the Squadron left for North Africa on its first overseas assignment. Amongst other things, part of the time was spent in learning how to put down American Waco gliders, in the event of the pilot being hit. It was all great fun, with plenty of circuits and landings to be tried, but keenest interest centred on speculation about the build-up of forces for the imminent invasion of Sicily, following the Axis collapse in North Africa. When it was launched in July, the men of the Squadron were disappointed beyond measure by the fact that their own unit was left out of the invading force. In a partial attempt to remedy this, eight of the more warlike amongst them actually stowed away, but were discovered in the gliders, prior to take off. Jim Taylor remembers that each of them had "a tin of 'bully', a packet of biscuits, a water bottle and a fighting knife." During the weeks that followed, there was a slump in Squadron morale, in particular a feeling of being terribly out of things but, as the momentum of the Sicilian campaign grew, so did it become apparent that the next stage would be an early invasion of Italy itself. When it came, two months later, Gough's Squadron had its first opportunity for action.

The invasion of the Italian mainland was a three-phase operation. The central prong of the attack was launched on 3rd September, when Montgomery's 8th Army crossed the Straits of Messina to Reggio. Six days later, the United States 5th Army, including British 10th Corps, began "Operation Avalanche" with landings on the west coast at Salerno. Simultaneously, the 1st British Airborne Division was conveyed, not in aircraft but in ships, to land on the "heel" of Italy at Taranto. In the vanguard of this right-hand prong was the 1st Air Landing Reconnaissance Squadron, by then under the command of Hackett's 4th Parachute Brigade.

Following an unopposed landing, it was determined that the Squadron's task would be to move up the east coast, feeling out the enemy. Three parallel routes were then chosen for the reconnoitring and two of those were made the responsibility of the Squadron. The main part of Gough's force was to take the centre position on a road that ran through Massafra and Mottola

* In those early days, correspondence arriving at the unit often revealed certain misconceptions on the part of outsiders. Jim Smith, who was Orderly Sergeant at the time, still remembers a variety of odd addresses, like 1st Air Launching Wrecking Squadron, or 1st Air Laundry Squadron

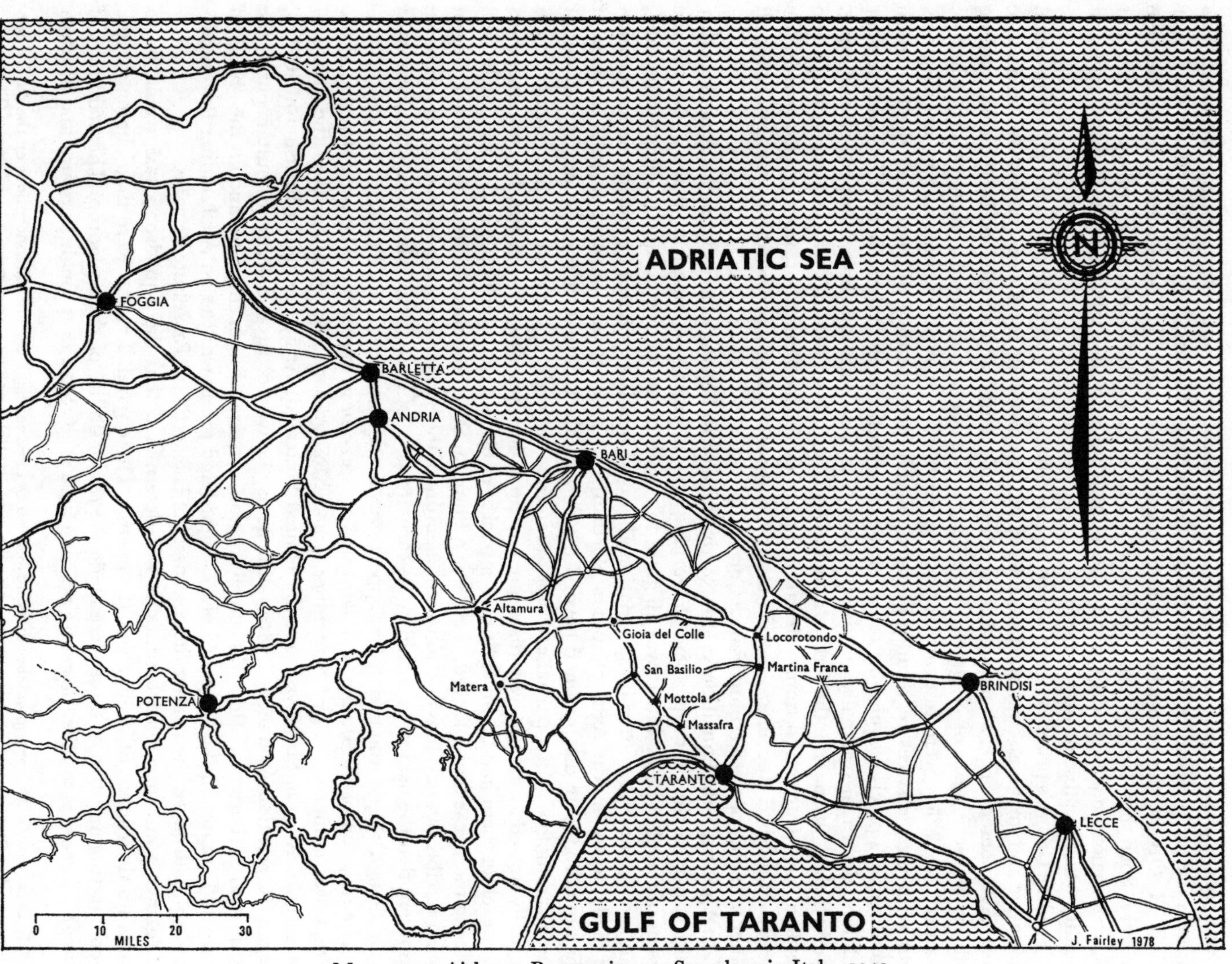

Map 1 1st Airborne Reconnaissance Squadron in Italy, 1943

to Gioia del Colle. B Troop of the Reconnaissance Squadron was to cover the right flank on a route through Martina Franca. The left flank was to be covered by the 2nd Special Air Service, and its job was to circle round by Matera and Altamura. Opposition permitting, the plan was for all three groups ultimately to converge on Gioia. One other unit, of a singularly much less orthodox kind, was also amongst the first to land. This was "Popski's Private Army", a group of mobile commandos under Lieutenant-Colonel Peniakoff, which had already established a colourful reputation as a freelance raiding force. Characteristically, it moved off immediately into the night, in the approximate direction of Rome!

On the centre route, the first Squadron contact came just north of Taranto, when the leading section of A Troop, commanded by Lieutenant Dougie Galbraith was fired on. Investigation led to the discovery that the adversary was an elderly Italian, who offered the rather threadbare excuse that he had been under the impression that they were Germans. Through an interpreter, the message was conveyed to him that, in the view of his British liberators, he was "a bloody old liar." Tom Firbank, the Troop commander, was later to recall that Galbraith, a lowland Scot, was very much attracted to the idea of a punitive demonstration: "Should we no' just lob a grenade in, and teach the bastard some manners?" From a purely disciplinary standpoint, such corrective action would undoubtedly have had a most salutary effect, but the notion was rejected on the grounds that it would be an unnecessary waste of ammunition. Instead, the old man was advised to get back to bed and behave himself, with the threat that, if he gave any more trouble, his house would be burned down.

In those early hours, groups of Italian soliders were also encountered at road blocks on the way. Officially, they were, by then, our allies and co-belligerents, but their loyalty was as suspect as their fighting qualities and neither the "Recce' men nor the SAS were disposed to trust any of them. So it was that, at the first encounter, the practice was initiated of making them lay down their arms, as well as submit to interrogation and search. Such caution proved to be wholly justified because, at the second road block, the British suddenly came under tracer fire. The firing was well wide of the mark but it was generally agreed that it was an unfriendly act, and it took all the linguistic persuasion of an accompanying SAS man, who spoke Italian, to persuade the hostile troops on the road block to desist. The opposition turned out to be a force of about a hundred Italian soldiers who, once the firing had stopped, were full of friendly, hand-flapping gesticulation and ingratiating smiles. The sudden transformation made little impression on the Reconnaissance Squadron men who, swiftly and at gun-point, relieved them of their arms and, in the process, handled the unprepossessing band in a manner that could only be described as "rough". Thereafter, the Squadron proceeded on its way, but took along an Italian officer whom it suspected might have knowledge of further ambush points. To ensure co-operation, as well as guarantee a measure of concentration on his part, the *capitano* was ordered to travel on the bonnet of the leading jeep. The tactic was successful, for the nervous agitation which he later displayed proved to be a clear indicator of hostile opposition ahead! And so it was that the Reconnaissance Squadron pressed on into the dawn at the beginning of its second day in Italy.

Just outside Massafra, on a straight open road, A Troop came under fire from long bursts of tracer. From the extreme accuracy of the shooting, it was obvious that the gun positions were manned, not by Italians, but by Germans and, indeed, although they did not know it at the time, the Reconnaissance men were up against the 1st German Parachute Battalion, soldiers of a calibre to match their own. Nonetheless, the encounter was a brief one for, under cover of an intense flanking fire put up by Galbraith's Section, the remainder of the Troop stormed in on their jeeps.

As the "Recce" boys entered at one side of the village, so did the Germans leave at the other. By the time the main body of 4th Parachute Brigade had caught up, Massafra was clear and the Squadron was already on its way to the next potential trouble spot, the village of Mottola.

Like Massafra and other villages of the Tulli district, Mottola stood high on a hillside, commanding the winding road that led up to it. Well ahead of the main brigade force, the Squadron's leading jeeps had begun to negotiate the hairpin bends on the lower section of road, when suddenly a hail of bullets swept across the convoy. Leading the party, Lieutenant Dougie Galbraith had them flick through his clothing, whilst others embedded themselves in the haversacks which were strapped to the bonnet of the vehicle. Immediate defensive action was taken, and all who could do so sought the shelter of the rocks and gullies of the hillside. There appeared to be two lines of defence manned by the enemy. The nearest was a group of trench positions on a small hillock; beyond that was a ridge with a more formidable row of pill-boxes. From both sets of German positions, a fair amount of fire, particularly that of machine-guns, was directed down towards the Squadron men, and this was supplemented by shell fire on the road.

In the circumstances, the logical move was to try to take the first set of German positions on the hillock, and this was tackled in style. Whilst one group of Gough's men produced well-sustained covering fire with the Brens, another detachment carried out a left-flank attack up the hill to the enemy emplacements on top. The move was completely successful and, under cover of smoke grenades as well as sustained bursts of Sten gun fire, the defenders were overrun. Following this, the Reconnaissance men consolidated their newly-won positions, pending the clearing of the pill-boxes on the ridge by the 156th Parachute Battalion. Not until this was successfully undertaken, would it be possible for them to relax, for there was still the danger of a German counter-attack.

Fears of this remained throughout the morning, and were heightened in the early afternoon, when it became evident that the ammunition reserves of the main attack force were dwindling. It was Craftsman George York, an attached member of the Reconnaissance Squadron who saved the situation. Very much an individualist, York, who really belonged to the Royal Electrical and Mechanical Engineers, was indistinguishable from the established members of the Squadron because, in preference to the insignia of his parent regiment, he wore instead, the Reconnaissance shoulder flash and cap badge. As an ex-London "cabby", he was an excellent driver and a first-rate mechanic; by his actions at Mottola, he demonstrated that he had the courage to match those gifts. Gough later described the event in which York was centrally involved: "At a critical moment, the 156th Battalion's 3-inch mortars were almost out of ammunition, but we ourselves had a reserve which was in a requisitioned Italian civilian lorry, just round a bend in the road, and refusing all efforts to start it. York went back, got it going and brought it up at speed, in full range of a German 88 mm gun, about 400 yards away. Nothing daunted, with shattered windscreen and bullet-holed canvas, he then helped to get it unloaded in record time. Miraculously, he survived without a scratch."

Both Brigadier Hackett and Lieutenant-Colonel Sir Richard de B. des Voeux, commanding officer of the 156th Parachute Battalion, were witness, together with Major Gough, to this very courageous act, and York was, there and then, immediately recommended for the award of the Military Medal. Characteristically, he later maintained that he had won it under false pretences, humorously adding that he had, all the time, been under the impression that the truck really contained blankets!

By mid-afternoon, the 156th Parachute Battalion had taken the ridge, following which it was the task of the 1st Airborne Reconnaissance Squadron to check for the presence of Germans in Mottola itself. David Christie remembers that this job was given to C Troop and that it was his own jeep which led the entry into the village square. Again the Germans moved out as the British came in, and it only remained to establish a working relationship with the local populace. This presented no difficulties whatsoever for, as Tom Firbank was later to recall, "We were subjected to a versatile Latin demonstration, which included an obese gentleman with a bunch of keys, dark-eyed beauties with bunches of grapes and their mothers with bottles of wine."

Shortly after the taking of Mottola, the decision was made to send out reconnaissance patrols towards San Basilio, in order to find out the new locations of the retreating enemy. On the way, A Troop met a German staff car, containing a Luftwaffe officer and two NCO's. They were taken prisoner, the first real Germans ever to be captured by the Squadron, and were marched off by their triumphant captors as a "present" for Freddie Gough. The contents of the suitcases which the Germans were carrying were sufficiently revealing to indicate that the trio, apparently oblivious to the turn of events, had set out with the intention of having a pleasurable weekend in Taranto. As one of the A Troop wits remarked, "They didn't just get a weekend off, they got a trip to England as well – jammy bastards!"

Inevitably, against troops of the quality of the German *Fallschirmjäger*, there were casualties. George Storrie of D Troop remembers that the first of those came, not long after they had started off down the road to San Basilio: "I remember that Mr Marshall went off on a single jeep patrol. He was driving, with his batman sitting beside him, and a wireless operator in the back. Just ahead of them, to the side of the road, were three trucks and, as we watched, German infantry appeared beside them. Unfortunately for the jeep, the truck convoy was concealing the presence of an armoured car, which opened up on them as they came within range." David Christie, who also witnessed what followed, remembers that the injuries inflicted were horrific. "One of them," he says, "had half his head blown off and the other was practically cut in half by bullets." George Storrie recollects that in the latter case, it was an MG 34 which caught the batman, just as he had swung his legs out over the side of the jeep in order to dismount: "From toes to waist, it just ripped the flesh from his body." Under covering fire supplied by Dougie Galbraith, it was the SAS man on attachment to the Squadron who volunteered to go out and help any survivors back to safety. Whilst this was happening, all three truck loads of German infantry came in for Galbraith's attention, and into one of them he poured a full Bren magazine, killing and wounding, in a matter of seconds, twenty-eight of the occupants.

At that stage, the Squadron had been in Italy for just over three days. On the morning after the unhappy episode involving John Marshall's jeep, they entered San Basilio, the Germans having once more faded away into the countryside beyond. The next objective was the agreed rendezvous point of Gioia del Colle, and it was near there, on that same day, that the main Squadron force ran into trouble.

In many ways, the initial contact was similar to that already encountered at Mottola. Once more they came under attack from the retreating Germans, who had again disposed themselves along a ridge of high ground to the south of the town. Caught in the open in a shallow cutting, the "Recce" men were pinned down by a merciless mortar bombardment, in a situation which deteriorated by the minute as the Germans gradually improved their aim. Only by scattering on the open ground and attempting to blend into the dun-coloured landscape were Gough's men able to restrict their casualties. Determined efforts were made to return the enemy fire, the most notable of which was an individual action on the Bren by Trooper Jim Taylor. Displaying a blend of coolness, tenacity and skill in weaponry, he did much to keep down the heads of the German mortarmen and so relieve the pressure. Taylor's courage was all the more commendable, considering that he was the only man left from a group of four, each of whom had been either killed or wounded. It was a left outflanking movement by the 156th Battalion that ultimately saved the day and brought help to the exhausted men of the Reconnaissance Squadron, who continued to lie in their exposed positions before realizing that, quite imperceptibly, the countryside had grown silent.

That night, they rendezvoused once more in San Basilio where, in the following few days, the pace eased a little. Understandably, patrols were still maintained, because there was the constant danger of a surprise German counter-thrust that could so easily drive the airborne men back along the way they had come. Besides, it was the unique task of the Reconnaissance Squadron to keep a finger on the German pulse, which is why reconnoitring was undertaken, not only in the immediate vicinity, but also by extended probes into enemy territory far beyond. Recalling this period, which was very much a mixture of rest, punctuated by intervals of intense "recce" work, David Christie, who was a Section Sergeant in C Troop, clearly remembers the details of one memorable foot patrol in which he was involved along with Lieutenant John Christie and Trooper Miles. At first, their reconnaissance was relatively uneventful until they were spotted by the enemy and had to take refuge in the outhouse of a farm. Mortar and machine-gun fire soon pinned them down and it was obvious that the only solution, short of surrender, was to shoot their way out. This they did successfully and with great rapidity, in spite of the bullets that zipped all around them as they ran out of the farm and down the road.

Minutes later, all three were scrambling for cover in a ditch, in order to avoid detection by a German armoured car. Thereafter, sanctuary was found in another farm which had a friendly proprietor and an absence of Germans. Unfortunately, no sooner had the Chianti been uncorked and mutual compliments exchanged, than British artillery shells began to land within twenty yards of them. "Whose bloody side are we on?" asked Miles, rhetorically. It was a valid point, for, no sooner had he spoken, than a particularly big bang took away part of the farmhouse roof. By the unspoken agreement of all three, it seemed as good a time as any to set out on their travels again, and so, making use of whatever cover was available in the adjacent vineyards and olive groves, they gradually worked their way back to the place where Squadron HQ had been earlier in the day. Numerous sightings of Germans were made on the way, which was why they approached with caution but, as Christie recalls, their "welcome" was even less orthodox than had been anticipated: "We moved cautiously forward and took a good look through the binoculars, to make sure that it was still our own and not a Gerry HQ. We could see several red berets lining the wall, and so we decided to walk straight in. We had just stepped from behind our cover, when a machine-gun rattled a burst over our heads. "You silly bastards!" yelled Lieutenant Christie, as we all dived for cover. We then started tossing our berets in the air, shouting, 'Recce-Recce!' and after that we were allowed into the HQ."

At that stage in the campaign, the Squadron could look back with some pride on its achievements. As spearhead of 1st British Airborne Division, it had undertaken a steady and aggressive advance of such rapidity that it had repeatedly bumped the rearguard of a retreating German airborne division. In general, it had been a highly successful and rewarding piece of sustained reconnoitring against enemy troops of a quality that was never in dispute. Nor was the Squadron's involvement entirely lacking in those touches of imagination and originality that can make even the quiet times memorable. Numbered amongst those must surely be the experience of

Lieutenant Michael Payne who, on the day after the landing at Taranto, was sent off to undertake a personal reconnaissance deep into German-held territory. He was away for the best part of a week, and got most of his information by talking schoolboy Latin to a retired Italian schoolmaster! All of it was of considerable value to Brigadier Hackett in planning the main attack on Gioia del Colle.

On 16th September, one week after the Taranto landings, the 10th Parachute Battalion took Gioia. Following this, the Reconnaissance Squadron took up fresh quarters in a large farm just outside the town, where, for the first time, news was received about B Troop, that part of the unit which had followed the most easterly route through Martina Franca. It was learned that, just beyond there, at Locorotondo, the party had run into a particularly bad ambush. It was something that was almost a natural hazard of "reconnoitring" and, in this case, the trap had been set up by the enemy at a Y-junction. As the Reconnaissance Corps jeeps reached the spot, the occupants came under frontal as well as enfilading attack from machine-gun fire and grenades. Corporal "Ally" Sloper, together with Troopers Tommy Quince and Henry Wood were killed almost immediately. Reg Burton, who took refuge below a jeep, lost a foot when an enemy grenade rolled in beside him and exploded. Many of the others were taken prisoner and only a handful managed, with difficulty, to extricate themselves. Cyril Simpson was one of those who escaped, suffering only a slight flesh wound in the back; he was later picked up by Popski's group.

The taking of Gioia marked the end of the opening phase of the campaign, and the Squadron members had an opportunity to overhaul equipment and catch up on some long-overdue rest. During the few days that followed, there was little in the way of enemy action but, at one stage, the farm went on fire in the middle of the night. The situation was complicated by the fact that the ammunition was stored in the cellar. To save it, the soldiers had to don respirators and work for hours to get it all to safety. At one point, the comic-opera fire brigade from Gioia provided entertaining light relief and, although it failed to make an impact on the fire, the antics of the fire-fighters did much to keep up the spirits of the men!

Long-range reconnaissance work carried out northwards from Gioia laid the foundation for the next order which was to press on to Bari and, if possible, take it. This time, the Squadron moved as a single force, with A Troop in the lead, followed by C, then D, with HQ Troop bringing up the rear. The run up to Bari was made in record time, the town was taken with no local resistance whatsoever, and, indeed, it was felt that the whole business had been disappointingly quiet. "Our jeeps," as Tom Firbank remarks, "took their place in the traffic, obeyed the police signals, and their occupants behaved with decorum. Short of an ill-mannered Wild West entry with guns blazing skyward, there was little we could have done to infuse drama into the situation."

As the vanguard of the victorious liberating forces, it was appropriate that the Squadron should take up residence in the best available accommodation. To this end, a school was commandeered, with Squadron HQ established only a hundred yards or so away in the Imperial Hotel on the sea front promenade. From this somewhat unorthodox base, the Squadron carried out its probes in the wake of the retreating German forces. Such, indeed, was its high mobility that, for a time, as Tom Firbank recalls, it was possible after a day's skirmishing with the enemy to return to the Hotel in the evening for a bath and dinner!

Soon afterwards, according to plan, elements of 78th Division began to advance through the Reconnaissance men, so that it was clearly time to be off again. The order was to press on to Foggia, by way of Barletta, which was further up the coast. Barletta turned out to be nasty, not so much on account of the German resistance encountered, as the activity of the mosquitos. "No one," says Jim Taylor, "got any sleep for them. They crawled inside clothing, up gaiters and bit us unmercifully – by morning, we were unrecognizable to each other, our faces and hands all swollen." It was with some relief that they got under way next morning, a day on which they were to make the longest run to date. Whether it was due to an impetus born of rage or simply a desire to be clear of the Barletta swamps is not clear, but by nightfall the Squadron had reached Foggia and there excelled itself. The orders called for a report on the position at Foggia airport, which the Germans were using as a base. Later that night, Major Gough was able to radio back that, not only were things just fine at the airport, but that he had pursued the matter to a logical conclusion by capturing and occupying it! Some damage had already been sustained as the result of an earlier attack by "Popski" who, it was said, had brought his men to the place in taxis! Nevertheless, the "Recce" boys found the airfield still functioning and actually caught the German ground crews still at work, servicing the Ju 88s. Once established, they commandeered the aircraft ammunition, stripped the guns from the planes and mounted them in pairs on their own jeeps. As Jim Taylor remembers, "They made a lot of noise, were not particularly accurate, but were a great morale-booster." As far as Reconnaissance Squadron tactics were concerned, this was a foretaste of the use of the more accurate Vickers "K" gun, which was to feature so prominently in their subsequent activity.

From a soldier's point of view, Foggia was a most satisfactory episode, for it was a blend of independent initiative and swashbuckling success, in which the victors emerged unscathed. What mishaps befell members of the Squadron were more attributable to Italian sanitation and the unhealthy nature of the terrain than to Germans. It was at Foggia that Sergeant George Storrie, who had distinguished himself in the earlier action and been "mentioned in despatches", was singularly unfortunate in contracting a virulent strain of malaria, which troubled him for many years thereafter.

By then, it was the end of September, and Foggia was to be the ultimate extent of the Squadron's advance. The divisional bridgehead was, by then, well established and, on the main fronts to either side of the Apennines, the allied forces were pressing on with their advance. Anzio, Cassino and the breaching of the Gustav line still lay in the future but, for the Reconnaissance men, the Italian chapter in their own unit's history was over. There followed some weeks of rest at Bari, clouded to some extent by the loss of Captain "Horsey" Waterman on a routine flight back to North Africa, until, eventually, the Squadron re-embarked at Taranto for the return to Philippville in North Africa. For a relatively small unit, which had never before heard a shot fired in anger, its success had been remarkable and, in a practical way, was a fitting tribute to the leadership, determination and drive of its commander. Together, they had proved themselves to be more than a match for the high-quality opposition, and a number, including Freddie Gough himself, earned well-merited decorations. Throughout it all, he had been an inspiration to the members of his Squadron, never flagging in his efforts, always in on the action and, by his very presence, constantly imparting the personal confidence that only a good commander can give. On the lighter side, Freddie Gough's distinctive impact was, in other respects, also unique for, all through the brief campaign, he wore a black eye patch, the result of concussion following a bad parachute landing in North Africa. As Jim Taylor was later to remark, "With his prematurely silver hair, he closely resembled a jeep-borne bishop turned pirate, much to the discomfiture of friend and foe alike!"

Sadly, of course, a price had to be paid for success – one familiar to any active "Recce" regiment – for, predictably, the casualty rate was high, and today, there are those who still lie buried under the warm sun that shines on Gioia del Colle. In December 1943, the unit was recalled to England, to be based in the village of Ruskington, just outside Sleaford in Lincolnshire. There, it was reorganized in a number of different ways. In the first place, the total complement was reduced from five to four Troops, with the roles of each reaffirmed in the light of the Italian experience. Central to the organization was HQ Troop. Like the others, it could be involved in the basic functions of reconnaissance and, when necessary, fighting. In addition, its administrative responsibility encompassed ration provisions, storage of ammunition and supplies, maintenance of radio links, interrogation of prisoners and care of wounded. Its subdivisions into various small specialized sections, such as Intelligence, Transport, Quartermaster and Signals, each under its own officer, reflected the diversity of function. There was, in addition, a Support Troop, much smaller than any of the others, alternatively designated as "Mortar" Troop, since one of its major purposes was responsibility for the Squadron's 3-inch mortars. In essence, it was really an extension of HQ Troop and worked in close conjunction with it.

The three other Troops within the new Squadron structure were those with the principal job of carrying out the forward reconnaissance work for which all personnel had been trained. Their task was to pass back information to Squadron HQ, which then relayed it, on its own rear link wireless, to Division. The operational Troops were respectively designated A, C and D, and the unusual lettering was a consequence of the loss of B Troop in Italy. It was never reconstituted.

Troops A, C and D, each consisted of about thirty men, organized into a Troop HQ and three numbered Sections.* Each Section was commanded by a subaltern, who controlled two vehicles, one of which was on a wireless link back to the Troop commander's own vehicle. A single vehicle's complement was four or five men which meant that there were approximately eight to ten per Section. One of those was the Section Sergeant, who was second-in-charge, and travelled in the other vehicle from the officer. Troop HQ also consisted of two vehicles, with the Troop commander in one, and the Troop Sergeant, who was the senior NCO, in the other.

In overall charge of HQ Troop as well as all three operational Troops, was the Squadron commander. His responsibility was the general command of Squadron activity, in terms of orders received directly from the Divisional commander. He was assisted in this by his second-in-command and his adjutant.

The second major change after Italy was even more fundamental. From the beginning of 1944, the Squadron entered upon a lengthy spell of intensive training, during which time it was gradually converted into what was mainly a parachute unit. As such, it still had to air land its heavy equipment from gliders, but it now had the additional capability of being able to despatch the bulk of its personnel by parachute drop.

The process of training members of the Squadron as parachute troops had, in fact, begun some time earlier, for even before the Italian campaign a number had gained their "wings", either on courses at Ringway or by undertaking the requisite jumps in North Africa. Alf Hazell was in the latter category, and still recalls it as a rather hazardous affair: "On our first drop of 'slow pairs', 'Jock' Pow was standing at the door, ready to go, when another aircraft flew past with a poor bloke dangling from its tail. 'Jock' saw this, and it must have given him a bit of a turn, but he jumped just the same and got down safely. The other one of my own "pair" was Bert Welham, and he dropped on his head. I remember, too, that we had to do one night jump, and how the

* The pre-Italy numbers were retained but, since B Troop had disappeared, it meant that the new organization did not include any Sections numbered 4, 5 or 6.

American pilot made a mistake by dropping us on top of an Arab village. Everyone was slightly hurt, but Gwyn Williams was unlucky enough to land in the middle of a cactus hedge. It was funnier for us than it was for him, because we were picking spines out of him for days afterwards!" Nor were the mighty exempt from the incalculable hazards of practice jumps, although it could still have its humorous side. Henry Venes still remembers Major Gough first appearing on parade with the black patch covering his eye injury and how, for months afterwards, in the privacy of the Sergeants' Mess, the CO was invariably referred to as "Long John Silver".*

But much the greatest effort in respect of parachuting was made following the return to England in December 1943. As a result, over a period of three months of concentrated and vigorous work, the unit gradually acquired a new tactical flexibility, in recognition of which it was renamed the 1st Airborne Reconnaissance Squadron. This was the title that it was to retain for the remainder of its existence. Nevertheless, not all the effort that went into the training of 1944 was parachuting and glider work. In a sense, these were the "glamour" aspects of the job, yet there were other things of equal importance that had to be done. Not the least of those was the maintenance of a level of physical fitness throughout the unit, appropriate to the exacting role which the Squadron was likely to have to undertake in future operations. For such reasons, everyone, including the CO, undertook a daily "run-walk" of anything up to ten miles, complete with all equipment, arms and ammunition. Even the water bottles had to be full!

Foremost amongst the leaders on such purgatorial cross-country forays was Freddie Gough himself. The silvery hair made for ease of identification but, in addition to that, he was always recognizable as the one with the dog! This was a Dandie Dinmont terrier, called "Swilly". Originally named "Robbie", such was his enthusiasm for the duty officer's daily inspection of the cookhouse swill bins, that it was changed to "Robert Swill". But the fact that this name was considered to be one wholly lacking in distinction soon led to a further change, and it was extended to "Robert Ramsbottom-Swill", in part after the name of a New Zealand Hurricane pilot with whom Freddie Gough was friendly. Understandably, perhaps, the dog's friends simply called him "Swilly" and, as his activities extended beyond the inspection of the bins and encompassed, amongst other things, all glider training flights, "Swilly" achieved the rare distinction of being the only dog to participate in the first night glider landing to be carried out in the United Kingdom.

On the technical side, one of the main features which distinguished the 1st Airborne Reconnaissance Squadron from other units of the Corps was the nature of its transport and associated armament. Ordinarily, the average reconnaissance regiment operated in advance of its division, using either the stylishly designed Light Reconnaissance Humber Mark IIIA armoured car, with a turreted Bren, or the stronger 7 ton Humber "Heavy", in particular the Mark IV, which took a 37 mm gun and had a top speed of 45 mph. For cross-country work, a regiment also habitually used the Carrier Universal, a light open-topped tracked vehicle which, under a variety of conditions, more than proved its worth, in respect of speed and versatility. "Soft" transport, like 15 cwt trucks, was also part of a regiment's complement, particularly for the movement of supplies or the swift deployment of an assault group in a situation where the information could, perhaps, only be obtained following a preliminary surprise attack.

By contrast, the characteristic transport and armament of the 1st Airborne Reconnaissance

* This was the patch, referred to earlier, which he wore throughout the Italian campaign. Later on, he discovered that he had had it on the wrong eye, but the net effect was that the injured eye got just the kind of exercise that it most needed.

Squadron was quite different. One major determinant, of course, was that it was normally expected to travel to battle by air, and so, like other airborne units, would have fewer men and less transport than comparable ground units of the same type in other divisional formations. The other was that, until late 1944, the British army was simply not equipped to airlift the range of transport which a standard unit of the Reconnaissance Corps would normally be expected to use. As a consequence, the basic vehicle type used throughout the Squadron was the Willys jeep, a highly mobile and manoeuverable general purpose vehicle that was ideal for quick reconnaissance sorties. So swiftly, indeed, could the Squadron move, that Alf Webb still recollects an evening in Italy when they suddenly came up fast on a German convoy, travelling ahead of them. "There was only one thing we could do", he recalls, "and that was to pull out and overtake them. We got past without any trouble."

Yet whatever advantages such vehicles might have possessed in terms of speed, there were comparable drawbacks, stemming principally from their lack of armour and open sides. As a result, only their own speed, combined with substantial weaponry, could help counter the vulnerability of the occupants, who were obvious sitting targets for enemy fire. Of such tactical weakness Major Gough was himself only too well aware, but the difficulty was that the Horsa glider, which was then the standard one in use, could not take a heavier vehicle. As events were to prove, this limitation was to be of decisive significance in relation to the Squadron's subsequent role at Arnhem. Not until the post-Arnhem period and the increasing availability of the heavy duty Hamilcar with its additional twenty-two feet of wing span was it possible for the Dingo armoured car to be included in the Squadron's establishment.

The other mode of transport which the Squadron used was motor cycles, conventionally designed, light in weight, and each with a two-stroke engine, capable of high speeds. These, however, were employed from Squadron HQ for the traditional despatch rider function that was not unique to a Reconnaissance unit.

As for the armament that was carried, the small arms were standard infantry equipment. For dismounted action, they tended to rely upon the Bren LMG,* the Sten gun Mark V and the Mark VII version of the well-tried and multi-purpose 2-inch mortar. All of these were popular weapons. They also had a variety of pistols, as well as the No. 4 Mark 1 Lee Enfield rifle, with the eight-inch spike bayonet. This last feature was to prove its worth in some of the Arnhem actions, although, for soldiers accustomed to the secondary functions of a bayonet as a tin opener or wood chopper, it was unjustifiably condemned! The Squadron also had an issue of a number of No. 4(T) rifles. These were standard Lee Enfields, fitted with a No. 32 telescope sight, and they later proved to be very effective in action.

Like other airborne units, the Reconnaissance Squadron was armed for anti-tank work, principally with the PIAT gun† and a range of grenades, which included that unique product of the British airborne forces, the "Gammon" bomb. Amongst other anti-tank missiles was the very effective Hawkins No. 75 grenade. This was oblong-shaped and had a crush igniter, so that it could be thrown or placed flat on the ground to act as a mine. For short range anti-personnel action, there was, of course, a plentiful supply of the classic No. 36 M grenade, last of a long line known simply as the "Mills bomb". This was the British equivalent of the famous German stick grenade, both having in common the feature that they were intended to be thrown by hand.

* Light machine-gun.

† An anti-tank gun which fired a 3 lb grenade and was effective over a combat range of 100 yards. The term PIAT derived from the initial letters of "Projector, Infantry, Anti-tank".

For screening purposes in action, bakelite smoke grenades were also carried. This constituted the range of smaller weapons that were carried into battle by the 1st Airborne Reconnaissance Squadron, and in nature they were not essentially different from those of any normal infantry combat unit within an airborne division. It was in respect of the heavier and more formidable weapons that there was, perhaps, a greater measure of divergence. This was notable in two ways.

In the first place, the Support Troop of the Squadron was unique in its fire power by having responsibility for two Polsten guns. The Polstens were really anti-aircraft guns of 20 mm calibre but, with a rate of fire of 450 rounds per minute, they were formidable weapons. Essentially cheaper versions of the famous Swiss Oerlikon guns, and each weighing approximately the same as a 3-inch mortar, they were towed on small gun carriages behind Support Troop jeeps. With all this fire power to add to that of the small arms carried by the men, it is hardly surprising that Lieutenant-General Browning, commander of the British Airborne Corps, was wont to refer jocularly to the Squadron's Support Troop as his "Chinese Cracker".

More conventionally, the Support Troop also had charge of two 3-inch mortars. These were the basic infantry support weapons of standard medium issue, as used in other Reconnaissance units. They were moved around by jeep and trailer because, although a team of men could carry such a weapon manually, its total weight of 126 lbs made vehicle transport desirable, and all the more so considering that each of the bombs weighed ten pounds. By the time of the Arnhem campaign, improved propellants had pushed the effective range of this weapon up to a distance of 2750 yards, with a rate of fire of ten rounds per minute.

As well as the Polsten gun, a second unique feature of the Squadron's heavier armament lay in the use of the Vickers "K" machine-guns, which were mounted on all its jeeps. These had at first been designed for use in RAF two-seater aircraft, and they were originally known as Vickers C.O. guns. With the decline in popularity of the open cockpit-type aircraft, the gun was gradually discarded. At the same time, however, it was adopted by certain of the less orthodox land units, especially for situations where sharp, concentrated fire power needed to be combined with speed and mobility. For the Long Range Desert Group and the Special Air Service, these qualities were of primary importance, and it was a tactical format which they shared with Gough's Reconnaissance Squadron. For that reason, by late 1944, the "K" guns had become, in a sense, the Squadron's most unusual yet most characteristic weapons.

By the middle of 1944, the unit had reached a peak of readiness and was eager for an opportunity to test its new structure, organization and armament. Understandably, therefore, there was acute disappointment when the 6th Airborne Division, rather than the 1st, was chosen for the key task of holding the flank to the north-east of Caen, at the time of the Normandy invasions. For the men of the 1st Airborne Division, there remained an irksome reserve role, in which training was maintained, and rumour fed upon rumour as the consolidation of the bridgehead on the French beaches made it apparent that the need for further airborne action would almost inevitably follow the break out.*

Despite this, the 1st Airborne Division's opportunity was to be a long time in coming for, in those thirteen weeks that extended from D + 5 to the second week in September, no less than sixteen major operations were worked out in meticulous detail, only to suffer, in all cases, last minute cancellation. In those well-intentioned yet abortive examples of military planning, there was never any lack of diversity. On one occasion the Division was briefed to drop on St Malo, in an operation code-named "Wild Oats"; in yet another instance, "Operation Transfigure" was

* Indeed, during the Normandy fighting, itself, four follow-up operations were planned and subsequently cancelled.

to be a joint Anglo-American attempt to take Paris. In most cases, the reason for cancellation was either the inappropriate timing of the operation and the possible jeopardizing of the airborne forces or else the swiftness of the allied advance that led, in a number of instances, to the ground forces over-running those very objectives that had been earmarked for airborne attack.

Throughout all of this – an incredible average of something like one cancelled operation every five and a half days – the Squadron remained split into two major elements. Based at Ruskington was the majority of the men who would be transported to the objective and then dropped by parachute. The smaller group, centred on Tarrant Rushton in Dorset, was the glider party, with responsibility for the Squadron's vehicles, trailers, heavy equipment and ammunition. Its job was to travel to the designated landing zone in gliders towed by powered aircraft and there to rendezvous with the main parachute party. Thereafter, the Squadron would immediately move into action as an integrated force.

In the constantly uncertain situation that developed as a result of the many cancelled operations, one of Major Gough's main problems was that of keeping his small force in a state of permanent battle-readiness. Sprung from one of Britain's most distinguished military families, no one could have been more eager than Gough himself to get into the fight. At the same time, he was sufficiently responsive to the reactions of his men to appreciate that, in many instances, their mounting frustration matched his own. It was fortunate for them that they had a commander of such sensitivity and individuality, for he was only too well aware of the need to keep up morale and to sustain it throughout a succession of anticlimaxes. Alf Hazell still remembers the consequences of one cancelled operation: "As usual, we were all briefed, and word came through that it was cancelled. Well, Freddie did his nut over that, so he took the whole Squadron off on a holiday to Weymouth. There was no reveille, no booking in, no guards, no bull – nothing!"

For Major Gough, this was undoubtedly a tension-relieving process, yet he and his men had to endure several more such disappointments in the weeks that lay ahead. The fact that everything and everybody had to be kept in an almost permanent state of readiness did not help, because, as far as the men were concerned, it meant confinement to camp in the period immediately prior to an operation. The irksome nature of such a restriction was felt more keenly by some than by others and, in consequence, there was those who, against all regulations, were prepared to break out of camp in order to relieve the monotony. Two such individuals were Troopers Frank Mann and Jimmy Bruce, both from Scotland, who, on an evening in early September, sought relief from boredom in a neighbouring Sleaford hostelry. Understandably, on their way back in the darkness along the straight road that lay between Sleaford and Ruskington, they were reluctant, for fear of discovery, to follow the normal practice of thumbing a lift. Vehicle after vehicle was allowed to pass, as each time they hid by the side of the road from the betraying beam of the headlights. This, in itself, was a tiring process, however, and it was hardly surprizing that two weary soldiers should eventually have decided to chance the possibility of detection. As Frank Mann recalls, "We saw this fresh pair of dimmed headlights appear far along the road and when they drew nearer we stepped out with our thumbs up. It was a small army truck, and when it stopped, Major Gough's voice said, "Get in!" That was all he said. We got our lift back to Ruskington all right – straight to a night in the guardroom!"

So it was that, alternately standing to and standing down again, the Squadron passed the long summer days. Each time, like all the other units comprizing the 1st British Airborne Division, it went repetitiously through the procedures leading up to imminent departure, only to have everything called off at the last minute. It was hardly surprizing, as some of his men still recall, that a frustrated Freddie Gough was overheard to refer irately to the "First British Still-born Division". For many, the successive briefings were producing a loss of credibility and a growing belief that it would never happen. In the second week in September came the warning of one more stand-by which, understandably, many regarded as "just another flap". They had no inkling that this one was to be different – its code name was "Market Garden".

Chapter 2 SUNDAY 10th–SATURDAY 16th SEPTEMBER 1944

"We may be going a bridge too far"

Operation "Market Garden" was an imaginatively conceived attempt to finish off the war in Europe by the end of 1944. From the time of the breakout at the Normandy bridgehead until the beginning of September 1944, the enemy had been thrown out of northern France, Belgium and Luxembourg. From the Seine to the Moselle and beyond, the 1st and 3rd United States Armies had pursued the retreating German forces whilst, further north, the 1st Canadian and 2nd British Armies had crossed the Somme to liberate the north-east corner of France and the whole of Belgium. So successful were the allies that they found their own lines of communication becoming increasingly stretched as the advance was pushed along at a rate which far exceeded what had been hoped for. An additional difficulty was that there were still insufficient ports in use to bring in supplies. Nevertheless, the German troops in the west had taken such heavy defeats that, in Montgomery's view, it required only one final decisive thrust to end the struggle in Europe.

The basis of his plan was that the 2nd British Army under Dempsey should drive northwards from the eastern border of Belgium, through the Netherlands to the Zuider Zee. From there, Dempsey could wheel to the right, outflank the Siegfried Line which extended only to Goch and, in one swift decisive blow, isolate Germany from its industrial base of the Ruhr and strike straight to the heart of the Reich itself. It was a strategy designed to rout an enemy still suffering from the major defeats of Caen and Falaise and the harassment of retreat before an allied advance that seemed, almost daily, to be gathering an increased impetus and momentum.

For the achievement of this grand plan, speed was vital. Such was the terrain, however, that there were formidable obstacles to be overcome. These were the numerous water crossings of Holland, which ran from east to west and which were likely to be stubbornly defended by the Germans. The three most important were the bridges over the Maas, the Waal and the Neder Rijn. To facilitate the advance of the 2nd Army, therefore, Montgomery proposed that troops of the 1st Allied Airborne Army, under Lieutenant-General F. A. M. ("Boy") Browning should in one simultaneous airborne operation, land beyond the enemy's front in order to capture and secure all the bridges and canal crossings that lay between 2nd Army and its initial coastal objective on the Zuider Zee.

Browning's total strength was to consist of a major part of the 1st Allied Airborne Army. Thus, under command he was to have two American Airborne Divisions, the 82nd and 101st, as well as two elements of his own Corps, the 1st British Airborne Division and the 1st Polish Independent Parachute Brigade Group. Aircraft and gliders were to be provided by 38 and 46 Groups of the Royal Air Force and by 9th United States Troop Carrier Command.

To the 101st United States Airborne Division under Major-General Maxwell Taylor was assigned the task of securing the canal bridges at Zon and Veghel in the Eindhoven area. Further north, at Nijmegen, the 82nd United States Airborne Division under Major-General James Gavin was to drop and secure the bridge over the Maas at Grave, the road and rail bridges over the Waal at Nijmegen and the Maas-Waal canal bridge south of Nijmegen. The task of capturing and holding the most northerly objective, Arnhem road bridge, was given to the 1st British Airborne Division under Major-General Roy Urquhart, with 1st Polish Parachute Brigade, led by Major-General Stanislas Sosabowski, under command. It was this third and most northerly objective that troubled Browning, especially when related to the distance of sixty-four miles which would have to be covered by the main force in order to link up with the British and Polish airborne troops. For this reason, he questioned Montgomery about how long his northern group would be required to hold Arnhem Bridge. To Montgomery's assurance that two days would be sufficient, Browning then made his now prophetic reply, "We can hold it for four, but I think we may be going a bridge too far."

Meantime, it had been decided that Browning's headquarters would be located somewhere in the Nijmegen area, from which base he would direct the anticipated two-day operation. It was also agreed that, following the consolidation of Urquhart's forces in the Arnhem area, 52nd (Lowland) Division, by then reorganized from its original mountain warfare role into one of air-transported troops, was to be flown into Deelen airfield, to the north of Arnhem.

The ground plan to accompany all this was that, from the start line of the Meuse-Escaut Canal, just thirteen miles south of Eindhoven, the 2nd Army would begin its advance at the same time as the airborne landings. Leading with the principal thrust would be 30 Corps under Lieutenant-General Brian Horrocks, with 12 Corps and 8 Corps respectively on his left and right flanks. Horrocks's Corps was to be led by the Guards Armoured Division. Once the water crossings were secured and guaranteed, this main force would then, in Montgomery's phrase, advance upon an "airborne carpet" that would take it all the way on its ninety-nine mile journey through Eindhoven, Nijmegen and Arnhem to the shores of the Zuider Zee. Once across Arnhem Bridge, the north German plain would be open and the final offensive would then take the war straight into Germany.

Such was the master strategy upon which Montgomery's hopes were pinned. On paper, it presented a pleasing simplicity of design but, as events were to prove, the optimism generated at Montgomery's HQ was wholly unwarranted. Objectives, however desirable, need planning according to a blueprint which, no matter how clear-cut it may be, has to be informed by an internal logic. It was this quality which, from the outset, "Market Garden" so demonstrably lacked, for too many imponderables remained unresolved and too many important questions were left unanswered.

For the planning of his own contribution to the operation Major-General Urquhart had precisely seven days, for it was fixed for Sunday 17th September. The briefing received in Browning's caravan had given him his broad remit in the most succinct of terms: "Arnhem Bridge and hold it." Roy Urquhart, very much the professional infantry soldier who knew his business well, had taken over the Division in December 1943. His distinguished record in North Africa, Sicily and Italy had preceded him, and, although he himself had no previous airborne

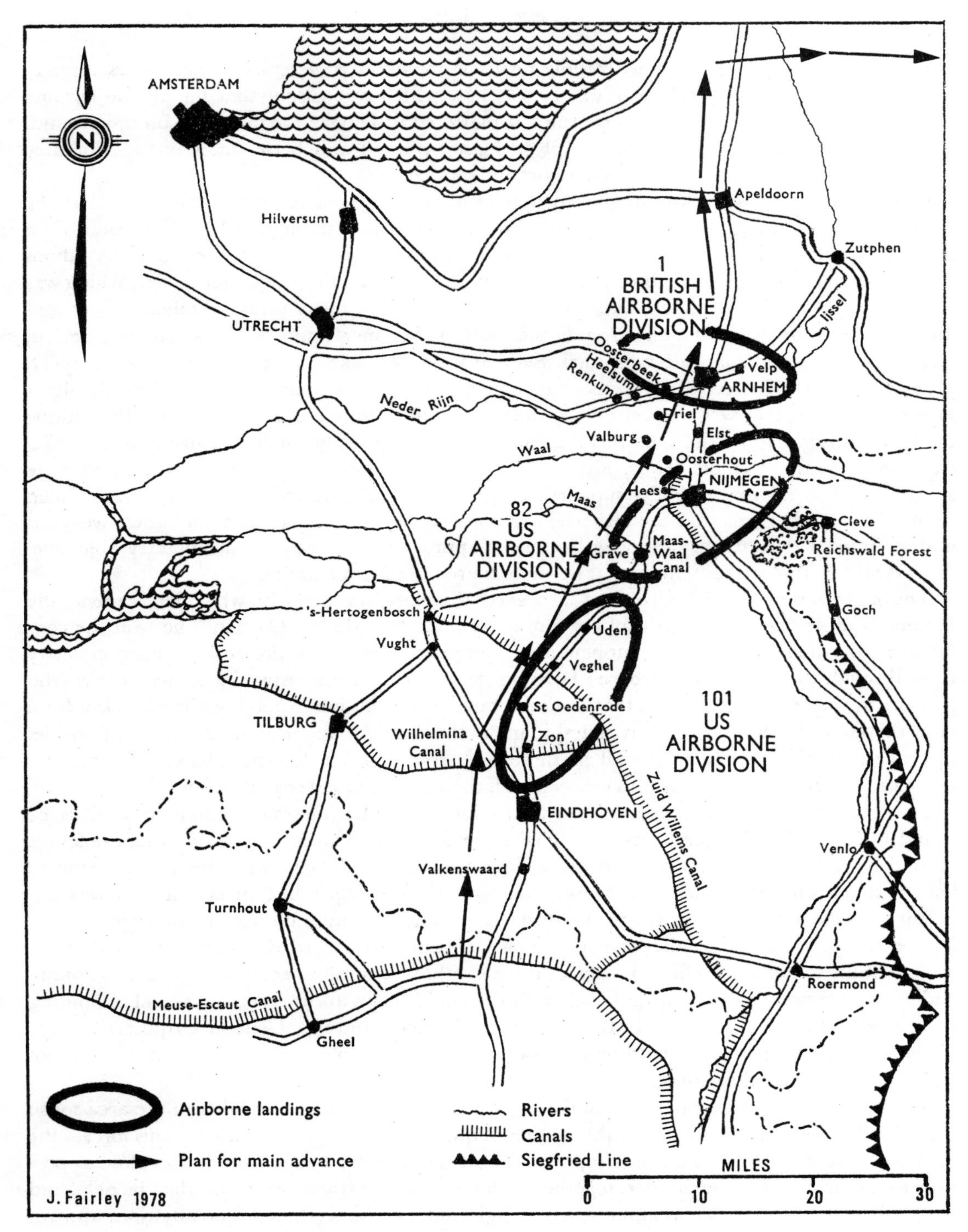

Map 2 Plan of Operation "Market Garden"

experience, he had been assigned to his new command in preference to brigadiers already associated with airborne-style warfare. It was felt, with justification, that for all the *mystique* which surrounded the notion of "airborne", it mattered little once the force was on the ground. Then it became, as it rightly was, simply a highly trained and better-than-average infantry division, backed up by the customary support and service units.

Basically, the structure was similar to that of a conventional infantry division, in that the airborne force consisted of three brigades. Two of those were parachute brigades, each of an approximate strength of 2,000 men, and each, in turn, composed of three combat battalions as well as brigade troops. The third was an air-landing brigade, slightly larger in size, which was transported to battle by glider; like the others, it was made up of three battalions. Over and above its three brigades, the airborne division also had support units, such as artillery, signals, engineers and reconnaissance personnel. Service branches, like medical, ordnance, transport, provost and REME were also represented, together with a divisional HQ staff. Certain significant tactical factors were, nevertheless, different, and these were determined by the unique mode of transport to battle. One was that the force was generally smaller in size than that of a standard infantry division. Thus, airborne infantry battalions were each of an approximate strength of 600 all ranks, whilst supporting arms and service elements were also very much reduced. The other was that the airborne division was forced to make do with lighter weapons and equipment than might otherwise have been appropriate for securing an infantry objective. After Arnhem, this was something that never again required emphasizing.

The organization to which Urquhart succeeded, therefore, was one with which he was generally familiar and, in the nine months of his command prior to "Market Garden", he won the confidence of his men and the loyal support of his officers. A man of no pretensions, his popularity right through the 1st British Airborne Division stemmed from the respect accorded to one who had already clearly demonstrated that he had competence in his job. Applying himself to this fresh task, therefore, he drew up the divisional plan for the Arnhem operation as rapidly as possible, in order that his brigadiers, as well as those with responsibility for specialized units directly answerable to him should be able to proceed with their own detailed organization.

Two other matters, however, imposed restrictions upon Urquhart's freedom to plan as he would have wished. The first was that RAF reports had indicated that German flak defences around both Arnhem Bridge and Deelen airfield were strong. There was subsequent reason to believe that such intelligence might have exaggerated the danger, but, at the time, it was sufficient to make a drop on or near to the Bridge itself unwelcome to the Royal Air Force. Since, for the transportation stage, airborne operations were officially regarded as subject to the decision or veto of the senior RAF officer involved, it meant that he could reject any proposed dropping and landing zones if it was felt that such a choice could mean an unacceptable level of landing casualties to the airborne force. In the case of the Arnhem landings, General Urquhart's initial decision was that his troops should be set down as close as possible to the target, but this was not agreeable to the Royal Air Force.

Accepting the rationality of many of the objections, such as the unsuitability of the area south of the Bridge for glider-landing, Urquhart then requested that one part at least, of his force – the 1st Parachute Brigade – should be dropped on both sides of the Neder Rijn and as close as possible to the Bridge. The remainder, together with glider-borne transport, could then be delivered to certain extensive clear areas about seven or eight miles to the west, and thereafter join up with the others as speedily as possible. This too was rejected so that Urquhart had no choice but to consider the "safe" areas for the landing of his entire force. The sole concession that he secured with regard to landings near the Bridge was the agreement that, from the second day on and provided that the flak had by then been eliminated, a small area, designated DZ "K", near the south end of the Bridge, could be used for whatever purposes were felt necessary.

Consideration of the need to bring in further troops after the first day was, in fact, at the heart of Roy Urquhart's other main problem, because the 519 aircraft allotted to him were insufficient for the conveying of his Division in one lift. In theory, this might have been resolved by a quick turn around and the operation of another landing later in the day, except that it would have meant a very late arrival for the second party. The practical drawback to this was a lack of experience in night flying by the pilots of 9th United States Troop Carrier Command. The upshot was that Urquhart had to plan for the delivery of his men in three instalments, with the initial landing limited to 1st Parachute Brigade, 1st Air Landing Brigade (less two companies of the 2nd Battalion South Staffordshires) and Divisional troops. On the following day, 4th Parachute Brigade was to come, together with the balance of 1st Air Landing Brigade and the remainder of the Divisional troops, leaving the Poles to be brought in on the third day.

For the first delivery, 1st Parachute Brigade under Brigadier Gerald Lathbury and 1st Air Landing Brigade under Brigadier Philip ("Pip") Hicks were to land on the two great open areas west of Wolfheze and on each side of the railway. These were Reijerscamp, to the north, and Renkum Heath, to the south. Divisional troops were also to land there. To assist in the landing of the gliders, to be followed a little later by the parachute forces, members of the 21st Independent Parachute Company were to drop on their own, approximately twenty minutes ahead of the main force, in order to lay out coloured celanese panels and ignite smoke canisters. Eureka homing devices for assisting the aircraft to locate the dropping and landing zones were also to be set going by this advance party.

Once on the ground, the plan was for 1st Parachute Brigade to make for the Bridge as quickly as possible, and to capture not only the road bridge but also a pontoon crossing slightly to the west of it. Thereafter, they were to hold the entire length of Arnhem Bridge and screen off the eastern approaches to it on both sides of the river. Three routes were chosen and allocated, one to each of the three battalions that made up the Brigade. The most southerly route, along by the river, was designated "Lion", and assigned to Lieutenant-Colonel John Frost's 2nd Parachute Battalion. The more northerly Utrechtseweg, to be known as "Tiger", was given to the 3rd Parachute Battalion under Lieutenant-Colonel John Fitch, whilst further north again, beyond the railway, Lieutenant-Colonel David Dobie's 1st Parachute Battalion was to find its way to Arnhem, principally by following the Ede-Arnhem road, code-named "Leopard".

1st Air Landing Brigade was not to be immediately involved in the attack on the primary objective, but was to guard the landing and dropping zones for 4th Parachute Brigade's arrival on the second day. By this arrangement, the 2nd Battalion South Staffordshires' under Lieutenant-Colonel McCardie, was to look after Reijerscamp, the 1st Battalion of the Border Regiment was to have the job of defending Renkum Heath, whilst Lieutenant-Colonel Payton-Reid's 7th Battalion of the King's Own Scottish Borderers was to seek out and guard the more westerly dropping zone of Ginkel Heath, which was to be used for the first time by 4th Brigade. Following the successful arrival of the second lift, it was then intended that Hicks's Brigade, less the 7th Battalion of the King's Own Scottish Borderers, should proceed to Arnhem to take up defensive positions on the western side of the town, comparable to those assumed by 1st Brigade on the east. The newly-arrived 4th Parachute Brigade under Brigadier John ("Shan") Hackett was also

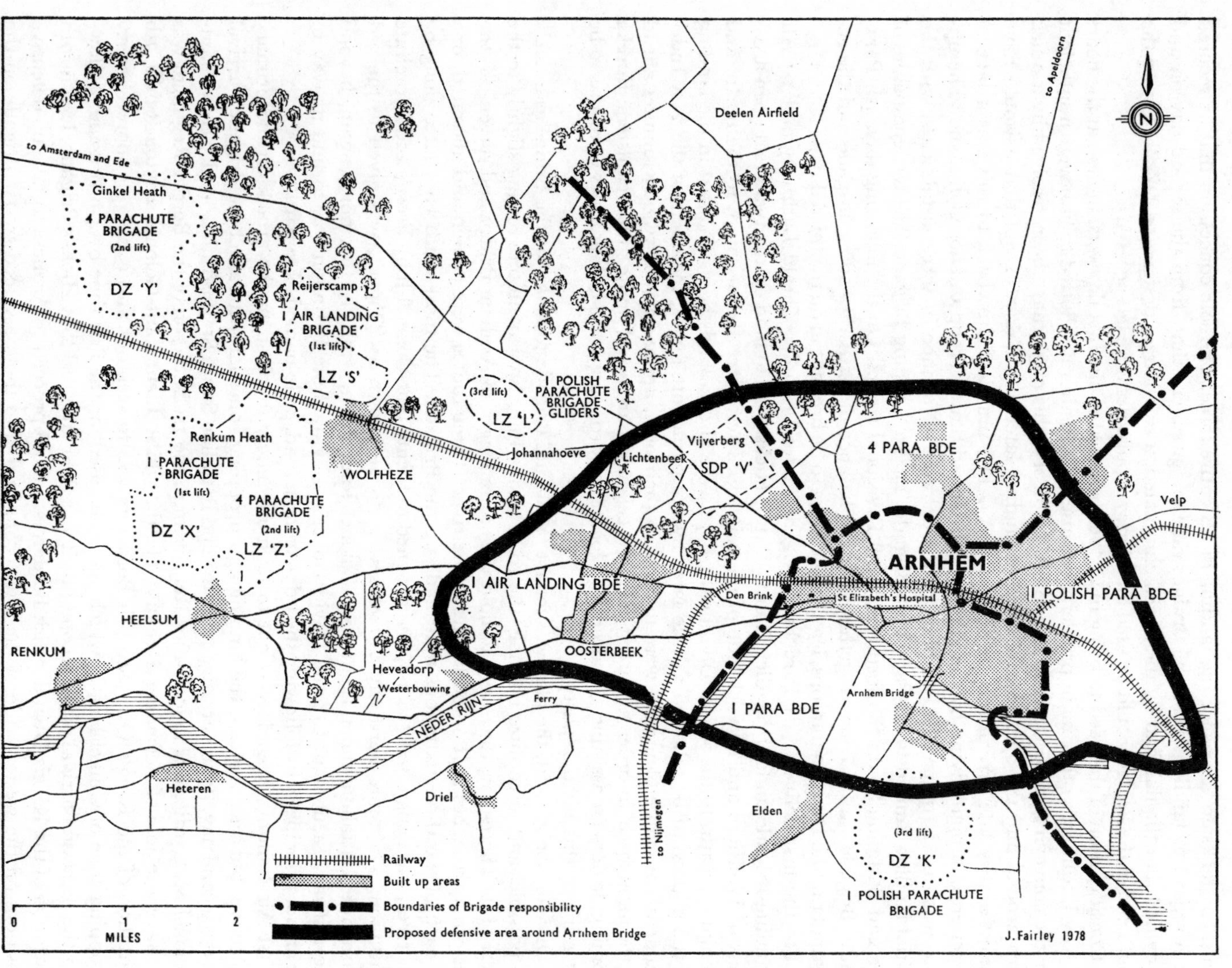

Map 3 Proposed layout for 1st British Airborne Division

to move on Arnhem, to occupy the high ground to the north and west of the town.

The third lift, which was to be undertaken on Tuesday 19th September, would bring in the 1st Polish Independent Parachute Brigade on DZ "K", the small area about a mile south of the Bridge. It was anticipated that they would then cross over to form part of the general defence line around Arnhem, by taking up positions to the north-east of the town. Their gliders would, however, be brought in just north-east of Wolfheze at LZ "L" in the Johannahoeve area. In anticipation of this, it was decided that the 7th Battalion King's Own Scottish Borderers would continue to undertake a role similar to that of the Monday, by keeping the Johannahoeve area free for the arrival of the Polish gliders.

There can be little doubt that the Divisional plan was basically flawed from the outset. Inevitably, the element of surprise, so significant in airborne operations, was initially in danger of becoming lost for the want of an opportunity to hit the main objective immediately after the landing. Nor was this in any degree compensated for by the strength of numbers, since the arrangement for piecemeal delivery of the force not only imposed an overall limitation on the total number to be taken on the first lift, but also ensured that something like one half of them would be tied up for the first vital twenty-four hours in the non-productive role of defending the landing and dropping zones. In a sense, General Urquhart was being placed in the position of a man who, having entered a card game, finds that the rules are not quite what he thought they were to be. The game can still be played, but it transpires that there are unforeseen hazards which no amount of *finessing* can easily overcome. In such a situation, there is always hope that his own skill and a measure of luck may see him through. But what if there should be a joker in the pack of which he is totally unaware – worse still, what if the joker should be in his opponent's hand?

According to Urquhart's information, the enemy did not have a particularly strong hand. Intelligence sources had accurately reported that he might expect opposition from a mixed bag of enemy units of varying quality. It was reported that to the west, *Generalleutnant* Hans von Tettau had been gathering together remnants and small detachments of defeated regiments whose personnel were, singly or in groups, making their own way east from the battlefields of France and Belgium. It was also known that there was an SS training school for NCO's, under *Oberst* Lippert and that 16th SS Panzer Grenadier Depot and Reserve Battalion was located in the Arnhem area. The presence of Dutch SS units was also known, together with the strength of the *Luftwaffe* force at Deelen airfield. Beyond that, it was not thought that the 1st British Airborne Division would encounter much opposition. "What about armour?" Major Freddie Gough had enquired, only to be told that, as far as was known, any such opposition was limited to a few beat-up old tanks which were too obsolete to be taken seriously.

In an atmosphere engendered by a feeling that at long last the Division might manage one operation that would not be aborted, it was all the more comforting to be assured that enemy opposition was likely to be light. It was true that in the early weeks of September messages were received on the intelligence network from the "Kees" and "Albrecht" underground resistance groups, to the effect that there were two SS Panzer divisions resting and refitting in the Arnhem area, but some of the messages were garbled and not taken seriously. In any case, it was adjudged that, even were it true, it was hardly likely that such heavily weakened formations would be capable of offering any serious opposition. Certainly, General Urquhart was not informed of those reports in advance of the operation and little credibility appears to have been given to them. Nevertheless, one man under Urquhart's command would certainly have been very put out had he known of their contents, for, at a previous briefing for Operation "Comet", Major-General Sosabowski had made it very plain that in his view one essential problem was being given insufficient emphasis. On that occasion, as General Urquhart had explained the detailed outline of that curiously artless plan to which he had fallen heir, he had been interrupted several times by Sosabowski's agitated exclamations, "But the Germans, General . . . the Germans!" In the context of the later "Market Garden", nothing could have been more prophetically relevant to the shortcomings and deficiencies of the top-level decision-making for, as the Dutch intelligence sources had correctly revealed there were indeed Panzer troops in the Arnhem area.

One grouping was that of the 9th SS (Hohenstaufen) Division under the command of *SS Obersturmbannführer* Walter Harzer,* with its headquarters at Beekbergen, a mere twelve miles north of Arnhem. The other was the 10th (Frundsberg) Division, based only a little further away at Ruurlo, and commanded by *SS Brigadeführer und Generalmajor der Waffen-SS* Heinz Harmel. Battered as they undoubtedly were by the fighting of the previous months, and in particular the great battles of Caen and Falaise, those were, nevertheless, no ill-assorted collection of "ear and stomach" line-of-communication troops, but seasoned, battle-hardened veterans with a great deal of fight left in them and backed by all the armour and equipment, howsoever depleted, appropriate to the most elite formations in the German army. Together, they constituted II Panzer Corps with a headquarters at Doetinchem, just fifteen miles to the east of Arnhem. In overall command was *SS Obergruppenführer und General der Waffen-SS* Willi Bittrich, one of the most astute and intelligent of all the German commanders.

Ironically, the fact that those crack troops were in the area at all was merely an accidental consequence of the decision that they be taken there for rest and reconstitution. The 9th Division, for example, had lost all its artillery, and its 19th and 20th Panzer Grenadier Regiments all their heavy weapons. In view of the losses, the decision had already been made to move what was left to Germany, there to rebuild a fresh formation around the nucleus of what had survived. It was a particularly cruel stroke of bad luck for the British that the Arnhem operation should have coincided with the temporary presence in the area of those two depleted but still formidable forces. Nevertheless, it was a fact of life, and the airborne troops, for all their heroism, would learn it in the hardest way possible. So it was that, for the game that was to follow, Roy Urquhart had no suspicion that there was not simply one joker in the pack, but two – and both of them were in Willi Bittrich's hand!

Finding himself in a situation in which his entire force would be landing miles away from its objective, Urquhart then adopted the plan of a *coup de main* in order that Arnhem Bridge might be seized as rapidly as possible and held, pending the arrival of the bulk of the Division. What was required was a small, heavily armed and highly mobile group which could speed rapidly to the task, straight from the landing and dropping zones. In this way, the element of surprise might not be totally lost. Once in possession of the Bridge, the *coup de main* party would then it was hoped, hold off the enemy until relieved.

To the 1st Airborne Reconnaissance Squadron fell the task of carrying out the *coup*. From the outset Major Gough was unhappy about the idea. In the first place, the *coup de main* proposal was essentially a "seize and hold" tactic and, whilst it was true that all Reconnaissance personnel were trained for undertaking such an action ahead of the main force, it was not primarily the work for which his men had been so intensively trained. To Gough, looking instead at the strategic

* In temporary command, owing to the fact that the Division's commander, *SS Brigadeführer und Generalmajor der Waffen-SS* Sylvester Stadler was wounded and in hospital. Harzer was Stadler's Chief of Staff.

design for a divisional advance upon Arnhem along the three major routes allocated to the parachute battalions, it seemed logical that each prong of that triple attack should be led by one of the three operational Troops of the Reconnaissance Squadron.

It is not difficult to appreciate the reasons why the Squadron was chosen to make the initial assault. The very speed and fire power normally employed by a Reconnaissance unit as it spearheaded forward in search of its information were the assets most likely to commend it to others for the carrying out of a *coup de main*. Yet, such reasoning was very much a confusion of means and ends. The fact that a regiment of the Reconnaissance Corps habitually employed tactics of that kind did not make it exceptional; it was not the method that was important so much as the fundamental purpose and uniqueness of its role. Gough's reasoning was that the function of any Reconnaissance unit, irrespective of how it was transported to battle, was the provision of information on whatever enemy dispositions and resources might lie in the way of the advancing division. He did not dispute the wisdom of a *coup de main* so much as the fact that it had been allocated to his force whose greatest military capability lay in the execution of a true reconnaissance role. They were respectable and logical arguments which he advanced, but they failed to convince Brigadier Lathbury. With the benefit of hindsight, it is now possible to say that if Gough had had his way, such forward-placed elements of his own unit as he suggested might precede each battalion of the 1st Parachute Brigade could have provided information in such a way as to compensate in part for the disastrous communication breakdown which subsequently afflicted the entire Division.

Having made his point, albeit unsuccessfully, Freddie Gough, like the committed soldier that he was, accepted the situation that the *coup de main* would have to be undertaken by his small unit and in the best way possible. What worried him then was the vulnerability of the jeeps. In a fast strike assault role, such as the *coup* on Arnhem Bridge inevitably had to be, it seemed to him essential to attempt to counterbalance the defensive weakness of his vehicles by stepping up their power. Already in North Africa and north-west Europe a comparably unique unit, the Special Air Service, had demonstrated the efficacy of the heavily armed jeep, in its attacks on enemy-held garrisons, supply centres and airfields. It was this tactical success which had already influenced Gough in the matter of equipping and arming his own vehicles. Impressed by the devastating results obtained in enemy-occupied territory by SAS jeep units armed with a combination of ·50 Browning and Vickers "K" machine guns, he had adopted the latter weapon as the mainstay of his Squadron's attacking strength. Certainly the Vickers "K" had already proved its versatility in a number of instances. Originally designed for employment as an aircraft gun, it was gradually withdrawn from use with the Royal Air Force, but its worth as an anti-aircraft weapon had been amply demonstrated by ground defences during the siege of Malta. Weighing a mere nineteen pounds and fed from an overhead drum of ninety-six rounds, it possessed two indisputable virtues for any British force. The first was that, in common with the Lee Enfield rifle and the Bren gun, it used standard ·303 inch calibre ammunition; the second was its rate of fire – no less than 1,050 rounds per minute!

In response to his submissions, and long before the Arnhem operation was ever thought of, Major Gough had succeeded in getting his jeeps equipped with the Vickers "K" guns. Special permanent mountings of tubular steel were devised for the vehicles, so that the guns could be operated from the front seat beside the driver. Provision was also made for the gun to be quickly removed from the mounting, in the event that the vehicles might have to be temporarily abandoned in the course of an attack. For the Arnhem operation, what was unsatisfactory about their use was the limitation of one Vickers "K" gun per jeep. In vain, Gough argued that, at the very least, each vehicle needed the fire power of a twin-mounted set. Indeed, it was known that in Italy, some SAS vehicles had been in action with as many as five such guns! His request was regretfully turned down, on the grounds that the problems of transporting all the ammunition needed would, under the conditions of airborne supply, be unrealistic.

Determined to explore all possibilities, Freddie Gough still persisted in his attempts to improve upon what he felt was an assignment with tactical drawbacks that were disconcertingly apparent. Never at a loss for ideas, his thoughts immediately turned to the possibility of supplementing his jeep transport with something more formidable: "I wanted them to let me have three Hamilcar gliders, with a troop of light tanks from the 6th Airborne Armoured Reconnaissance Regiment, because I said that I didn't see how we could really do this *coup de main* unless we had some armour." What he had in mind was the Mark VII Tetrarch, something like a half-dozen of which had previously been glider-landed into Normandy on the eve of D-Day 6th June; these had subsequently given valuable support to the parachute forces. For the initial attack on Arnhem Bridge, it was his view that even two such vehicles would allow for cross-country work as well as help deal with any unexpectedly difficult opposition. It was an imaginative notion which, in terms of glider availability, was practical and feasible It was true that, of the total glider force of 694 scheduled for use on the three planned lifts, most were Horsas and a mere thirty were of the Hamilcar type. Nevertheless, in the distribution table for the second lift, two gliders were unalloted, and both were Hamilcars. "I'm sure", said Gough, "that the boys from the 6th would have volunteered right away, but I don't think that any real effort was made to ask for them."

Such were the trials of a squadron commander whose senses, experience and instincts told him that, however desirable might be a successful *coup de main*, his unit was ill-prepared for the task. Events were subsequently to prove him right and yet, it was in a spirit of optimism that the men of the 1st Airborne Reconnaissance Squadron made ready once more for a divisional operation. All of them were confident of the wisdom, initiative and imagination of their commanding officer, and each knew that he was under the direction of an able and experienced soldier. If Major Freddie Gough had any faults as a commander, his men were not aware of them. But there was one minor shortcoming which he did have, and that was a reputation for unpunctuality, particularly at General Urquhart's briefings. It was a trait that was perhaps understandable in one of such exuberant vitality that each minute of the day had to be filled. It was even more understandable that the General should have found it a trifle irritating and in the days leading up to "Market Garden" it earned Gough a mild reproof. Both men were later to recall this incident in the strangest of circumstances.

Chapter 3 SATURDAY 16th–SUNDAY 17th SEPTEMBER 1944

"Freddie's Flying Circus"

Of the 358 gliders available, twenty-two were alloted to the Squadron and by 15th September they had been packed. They were of the type Airspeed Horsa Mark II, more colloquially referred to as the "White Horsa", and their main advantage over the recently displaced Mark I type was that they had knock-off tail units. Until just a short time prior to the Arnhem operation, all flying had been done with the earlier model, which had to have its loads manhandled on and off through a door in the side. With the new type, side loading continued as before, but for unloading purposes on the landing zone, the tail was dropped off. This process was facilitated in a number of ways by the modified design of the Mark II. The entire tail unit was attached to the main fuselage by four clamps which, when hit firmly, unthreaded and moved out of position, allowing the whole tail assembly to fall away. Before the clamps were struck, however, it was necessary to cut through the control cables, which ran from the front cockpit to the rudder and elevator at the rear. These were of steel hawser, approximately 3/16 inches thick, very hard, but treated for about three inches of their length just inside the tail section in order to make them easy to sever. This "soft" section was painted white for easy identification, and hanging near to it was a set of tools – heavy wire cutters, axe, hand saw and machette – which were used to do the cutting. Once the business of severing cables and striking clamps had been carried out, there only remained the jointing fabric between the round body of the main fuselage and the tapered section of the tail. In practice, of course, things did not always go by the book. A tail unit could easily become jammed due to a bad landing, in which case the axe and machette had then to be freely used in order to smash it away.

One of the most responsible of all jobs was that of preparing the gliders, because the safety of those who were to accompany the transport in them was in large measure dependent upon the care and skill that went into the loading. In the case of the Reconnaissance Squadron, prime responsibility lay with Captain Tony Platt, assisted by Sergeant Ken Lapper. The first task, as Lapper recalls, was to determine the exact weight of every single item that was to go. "What I used to do", he says, "was to 'armour' a vehicle exactly as it would be going into action. We'd load it up with its guns, ammunition, wireless set, rations, water and anything else that it was to carry. We would then take it down to the public weighbridge at the local railway station and take careful note of the total weight. Only then did we get down to working out the loading stations."

The loading stations were the precise positions which would be allocated in the glider to specific items of transport and equipment, and they were calculated in relation to the fulcrum point of the unloaded aircraft. It was vital that the load should be balanced on this central point which, in the case of the Horsa, was just a little forward of the main spar. Understandably, the weight which could be disposed over the area of any one loading station was determined not only by the lifting capacity of the glider but also by the dispositions to be made elsewhere in the craft. Frequently, the weight differential was so critical that a jeep or trailer transported forward of the fulcrum in one glider might have to be loaded to the rear of the centre point in another. Even the direction in which a jeep faced could be significant. It might be desirable that, for unloading purposes, the vehicles should face the tail unit, but the weight of the jeep's engine in relation to the chosen loading station might make it necessary to have it facing towards the front.

Once positioned in the aircraft, a vehicle's weight had to be taken off its springs by the lodging of a wooden wedge block between spring and body. This allowed for good firm fixing to fore and aft, with final adjustments carried out by means of screw shackles which joined the stay lines to the glider. Understandably, it was very necessary for the wedges to be removed before a jeep was driven off, or the driver was in for a rough ride! The final test, after loading was completed, was always made by the senior glider pilot, who would jump up and catch hold of the tail to check that he could still pull the nose up off the ground.

Of course, not all glider loads were identical. One might carry two jeeps and a trailer, another might have a single jeep, a trailer and a Polsten gun or, perhaps, be loaded entirely with trailers. In the circumstances, some possibilities were viewed with less enthusiasm than others. Cyril Belcham, for example, clearly remembered that he had to travel to Arnhem in a glider which contained not only a jeep and trailer, but also the Squadron's reserve petrol supply and a hamper filled with 2-inch mortar bombs! As he later remarked, with a degree of understatement, "It was a combination which I was not particularly happy about."

In charge of the whole glider-borne party was Captain David Allsop, the second-in-command of the Squadron. His task was to lead them to the rendezvous point, a little in advance of the main parachute party under Major Gough. Something like two or three men per glider had been allocated to travel with the vehicles and guns and, of the two possibilities, theirs was probably the least enviable task. Parachuting from an aircraft always carried with it the attendant risk of a landing accident, but most of those were usually of a minor kind. With flimsy gliders being belly-landed at speeds of something like ninety miles per hour, there was always the chance of heavy equipment becoming detached from its anchors, or even of the whole glider flipping over on to its back. When that happened, the possibility of death or serious injury was high.

Even on the night before the operation there was still a degree of understandable scepticism in the minds of the personnel of both glider and parachute parties. For men who, in a little over three months, had experienced the build-up to sixteen operations, all of which had then been cancelled, it was difficult to accept that the next one was assuredly going to be different. Not surprisingly, there were some who said that they would not believe it was "on" until their feet actually touched the soil of Holland. Considering that one previous operation had not been cancelled until they were actually in the planes awaiting take-off, there was every justification for thinking in that way. It was on that occasion that the 21st Independent Company had itself actually become airborne and begun heading towards the objective!

Nevertheless, there was little of high spirits manifested on that Saturday night. Some wrote letters home, others sat in groups, talking quietly. Kit was checked and double-checked and, in a number of cases, attempts were made to try to resolve any last-minute problems. Arthur Barlow, who was a member of the parachute party, was especially concerned about the contents of his equipment kitbag. The problem stemmed from the standard arrangement whereby small items, like Bren guns, PIAT projectors and certain wireless sets were not taken by the glider party, but by individual parachutists. The method was to pack these things into large kitbags, with a man made responsible for each of them. The bag was attached to the man's waist by a rope, five yards in length, which was coiled and temporarily accommodated in a special leg pocket. As the parachute "stick" left the plane, the soldier held the kitbag against his body but, once out, began immediately to pay out the rope from the pocket until it had reached its fullest extent. This meant that the bag hit the ground first, and the landing speed of the parachutist was not affected. The soldier had to work fast, for there was little enough time to carry out the operation, and a failure to complete it could mean hitting the ground at a speed far in excess of what was desirable. At the least, he would probably be lucky to get off with a broken leg. The system, of course, had the advantage of providing the jumper with a check on his distance from the ground because, as soon as the rope went slack, he knew that he had less than fifteen feet to go and was able to prepare for the bump.

What was worrying Barlow was not so much the paying out of the rope – something which had been well-tried on numerous practice jumps – as the provision that his kitbag was to contain the small 38 set transmitter, together with three 4-foot sections of tubular steel aerial rod. The trouble was that the rods projected for about eighteen inches out of the top of the bag. As he says, "I was petrified in case the kitbag landed in an upright position and I impaled myself on the aerials." Because of this danger, part of Barlow's pre-operational preparations, that Saturday night, was to try to ensure that the bag would land on its side. He is still able to remember what he did: "I packed the 38 set and the aerials tightly to one side of the kitbag, and placed dozens of packets of spare Sten gun ammunition around them. On the opposite side, I put clean underwear, a shirt, a towel and several shell dressings. The theory was that the heavier half of the kitbag would fall flat, with the set and aerials next to the ground, and the 'soft' washing would be on top for me to fall on. When it was packed, I pushed the bag off the billet table half a dozen times, much to the disgust of those already in bed getting an early night. To my great satisfaction, the kitbag fell just the way I wanted it each time."

For the most part, however, it was not so much the immediate practical hazards of this kind that concerned most of them, as the thought that in a few short hours they would probably be face to face with the enemy in situations where each would have to rely upon all the slowly acquired expertise and experience. All were conscious of what it would mean to be landed or dropped well behind the conventional front line and this awareness had been heightened by the issue to each man of official items of escape equipment, which included a silk map of western Europe, a file and an ingenious compass made from two trouser buttons. There was also an issue per man of a sum of Dutch currency. These, however, were seen as nothing more than sensible precautions, simply a form of over-insurance to allow for unlikely contingencies. Already, in the autumn of 1944, the scent of victory was in the air, and there were few on the eve of "Market Garden" who seriously considered the possibility of defeat or capture. Whatever form the individual's personal apprehensions may have taken, there was not a man of the Reconnaissance Squadron who did not wish to be a part of the action destined to begin on the following morning. Foremost amongst them was Freddie Gough himself, and it was in character that, on the evening prior to the operation, Gough, newly turned forty-three years of age, should have visited his men in their billets. He sensed and understood the underlying feelings of excitement, coupled with hope that this time there would be no last-minute cancellation. There was a bit of small talk, and he wished them well. "Let's make it a good one, boys," he said and, as he turned away, paused to add, "You know, today's my birthday – and the best present you can get me tomorrow is a dead German."

As dawn broke over the fields and villages of southern England, the departure aerodromes came alive with the unique bustle of a major military operation getting under way. At Tarrant Rushton, the members of the Squadron's glider party fitted into this ferment of activity, each one increasingly anxious to be off, as the hour for departure drew near. Morale that morning was high, with an almost festive atmosphere in the air. From the mobile canteens men bought "tea and wads", the traditional sustenance of the British soldier. Lined up in the background, were the towing aircraft and, behind them, the Horsas which they would take with them into the air. Against the camouflage paint of the gliders, the wing markings and the coloured rondels stood out with a conspicuous clarity in the morning sun. So too did the writing which had mysteriously appeared overnight, for on the fuselages men had chalked their own personal inscriptions. David Christie of C Troop arrived to find his Horsa already embellished with "Minnie the Moocher", the title of a popular song which examined the paradox of the professional lady with the heart of gold. Henry Venes, with the foreknowledge that his glider would soon be landing on the mainland of occupied Europe, had done his bit for the post-war tourist trade by extolling the scenic beauties of Bethnal Green. Yet another of the Reconnaissance gliders alluded in mild but acceptable disrespect to "Freddie's Flying Circus".

Astonishing as it must now seem, this "graffiti" was later carefully noted by the Germans, and examples were incorporated in *SS-Sturmbannführer* Sepp Krafft's intelligence report which was sent directly to Berlin for the personal attention of Himmler himself. It would seem that Krafft was circumspect in his choice for he avoided reference to those chalked observations that did less than justice to the characters, habits and physical appearance of the Führer and his closest advisers. Today, it is Krafft's comments upon them rather than his choice of inscriptions that are of greater interest. These, in all teutonic seriousness, he enshrined under the general heading of "Political Convictions", from which the following is an extract:

> . . . not much information on political convictions has been gleaned but it is known that in England, when the truth conflicts with the military powers, the truth is withheld. In this respect, chalked inscriptions on the gliders are interesting:
>
> "We are the Al Capone gang"
> "Up with the Reds"
> "Up with the fräuleins' skirts"

It is then that the laboured prose yields up a priceless gem such as would have graced the script of a Tommy Handley radio show for, in allusion to the first two examples, he continues by saying that, "How far this is connected with the political convictions of the troops themselves, or whether it is due to Bolshevist or American influences is not known." Krafft makes no specific comment on the third quotation of his choice, perhaps in the belief that one of such sensitivity as Heinrich Himmler could only have been repelled by any suggestion that the sanctity of German maidenhood was somehow in peril. Lacking in the social education provided by such essentially British institutions as Ted Kavanagh's ITMA all the way down to the fruitier products

Stirling, with Horsa in tow, leaving for Arnhem
(Imperial War Museum)

2 Section, A Troop on practice jump, prior to Arnhem
L–R: L/Cpl. C. King, Tpr. A. Palmer, Cpl. J. Taylor MM, Tpr. W. Fraser, Lt. D. Galbraith, Tprs. A. Auld, W. Rew,* M. Gassett, Sgt. G. Williams, Tprs. E. Ogden, F. Sylvester, M. Weaver, J. Bruce, J. Cooper
* Killed, minutes later on this jump

(R. Guthrie)

C Troop, 1st Airborne Reconnaissance Squadron, Ruskington 1944
Back row: Tprs. Speller, McSkimmings, Southwell, Garwood, Brawn. *Second back row:* Tpr. Kellet, L/Cpl. Palmer, Tprs. Tickle, Cross, Edmond, L/Cpl. Morris, Tprs. Giles, Fergus, Pearce. *Second front row:* Tprs. Goulding, Gorringe, Miles, Minns, Macro, Barlow, Crowder, Brumwell, Hares, Hasler, Chandler. *Front row:* L/Cpl. Thomas, ——, Sgt. Winder, Lt. Bucknall, Capt. Hay, ——, Lt. Bowles, Sgt. Stacey, L/Cpl. Baker. [Missing: Sgts. Christie and McGregor]

Officers, 1st Airborne Reconnaissance Squadron, Ruskington 1944
Back row: Lts. Lickerish, Bowles, Voss, Wadsworth, Pascal, Hodge, Ladds. *Centre row:* Lts. Guthrie, ——, Marshall, Galbraith, Bucknall, Christie, Capts. McNabb, ——, Lt. Stevenson. *Front row:* Capts. Poole, Park, Hay, Allsop, Major Gough MC, Capts. Costeloe, Grubb, Clark, Lt.-QM. Collier

of the sergeants' mess concerts, Sepp Krafft, for all his excellence as a soldier, was unable to comprehend that, far from being political statements, these were no more than morale-boosting catch phrases. One can only speculate on what he succeeded in making of two other inscriptions left on the A Troop gliders of the Reconnaissance Squadron. One was a prophecy – "West Ham for the Cup", the other a domestic exhortation – "Get up them f- - - - - - stairs!"

By ten in the morning, the tug and glider pairs were all set to go and, at twenty minutes past the hour, the Squadron's complement took to the air. Army comrades, as well as Royal Air Force personnel, both men and women, lined the runways to wave them goodbye and to stand until the last glider had become a dwindling speck in the sky and the sound of the aircraft engines had finally faded into the Sunday silence.*

In the meantime, about 170 miles to the north, the main body of the Squadron had been transported to Barkston Heath, an aerodrome near Grantham in Lincolnshire. It was a dry morning, although there was a broken cumulus cloud base extending from 500 to 2,000 feet, so that flying and towing conditions were far from ideal. Still, it was obvious that, as far as weather conditions were concerned, there was nothing to prevent the operation from going ahead as planned. For all those involved, that was what mattered.

Each man in the jumping party wore standard issue battledress with the Denison smock over the top. This was a loose-fitting camouflage garment in green and brown, with a lining of blanket material which made it windproof, even although it was not wholly waterproof. It featured four large patch pockets and a front-fastening zip. A tailpiece was brought from the rear, between the wearer's legs, to the front and fastened with press studs. Over this, the men wore normal webbing equipment – waist belt, pouches, straps and small pack. Each also had a rimless helmet with a green string net camouflage cover, a softer loosely woven camouflage face veil, usually worn as a scarf, and the inevitable body accoutrements of the active-service infantryman – respirator, water bottle, bayonet, entrenching tool, toggle rope and bandolier of small arms ammunition. Strapped to the right leg was a knife, similar in design to the commando fighting knife. Its main purpose was to allow the soldier to cut himself free of entangling parachute harness but, if necessary, it could also be put to effective use in hand-to-hand combat. To obviate the danger of all the equipment fouling up the parachute harness during descent, a "jump jacket" was worn over everything else. This was a simple sleeveless gaberdine garment, over which the parachute was fitted and which, like the 'chute, was discarded on landing.

One other interesting piece of equipment which was worn by some was the body armour. This had first been issued as standard equipment during the preparations for a previous operation. A set comprized two steel sheets covered in khaki denim material, the larger of which was a chest protector, slightly curved and about fifteen inches long by about twelve inches deep. A smaller sheet, about seven inches square, was attached by a pair of straps to the lower edge of the larger one and was intended as protection for abdomen and genitals. The initial reception which this contraption received was a cool one for, at first glance, it seemed much too thin and lightweight to be capable of stopping anything. Stan Collishaw remembers how he took his armour out to the area at the back of the Nissen huts at Ruskington and hung it on a tree. "Spud" Taylor, whose prowess in small arms was second to none, was then asked to test its effectiveness. In doing so, he managed to make a dent in the breastplate, but did not succeed in penetrating the metal. Barlow and McSkimmings, with equal concern, produced the same result when they went down to the firing range and loosed off at a set with a Sten gun from a distance of twelve paces.

At Barkston Heath, eight C 47 Dakota aircraft had been placed at the disposal of Major

*Freddie Ladds, the Signals Officer of the Squadron, remembers how they sang, "We'll meet again", as the planes took off.

Gough's men. When the time came for them to line up and enter the aircraft, they did so in "sticks" of about twenty. Once aboard, they took up position facing inwards and seated along both sides of the fuselage. Packing themselves into the space provided was a feat in itself, for, with all the equipment and body luggage that they carried, each was as loaded as an itinerant pedlar of old. In addition to all his own personal webbing and the parachute itself, each man also had responsibility for either an equipment kitbag or a rifle valise. These cumbersome objects then had to be tucked into the limited floor space between one man and the next, or else wedged between a man's knees, in a position which guaranteed little opportunity for the stretching of cramped leg muscles. Something like 160 members of the 1st Airborne Reconnaissance Squadron were installed in this way, settled with what ease they could manage on the bare metal seats of a plane which, whatever other virtues it possessed, was assuredly not built for human comfort.

At 1015 hours, the pathfinder aircraft of the 21st Independent Parachute Company took off from Fairford, and three-quarters of an hour later, the Squadron's parachute party took to the air on the first stage of the journey to a rendezvous with their glider-borne comrades in Holland. The designated spot was a field not far to the west of the small town of Oosterbeek. Few had ever heard the name before. For the rest of their lives, it was one that they were unlikely ever to forget.

By the time the parachute party had taken off, the gliders were already well under way on the first stage of their journey. For the glider troops, everything had gone very smoothly and, of the 358 gliders which had taken off behind their towing aircraft only one had failed to become airborne. It is true that there were a number of other mishaps which led to some having to force-land in England but such instances were relatively few. One such set back, however, was experienced by Bill Cook, a driver operator with HQ Troop, who was with Lieutenant Graham Wadsworth and Sergeant George Kay. "I was sat," recollected Cook, "at the rear, on the right of Sergeant Kay, and, as we swung out to sea, I well remember a feeling of apprehension which made me reach for the bottle of rum that "Judd" (Kay) was swigging. The next glance out of the port side turned that apprehension into fear, for I saw part of the wing fabric – a strip about a foot wide – rip off from the leading edge right to the back. At that point, it disappeared, leaving an ugly gaping hole and a wing that started to billow out. 'God,' I thought, 'this is it,' and had visions of the whole wing disintegrating. I let "Judd" into my discovery and somehow we got Lieutenant Wadsworth, sitting at the front, to understand our predicament; he in turn passed the news to the glider pilots. 'Did we think we could make it?' was the cool, delayed response, to which our unanimous reply was, 'Get the bloody thing turned round and put her down!'" The result was that they returned to Tarrant Rushton and, after a quick patch up with glider fabric, took off again in just over a quarter of an hour, in an attempt to catch the tail end of the glider force. Failing to succeed in this, they returned to base for a second time. Later that evening, in the deserted billet, Bill Cook heard the radio announcement of the landing at Arnhem.

Out of the total force of gliders which left that day, a little over six percent had to take similar action. Two of those carried Squadron personnel and equipment, which meant that, of the original allocation of twenty-two, twenty were set safely on course for their objective. Ralph Foulkes, who was a Section officer with C Troop, remembers looking down at the spread of Bournemouth, and then they were into the thick cloud base, with a very bumpy ride to the rendezvous point over Hatfield. He then recollects the gradual thickening of air traffic, as scores of tugs and gliders from other departure points began to converge, ready for the combined swing east and the crossing of the Suffolk coast at Orford Ness. By then the airborne force was at its most concentrated and, for an hour and a half, the great winged armada throbbed through the sky over the patchwork fields and the familiar towns of southern England. From the ground, thousands stood to watch the unforgettable sight, knowing that something momentous was under way and, as the airborne army streamed out over the sea, wishing God-speed and safe return. As the *Daily Express* was later to report, "All the streets were crowded. Women left their Sunday lunch. Traffic stopped. Ships in harbour blew a greeting on their sirens. Congregations leaving church went back to say a prayer. So great was the roar that no one could use the telephone till the planes had passed."

Once out over the sea, the cloud dispersed and under a clear blue sky flying conditions were excellent. Despite this, four gliders from the total divisional force had to ditch in the sea and one, prematurely released due to tug engine failure, landed on Schouwen island, just at the crossing point on the Dutch coast. None of the Reconnaissance Squadron's gliders was involved in any such mishaps. Throughout the crossing there was, in general, little enemy action directed against the tugs and gliders as they flew over and beyond the Scheldt estuary to the Arnhem area. Fighter cover protected them all the way, and in only a few instances were the airborne men conscious of fire by the German "ack-ack" coastal batteries.

Following the main glider element at a short interval of time, came the planes that carried the parachute troops. Like their comrades in the gliders, they too were to find the crossing relatively uneventful. Conscious of the security afforded by the supporting fighter escort planes above and the well-positioned air-sea rescue ships below, they were able to settle down to a flight that was not in any significant sense different in character from a straightforward routine exercise. There was a certain amount of initial interest in picking out landmarks, but most then eased down to relax for the remainder of the journey. Some, like Reg Hasler, slept for a good part of the way, for the drone of the engines tended to encourage this. Others engaged in good-humoured exchanges of the kind that soldiers on the eve of battle have always indulged in. Inevitably, too, there was singing – a varied repertoire ranging from current favourites such as "Paper Doll" to those with lyrics of a more robust literary quality. Foremost amongst the latter was a vocal gem which, set to the tune of Colonel Bogey, opened with the poetically memorable line, "Hitler has only got one ball!"

In retrospect, some of the humour of the journey had a bitter irony to it, particularly in the light of subsequent events. With memories of the occasion on which they had tested the body armour, Arthur Barlow leant across the plane at one point, to ask his friend, Ray McSkimmings, if he was wearing it. "Too true," was the reply, "in fact I've got two sets on, one front and one back – I don't want any stray bullets up my arse as we go over." Alas, just forty-eight hours later, McSkimmings was to die – by a bullet through the head.

And so the time passed as, munching, chewing, singing, sleeping, telling stories or just sitting, quietly thinking, the paratroops of the 1st British Airborne Division left England far behind and headed out over the North Sea. In time, the Dutch coast appeared and the flooded areas were clearly discernible below. Once again, light "ack-ack" fire was put up by the Germans as this second wave of planes crossed the Scheldt – Alf Hazell remembers it as sounding like pebbles hitting the bottom of the aircraft – but no one was unduly troubled. Then, as the flat Dutch landscape slid past, they could see the roads and villages and, here and there, a watcher drawn to look joyfully skywards at what was generally believed to be the start of the liberation of Holland.

For one soldier, perhaps more than for anyone else in that entire allied force, the crossing had something of a unique significance. Over 500 years previously, in an army of comparable size and quality a brave fighting man had followed his king to France and had there distinguished himself upon the field of Agincourt. His name was Matthew Gough, one of a number of illustrious ancestors from whom the Squadron's commanding officer could claim direct descent. It would have been strange indeed, if Freddie Gough had not noted the uncanny similarity between his own situation and that in which his gallant predecessor had been involved five centuries before. Nor was such reawakening of the spirit of the past to end there, for, in the course of the battle that was to follow at Arnhem, one more proud chapter was to be written into the record of a distinguished and honourable family. To no one would Shakespeare's words, penned in memory of that earlier struggle, be more appropriate than to Freddie Gough himself:

> "Old men forget; yet all shall be forgot,
> But he'll remember with advantages
> What feats he did that day . . ."

At just after 1330 hours in the afternoon, the gliders arrived over their destination point and the landings began. There was always an element of the unpredictable involved in the process of landing a loaded craft of such size and, for that reason, the men of the Glider Pilot Regiment had to be amongst the most skilled specialists in the British army. On that day, it transpired that the unpredictable element was the nature of the landing zone itself. Lengthy study of aerial photographs prior to the operation had created the belief that the LZ was a stubble field which would provide a firm area on which to land. Having to bring down their engineless planes on what turned out to be a ploughed potato field was a job which tested to the full all the expertise of the glider pilots involved. David Allsop still has a personal recollection of the difficulties: "I remember my glider pilot, Robbie Boyd, suddenly shouting, "God – I've bogged it," when he realized that he was coming in too steeply for the soft ground. Just then, the floorboards came up and hit us in the face."

Some landings had much more serious consequences, particularly if, having buried its nose into the soft soil, the glider then flipped over on to its back. When that happened, the occupants had little chance, and Henry Venes was one of those who saw a nearby Hamilcar end up in that way, with the two glider pilots crushed to death inside. An attendant hazard was the presence of nearby wooded areas, and a number of gliders crashed into the trees, sustaining damage of various kinds with accompanying death and injury to the occupants. One Reconnaissance Squadron glider of HQ Troop landed fairly high up in the foliage of one group of trees, as a result of which Squadron Sergeant-Major Bill Meadows suffered a fractured spine. Cyril Belcham, who was with him, remembered having to administer a morphine injection before scrambling down the tree and jumping to the ground. For the later arrivals, there was also the additional difficulty that, as the landing proceeded, the zone gradually took on the appearance of an overcrowded car park. "For between fifteen and twenty minutes," recalls John Stevenson, "there was the constant crashing of those things coming down – great woofted birds, all over the place."

But soon the last of the gliders had come to rest and their towing aircraft had turned for home. The droning in the sky gradually faded to a whisper and then to nothing. On the ground, all was astir, as men applied themselves to the well-practised drills of unloading the vehicles and equipment. Then at 1400 hours, just a half-hour behind the gliders, the faint pulsing of aircraft engines was again heard from the west. Within ten minutes it had swollen to a mounting crescendo of vibrant intensity as the C 47s carrying the bulk of the personnel of the 1st British Airborne

Division appeared in the sky, heading in on their final bearing to the landing and dropping zones. Suddenly, from the ground it was possible to see clusters of tiny black dots appear, silhouetted against the sky. Then like great blossoming flowers unfolding their petals, the parachutes began to break out over the fields of Renkum and Reijerscamp.

From each of the planes overhead, every man jumped on the pre-ordained signal. As the red light beside the door flashed on, the subdued conversations dwindled to a silent expectancy. In an instant, came the "green" and they were moving swiftly out into the slipstream of the aircraft. One followed the other without hesitation, so that the "stick" flowed out with all the smooth perfection of a well-functioning machine. As the cold air currents tore at their clothing, all of them felt the familiar sensations of exhilaration, apprehension and helplessness that always accompanied the plunge into that curious temporal limbo and the long agonizing seconds that it took for the parachute to unfold from its pack. An eternity later, came the comforting tug and the welcoming sight of coloured silk ballooning out against a light blue sky.

With a swift glance over the rigging to check for twisted lines, each man then paid out his kit bag by unwinding the rope attached to his waist and, for just a few brief seconds of the descent, it was then possible to relax and to take a quick look at the surrounding countryside below. The green woods to east and west stood out in verdant contrast with the purpling heathland to the north, and the furrows of the great flat expanse of the dropping zone. Here and there, an occasional farm or church spire could be seen and, in the middle distance, the small town of Oosterbeek, sitting neatly on the calm, dark ribbon of the Neder Rijn. Celanese panels, laid by the pathfinders to mark the dropping zones, could be seen, with scattered plumes of coloured smoke wisping upwards from the mustering points. Scattered thickly on the ploughed fields below were scores of fawn-coloured gliders their broad black and white striped wing markings and coloured rondels clearly discernible from the air. Men could also be seen bustling around the grounded craft and, with all the jerkiness of children's toys, military vehicles that had already been unloaded, lurched bumpily across the uneven surface of the field to pre-arranged rendezvous points.

To the watchers below, there seemed to be no end to it all for, as the noise of the throbbing aircraft mounted to a thunderous climax, cluster after cluster of burgeoning colour splashed the sky with combinations of khaki, white, orange, blue and yellow. And all the time, like a great moving canopy, hundreds upon hundreds of airborne soldiers and containerized equipment floated down in a harmonious unison of movement until, at the moment of contact with the ground, each man sought to free himself as rapidly as possible from the harness, thoughts already turned towards the more conventional tasks of soldiering.

For the Dutch in the adjacent town of Oosterbeek, the magnificently arresting spectacle heralded the long-awaited spring time of liberation. Throughout years of depressing and detested enemy occupation they had dreamed of such a day, when Churchill's promise to return would be fulfilled and the blight of German oppression brought to an end. Now, unbelievably, it was happening, but who could ever have predicted that it would come in such a dramatic way? Never was a liberating army welcomed with such fervour. Some cheered, others wept, openly overcome by the emotion of an experience that was one of unforeseen joy, whilst most contemplated the unfolding drama with a glow of inner content and resurrected faith. Suddenly the nightmare was over, they were free once more and the dreary, interminable days of fading hopes had come to an end. For those who had so long endured the privations and uncertainty that had become so much a part of their lives, it was a time to be savoured and remembered – something to tell of, again and again, in the years that lay ahead.

From the viewpoint of the airborne men themselves, it was a good jump and there were few landing accidents. Frank Mann's recollection of it as, "the best landing ever," is typical of the reaction of most who parachuted in that afternoon. To a considerable extent, this was due to the calmness of the day, for even a slight breeze could play havoc with a drop, producing not only physical injuries but also a scattering of personnel over a wide area. Another reason for the success of the jump was the high quality of the "X"-type statichute in use at that time. The degree of control that he could attain by manipulation of the lift webs together with the even disposition of the parachutist's weight in the harness, made the British airborne soldier infinitely less vulnerable to the body bruising commonly suffered by his counterpart of the *Fallschirmjäger*. But, there were still potential hazards to be overcome, and some were encountered even before the ground was reached. In some cases, it was desultory firing from the woods, although this was not the nuisance that it was to become for the following lifts. In other instances, the trouble could be nearer at hand, as Arthur Barlow discovered when there was a sudden bang and a high-pitched whistle near him during his descent. The noise was that of a grenade, inadvertently released by another parachutist in mid-air, the explosion being followed by the whine of the fuse cap as it whistled off into space. Barlow's immediate worry, however, was still the kitbag with the three steel aerial rods of the 38 set protruding from the top for, as it hit the ground, he saw, to his dismay, that all the barrack room experiments of the previous evening had been in vain. Far from falling flat, as he had hoped it would do, the bag had thumped itself securely into an upright position between the fresh furrows of the potato field, with impalement an immediate possibility. By good luck he missed that unhappy fate, but with no more than a yard to spare!

Inevitably, some were unlucky. Alf Hazell had his own troubles on the way down, when his rifle became temporarily caught up in the parachute rigging. With vivid memories of the pre-Arnhem exercise in which young "Ginger" Rew of Bannockburn had "roman-candled" to his death in similar circumstances, Hazell's sole concern was to extricate himself as rapidly as possible. It may be that the need to untangle the parachute shrouds left him slightly off balance at the point of impact with the ground. Whatever the reason, Alf Hazell's first contact with Dutch soil resulted in that commonest of all parachuting accidents, a broken ankle, so that he was out of things right at the start. Fortunately, such mishaps were few in number, and the general mood of optimism was, if anything, reinforced by the relatively effortless nature of the operation thus far. Few could have predicted that within a matter of hours the situation would change dramatically, beyond all recognition.

Chapter 4 SUNDAY 17th SEPTEMBER 1944

AFTERNOON

"Tell my wife I love her"

Thus it was that the Reconnaissance Squadron, in company with just over one half of the 1st British Airborne Division landed in occupied Europe. In many ways, the quiet landing perhaps accentuated rather than diminished the initial unreality of a genuine airborne operation. Traditionally when soldiers had gone to war they had done so in certain commonly recognized ways, either by troopship or perhaps overland, as part of a mechanized force. Often too, considerable parts of the journey might have to be covered on foot. In all such transitions from peace to war, the change was usually a gradual one, but for the airborne soldier this was no longer so. Now, in a dramatic compression of time he found himself suddenly plucked from the peaceful unscarred world of rustic England to be set abruptly down far behind the enemy's front line positions. For those who, a mere three hours earlier, had driven past the shuttered shops in the quiet Sunday streets of an English town, who had, that very morning, posted letters home, who had queued for tea at the WVS trolley and had looked out on the well-loved landscapes of Lincolnshire, it could hardly have been other than a period of initial disorientation. The Dutch countryside west of Arnhem was not characteristically unlike that of many parts of Britain, and yet the airborne men had immediately to accept that, in reality, their new situation was as different as it could possibly be. Here, in spite of the presence of the familiar oaks and beeches, the pink heathland and the neat farmsteads, they had entered a world of hostility, danger and death.

Now, like actors on a stage, they had already taken their places at the start of the final act in the story of Europe's liberation and survival. As the curtain rose, few could have had any proper preconception of the drama that was about to unfold or of the unique part which they themselves would come to play in it. On that Sunday afternoon, the sun shone upon a scene of deceptive calm but, for the men who had come from the sky, it was the few long agonizing days that followed which were speedily and cruelly to become the new and the true reality. Then, as they battled with an enemy who had yet to come to terms with the inevitability of his own impending defeat, pastoral England, and for the Reconnaissance Squadron in particular the quiet village of Ruskington, was to become a fast-fading and almost unbelievable memory.

But all that had yet to come. To begin with, everything had gone well and there appeared to be few losses, either of men or equipment. Already, as the last of the troops were freeing themselves from their parachutes, the landing and dropping zones had taken on an air of packed and bustling activity. Glider-borne vehicles were being driven to their specified assembly points, to meet up with those who had come by parachute. Throughout the area, men had started to gather in groups, the rendezvous recognized as much from the memory of air photographs carefully studied on pre-operational briefing sessions as from the plumes of coloured smoke which rose to guide them. There were other ways, too, in which some were brought together, like the skirl of "Blue Bonnets over the Border" from the piper of the 7th Battalion King's Own Scottish Borderers, or the strains of John Frost's hunting horn as he rallied together the men of his own 2nd Parachute Battalion. The hulks of the gliders, the brown-green smocks of the men, the camouflaged helmets and red berets all blended into the subdued colours of the Dutch landscape yet it was a picture that was constantly changing, as all over the vast areas of Renkum Heath and Reijerscamp came the activity and ferment of thousands on the move, each loading up and taking himself to his own designated start line.

Out of the fight before it had begun, and propped up against a hedge by the side of the dropping zone, Alf Hazell waited for medical attention and watched the scene. "I can still remember," he says, "all the bustle of the unloading and mustering at the rendezvous points. Freddie (Gough) passed by and said, 'Hard luck – I'll see you later,' and I clearly recall that, whilst all this was going on, the Dutch girls and women were running out of the woods to grab the parachutes, whilst the recovery squads of the RAOC tried to stop them. Some of the boys, like "Spud" and "Gunner' were on the side of the ladies, and we were encouraging them to get the best of the silk ones whilst they were there. There was one farmer, I remember, who had his whole family organized to dash about collecting as many as they could and they were all running with the parachutes to a nearby barn."

The Squadron's rendezvous was topographically conspicuous as the corner of a large wood about 750 yards south of a railway level crossing, and it was to that point that those who had dropped came to meet up with their vehicles. For Major Gough, everything looked to be going well, as from all directions of the vast landing area, came vehicle after vehicle, each bearing on its front wing the distinctive "41" of the Reconnaissance Corps. Bren guns, PIATS and 2-inch mortars were removed from kitbags and made ready with swift efficiency, and it was particularly unfortunate that, in all of this activity, Lieutenant Bob Guthrie of A Troop, a young architect from Tunbridge Wells, became the first shooting casualty when he accidentally discharged his own Sten gun and shot himself through the hand.

In addition to this, A Troop was having other difficulties. By a combination of circumstances that were quite coincidental, it appeared that, unlike the other Troops of the Squadron, much of the A Troop transport was either completely missing or temporarily inaccessible. As a consequence of bad crash landings it had not been possible to remove the four vehicles of 1 and 3 Sections from their gliders, nor one of the vehicles of A Troop HQ. Worse still was the fact that 2 Section's jeeps had not arrived at all. For Captain Mike Grubb, the Troop commander, it was a trying start, yet not too serious, because it had already been decided, at the planning stage of the operation, that A Troop would remain in reserve on the dropping zone and not participate in the *coup de main*. If there had to be losses or delay, therefore, Grubb's troop was the one which could most readily accept them without prejudice to the original plan.

In other respects, the Squadron's strength was almost complete. HQ Troop was only lacking one vehicle, in consequence of Graham Wadsworth having to turn back to Tarrant Rushton; C Troop despite some bother in getting two of its vehicles out, turned up at the rendezvous in its entirety. D Troop had two vehicles which could not immediately be extricated, and so was a little below its full complement. Taking the Squadron as a whole, the situation was that, not only were the figures for initial casualties well below the acceptable level, but the non-arrival of two Reconnaissance Squadron gliders from an allotment of twenty-two was statistically compatible with total divisional losses (30 out of 358) on the whole first lift. Certainly, as far as the *coup de main* was concerned, twenty-eight out of the thirty-one jeeps earmarked for it were mustered. One serious organizational flaw did emerge, however, in relation to sub-unit co-operation, but it was the fault of neither of the units concerned. It arose because the four jeeps of 9 Field Company Royal Engineers, which were to have accompanied the Reconnaissance Squadron on the *coup de main*, were not sent in the flight serials next to the Squadron nor were they even landed in the same zone! The result was that when the Engineers did get away, they made no link up with the Reconnaissance men.

At 1540 hours the Squadron was ready to go and, apart from the A Troop reserve, only a small Squadron Rear HQ under Lieutenant QM Collier was to be left on the dropping zone. C Troop was to lead, followed by HQ Troop, with D Troop and the smaller Support Troop, with its Polsten guns, bringing up the rear. All were anxious to get under way, none perhaps more so than young Peter Bucknall, a single-minded and dedicated officer who, as commander of C Troop's number 8 Section, was very conscious of the crucial role which had been given to his own Troop. Personnel had been detailed off at briefing time for specific vehicles, but so anxious was Bucknall to be quit of Renkum Heath that he disregarded those arrangements and took on to his jeep the first three available men of his Section. These were Troopers Goulding, Brumwell and Gorringe. As the order to move out was given, Bucknall took off immediately with them, leaving his sergeant, Tom McGregor, to follow as rapidly as possible with the other members of the Section. It meant, of course, that there was a slightly uneven spread of personnel, in so far as Bucknall's jeep carried only four men and McGregor's had to take six, but this was of no tactical significance, since the men of the Squadron were used to such flexibility. As events were to prove, however, it is certain that Peter Bucknall's last-minute rearrangement assuredly saved at least one man's life.

McGregor, meantime, lost no time in getting his men aboard. With him, he had Lance-Corporal Thomas and Troopers Pearce, Minns, Barlow and Hasler and, by putting on a spurt, he succeeded in catching up with his Section officer. Ahead of Bucknall's two jeeps were the four of Sections 9 and 7, whilst the two vehicles of C Troop HQ brought up the rear. Already, they were making good progress and they knew that the plan was to run parallel to the railway by the minor road that went through the northern suburbs of Oosterbeek, and from there to the primary divisional objective of Arnhem Bridge. In theory it seemed quite straightforward – at the most a twenty minute run, then a short period of holding at the Bridge until the foot soldiers arrived. All very good – all too good perhaps – too good to be true!

In an atmosphere of well-organized dispersal, the other units of the Division were, one by one, confidently moving off in similar fashion to their allotted tasks. To the west, units of 1st Air Landing Brigade were already marching towards Ginkel, whilst the three battalions of Lathbury's 1st Parachute Brigade were also getting under way to move in the opposite direction towards Arnhem town. Divisional elements, too, like field ambulance, engineers and light artillery were all well ahead in preparation for undertaking their own specialized tasks, and it was with an air of cautious optimism that the 1st Airborne Reconnaissance Squadron set out likewise on its own unique mission. Some wore their rimless helmets with green camouflage covers, but there were others who disdained those, preferring to wear their red berets, each bearing the spearhead and lightning badge of the Reconnaissance Corps. Jeep engines increased speed, and wireless operators crouched over their 22 sets, red pilot lights aglow, HP units humming, each Troop HQ already successfully netted in on the Squadron's frequency, and in disciplined response acknowledging, in turn, the familiar call of, "Hello all stations Fox Baker Charlie, report my signals, Over." As the convoy gathered momentum, it was inevitable and entirely appropriate that someone from one of the vehicles should have shouted that unofficial yet universally acknowledged battle cry of the Corps, "Bash on Recce!"

The short distance up by the wood to the railway line was accomplished in minutes. Then came the right turn eastwards and the drive along the sandy but well-bottomed track that ran straight beside the railway to Wolfheze station, a solid two-storeyed building of pink and yellow brick. Just before the station, in extensive grounds to the right of the road, was a large psychiatric hospital. It had been bombed by the Royal Air Force that morning, as it was believed that the Germans were in occupation of a part of it and were using it for military purposes. Notwithstanding their recent unhappy experience in the bombing, the hospital staff showed no sign of animosity towards the British, and Sam Bowles, lieutenant in charge of 9 Section, still remembers how they were met by the nurses, who ran out, "with gifts of apples and warm smiles," to give what information they were able to offer about enemy troop movements in the area.

The reality of the enemy's presence had already become apparent within minutes of the move away from the landing zone for, just on the edge of the hospital grounds, an 88 mm Flak gun had been destroyed in the air attack and two of its crew were dead beside it. Henry Crowder remembers how, against the background of a section of the hospital that was still on fire, one of the dead Germans sat, propped up against a fence, "with his own blood congealed all the way down his front, from his nose to his feet." Bill Chandler also recalls how his mate, "Midge" Miles investigated further by lifting back the man's helmet from his face. It was then that David Christie, 9 Section Sergeant, spotted a live German crawling out from behind the cover of the dead man, with his hands up. It was an episode of no great significance, but it was "first contact" and, with a jerk of the thumb, the sergeant ordered the German to "Double!" in the direction of Renkum Heath. Christie can still remember with clarity that the order was quite incomprehensible to the enemy soldier, but that instant communication was established when he repeated it, to the accompaniment of a quick Sten burst that zipped into the ground near to the German's feet. As he was to comment soon afterwards, with an ironic economy of words: "He understood then alright!" Meanwhile, in an almost simultaneous incident, just by the western side of Wolfheze station, Christie's fellow sergeant, Bill Stacey of 7 Section, shot a German who attempted to escape into the woods adjacent to the road.

From the start, the time during which these initial contacts were made could not have exceeded ten minutes, so that the Squadron was making good progress. What they were unaware of was that, despite the successful beginning on the *coup de main*, a very odd rumour had arisen back at the landing zone. Understandably, in any situation containing the kind of confusion such as could hardly have been avoided in a massive airborne landing, there was almost inevitably bound to be a degree of misreporting. A certain proportion of conflicting accounts, guesswork and rumour are almost unavoidable by-products of any military operation of such a size and scale. Yet, however easily rumour may germinate and feed upon itself, it ought, logically, in the face of tangible evidence, to be the more readily corrected. In this instance, no such logical process was followed for, despite the Squadron's successful muster and subsequent despatch, it was being said that, as a result of glider mishap, it had lost most of its vehicles and was, therefore, no longer in a position to undertake the race for the Bridge. It was a damaging rumour, and just when it began and how it originated remains to this day a mystery. The likeliest explanation is that the various initial difficulties of A Troop were somehow reported in exaggerated form as applicable to the Squadron as a whole. A quick wireless query to the Squadron's "Sunray" (i.e. its commanding officer's HQ) could certainly have scotched the rumour, but already poor radio communication was introducing a major complication into the direction of the battle and it was becoming unhappily apparent that, for all their skill, Roy Urquhart's signallers at Divisional HQ were experiencing the greatest of difficulty in keeping contact going with the operational units. Part of this was undoubtedly due to the inadequacy of the wireless sets themselves, but it was mainly because the heavily wooded territory was acting as a screen against the reception of signals from sets transmitting on simple rod aerials. Thus, from the outset, the Divisional commander found himself out of radio communication with many of the major elements in his command. From the sources available to him, as well as from personal observation, General Urquhart was confident that Gerald Lathbury's 1st Parachute Brigade was on course for the objective, but no news had been received about the progress of Brigadier Hicks's 1st Air Landing Brigade. As a result, he paid a personal visit to the latter's HQ, only to find that Hicks, in similar plight, was doing exactly the same and going forward personally in order to get information about his battalions. It was whilst he was there, however, that Urquhart was brought information about the Reconnaissance Squadron's supposed losses. In the circumstances, he had no reason to disbelieve this totally false report. No doubt Mike Grubb or Tom Collier who were still working at their respective jobs on the dropping zone could have corrected the story, but the assumption of credibility seems to have been fairly general at Divisional HQ, so that neither officer was approached for confirmation. It would, in any case, have been a daunting task to have attempted to identify a small group of residual Reconnaissance personnel amongst the mass of troops and vehicles with which the dropping and landing zones were still well crowded.

Prompted by a natural anxiety to save as much as he could of the original plan and to compensate for a *coup de main* which he believed to be a non-starter, Urquhart's immediate priority was to inform John Frost of the situation and urge him to press on with all haste, in order to get his 2nd Parachute Battalion to the Bridge without further delay. The General also issued instructions that, in the circumstances, he wished to see Major Gough as soon as possible. As events were to determine, the meeting was never to take place, but the request, once made, was to prove to be one of significance for the Squadron's future contribution to the battle.

Meanwhile, totally unaware of the unfortunate rumours that had filtered through to Divisional Headquarters, the Squadron's leading jeeps were grouping at Wolfheze crossing. It had been decided that, at least initially, standard "leapfrogging" reconnaissance practice would operate. This meant that, according to circumstances, either the twin vehicles of a single section themselves alternated, each in turn acting as leader, or else a whole section would fall back to let another come through and take its place in the lead position. Once overtaken, those behind then assumed the role of protecting the rear and flanks of their own forward elements. It was a system which provided for the maximum level of operational efficiency, and it had been agreed that, after the initial run of just under two miles, which would take the Squadron from its rendezvous point to Wolfheze, Peter Bucknall's 8 Section would take over from 9 and move into the lead. With this in mind, Sam Bowles clearly remembers executing the standard manoeuvre, by pulling his Section into the cover of trees by the side of a road which by then had dwindled to little more than a narrow dusty farm track. It was from there that Bowles still recalls seeing Bucknall's two

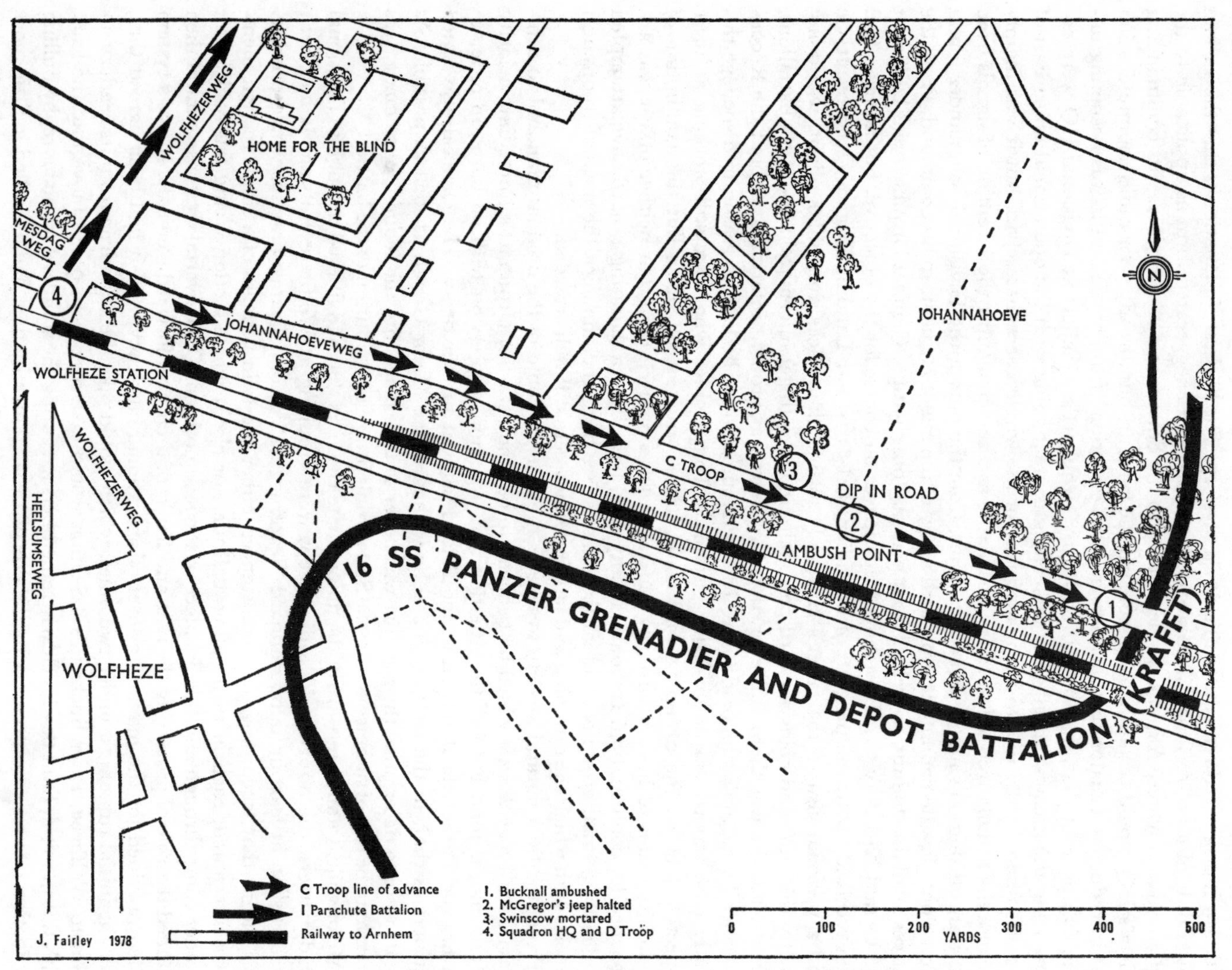

Map 4 Ambush of C Troop at Wolfheze: Sunday 17th September 1944

8 Section jeeps come through at speed, with 7 Section, led by Ralph Foulkes, immediately following. This had the effect of leaving Bowles's Section and the C Troop HQ under Captain Hay with the main covering role. Behind them, was the remainder of the Squadron.

Until then, the Reconnaissance Squadron had been on the south side of the railway line, but at Wolfheze level crossing it moved over to the north and on to another lane, rather grandiosely named the Johannahoeveweg. From the station, this ran eastwards as a narrow avenue through a grove of oak trees. About a third of a mile beyond Wolfheze junction, it took a fairly steep dip down into an open area, on each side of which many of the trees had been cleared. As a result, the available cover was sparse. Alongside, to the right, the main railway line to Arnhem still ran parallel but no longer on a level with the route being followed by the Squadron. Now, the railway commanded the open territory in and around the dip, for it ran along the top of a steep embankment, the northern edge of which was overgrown with close-packed hawthorn bushes. After the dip, the road rose up again in a gentle incline, to continue its straight course in the direction of the town. In the lengthening shadows of that pleasant Sunday afternoon, the way ahead ran clear and inviting. Gough's men had no suspicion that behind the innocent hawthorns adjoining the railway, and up ahead in the shady trees that flanked the road as it crossed the little valley, lay the men of the 16th SS Panzer Grenadier Battalion.

The commander of this German unit was *SS Sturmbannführer* Sepp Krafft, an able and perceptive junior officer with a flair for military strategy. Once informed of the landings, he had worked out that the most probable line of the British advance would be through the woodland between the railway and the more southerly Utrechtseweg, along which Fitch's 3rd Parachute Battalion was to go. It was as a result of this reasoning that Krafft had spread his Battalion out in a defensive line, along the eastern side of the Wolfhezerweg all the way from its junction at Utrechtseweg, northwards almost to Wolfheze station. As part of this defence, his Reserve Platoon was detached from the rest and positioned in the woodland to the north of the railway, in order to protect his Battalion's right flank, as well as to cover the railway itself. It was an effective deployment of a relatively small force and, ironically, it was, in these initial stages, all that stood between the British and their primary objective at Arnhem Bridge. The time was then just a little before 1600 hours in the afternoon.

Unsuspecting, Peter Bucknall's lead vehicle swept down into the dip and up the other side. As it disappeared from sight amongst the trees, firing broke out, at which point the second 8 Section vehicle, commanded by Sergeant Tom McGregor, had almost reached the lowest point of the dip. As McGregor and his men came into the open, Minns, hit in the stomach, tumbled out of the jeep. More firing immediately followed, and it appeared to be coming from several directions. In the wooded front ahead, Krafft's SS were using at least one heavy machine-gun and intensive fire from the embankment was being directed to the side and rear of the C Troop men below. McGregor, following standard procedure and perhaps conscious of what had already happened up ahead to Bucknall and the others, ordered dismounted action, and his men ran to take up whatever firing positions they could find in the unpromising and exposed territory that lay to each side of the road.

There was no time for deliberation on the matter. Thomas and Hasler followed the wounded Minns and dived beneath the jeep. The other three scattered for cover in the sparsely wooded area to the left of the road. There, McGregor threw himself into a shallow ditch, whilst Pearce and Barlow found protection behind the trunks of a pair of slender oak trees. One difficulty about engaging the enemy was that, although the Germans up ahead could be seen quite plainly moving about among the trees, those on the railway who were pinning the Reconnaissance men down were screened by the bushes and could only be detected occasionally by the muzzle flash from their guns.

Arthur Barlow remembers what happened then: "I began firing around the side of the tree, and straightaway a machine-gun started to remove large chunks of bark just above my helmet. I remember seeing Sergeant McGregor rear himself up on his hands to have a look around. He fell flat on his face and died without making a sound. On top of the railway embankment, a German soldier was letting off single shots at Pearce and me. One of his shots hit the body of my Sten gun and went right through the cocking-handle slot, ruining the breech-block spring." It was a very near miss for, at the time, Barlow had the Sten in the shoulder-firing position, with the cocking-handle no further than six inches from his nose!

From his meagre cover beside Barlow, Pearce heard Minns shout that he had been shot in the leg, and it was obvious that he was in great pain. Almost immediately, the others sheltering beneath the jeep were also hit. In making a move to put the radio out of action, Thomas got a bullet in the foot and Hasler sustained a serious leg injury. Pearce, meantime, already scorched by bullets in two places, had his fingers deeply grazed when the Sten was blown out of his hands. Barlow was also slightly injured when he received a superficial flesh wound in the thigh. With McGregor dead, and the rest of them wounded, the C Troop men had no alternative but to surrender. Lacking any kind of defensive cover, it was inevitable that they would simply be picked off, one by one. Someone beside the jeep put up a white flag and the firing stopped. Barlow remembers how, almost immediately, a German sergeant then called to them to come out with their hands up. He also assured them, in perfect English, that if they left the dead and seriously injured, they would be properly looked after. An attempt by Barlow to return to the jeep to retrieve his haversack, which contained razor, soap, mess tins and other personal belongings was blocked by the German, and he still remembers with great clarity, how, as he stood several paces away from the vehicle, he could hear the disembodied voice of Control station operator crying from the discarded headsets of the wireless, with a total disregard for standard transmission procedure, "For Christ's sake, Oboe Two, give us your position!"

Tom McGregor had to be left, and Minns was too gravely hurt to be manhandled by his comrades, all of whom had, themselves, been hit. Still, it was agreed that, despite the German sergeant's instructions, Hasler should be taken along. "We had to carry him", says Jimmy Pearce, "and I took hold of a stick for support – a bit of old tree branch, it was – and got Reg up and leaning on my shoulder. After that we just kept going and took it in turns to carry him. I can still remember as he rested on my back, how Reg said that it was like being a bleedin' rear gunner in the Camel Corps!"

And so, the group for whom the war had so speedily ended limped away from the scene of the ambush. They were wounded, exhausted and shocked but, as they shuffled along, Pearce noticed the end of a large sausage protruding slightly from their German escort's pocket. Working himself gradually over to the German's side, he was able to remove it without detection. The sausage was then quickly shared out amongst the others in the party. One of Pearce's most treasured memories is of how they laughed when young Reg Hasler, in the indomitable spirit of the native-born Londoner suddenly shouted out, "Hey – square-head – ain't yer got no bleedin' salt for this end of sausage?"

From the beginning, the action involving 8 Section could not have taken more than a few minutes, and certainly by the time that number 7 Section, which was immediately following, had come on the scene, it was by no means over. Ralph Foulkes recollects that, having drawn the two vehicles into the cover of the trees, his Section then moved forward on foot to investigate, and one of the first things which he saw was McGregor's vehicle, with the men still lying around it. Foulkes moved back and reported the situation to the Troop commander, Captain John Hay, who then made two decisions. One was that 9 Section should move to the south side of the railway, in order to guard the Squadron's right flank, the other that 7 Section should move nearer to the scene of the action and undertake a foot reconnaissance to discover precisely what had happened.

As a result, Ralph Foulkes led his Section down the slope towards the dip. The men were fanned out on each side of the track, using whatever cover was available, with some more advantageously placed than others. Henry Crowder remembers that he was in the lee of the embankment and much less exposed to enemy fire than were his comrades on the other side of the road. Sergeant Bill Stacey was one of those who deployed to the left, and Ted Hares still recollects Stacey attempting a solo reconnaissance down towards McGregor's vehicle, only to be shot at from a point on the railway somewhere to his right. As Stacey lay in the road with a stomach wound, Hares recalls how he shouted, "Stay back – I've been shot, but try to help me." Calling for assistance, Lieutenant Foulkes, who was only a short distance away, ran over with Trooper Dodson. Unfortunately, they found Stacey too heavy to move and, as the bullets kicked up the earth around them, he was hit again, this time more seriously. Astonishingly, neither Foulkes nor Dodson was hit, but they had to withdraw, leaving Stacey still lying in the road.

Squadron Headquarters was only a few hundred yards to the rear, and it was at that point in the action that Major Gough received the message that the General wished to see him. With his forward elements already engaged in a critical action, it was an unfortunate position for any squadron commander suddenly to find himself in; nor was Gough to know that the summons was a direct consequence of the "lost vehicles" rumour. His dilemma was a very real one, but he concluded that as his unit looked to be well pinned down, for a short time at least, it would only be a matter of minutes, there and back, to make the journey to Renkum Heath in order to report to the General. So it was that, leaving the Squadron under his second-in-command, Captain David Allsop, Gough turned around and headed back towards Divisional HQ. With him he took some officers and men of his own Squadron HQ, including Tony Platt, the officer commanding HQ Troop and Trevor McNabb, his Intelligence Officer; he also took along some men of D Troop on one of their own jeeps.

Rapidly, the small group of vehicles covered the short distance back to the dropping zone, but luck was not with Gough, for he arrived only to learn that Urquhart had gone off just prior to his arrival. In anticipation of this, the General had left word that he would be with Brigadier Lathbury who, by then, was taking his own Brigade HQ along the lower route to Arnhem in the rear of Frost's 2nd Battalion. Like other commanders who were much dependent upon successful and well-sustained wireless links, Major Gough was beginning to realize that the elusive nature of his attempts to contact both the Divisional and Brigade commanders was a consequence of serious breakdown in radio communication. He also sensed that his predicament was by no means unique. Already it was only too evident that the circumstances forcing General Urquhart to go chasing after his own troops in order to find out anything at all, had created an impediment of major significance. But, it is difficult to see how Urquhart could have done otherwise, and his plight simply mirrored what had developed at all levels throughout his

Division. In the main, radio communication at battalion and company level appeared to be working no better than higher up the chain of command.

And so, following the trail of the General, Freddie Gough set off once more with his three jeeps. As he travelled on the circuitous route by Renkum crossroads, it was hardly surprizing that inwardly he was becoming increasingly anxious about the fate of his own unit. Conscious of his lengthening absence from it, and in a state of mounting frustration, he was not to know that it would be many long months before he would again meet either General Urquhart or the officers and men of the Reconnaissance Squadron, whom he had left, for what he imagined would only be a short interval of time, fighting in the dip beyond Wolfheze station.

Back there, matters had not improved. David Allsop, in overall command and occupying what he believed would be a caretaker role of short duration, had wisely decided to leave John Hay to try to make what progress he could with C Troop. Unfortunately, the situation was showing signs of further deterioration, for number 7 Section, in its vulnerable forward position had also come under heavy attack, with mortars added to the small-arms and machine-gun fire of the SS troops. One serious difficulty was the steady sniper action directed at them from a position not too far away, but undetectable. This was accurate and persistent, making it very hard for the Section to move back from the thin cover to the shelter of the woods through which they had come. Faced with a tactical situation that had all the ingredients of a developing stalemate, Captain Hay decided to withdraw Lieutenant Bowles's 9 Section from the defensive flanking position which they had been occupying to the south of the railway, and use them instead to relieve the hard-pressed 7 Section. Already Bowles and his men had been keeping their reserve position for over an hour, and Hay obviously thought that, since they were fresh, they might be able to cover the withdrawal of the others and also, perhaps, succeed in one final attempt at a breakthrough.

The first part of the plan was carried out with relative ease. 9 Section moved with speed to the north side of the railway, came to within twenty yards of 7 Section's rear and then laid down a thick smoke screen in order to cover the remainder of its advance. David Christie noted at the time how, under cover of the smoke, they were then able to move forward and take up new positions about fifty yards in front of the 7 Section men. Despite that, Stacey, who was lying wounded and had been unable to move back with the others, was still a short distance further on. It was in the course of this move that a significant observation was also made by two of the 9 Section men, one of whom was Trooper Bill Chandler: "I remember," he says, "that we were down the slope, looking across the dip to the German side, when 'Midge' Miles spotted a burning jeep amongst the trees. We worked our way through the cover, and came out further down the slope; it was then that I could see Gorringe in it – he was dead." Miles and Chandler had glimpsed Bucknall's ambushed vehicle with the body of one of those who had been on it. They had no opportunity to investigate any further, because just then Chandler was hit for the first time. Recalling the episode, he says, "I remember dodging to left and right with 'Midge', when suddenly my helmet was cut by a bullet on the side and, as I lay on the ground, I realized that I had a trickle of blood running down the side of my head. 'Midge' said, 'We'll laugh at this when we get back,' so I swapped the damaged helmet for my red beret, picked up my Bren and got back into cover behind a tree."

Soon, in the face of renewed and intensive enemy fire, it became apparent that Sam Bowles's section was going to be no more successful in its attempts to break through than the others had been. Realizing this, Captain Hay issued an order for the recovery of the wounded, to be followed by general withdrawal. It was assumed that, in terms of the Geneva Convention, the former process could be carried out by the Squadron's Medical Officer and his orderlies. Bearing a Red Cross flag and with arm brassards that clearly indicated their purpose, Captain Douglas Swinscow and his men moved out quite openly with a stretcher, in order to fetch in the wounded Stacey. They were instantly fired on and forced to withdraw. Seeing this, the Troop commander then decided to try to recover the injured sergeant under cover of another smoke screen. David Christie's account takes up the story: "The smoke was laid down and we advanced. We reached a point about twenty yards from the wounded man, when the Huns started sending heavy machine-gun fire into the smoke. Snipers opened up on our right and left flanks, and we found ourselves in a very precarious position. We dived for cover and immediately returned the fire." From the position behind the tree to which they had already retreated, Miles and his companion were also covering the German positions across the dip, with Bill Chandler still congratulating himself upon his narrow escape. Chandler's luck, however, had run out: "'Midge' and I opened up again, with, perhaps, three or four Bren magazines into the woods ahead of us when, all at once, I was hit in the thigh. It was a terrific blow, like a red-hot poker going in, and I thought it had come from behind, from one of our own men." It was an understandable assumption for Chandler to make for he obviously did not realize that Krafft's 4th Company was enfilading the Section from the embankment. No sooner had Chandler been put out of action, however, than a shot took away two of the fingers of Miles's right hand. To this day, Christie recalls how Miles immediately switched his gun over and continued the firing with his left hand!

Concerned primarily for Chandler, Miles then shouted for the stretcher bearers but, in the light of what had happened earlier to Captain Swinscow, there was initial reluctance on the part of the medical orderlies to run out. Undaunted, and with the blood pouring from his shattered right hand, Miles then set out himself to get a stretcher, only to be hit again, this time in the lower abdomen. By then, the Troop had run out of smoke bombs for its 2-inch mortars and had to fire ordinary high explosive to cover the disengagement. Recovery of the wounded had not been a success, and it had become a matter of withdrawing in accordance with the Troop commander's decision. In Christie's words, "We crawled for about forty yards and then decided to get up and make a run for the last ten to twenty yards. In doing this, Edmond, the Scots lad from Musselburgh, was hit in the back and dropped about five yards from the edge of the wood. We then took up a defensive position in the wood and weighed up the situation." Their dilemma was that, whilst unsuccessful in the attempt to recover the wounded of other Sections of the Troop, they had still to try to save the two wounded men of their own Section, Chandler and Edmond. It was not going to be an easy job, because although the two of them were nearer to safety than Stacey was, they were so exposed as to make rescue attempts extremely dangerous.

The wounded Miles had, in the meantime, contacted Captain Swinscow. Christie remembers how, despite the fact that he had a shell dressing on his shattered hand and was obviously in great pain, Miles insisted on helping the MO with the stretcher in order to go back for his friend. Swinscow, nevertheless, also took out one of his own stretcher bearers and the three of them succeeded in getting to Chandler. Douglas Swinscow tells of what happened next: "At that point, the other two were a little way off, so I was by myself with the wounded man, when the Germans opened fire on me. It was obvious that they were using a mortar, and six bombs were fired in succession. The first one landed in front of me, and I lay on the ground. Then a second fell behind me, and after that four more in succession, so that all six made a neat little circle around me. I remember wondering two things. The first was whether it was possible to see a mortar bomb in the air, and I remember, as I heard each detonation from the woods, looking up to see if I could catch it in flight. The second thing that I wondered was, 'When is this man going to hit the centre of the circle?' Well, he didn't, and after six bombs had fallen there was a pause, during which time I signalled to my stretcher bearer. He came over and we put the wounded man on the stretcher and together we picked him up. Much worse then followed, because then we came immediately under machine-gun fire and some bullets hit the stretcher, which was made of aluminium. Fragments of it splintered off, and two pieces embedded themselves into my back – into muscle on either side of the spinal cord. I was extremely lucky but, although no serious damage was done, it did bowl me over and, of course, in falling, I dropped my end of the stretcher." Nor had the patient escaped further injury for, as Chandler, already wounded in two places, lay face down and fully conscious on the stretcher, he was hit for the third time. "I got one in the back," he recalls, "and it went through a bullet-proof vest that I had, finished up a quarter of an inch from the spinal column, and knocked me off the stretcher. I thought 'Please God – I hope I don't die now'."

Somehow or other, Douglas Swinscow and the others managed to take advantage of a lull in the firing to get Chandler in under some cover. Meantime, Lieutenant Bowles and his Section Sergeant, David Christie, had gone out after Edmond. It was generally believed that the sniper responsible for shooting Chandler was the one who had also got Edmond and, certainly, as they dragged him to cover, Bowles and Christie suffered a number of near misses and were made very conscious of the accuracy of the German's shooting. Despite all this, both wounded men were brought safely back, each was given morphia and had his wounds dressed. It was obvious that Edmond was the more serious casualty, as he had been hit in the left lung and had lost a lot of blood. Laid out on a stretcher, he was placed on Christie's jeep and, with Miles and Palmer in the back, they set out for the regimental aid post. On the way back, Edmond kept asking for water and saying that he was going to die. "You won't die, Jock," Christie kept assuring him although, as he adds, "I didn't believe a word I said." They arrived at where the RAP had been just three hours earlier to find it gone, and so, there was little that they could do except unload the casualties and treat the wounds as effectively as possible under Douglas Swinscow's direction. Miles, by then, had passed out, so he was taken off first and given a shot of morphia. Later, at the dressing station in the Tafelberg Hotel, he was to be put out with the dead for burial, only to revive sufficiently in time to be able to crawl back inside again. By the end of the short journey, Edmond, too, was unconscious and, when Christie cut away his clothing, he found a three inch hole in Edmond's back. "The wound was sucking in air," says Christie, "and making a noise just like someone pressing the air from a cycle tube. I took a field dressing and pushed it right inside the hole, and then covered it with a shell dressing. Just after I had finished this, I gave him a drink of brandy from the flask that I carried, and shortly afterwards he recovered consciousness for about two minutes. During that time he said to me, 'Jock, I'm dying. Tell my wife I love her and go and see her for me.' 'Yes, Jock, I will,' I replied. He lost consciousness after that, and died the following morning."

With Miles and Chandler off to casualty clearing station, and Edmond mortally wounded, Sergeant Christie and Lance-Corporal Palmer were the only two left from their vehicle's complement. In rear of C Troop, Squadron HQ and the Support Troop had not become directly involved but, because of mortar fire which had been directed their way, had been forced to adopt defensive positions. Personnel of D Troop, in support of C, had exchanged some small arms fire with the enemy on the embankment and, at no cost to themselves, had been able to record a number of hits. For all that, it had undoubtedly been C Troop's day and it had been a rough one.

At 1830 hours, orders were received from Divisional HQ to disengage, and the Squadron's position, just east of Wolfheze, was taken over by men of the Glider Pilot Regiment. This relief force arrived in the middle of a heavy mortar "stonk" but, for the new arrivals, it was to be a relatively peaceful assignment. Already, the light of the day was passing and, as it eventually faded, Krafft, under the wholly mistaken impression that the British had surrounded his force with a view to annihilating it, quitted the area by making what he believed to be a "break-out" to the north. It was then approximately 2130 hours.

Chapter 5 SUNDAY 17th SEPTEMBER 1944

LATE AFTERNOON TO EVENING

"We're going to take a hell of a bloody hammering"

On the dropping zone, throughout that first afternoon, the members of the Squadron's A Troop had no knowledge of what was happening to their comrades. They had been left as reserve under divisional orders, and, as the Troop with the highest number of badly crashed gliders, their main practical task remained that of extricating their vehicles. In some instances, this took most of the remaining hours of daylight. For Lieutenant John Stevenson, who was number 1 Section officer and had travelled with his own jeeps, it was to take four and a half hours to get them out. He arrived on the landing zone about twenty minutes before the first parachutists and still remembers having a reasonable touch down, followed by a fairly long run into some trees, "with a good hard bump at the end." With his companion of the journey, Lance-Corporal King, Stevenson then discovered that the glider's nose had dug itself into the soft soil, so that the tail was about fifteen to sixteen feet in the air. Getting the Horsa tail off under normal conditions was, in itself, a tricky operation. It needed two men, operating in perfect synchronization, to remove paired pins and shackles simultaneously from both sides. It was a skill that was learned with practice, but to have to carry it out at such a height and angle made the whole thing so very much more difficult. What was worse, the perforated steel ramps which, in theory, were supposed to lead, by a relatively gentle slope, from the back of the opened glider to the ground, were just not long enough to reach. "I remember", says Stevenson, "we had to get out the big panniers which had all our equipment in them, and place them below the tail in such a way that the ramps could run from the glider to the panniers. Even at that, the ramps were nearly vertical so that we had to take both vehicles down, and then bump off the panniers to the ground." Understandably, his fear was that as the jeeps hit the ground, something might give. Fortunately, nothing did, but the whole business was a long sweat-inducing job that was not completed until 1750 hours.

Two others had comparable difficulty after their own rather unorthodox landing. Sergeant Henry Venes and Trooper Ken Hope discovered, soon after touching down, that their glider had a distorted tail, as a result of which the release mechanism would not function. As Hope remembers it, "Henry and I hacked and battered for hours, but the tail stubbornly refused to budge . . . Henry's language was frightful!" Eventually, with the assistance of Lieutenant-Colonel Murray of the Glider Pilot Regiment and two of his subalterns, the back was knocked away and the A Troop HQ vehicles were unloaded, with nothing more serious than one fractured exhaust pipe.

It had taken most of the afternoon to accomplish and they were just five minutes ahead of John Stevenson in getting their jeeps out and on to the ground.

During this time, Squadron Rear HQ under Lieutenant-Quartermaster Tom Collier was coping with its own problems. Collier had about ten men with him, and his first main task was to gather in and stockpile the supplies for which he had particular responsibility. In the main, this was ammunition, but the Squadron's containers were widely scattered over the dropping zone and obviously had to be collected and taken to a central point. Collier decided to set up his base at Klein-Amerika farm just a little under a mile along the road that ran southwards from the original rendezvous point. The task of retrieval then began, with two Reconnaisance jeeps, each pulling a trailer, sent to transport the containers from the field to the farm.

One foreseen difficulty was that whilst the limited amount of transport available for the job was sufficient for a gradual shifting of the total supply of ammunition, it was obviously going to be inadequate in the event of a hurried move away. Collier knew this only too well, and had already given thought to the problem. As a regular soldier of some experience, his natural inclination was to try to "find" transport on the ground. With that in mind, he left the collecting of the containers in the capable hands of Lieutenant Bertie Lickerish, whilst he set off with about a half-dozen men to forage for extra vehicles. Following a short and unsuccessful search in the direction of Wolfheze, the group walked the few miles to the village of Heelsum. There they found transport, but it had all been very efficiently immobilized by the Germans. "As we were looking over that lot," he recalls, "the local population came out to greet us with wine and fruit. This was very welcome, and we stood around in a group on the pavement eating and drinking and chatting to the Dutch people. Just then, we heard the sound of a vehicle engine starting and a few seconds later saw a lorry coming down the road towards us – loaded with German soldiers. As it passed, we stood on the pavement and gazed at them, and they stood on the lorry and looked back at us. No one said anything, they didn't stop and nothing happened – not even an exchange of "V" signs! Shortly afterwards, from the same direction, came a motor bike and sidecar, with two German soldiers, the private driving and the officer in the sidecar. This time we were more prepared and so we opened fire and wounded the officer. It was as we were dressing his wounds that the lorry then reappeared. By then we'd realized that they were SS, so we beat a very quick retreat out of it with our prisoners and returned to Rear HQ. We got back at 1815 hours."

Fifteen minutes later, the bulk of the Squadron began its disengagement from the Wolfheze action, with its commander still missing. D Troop, lacking one jeep in consequence of Major Gough's departure, had meanwhile discovered that one of its other vehicles, although last seen at the rendezvous point, had not arrived at Wolfheze. This was the jeep belonging to 10 Section officer, Lieutenant John Marshall, and the explanation was that, as one of the last Reconnaissance vehicles to leave the landing zone, he had simply gone off in the wrong direction! Later, in retrospect, he was to realize that he had become disorientated in relation to the original rendezvous point at the corner of the wood. As a result, instead of heading north towards the railway, he had taken his jeep south in the direction of Renkum itself. Despite Tom Collier's experience, the Heelsum/Renkum area was still relatively free of any kind of German troop concentration, so that Marshall, who was accompanied by Trooper "Joe" Irala, had only one distant encounter with the enemy: "I saw this German armoured car," he recollects, "somewhere up on the horizon and, as I didn't think that jeeps and armoured cars really went together, I said to Irala, 'Let's get the hell out of it.' By then, they were shooting down the road at us, so we backed out, skedaddled away and found another road for ourselves."

In his attempt to find the Squadron, John Marshall, perhaps logically, headed towards Arnhem. As he worked his way gradually eastwards, he heard, at one stage, the sounds of a major engagement, somewhere in the direction towards which he was travelling. He saw nothing of it, but eventually arrived at the junction of Utrechtseweg and Wolfhezerweg. There, hanging dead out of the ruins of his bullet-ridden car was *Generalmajor* Kussin, German area commander of Arnhem who, at the end of a short visit to Krafft's headquarters, had been returning to the town. Krafft's advice to Kussin had been that he should go by the road parallel to the railway line but, unwisely and with fatal consequences, he had neglected to do so.

By then, it was after 1800 hours, and Marshall would have been surprised to learn that only two miles up the road along which Kussin had driven to his death just an hour earlier, the 1st Airborne Reconnaissance Squadron was in the final stages of its engagement with the troops of Krafft's right flank. During the following thirty minutes Marshall and Irala somehow worked their way, by various secondary routes, down to the river road, in time to witness the blowing up by the Germans of the railway bridge that carried the line across the river to Nijmegen. From his estimated position, about a mile and a half to the east of the Driel ferry on Benedendorpsweg, it would appear that Marshall was very close to Frost's 2nd Parachute Battalion, which was making all speed to the main objective. It is ironic to think that had John Marshall, whose prime concern was simply to rejoin the Squadron, continued eastwards, he would almost inevitably have been one of the first members of the entire British force to arrive at Arnhem Bridge.

At that point, of course, no one had come near to arriving at the primary objective. Krafft had effectively blocked the *coup de main* at Wolfheze, and Frost still had some way to go on the river route. However, things were going reasonably well with 1st Air Landing Brigade under Hicks. In the course of the afternoon, the Brigade had successfully taken up defensive positions on Reijerscamp and Renkum Heath, in readiness for the arrival of 4th Brigade on the following day. What fighting had taken place had occurred out at Ginkel Heath, where the 7th Battalion of the King's Own Scottish Borderers had had several sharp skirmishes with the Dutch SS battalion of *SS Obersturmbannfüher* Paul Helle.

But, for 1st Parachute Brigade, progress had been much less satisfactory, and especially so with the three-pronged thrust on the Bridge. The Brigade was simply not making the speed of advance that had been hoped for and, by early evening, two parachute battalions, the 1st and the 3rd, had run into very serious difficulties. Paradoxically, two contributory factors were the smoothness of the landings, which had been almost unopposed, and the hospitality of the Dutch people. The easy landings had helped to induce a false sense of relaxation and an acceptance of the validity of intelligence assertions that enemy opposition would be light As for the Dutch people, bedecked with orange favours, they emerged from their homes to ply the British troops with food and drink, as they passed along on their various routes into town; the inevitable exchange of courtesies which accompanied this, eroded still further the precious time in needless delay.

On the northernmost route, "Leopard", David Dobie's 1st Parachute Battalion had set out as planned from the dropping zone at about 1600 hours. His first objective was to reach Wolfheze station, and he did so during the time that the Reconnaissance Squadron was still engaging Krafft. Had it not been for the opposition which Gough's men were holding, Dobie might then have pressed on along the route parallel to the railway, up to and beyond the point at which the ambush of C Troop had taken place. Instead, having met Major Gough on his way back from Wolfheze to look for the General and as a result of what he learned from him. Dobie detoured immediately northwards from the rail junction, towards the Ede-Arnhem road. It was there, at

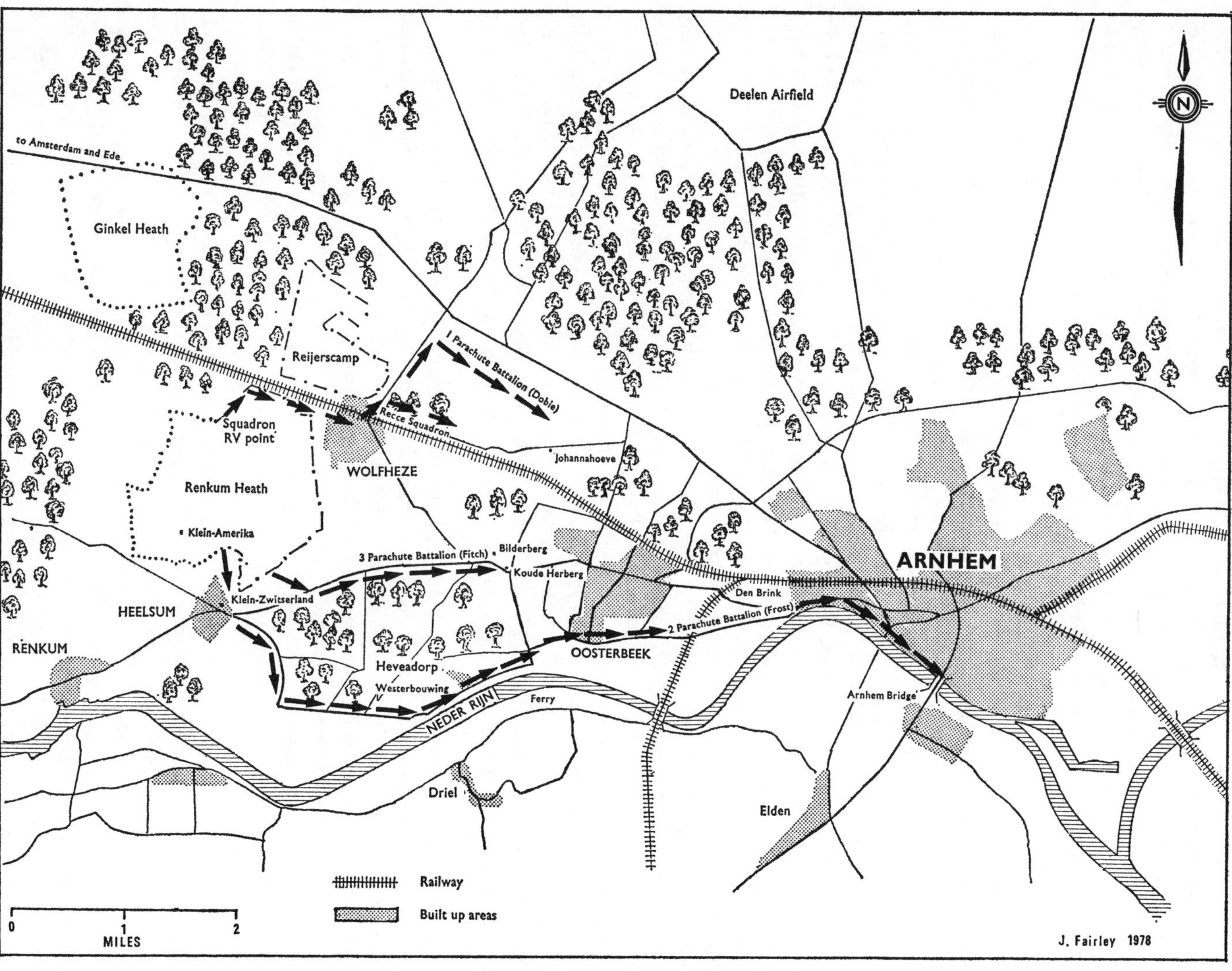

Map 5 The position at the end of the first day

the end of the Wolfhezerweg, that his leading company encountered stiff and totally unexpected armoured opposition. In the face of this, he made a second change of plan and took his Battalion cross-country in an attempt to reach the road at a point further east. There, in the woods just to the north-west of Johannahoeve, a further concentration of armour was met and beaten off. By then, it was 2200 hours and, with one of his companies already reduced to fifty per cent of its operational strength, Dobie decided to dig in for a time before renewing his attempts to try to get through to the town.

On the centre route of the Utrechtseweg, code-named "Tiger", Fitch's 3rd Parachute Battalion had its first action at the junction of Wolfhezerweg. As the Battalion arrived there, Kussin, whose timing could not have been worse, ran straight into the path of the airborne men. They opened up with Sten guns and he, with the other occupants of his vehicle, was immediately killed. It was the aftermath of this which John Marshall was inadvertently to come upon a little later in the afternoon. Following upon the Kussin incident, however, Krafft's 2nd Company, which was on the left flank of this extended position, put down a heavy mortar barrage that held Fitch up for at least an hour. By then, first Lathbury, and then Urquhart, who had been attempting to encourage speedier progress down on the river route, had both joined up with Fitch. Many casualties were sustained, and Urquhart himself had a narrow escape. As he was returning to his jeep in order to try to raise his own HQ on the radio, the vehicle was struck by a mortar bomb and his signaller seriously wounded.

Fitch eventually extricated himself from what was clearly a suicidal position, accurately ranged by Krafft's mortar fire, but he could make little further progress. He was then in a location almost due south of the 1st Parachute Battalion's position and, like Dobie, he was also encountering armoured opposition. As a result, 3rd Battalion had little alternative but to dig in for the night, near the Koude Herberg café, a small unpretentious building with a partially glassed-in verandah, which stood at the junction of Utrechtseweg and Valkenburglaan. General Urquhart and Brigadier Lathbury had, meantime, decided to remain with Fitch and together they passed a few uneasy and anxious hours in a house on the opposite side of the main road.

The ultimate joint experience that day of both 1st and 3rd Battalions had been similar, yet entirely unexpected. Both battalions had been halted by a strength of German armour that had been unanticipated and that in no way correlated with the intelligence briefing reports given to the Division prior to the start of the operation. The seriousness of the situation was something that the British were to become increasingly aware of over the following twenty-four hours, for this, indeed, was the unpredictable element that men like Sosabowski had feared. In fact, both Dobie and Fitch had already made their first contact with units of Harzer's 9th SS Panzer (Hohenstaufen) Division.

Almost from the time of the first sighting of British planes and gliders, Bittrich had been sufficiently perceptive to guess at the object of the operation. His views were supported by that equally astute veteran of airborne warfare, *Generaloberst* Kurt Student, commander of the German 1st Parachute Army. In confirmation of their joint opinion, it was claimed that most of the essential details became known to Student by mid-afternoon, when all the plans of "Market Garden" were discovered by the Germans in a crashed American glider and delivered into his hands at his HQ in Vught.* Even as the British were still in the process of quitting the landing and dropping zones and 1st Parachute Brigade was setting out for the Bridge, Bittrich had already issued orders to his two SS Panzer divisions. They were:

*No evidence has ever been produced to confirm this story, which must be regarded as highly suspect.

Scene of ambush at Wolfheze, Sunday 17th September 1944

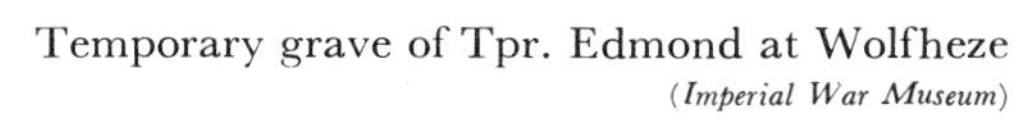

Temporary grave of Tpr. Edmond at Wolfheze
(Imperial War Museum)

Sergeant Tom McGregor

No. CPR Army Form B. 104—82.
(If replying, please quote above No.)

ROYAL ARMOURED CORPS Record Office,
DRILL HALL, BARNET, HERTS.
6th October 1944.

Madam,

It is my painful duty to inform you that a report has been received from the War Office notifying the death of :—

(No.) 14596517 (Rank) Trooper
(Name) BARLOW Arthur Ebenezer
(Regiment) 1st Airborne Reconnaissance Squadron, R.A.C.
which occurred in the North West European Theatre of War
on the 17th September 1944.

The report is to the effect that he Was Killed in Action.

I am to express the sympathy and regret of the Army Council.

I am to add that any information that may be received as to the soldier's burial will be communicated to you in due course, by the Directorate of Graves Registration and Enquiries, War Office (A.G.13), 32 Grosvenor Gardens, S.W.1, to whom all enquiries with regard to graves or places of burial should be addressed.

I am,

Mrs. D.B. Barlow,
24 Forfield Road,
Coventry,
Warwickshire.

Madam,
Your obedient Servant,
A. Holford Walker
Colonel
Officer in Charge of Records.

(27305) Wt.15457/2574 ,000 5/44 A.& E.W.Ltd. Gp.698 Forms/B.104-82/6. [P.T.O.

Official notification of Tpr. Arthur Barlow's death

Army Form B. 104—83A.

No. CPR
(If replying, please quote above No.)

REPLY TO THIS CORRESPONDENCE MUST BE ADDRESSED TO THE O.C. CAVALRY & R.A.C. RECORDS AND NOT TO ANY INDIVIDUAL

CAVALRY & ROYAL ARMOURED CORPS RECORD OFFICE 18 APR 1945 BARNET HERTS

Record Office,
Station.
19

SIR OR MADAM,

I have to inform you that a report has been received from the War Office to the effect that (No.) 14596517
(Rank) Tpr. (Name) BARLOW A.E.
(Regiment) 1st Airborne Reconnaissance Squadron
is a Prisoner of War now known to be at STALAG IVB GERMANY on 22nd October 1944
His prisoner of war number is 92593

Should any other information be received concerning him, such information will be at once communicated to you.

Instructions as to the method of communicating with Prisoners of War can be obtained at any Post Office.

I am,
SIR OR MADAM,
Your obedient Servant,

Mrs D.B. Barlow,
24, Forfield Rd,
Coventry,
Warwickshire.

Officer in charge of Records.

IMPORTANT.—Any change of your address should be immediately notified to this Office. It should also be notified, if you receive information from the soldier above, that his address has been changed.

Wt.30241/1250 500M. 9/39. KJL/8818 Gp.698/3 Forms/B.104—83A/6

Notification of Barlow as Prisoner-of-War in Germany

C Troop men: Duitsekampweg: Monday 18th September 1944. *Background:* Tpr. F. Brawn (Bren). *Foreground:* Tpr. J. Cooke (PIAT), Tpr. D. Evans (Rifle and Bayonet)

9th SS Panzer (Hohenstaufen) Division
1. Division to reconnoitre in the direction of Arnhem and Nijmegen.
2. The Division to go immediately into action, occupying the Arnhem area and destroying the enemy forces which have landed to the west of Arnhem and Oosterbeek. Immediate attack is essential. The aim is to occupy and firmly hold the bridge at Arnhem.

10th SS Panzer (Frundsberg) Division
Division to proceed immediately to Nijmegen, occupying the main bridges in strength and defending the bridge-heads.*

Bittrich had acted with a speed and initiative which matched his own perceptive skill as a first-rate professional soldier. His decisions were endorsed later in the afternoon by *Generalfeldmarschall* Walter Model who, as Commander-in-Chief in the west, was also in local command of Army Group B. Thus, 10th SS Panzer Division would effectively reinforce the forces of Kurt Student in blocking the path of 30 British Corps, but it was the 9th SS (Hohenstaufen) Division that would provide the main resistance to the lightly armed soldiers of the 1st British Airborne Division.

Following its withdrawal from the engagement at Wolfheze, the Squadron reported back to Divisional HQ at Renkum Heath, where David Allsop was informed that Major Gough was at a large house called Klein Zwitserland, situated just to the north of the village of Heelsum. Allsop, therefore, moved out to attempt to contact him, but was unsuccessful and eventually returned to the Divisional HQ area for the night. One last duty was then asked of the Squadron, which was to undertake a reconnaissance in order to try to find out what was happening to Dobie's 1st Battalion. D Troop was given the task, and set out in the dark along Utrechtseweg, with the ultimate intention of finding a way up to the railway. Inevitably, of course, they ran into Fitch's 3rd Battalion, which was engaging the enemy in the area of the Koude Herberg and the nearby Bilderberg Hotel. After two hours of vain and frustrating attempts to get firm information about Dobie, they finally returned to harbour. This coincided with the arrival of Lieutenant John Marshall and Trooper "Joe" Irala in the missing D Troop vehicle. Having been on their own for most of the day and, indeed, having gone almost to Arnhem Bridge itself, the two, by some miracle of nocturnal navigation, had somehow managed to become reunited with the Squadron.

Meanwhile, in his search for the General, things had not gone well for Major Gough. It was bad enough to have to cope with an almost total breakdown in wireless communication, but to be moving through unfamiliar territory towards an unknown – or at the least unpredictable – rendezvous, was making the whole task immensely more difficult. The fact, too, that the maps which had been provided were not at all accurate did not help. Naturally, this affected progress, as did the necessity for observing caution in a situation where the enemy could be encountered at any time in strength. At one stage, Gough was saved from running straight into German-held positions by a warning from Major Dennis Mumford, who commanded the 3rd Light Battery. Each set-back of this kind meant the inevitable detour and, in that instance, he had to go the long way round by Renkum crossroads, in order to get on to "Lion" route from another direction. As dusk began to creep in, Gough headed eastwards along the river route and, at just after 1830 hours, finally caught up with the rear section of 1st Parachute Brigade HQ. By then, of course, both Urquhart and Lathbury were with Fitch, but at last Freddie Gough was able to find out

* Harmel, the commander of the 10th SS Panzer Division was in Berlin at the time of the landings and had to be hurriedly recalled.

precisely why the General wanted to see him. "He wanted you to bring your Squadron along this road to follow Frost," was the information which he received from Tony Hibbert, the Brigade Major. The problem then was how to re-establish contact with the Squadron, for he had no longer any sure knowledge of its whereabouts. Just then, by apparent good fortune, Brigade HQ at last succeeded in getting through by radio to Lathbury and Urquhart. This seemed to indicate that the HQ had, perhaps, entered an area in which reception and transmission were clearer than elsewhere. With this possibility in mind, Gough requested that an attempt be made to raise Divisional HQ, in order to have his men redirected. Unfortunately, the brigade signallers had no further success, so that he could do no more than follow the General's orders with the very small force that he still had under his immediate command.

To some extent, "Lion" route was the loophole in the screen which Bittrich had begun to erect so quickly between the British forces and their objective. This did not mean that there was a total absence of enemy opposition on the river route. On the contrary, although progress was fairly steady, there was still sporadic action at a number of points on the way. At Heelsum, the 2nd Parachute Battalion ambushed a party of Germans in lorries and cars, and took twenty prisoners. Shortly afterwards, the convoy was held up again, to the south of the Doorwerth woods. Trooper Robert Coldicott, a young farmer from Stratford-on-Avon, who was with the small Reconnaissance party recalls the latter incident as his first experience of being under enemy attack: "I was with Lieutenant Platt, when we came under heavy fire, so we immediately dismounted and scattered. I remember diving off and trying to get cover by the side of the jeep and how the bullets were coming all ways – over the top as well as underneath." As it happened, he was unable to rejoin the group, and had to spend a night in the woods before reporting back, next day, to Squadron HQ.

Afterwards, 2nd Parachute Battalion had an engagement with an armoured car; this too, was successful, and some SS men were captured. Frost then detached his C Company in an attempt to capture the railway bridge over the river but, as they approached, the enemy blew it up. Unfortunately, C Company paid dearly for this because they were subsequently blocked off by the Germans and prevented from catching up with the main body of the Battalion which, in the meantime, had made good progress towards Arnhem Bridge. B Company of the 2nd Battalion was also given a special task – that of capturing Den Brink, a commanding piece of high ground to the north of the Utrechtseweg and just beyond the railway line running south to Nijmegen. Their success in achieving this allowed the Battalion's leading A Company under Major Tatham-Warter, together with Frost's own HQ, to make good speed by Onderlangs and Oude Kraan to the immediate area of the Bridge itself. As Frost's men raced down Weerdjestraat and across Eusebiusplein, suddenly the great curving single span of the road bridge came into sight. It was an impressive structure of superb architectural design, and was approached from the north by a great concrete ramp, which carried the traffic up and over the top of the riverside roads that ran between the supporting pillars below. All around, was the old congested part of the town, and the houses which were clustered together in the narrow, irregular streets stood hard by the ramp approach as it soared up past their rooftops to link up with the Bridge itself. As the men ran towards it, they could see that the Bridge was intact, with German traffic still passing southwards across it. By 2000 hours, the leading troops of John Frost's Battalion had reached the north end. There they occupied area A (see map) beneath the ramp and, to the consternation of the inhabitants, began rapidly to set themselves up in the houses to either side of the great ramp approach. Houses 8 and 10 were, in particular, regarded as of prime strategic importance.

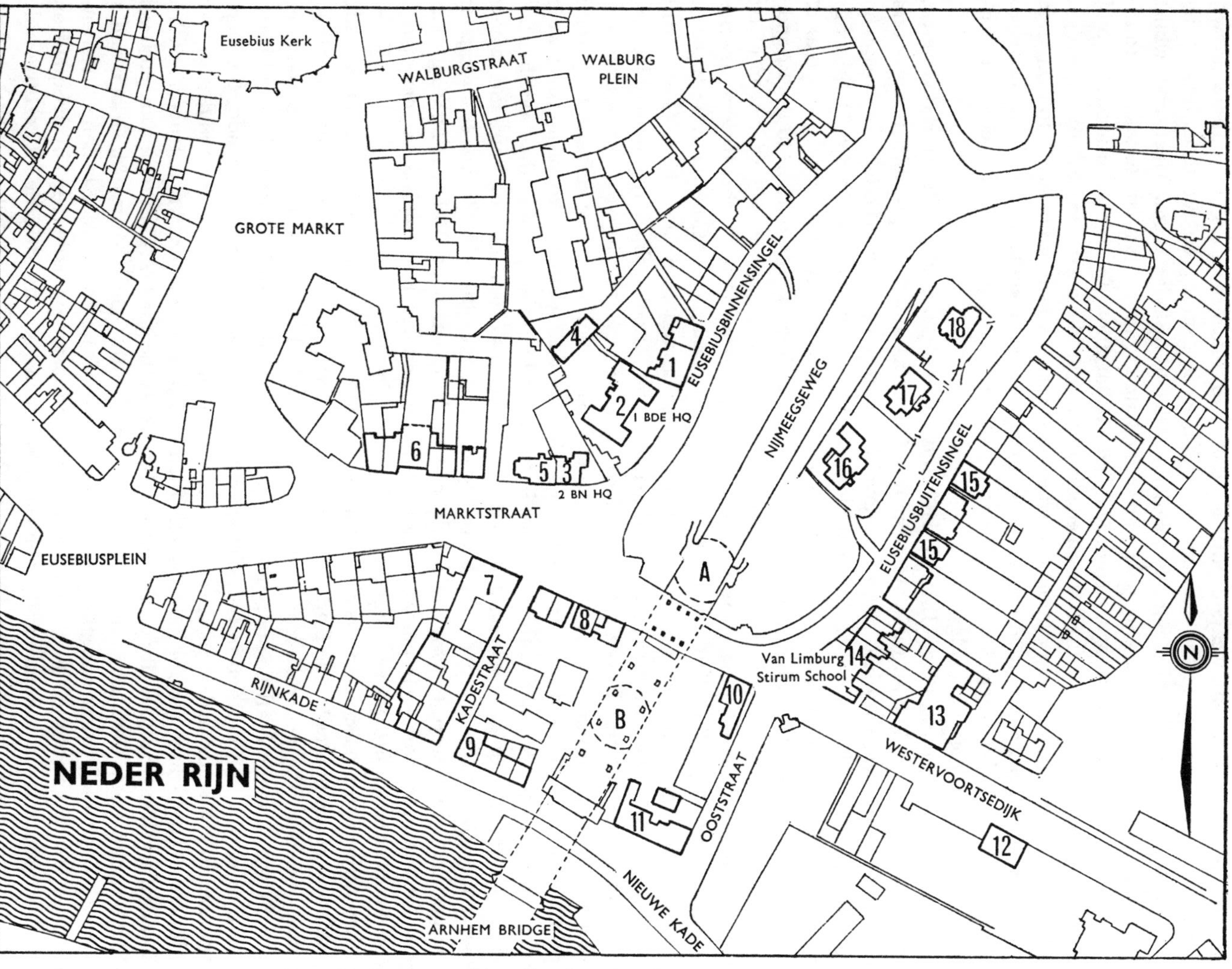

Map 6 Arnhem Bridge: Sunday 17th–Thursday 21st September 1944

Once occupation had begun, weapon butts were used to smash the glass out of the windows, and furniture was moved up to the openings as the airborne troops prepared to withstand the attacks which they knew would inevitably follow in order to dislodge them. Meantime, whilst the defensive preparations were taking place, an immediate attempt was made to take the south end. This was led by Lieutenant McDermont of the 2nd Battalion, but it was unsuccessful and casualties were sustained through fire from an enemy pill-box on the north-west side of the Bridge, as well as from an armoured car positioned further across it. It was in an attempt to overcome this difficulty that Frost then gave orders for B Company to be contacted and instructed to quit Den Brink, in order to cross over to the south of the river by way of the secondary objective of the so-called pontoon bridge.

Whilst all this was taking place, Brigade HQ and various other sub-units were themselves approaching the Bridge. For all their attempts to advance as quietly as possible, many found that, once into the town, they had frequent unavoidable encounters with Dutch civilians, who would rush out of their houses in order to shout loud welcomes to the British troops. Despite this hazard, most arrived with relatively little difficulty and placed themselves at the disposal of Frost who, as senior officer, had assumed command of Brigade HQ. In addition to the Brigade HQ and its Defence Platoon, the main elements involved were a platoon of RASC, men of 1st Parachute Squadron Royal Engineers and the small detachment from the Reconnaissance Squadron, led by Major Freddie Gough. As Frost's own Battalion was at that point reduced in strength by two companies, he was particularly pleased to welcome the others. Gough still recollects that Frost's words to him just after he arrived were, "Look – this is the main objective, so this is where we stay. But I need every man I can get, because tonight we're going to take a hell of a bloody hammering." Some of the newcomers, particularly those of Brigade HQ, were not primarily equipped for the situation in which they found themselves, for a number were orderlies, batmen and clerks. Yet, they were soldiers first and foremost, and in the days that followed proved themselves to be as courageous and resourceful as those of their comrades whose roles were more obviously of a combatant kind. Many, too, brought with them useful weapons and equipment which were to prove of worth in the subsequent house-to-house fighting. The sappers, for example, had their portable flame throwers and the Reconnaissance men had a variety of concentrated fire power, not least the Vickers "K" guns.

As they arrived, the reinforcements either joined those members of the 2nd Battalion already in occupation of the houses by the Bridge, or else took up fresh positions under Frost's direction. The map indicates the general dispositions. Gough detached a few of his men to reinforce Bernard Briggs, Brigade Staff Captain, at the eastern side of the Bridge approaches. With the rest, he then occupied a position in the Rijkswaterstaat building on the western side; the jeeps were parked in the courtyard at the back. This is shown on the map as House 2 and, together with Houses 1 and 4, was the established base for Brigade HQ. House 2 itself was a structure with a high flat roof and it stood about fifty yards from the Bridge, at the junction of Eusebiusbinnensingel and Marktstraat. From the attic position which he shared with Dennis Mumford, Gough had a fine view through the girders and along the entire length of the great arched span. A Reconnaissance 22 set was established in House 4 and an optimistic attempt made to net in on Squadron HQ. Predictably, this was a failure and, from the same room, only the Brigade HQ set was able to make any radio contact at all. As it turned out, this was only with 2nd Battalion HQ, a mere thirty yards away in House 3!

Intermittent German attacks took place on the north side during those early stages, but the most serious opposition came from the south side of the Bridge. From there, Harzer's Panzer grenadiers took the offensive and, shortly after the repulse of a second British attempt to take the southern end, this time led by Lieutenant John Grayburn of the 2nd Parachute Battalion, they launched a heavy mortar "stonk". This was followed by an infantry attack, in which the German soldiers attempted to make use of the Bridge girders to screen their advance. It was not successful.

Meantime, the main obstacles to any British attempt to move to the other side were the pill-box, whose 20 mm Flak guns had successfully halted earlier efforts, and the armoured car, which was still positioned further across the Bridge. Frost estimated that if the pill-box could be knocked out, then perhaps an anti-tank gun might be able to do something about the armoured car. The action which then followed is best narrated in Freddie Gough's own words, for he had a grandstand view of the whole affair: "When I got to the Bridge, there was a hell of a battle going on, because the Germans had this pill-box with the twin-mounted gun. Well, we got the sappers who'd come with Brigade HQ to bring one of their flame throwers to bear on it from their own position at the north end of the Bridge. Behind the pill-box, however, was a row of wooden huts and, although we didn't know it at the time, that was where they kept all the 'ack-ack' ammunition for the guns. What happened then was that although the engineers aimed at the slit in the pill-box, they missed, but hit one of the huts instead and set it alight. Immediately afterwards, up went the rest in an enormous explosion and in no time at all the fire had spread to the Bridge itself. Fortunately, it was only the paintwork that caught, but all of it was burned off at our side and, in the process, the electric leads were damaged." In the light of what was to happen two days later, this last consequence was of special importance for, when a captured German officer was subsequently interrogated by Frost and Gough, it was discovered that he had been sent down to operate the emergency detonation system. Since he was unsuccessful and the Bridge remained intact, it is possible that, at the outset, the leads were damaged in the fire.

It was Lieutenant Vlasto of the 2nd Parachute Battalion who eventually put the pill-box out of action with a PIAT, but before the British could organize a fresh attack, they had to repel another German attempt to retake the north end. This time, the enemy sent over lorries filled with infantry troops, but most of them were taken prisoner and the lorries were set on fire. Meanwhile, in the lulls, the British took the opportunity to strengthen their positions. The arrival of a troop of 1st Air Landing anti-tank guns under Major Arnold was a considerable boost to Frost, and his own men also succeeded in setting out mines on the embankment adjacent to the Bridge.

In the face of all the German attempts to dislodge him, Frost had been able to consolidate. Only his attempts to take the south end of the Bridge had been unsuccessful and yet, ironically, just four miles to the west at Heveadorp, near the point where his advance had been temporarily held up, the Driel ferry, a sizeable vessel capable of taking vehicles as well as passengers, had been plying back and forward as usual all day. It was no distance at all from the road along which he had travelled, but sufficiently far over the polder land as not to be easily spotted, especially by someone who had been given not even a hint of its existence. Frost did not know about it nor did those at Divisional HQ, but the Dutch ferryman whose job it was to take the local people from Heveadorp to Driel and back continued to do so, despite the battle, until sometime on the Wednesday. One man on the spot who did discover the Driel ferry was Lieutenant John Marshall of the Reconnaissance Squadron's D Troop. Because he took the wrong turning off the landing ground, Marshall eventually finished up in the area of Westerbouwing. To this day, he distinctly remembers seeing the ferry in operation, a flat raft-like structure, with deep rails at each side, but open at the ends. He remembers equally well reporting the fact later to Divisional HQ. For a brief period from Tuesday onwards, this information was to take on a new significance when consideration would be given to establishing an alternative bridgehead based on the Neder Rijn at Heveadorp.*

Sixty-four miles to the south, at just a little after half-past two in the afternoon of that first day, 30 British Corps, under Lieutenant-General Brian Horrocks, began the main ground advance of Operation "Market Garden" from the base line of the Meuse-Escaut canal. Its own artillery provided a moving barrage ahead, to ease the way for the Irish Guards in the van of the attack. Against the entrenched German anti-tank defence guns, Royal Air Force Typhoons were sent in, and the advance continued up the road towards the first objective, Eindhoven, only thirteen miles further on. The fields around were already flooded, so that there was little opportunity for flexibility for the heavy armour. It soon became apparent that, silhouetted as they were on the dyke roads, the great cumbersome tanks were like targets moving along the back of a shooting gallery. And so, right from the outset, none of the optimistic assumptions about a sharp, rapid thrust of the main army were realized. Instead, it emerged as a sluggish, bitter grind, with one hard engagement after another occupying, in particular, the leading elements of Horrocks's force.

Thus it was that, in the face of a strong and well-sustained enemy defence, they covered a mere seven miles that day. At nightfall they harboured at Valkenswaard with six miles still to go before reaching Eindhoven. As a pointer to future success it was not good, for the favourable conclusion of the entire operation depended upon speed and a consolidation of the corridor at each stage of the advance. Lacking the necessary momentum and the capability of overcoming an enemy opposition that was already proving to be more formidable than had been anticipated, the forward progress of 30 Corps ground to a premature halt. Within hours of the start of Operation "Market Garden", the main drive was already seriously behind schedule. At that stage it would not have been possible to say with any certainty that the efficacy of 30 Corps as a relieving force was already in dispute. Nevertheless, it was an inauspicious start and one that did little to sustain the optimistic forecast of a speedy link-up with the men whose task it was to seize and hold the bridge at Arnhem.

* Unfortunately, as it happened, the ferry ceased to operate at some time on Wednesday 20th September, when its moorings were severed and it drifted downstream.

Chapter 6 MONDAY 18th SEPTEMBER 1944

"What a funny lot you English soldiers are!"

From the outset, it had been arranged that, following the *coup de main*, the Squadron would cease to be under command of 1st Parachute Brigade and would resume its normal divisional function. So, from the time that it disengaged at 1830 hours on the Sunday evening, it became answerable once more to the Divisional commander. Thereafter, for a little short of three days, it was to find itself operating in a manner as near to an effective reconnaissance role as it was ever to experience throughout the entire battle.

Divisional HQ moved position twice between Sunday night and Monday morning, but as dawn broke and the General had still not returned, his GSO(1) Ops, Lieutenant-Colonel C. B. Mackenzie, in conjunction with Lieutenant-Colonel R. G. Loder-Symonds, the CRA, had to take some vital decisions. Already Mackenzie had begun to think about the General's orders to the effect that Brigadier Hicks was to be regarded as his replacement in the unlikely event that both he and Lathbury should be put out of action. Since this very contingency appeared to have come about, Urquhart's emergency instructions were implemented and, at 0915 hours on that Monday morning, Hicks officially took over command of the 1st British Airborne Division. In the meantime, specialist troops under Divisional orders had already been given instructions and it was in consequence of this that Captain David Allsop, by then the acting Squadron commander, had been asked to organize a reconnaissance of the Utrechtseweg, between Heelsum and Arnhem.

Heelsum, the town in which the Squadron had spent the night, lay approximately six miles to the west of Arnhem, and the task called for a reconnaissance of "Tiger" route, the one along which Fitch's 3rd Battalion had moved eastwards after the landing. It was decided that the entire unit, less C Troop which had taken the brunt of the previous day's fighting, would move out of harbour at 0630 hours. For the time that the Squadron was to be on this assignment, it was arranged that C Troop should come temporarily within 1st Air Landing Brigade and be left to help the 2nd Battalion South Staffordshires guard the Wolfheze side of the Reijerscamp landing zone. It was understood that its members would require to be on the alert, but it also seems to have been assumed that this would be a less onerous task than the one which the remainder of the Squadron was likely to encounter, especially since this would take it into the area of the previous evening's battle around the Koude Herberg café and the Bilderberg Hotel.

In truth, of course, things had quietened down in that part of western Oosterbeek, and both

1st and 3rd Parachute Battalions had been under way for some time. Shortly after midnight, under cover of darkness, Dobie's 1st Battalion had slipped quietly past the German armour, by moving stealthily south-eastwards. Dobie was already considerably reduced in strength, and progress cross-country, through the difficult wooded terrain, called for a considerable effort. Despite further casualties, his Battalion moved to the south of Lichtenbeek and reached Utrechtseweg ("Tiger") at 0430 hours. There, at a point about a quarter of a mile to the west of the overhead railway bridge, Dobie's leading company ran into a fierce engagement with a mixed infantry and armoured force, as a consequence of which more heavy losses were suffered. The outcome was that at 0830 hours, a badly depleted 1st Parachute Battalion eventually came to a halt, south of Utrechtseweg, in the area of the railway line south to Nijmegen.

3rd Parachute Battalion had, meantime, disengaged and, about two hours before dawn, Fitch left the area of the Bilderberg Hotel. Like Dobie, he moved off in a south-easterly direction. His object was to attempt a breakthrough to the Bridge by "Lion" route, the one already used successfully by Frost on the previous evening. Despite the fact that in the dark the Battalion lost touch with its transport, initial progress was good, with over two miles covered, and it was not halted until reaching a position about 300 yards west of St. Elisabeth's Hospital. With Fitch went General Urquhart and Brigadier Lathbury and, at the point of the hold-up, they were only about a half-mile's distance away from Dobie's 1st Battalion. In this small area of western Arnhem, 3rd Battalion then made contact with some men of 2nd Battalion's "lost" C Company, whilst some of Fitch's transport as well as his A Company, which had also become detached caught up with and joined forces with Dobie!

Two things were becoming obvious. The first was the degree of confusion that was already emerging as a major characteristic of the operation. An interesting aspect of this was that, despite the general inter-penetration and the occasional link-up of detached groups, Lathbury, the Brigade commander, who was moving with Fitch's 3rd Battalion, was to have no inkling of the presence of Dobie's 1st Battalion in the same area until 1315 hours that afternoon. The second was that the loophole in the hurriedly prepared German defences, through which Frost had slipped on the previous evening, was by then closed, and down by those western outskirts of the town of Arnhem, the Germans were already established along the railway line and in occupation of the high ground at Den Brink. Throughout that Monday and for the whole of the following day, their positions were to be further consolidated, with disastrous consequences for the airborne troops.

The movement of the two parachute battalions to the same area of western Arnhem, and the enemy's obvious concentration of armour at that point in anticipation of their arrival had, nevertheless, relieved the situation further to the west. So it was that, when the Reconnaissance Squadron moved eastwards towards Arnhem on Utrechtseweg, it encountered no serious opposition at the points where Fitch had "bumped" so badly on the previous evening. D Troop led, followed by Squadron HQ, then a still very much depleted A Troop, with the small Support Troop bringing up the rear. For the first part of the journey, the road ran long and straight, with tall woodland to either side. At the intersection of the Wolfhezerweg, they met no enemy opposition at all, for Krafft had already withdrawn to the north-east, on the mistaken assumption that the British had earlier been attempting to surround him. Only the dead bodies of Kussin and those who had accompanied him on his last journey were still beside the wrecked car on the crossroads. John Stevenson tells of how the body of one of the dead Germans, which was lying in the centre of the road, was pulled by its feet to the side to prevent it from being run over by passing vehicles. "Later on," he says, "when we had to pass the same point, we found that, for some unaccountable reason, someone had put it back into the middle of the road again."

With no sign of the enemy, the Squadron pressed on with its assigned reconnaissance task to the point where the main road took a bend to the right and the large villas of western Oosterbeek began to appear, each in its own patch of woodland set well back from the road. To the left, through a gap in the trees, they could glimpse the white frontage of Bilderberg and, as the woodland began to thin out, they arrived at the Koude Herberg café, scene of such bitter encounter only a short time earlier. There they found much evidence of the recent fighting, and Alan de Looze, who was with the Support Troop still has memories of the scene at the nearby lodge of the Bilderbeg Hotel: "There was a lot of blood on and around the front door, the body of a British paratrooper on the bed inside, and the landing window broken, with a Bren gun barrel lying beside it."

Beyond the junction of Valkenburglaan was a triangular area of grass, bordered on its north side by more handsomely styled houses. Each of the large villas looked across to a well-placed and gracefully proportioned white building, set in parkland a little way back from the road. This was the Restaurant Park-Hotel Hartenstein, fated to occupy a central position in relation to the events that were to follow. About a hundred yards further on and slightly downhill was the main crossroads of Oosterbeek, with two imposing hotels flanking its north and south-east corners. On the right was the two-storeyed Hotel Schoonoord, with its long glass-windowed extensions fronting on to the pavement. Over the way, in a pleasant garden and set at an angle to the crossroads, was the attractive cream-painted Hotel Vreewijk. Each, with its adjacent buildings, was to serve as a dressing station throughout the battle. That morning, the crossroads, which would ultimately become one of the most tightly held parts of the final British perimeter, was still relatively peaceful. As they drove through it, past the row of shops, with the local civilians standing to wave from the pavement edge, it was for all the world like being on an exercise in England. Seated sideways, with their legs dangling over the sides of the jeeps, the "Recce" men waved back, and for a brief interval of time the war seemed far away.

At 0800 hours, 12 Section of D Troop, which was leading the procession, ran into machine-gun fire at the junction of Utrechtseweg and Grindweg, three-quarters of a mile to the east of Oosterbeek crossroads. In this action there were no initial casualties, except for an unfortunate German despatch rider who was hit by fire from his own guns and crashed in the middle of the road. The area was residential, and the wide road was lined with ancient beech trees whose roots had pushed the red pavement bricks up into a succession of distorted humps. On the left side of the road was a steep bank, with long flights of steps leading up its face to the villas that were perched in a commanding position on top. At that point, the Squadron was just 700 yards west of the railway bridge over the main road, and in the same general area where the Germans had halted Dobie's 1st Battalion about four hours earlier.

Dismounted action was immediately taken by both D and A Troops and foot patrols were despatched in a number of directions to try to ferret out the enemy. Much of the time was spent in working through houses and gardens, and Ernest Jenkins, who was 10 Section Sergeant, clearly remembered how one or two of the houses were found to have Nazi posters and other forms of propaganda. Prominent amongst those was Hitler's picture and, not surprizingly, the airborne men were not slow in seeing to it that "Corporal Schicklgruber" received an appropriate and well-merited "face lift".

Throughout all this search activity, A Troop made no contact and was eventually ordered back to deal with enemy infiltration to the rear. At about 0900 hours, D Troop at last located the Germans in a narrow strip of woodland, north-east of the road junction. The Troop immediately engaged and, in the course of the action, Trooper Fred Chilton of Dagenham was shot and seriously injured. He had six bullets in the thigh, and Jenkins remembered giving him morphia and marking the time and dose on his forehead with indelible pencil. Helped by James Pyper, the Troop Sergeant, Jenkins then laid Chilton in a ditch whilst medical aid was summoned to take him to hospital.

Shortly afterwards, Trooper George Adams became the second casualty of the morning. Adams was standing beside his Section officer, Lieutenant Alan Pascal, just a few feet from their stationary vehicles. They were on Utrechtseweg at the time, and he remembers how both of them were using the large beech trees as cover from enemy fire. As he sheltered from what appeared to be the probable location of the enemy, Adams recollects that he looked over a low wall into a garden, where conifers and rhododendrons were interspersed with more of the beech trees. The house itself, a large imposing red brick building called De Vergarde was set well back from the road, but parked outside the front door was an ambulance. He recalls that the ambulance attendants were dressed in civilian clothes, but standing beside the vehicle was a group of armed German soldiers. "It looked to me," says Adams, "as if they were about to get into the ambulance and head off somewhere, so I told Mr Pascal what I thought was happening. He didn't waste any time at all in making up his mind what to do. 'Open fire!' he snapped out, which we did. Just what happened then I don't really know, because as we opened up, so did someone from the houses on the other side of the road, and almost right away I got a bullet in the arm. What I do remember is that just then the ambulance drove out very fast through the gate of the big house and headed off in the direction of Arnhem. By that time, there were no German soldiers in sight at the front of it."

Were the Germans using ambulances to move armed troops? Certainly there has been no indication that they regularly violated the Geneva Convention in this unacceptable way. Nevertheless, isolated incidents of an unpleasant nature, such as the attack on the medical officer at Wolfheze on the Sunday ambush, did occur, so that the possibility cannot be entirely dismissed. At the very least, evidence of this kind leaves the suspicion that some Germans, less scrupulous than most, could well have decided that there were obvious advantages to be derived from using the medical services for military purposes.* They could, of course, have been walking wounded, but in that case should not have been carrying arms. The possibility, too, that the Germans made a fast move back into the house should not be overlooked, for, understandably. George Adams's attention was for a time distracted, and Alan Pascal, who might have been able to tell what happened, was not to survive the battle. Adams, in the meantime, was driven by Trooper Bell up to a house near the Schoonoord Hotel, and later transferred to Captain Doyle's dressing station in the school in Paasberg. He was still there when the building was completely destroyed on 21st September and Captain Doyle was killed. During his time there, he also saw Chilton, who died on that Monday evening as a consequence of clinical shock.

In the course of the action. A Troop had pulled back a little to investigate reports of enemy infiltration from the direction of the main Oosterbeek-Arnhem railway line. Whilst doing so, they had come under machine-gun and sniper fire at the corner of Reuvensweg and Stephanie-

* An interesting item relating to another incident subsequently appeared in the Divisional war diary: "24th Sep 0710 BBC correspondent goes through German lines under the Red Cross flag to fetch water for wounded. On returning reported that there were 150 German troops collecting in the hospital."

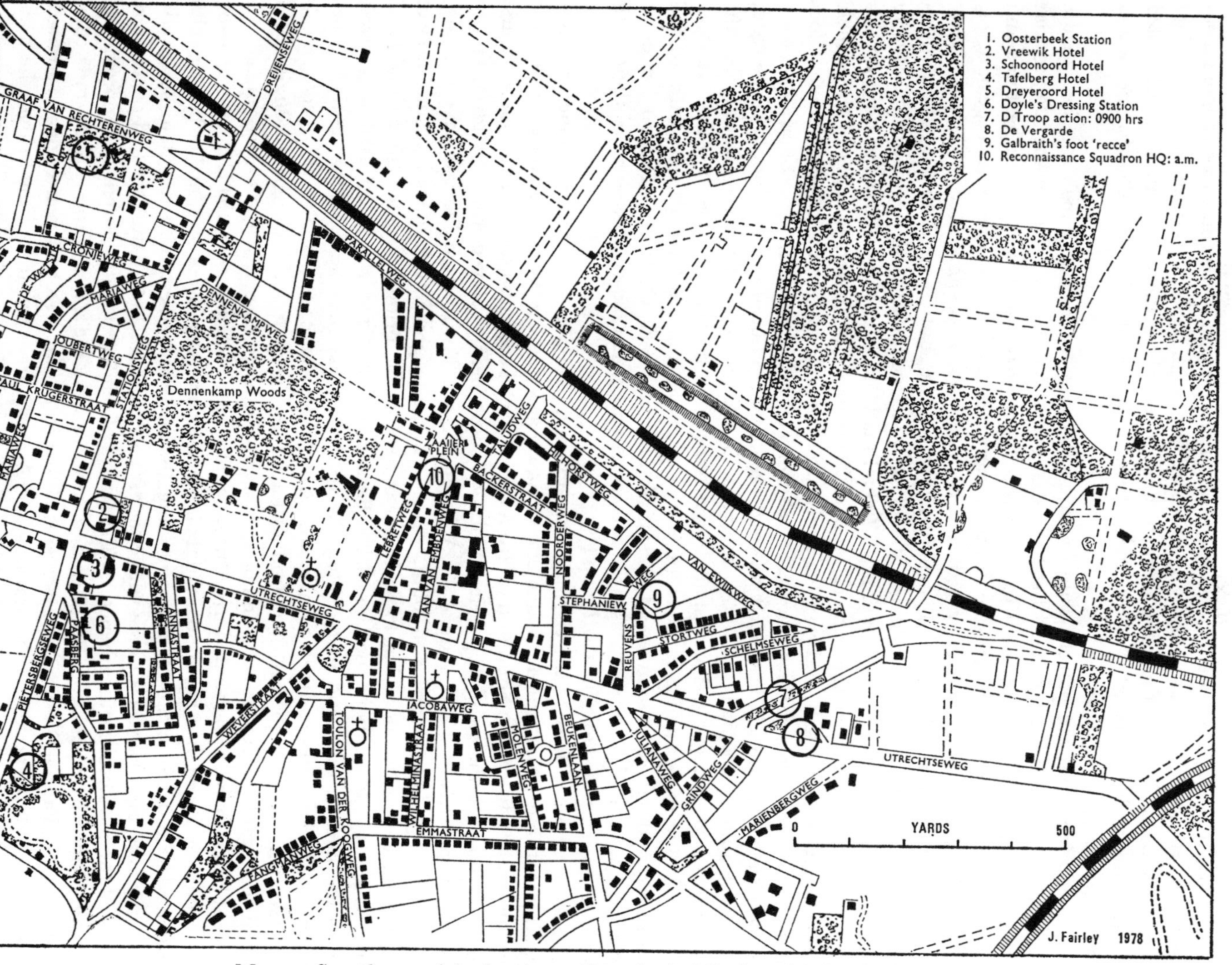

Map 7 Squadron activity in eastern Oosterbeek: Monday 18th September 1944

weg, as a result of which, Lieutenant Dougie Galbraith, 2 Section officer, undertook a foot reconnaissance northwards as far as the railway, in an attempt to pinpoint the enemy positions. What followed from this had certain of the elements of drama perhaps more appropriately associated with the vintage Hollywood "Western", but it was characteristic of Galbraith that he should have chosen to handle it in the way he did.

It was decided that the patrol would move up Reuvensweg, a road which rose in a gentle incline and ran between neat rows of red-brick cottages. Each had its door at the side, so that windowed frontages were presented to the street. There were small lawns, with heathers and evergreen conifers, but on neither side did the front gardens offer any cover worth speaking of; on the other hand, every boundary wall and outhouse was a possible position for an enemy sniper. In the event, nothing of great significance took place, but Gwyn Williams of Pontycymmer, who was Galbraith's Section Sergeant, still has vivid memories of an occasion which, for all its anticlimax, lacked nothing of tension: "We had made an advance by jeep and run into this heavy machine-gun fire on the corner. Trooper Blackman, our driver, was out of the vehicle even before it came to a halt, and we all of us dived for cover. It was then decided to mount a foot patrol, in order to avoid further risk to the vehicle. The result was that with 'Spud' Taylor on the right pavement, myself on the left side and Lieutenant Galbraith in the middle of the road, we walked quite deliberately for about 100 yards in the direction of the area from which the firing seemed to be coming. This I shall always remember, because at every step that we took, I expected to hear the sudden rattle of a German machine-gun. But the gods were with us, and we suffered nothing worse than a cold sweat!" Ten minutes later, Galbraith's Section did locate the enemy in strength at a position on the railway embankment; there they engaged them with grenades, until ordered to return to Troop HQ.

To those who had flushed the Germans out, this sudden order to withdraw came as a disappointment, but it was issued because of civilian reports that enemy patrols to the north were working around to cut the Squadron off from the rear. D Troop also disengaged, but were first able to radio back the enemy's position. This was subsequently relayed from Squadron HQ to Division, together with particulars of the A Troop contact. For the remainder of that morning, the Squadron probed to north and south, trying to find a loophole, with the object not simply of locating the enemy but of trying to find a clear route to the Bridge, if such a thing should still exist. As a result, from about 1000 hours, the Reconnaissance Squadron based itself at the west end of the Backerstraat, and investigated the roads in every possible direction, testing, penetrating and looking all the time for a way through. "Everywhere we went, we 'bumped'," recollects Geoff Costeloe, who was Squadron Adjutant and accompanied Dougie Galbraith in a jeep as they searched fruitlessly up and down the tight little streets of eastern Oosterbeek.

What had happened was that, during the night of 17th-18th September, the Germans, moving with incredible speed, had begun to build their blocking line, to prevent any further link up with the defenders at the Bridge. By Monday morning, the line was well-established and, although still weak in places, especially in the area where the 1st and 3rd Parachute Battalions had penetrated, it was all the time being strengthened by the arrival of reinforcements. Within the approximate triangle formed by Apeldoorn, Zutphen and Arnhem were the bases of the various units comprizing 9th SS Panzer Division, and elements of that formation had been converging in strength since the start of the action on the previous day. Already, from the area of the Bridge, the main German line extended by Roermondsplein and Nieuwe Plein, past Arnhem Station and along the railway in a westerly direction. Between there and the river, as far as the southern rail branch off to Nijmegen, the enemy held strongpoints, which was why Dobie and Fitch were encountering serious opposition not far from where the Reconnaissance Squadron had first made contact with the enemy that morning. Westwards, beyond the junction of the two railway lines, the Germans were building up their strength throughout the day, along the main Utrecht-Arnhem railway track as far as Oosterbeek station. It explained why Galbraith's Section had made the contact, following its foot reconnaissance. From Oosterbeek, the blocking line then took a turn to the north along Dreijenseweg, as far as Amsterdamseweg. It was this last part of the German line that was to prove particularly troublesome later in the day.

Back at Divisional HQ, Brigadier Hicks, in the continued absence of General Urquhart, had taken over command. Half an hour later, at 0945 hours, he made the first of a number of significant changes to the overall strategic plan, by detaching the 2nd Battalion of the South Staffordshires and ordering it to help with the main drive to relieve the men at the Bridge. This meant that the South Staffs came immediately under command of 1st Parachute Brigade and so relinquished its allotted task of holding Reijerscamp for the later arrival of 4th Brigade. As a result, the holding job was left to C Troop of the Reconnaissance Squadron, together with a platoon of the 21st Independent Parachute Company and a force of about fifty men of the Glider Pilot Regiment. C Troop, in view of its earlier losses, had been given a small reinforcing detachment from HQ Troop, under Lieutenant "Jimmy" Pearson.

As well as helping to guard the landing zone, one of the secondary tasks for C Troop was to attempt to recover the dead of the previous evening's ambush and, understandably, there was a certain amount of apprehension at the prospect of returning in broad daylight to the scene. The particular worry, of course, was that they had no sure knowledge that the enemy was not still occupying the position. Sergeant David Christie was one of the party: "I was leading jeep," he says, "and I was never more scared of anything. I remember that we drove slowly down into the valley where we found one of the 8 Section jeeps. The only member of the crew visible was Sergeant Tom McGregor, who was lying about five yards from the vehicle, with two bullet holes through his head and about seven in his chest. He still grasped his Sten gun in the hip position, with his left arm folded under him. We found Sergeant Stacey also dead. He had one bullet in the back and two in his stomach. By the pool of blood around him, it was obvious that he had bled to death."

In the meantime, Lance-Corporal Alan Baker, in a following vehicle, had discovered Dick Minns lying in a ditch by the side of the road. He was still alive, and Baker wasted no time in getting him off to a dressing station. Having been regarded as too seriously wounded to be moved, Minns had been left behind, still sheltering beneath McGregor's jeep, when the others were marched away by the Germans. The assurance given by the German sergeant that the British dead and wounded would be looked after had not materialized, and so he had lain for hours before starting to crawl away in order to reach the trees under cover of darkness.

It is not possible to say whether the promised German medical help would have made any difference in Stacey's case, but clearly Christie was correct in his judgment that if Krafft's SS men had not fired at the British medical orderlies during the course of the action, it is possible that his life might have been saved. It was hardly surprizing, therefore, that the recovery party was in a grim mood as it moved up the rise and into the wood on the other side of the dip. There they found Peter Bucknall's group, a sight which Christie has never forgotten: "They were laid in single file, about one yard between each man. None of them was wearing any equipment, nor had they any weapons. All had about ten bullet holes in the back or on the neck.

We later found their equipment on the jeep. From this, it was obvious that the Germans had taken them prisoner and then shot every one in cold blood. Lieutenant Bucknall had his face burned right off. I could recognize him by the blue polo-necked sweater he had been wearing and by his identity discs."

Recognition of the others was less straightforward, but battledress jackets were found in the jeep, each with a name on it, and it was wrongly assumed that they belonged to the dead men. These had been stowed in the vehicle by the owners at the landing zone but, since Bucknall had taken on to his jeep the first four of the Section who were ready, some of those to whom the jackets belonged were left to follow on in McGregor's vehicle. Lieutenant Pearson did not personally know any of them other than Bucknall, for he had only recently rejoined the Squadron after a lengthy period as a prisoner-of-war. As a result, undue reliance was placed on the evidence of the jackets and serious mis-identification took place, with Reg Hasler, who had been with McGregor in the following vehicle and had been wounded, mistakenly reported as killed. It was only afterwards, when word came through that Hasler was alive as a prisoner-of-war in Germany that the error became apparent. The same mistake was made in the case of Dick Minns, despite the fact that he had already been picked up and taken off to a dressing station. Similarly Arthur Barlow, who had been captured at the same time as Hasler and the others, was also reported as dead. The fact that Barlow was Bucknall's regular driver only served to reinforce the misunderstanding. In human terms it caused a great deal of anguish, and Daisy Barlow still has the War Office AFB 104-82 informing her of her husband's death in action. It was an error which was to take six and a half months to rectify, and only after that lapse of time did she ultimately learn that he was alive and well in Stalag IVB. In time, most of the errors were cleared up, although not entirely so. Today, Bucknall, Goulding, Brumwell, Edmond and McGregor are laid in a row in Oosterbeek War Cemetery, but there is one adjacent grave belonging to an unknown soldier. Since Edmond and McGregor were not with Bucknall's party, only three of the four that made up his jeep complement are here accounted for. It would, therefore, be a reasonable assumption to draw, that the unknown soldier is probably Ted Gorringe.

The most intriguing problem surrounding the discovery of the bodies of Bucknall and his men is that it raises the question as to whether or not a wartime atrocity did take place in the woods of Wolfheze on that late Sunday afternoon. At the time, many C Troop personnel believed that it did, pointing in particular to the absence of weapons and equipment on the bodies as well as the presence of extensive bullet wounds in the backs of the victims. These things in themselves, however, are by no means conclusive for both are open to an alternative explanation. In the first place, Krafft appears to have had a keen appetite for detail, and in his post-battle report to Himmler even included precise comment upon the thickness of the field telephone cable used by the British. With this in mind, it is possible to accept the explanation that equipment and weapons could well have been removed for inspection by the Germans. Furthermore, one needs also to consider the matter of timing. These, after all, were the first British troops contacted, and it would have been very strange had the Germans not taken the opportunity to go through all the clothing and equipment in search of maps or orders which might yield clues as to the purpose of the British operation.

The shots in the back, could be explained in a number of alternative ways. One belief, still held by certain former members of the Squadron, is that, having run into the ambush, Bucknall and his men were taken prisoner, but were almost immediately afterwards shot whilst trying to make a break for it. This could certainly account for the shots from behind, but the probability of all four men attempting a simultaneous escape under conditions which offered virtually no hope of success is most unlikely. Furthermore, such a theory does not satisfactorily explain the burning and disfigurement of the faces.

It is the burning which may well provide a clue to the mystery. Some, in seeking to explain it have done so by suggesting that the bullets caused the ignition of smoke bombs in the mens' pockets. They did have those with them, but there is little evidence to support the belief that this is what happened. The main purpose of the smoke grenade was as an anti-tank weapon, and the tactic was to generate dense clouds of white smoke in order to force out the crew of an armoured vehicle. It is difficult to imagine how the ignition of such devices in any quantity at all could have escaped the notice of those others who were following on behind, yet no reports of white smoke have ever been given. Another possible explanation is that, as it ran into the ambush, the vehicle's petrol tank was hit. Several independent witnesses have spoken of Bucknall moving forward at speed, in which case it is conceivable that the jeep's momentum could have caused it to overshoot the ambush point, making it necessary for the Germans to shoot, first at the side and then at the rear of the vehicle. This could have led to the igniting of the tank and perhaps accounted for both the burning and the placing of the shots. On the other hand, a petrol tank set alight in this way would have gone up like a bomb, with an explosion which would probably have disintegrated the jeep. Towards the end of the ambush Chandler saw the vehicle on fire with Gorringe lying across it, but it had not been destroyed. Besides, any burning sustained in consequence of an exploding petrol tank would hardly have been confined to the faces of the men who were, in any case, sitting facing the front.

The likeliest explanation for the burning is that the enemy was using a portable flame thrower. Assuredly, the German army had them as standard equipment, and Krafft's battle report does mention that they were included as part of his own armament. On the basis of this assumption, therefore, two rational possibilities present themselves. The first is that the men were deliberately executed after capture, presumably by being shot in the back as well as having the flame thrower turned on them. Krafft's unit was a bit of a hotch-potch, containing not only older men, regarded as unfit for front-line service, but also fanatical young Nazis whose battle ethics were highly suspect. It is also true that during the same action, some of those under Krafft's command had clearly demonstrated a readiness to react under fire in ways that were criminal. It may have been that they were inspired by a fear which produced over-violent reaction but, inevitably, their callous behaviour on that Sunday afternoon, in mortaring the medical officer and his stretcher bearers, leaves the suspicion that Bucknall and his group could well have met with an unorthodox end.

On the other hand, it could be argued that Bucknall's value for interrogation purposes is likely to have made him too desirable a prize to warrant such summary execution. The unlikelihood, too, of an act of that kind being carried out deliberately on the very spot where the men were captured perhaps makes the atrocity story less acceptable. So also does the fact that Pearce and the other captured men were well treated by soldiers of the same German unit. The second alternative therefore, is perhaps the more likely, because it probably comes closest to matching the available evidence. Given that Peter Bucknall's jeep ran swiftly through the dip and into the trees on the far side, it is conceivable that the waiting Germans could have directed the flame thrower at it, inflicting the burning injuries to heads and faces. Then, as the British soldiers, with the exception of Gorringe, jumped from the vehicles to run for cover, they could have been gunned down from behind. One thing which supports this view is that, according to the reporting of those who were following close behind, firing broke out almost as soon as Bucknall's jeep reached the wooded crest on the far side of the dip. If these were the only shots that were fired, then the "atrocity" theory has to be rejected. In the final analysis, however, one can do no more than speculate, for only those responsible for the killings were witness to them. Whether the British soldiers were slaughtered in cold blood or whether they simply ran into a packet of trouble, we shall probably never know.

When the bodies of the dead had been recovered, each was wrapped in a grey army blanket and laid to rest in temporary graves in Duitsekampweg. A short service was conducted by one of the Roman Catholic padres, and Jimmy Cooke can still recall how, at the end of it, the padre turned to them and said, "I think you've done your bit – now I'll do the rest." Thereafter, the recovery group rejoined the Troop in the allotted positions, which extended north from Mesdagweg.

It was not all stationary defensive work, however, for there were still opportunities for reconnoitring, and patrols were sent out. Cooke recollects accompanying his officer, Lieutenant Pearson, in three reconnaissance jeep sorties up the Wolfhezerweg to its junction with Amsterdamseweg. This was the place at which Dobie's 1st Parachute Battalion had suffered such heavy casualties on the previous evening, and the dead were still lying on the road. Nor had the danger by any means passed away, for the Germans still seemed to have a mortar ranged on the crossroads and, from time to time, they would suddenly plaster it with a cluster of bombs. Cooke remembers the feeling of vulnerability that they had on that open crossing and the consciousness of being in what was obviously a potential hot spot.

It was there, on the third sortie, that they narrowly escaped capture: "Mr Pearson took three of us back up to the crossroads," says Cooke, "where we harboured the jeeps under the trees. Two of us then set off with him on foot to reconnoitre the main road to the west. Mr Pearson was about six yards ahead, then came the other men, then myself. Suddenly I saw him signal back to us before disappearing fast into the woods. Where we were, we didn't have any cover at all, so we lay down in the ditch and pretended to be dead, like all the other British soldiers who were lying around. It was an SS patrol of about twenty men, walking on a path beside the ditch, and they actually marched right past the chap who was lying down further ahead of me. About ten yards or so before they got to me, they crossed over to the other side of the road and into some gorse. We lay faking 'dead' until they'd passed on a bit, then made as quietly as possible for the shelter of the woods. Fortunately the chap on the jeep had spotted what was happening and came up fast to collect us. By then, Mr Pearson was nowhere to be seen, but he managed to get out all right, although he had to run all the way back to our base on foot."

Whilst these hazardous "recce" sorties were taking place, the remainder of the Troop continued to maintain static positions of defence at the landing zone, in anticipation of the arrival of the second lift. The empty gliders of the previous day, each like an enormous discarded chrysalis, still littered the deserted area of Reijerscamp, but of the enemy's presence there was little sign, save for the occasional snap of a sniper's rifle. The response to this troublesome activity was the sending out of patrols and, as a result, four very frightened Germans were brought in. At about 1100 hours, planes arrived overhead, which everyone assumed were British. Bursts of cannon fire on the positions soon dispelled that notion but, although the Messerschmitts used up a lot of ammunition, they inflicted no damage, except upon the empty gliders, many of which were set on fire. This apparently pointless attack was possibly prompted by the suspicion that one of the brigade HQ's might be using the gliders as a base.

At Arnhem Bridge, the defenders were still holding on to their positions, and at 2 a.m. had been joined by a group of men from Fitch's 3rd Parachute Battalion. During the hold-up of the previous evening at Koude Herberg, Fitch had detached this group with orders to try to find a by-pass into Arnhem from the north. Those who managed to get through had come into the town by the railway line, and must have passed the point at which, later in the morning, Galbraith and his men were to engage the enemy. In the small hours of that Monday morning, Fitch's men passed through the main line station at Arnhem, with no greater mishap than a rather noisy collision with a collection of milk churns. Thereafter, following a brief encounter with a German tank, they passed on down to the Bridge. Unfortunately, their journey had a most disastrous end, as 1st Parachute Brigade diary was later to record: "One platoon immediately vanished whilst Major Lewis was giving his orders, another platoon was ordered to occupy a house near to the Brigade Defence Platoon and was never seen again. The third platoon joined Major Lewis in the school to the east of the Bridge, but was badly cut up before they reached it."

By contrast with the west side of the Bridge, the east appears at first to have had to cope with enemy forces in greater strength, as Captain Mackay and his RE sappers discovered during their own move to occupy. Having passed under the ramp, he took over two houses on the east, only to discover that the next one, only fifteen yards away, was a German company HQ. As a result, his men were hardly into position before the enemy attacked, by throwing grenades in at the windows and entering the basement. As Mackay reported, however, "determined hand-to-hand fighting with fists, boots, rifle butts and bayonets dislodged them . . . the enemy had no stomach for cold steel and retired to the house next door, where we followed him up with grenades." At that stage, nothing like this appears to have taken place on the other side, where Gough was. Whilst it is not to be taken as meaning that the German presence was not there, it does indicate that, even from the start, some defensive positions were more dearly won than others. In such circumstances, this could well account for the disappearance of Fitch's men, who had been directed to the east side.

In the early hours of that day, a second group of three lorries of Panzer grenadiers drove slowly past the Bridge positions. This time, Frost deliberately withheld the order to fire until the Germans were between the British on either side of the ramp. On a signal, the airborne troops opened up, and all the enemy were successfully despatched, with the exception of two seriously wounded Germans who were taken prisoner. Throughout the remainder of the night, things quietened down, and the British had the opportunity to lay a "daisy chain" of paired Hawkins 75 grenades out on the road, with a PIAT covering the position. It was believed that the Germans might make further attempts to retake the north end, perhaps by using heavier vehicles. The prediction turned out to be correct.

At 0500 hours, B Company of the 2nd Parachute Battalion arrived at the Bridge positions. Its mission, to take the pontoon bridge, shown clearly on the map as crossing the river a little to the west, could not be carried out, for that bridge was no longer in use, and the floating centre section of it had long since been removed. The new arrivals occupied buildings on the west side of the ramp. But it was not all disappointment for, at that time, one very useful decision was being made which was to be of great help to the defenders. Major Dennis Mumford, commander of the 3rd Light Battery, was sharing the attic of Brigade HQ with Major Gough. Like Gough, he had also become separated from his unit, which was still in position south of Wolfheze. Just before dawn, he sent off his own Captain Harrison, to try to contact the Battery and, if possible, get the guns brought within range of the Bridge. It was a hazardous assignment, but one which Harrison successfully completed. As a result, the guns moved down to near Oosterbeek Laag church, where they stayed throughout the duration of the fight at the Bridge. From over three miles away, Mumford was able to use a reliable 22 set link to bring their fire on to observable enemy positions at the Bridge. It was a move which also owed much, not only to Mumford's initiative and Harrison's courage, but also to the speedy reaction and skilled direction of Lieutenant-Colonel "Sheriff" Thompson, CO of the 1st Air Landing Light Regiment RA.

At 0900 hours, observers reported that the Germans on the south side appeared to be forming up some kind of convoy. It was in anticipation of this that the Hawkins mines had already been laid, and it was apparent that a more serious attack was about to be launched. The British discovered later that the attack force was the reconnaissance battalion of the 9th SS Panzer Division, under its commander, *SS Hauptsturmführer* Paul Grabner. On the Sunday night, one hour before Frost's arrival this specialized German unit had crossed over to the south, in order to assess the strength of any airborne invaders in the area between Arnhem and Nijmegen. Having covered the assigned territory and drawn a complete blank, Grabner had then returned to the southern end of the Bridge, and at 0930 hours, it was his armoured cars, with half-tracks and supporting infantry, that suddenly began to move back at speed across it.

The front vehicles successfully avoided the German lorries, which were still burning and littering the north end as a result of the earlier assault. They also eluded the Hawkins mines, only one of which was set off. The result was that the five leading vehicles – all armoured cars with machine-guns blazing – successfully penetrated the British defences and emerged on the other side. Against such a well-protected attacking force the airborne men could do little, but in the wake of the armoured cars came a string of half-tracks, vehicles of the *Schützenpanzerwagen* class, whose lighter armour and open tops made them much easier targets. The semi-tracked vehicles, which could normally develop a top speed of about 40 m.p.h., were travelling flat out and, as they emerged from below the bridge span and on to the northern ramp itself, the occupants were immediately exposed to fire from the adjacent houses. The fact that the top storeys of the houses rose above the level of the ramp made the German force even more vulnerable and, from their commanding positions, the British were able to direct their fire straight down on to the attackers in the open-topped vehicles.

From the east side, Mackay's men took first blood, by dropping a grenade into the first half-track and shooting the driver and front-seat passenger of the second. By then, the British had opened up on the Germans with everything they had. The broken chatter of Bren guns, the banging of PIAT bombs, the loose rattle of Stens and the bark of rifles was punctuated by the crump of mortars and the sudden reports of exploding 36 grenades and "Gammon" bombs. Each vehicle had a crew of six and, as the survivors scrambled out to try to seek cover, they were picked off one by one. Still the German reconnaissance column pressed on and, as the third half-track came within range, its driver was also shot and wounded. In a panic, he did the worst thing possible by stopping and trying to reverse. Almost immediately he collided with the vehicle behind, so that, locked together with one in flames and neither able to move, they effectively narrowed even more the path which those at the rear of the column had to follow. A multiple pile-up developed and, as the noise of crashing vehicles was overlaid on the sounds of the firing, the confusion mounted. Throughout it all, the British poured a pitiless fire into the midst of the attackers. Freddie Gough, himself, was behind a gun which he had removed from one of his jeeps: "As these armoured things came across", he recalled, "they started piling up on each other. I was firing at them with one of my 'K' guns, and it was the best shooting I've ever had in my life, because our targets were absolutely unimpeded." For one whose ancestor had once distinguished himself in the defence of London Bridge against Jack Cade's Kentish rabble, no situation could have been more appropriate, and of Gough's own soldierly gratification there was no doubt whatever. John Frost was later to report that one of his memories of the affair was of looking over during the action and seeing Gough behind his gun, his face flushed and beaming with pleasure.

Indeed, it was a fight which most of the British participants enjoyed and in which everyone who could do so joined in, including the drivers, the batmen and the clerks. On the German side, there was no comparable satisfaction, for the crews of the half-tracks stood little chance of escape once their vehicles had been halted. As vehicle after vehicle accelerated from behind in a desperate attempt to outrun the trap, the chaos mounted. One after another, they crashed into the stricken carriers which were already out of action and slewed across the Bridge. Six vehicles toppled out of control over the edge of the embankment, some to land in the street below. As their cover disappeared, the supporting infantrymen who had been advancing behind on foot, were also mercilessly exposed to the British fire. Some Germans huddled up to their blazing vehicles, impossibly seeking cover in a position where they found themselves between two lines of crossfire. Those few vehicles which did manage to run the gauntlet fetched up close to the school on the east side from where Mackay's men fired straight down into them, either killing the occupants where they sat, or else picking them off as they sought shelter in the bushes by the side of the Nijmeegseweg.

Two other factors had materially aided the British success. One was that Major Arnold had managed to get his four 6-pounder guns ranged on the column. The other that, as the battle developed, Major Dennis Mumford, from his observation post overlooking the Bridge, had been able to call on supporting fire from the light artillery, which was set up in the new position at Oosterbeek church. As a result, Grabner's column, the forward elements of which could eventually move neither forward nor back, suffered much from well-placed and accurately directed shelling. In reporting the action, 1st Parachute Brigade diary later credited the PIATS and 6-pounders alone with having knocked out or scored hits on a total of two armoured cars, eight to ten half-track vehicles and five or six lorries following up behind. On the whole, it was very satisfactory and, indeed, one senses from the Brigade diary record that a certain sporting atmosphere even crept into the proceedings: "(the Germans) provided very good target practice for the Brigade HQ personnel who were in the attic. The highest individual score was reported to be Lieutenant Harvey Tod who claimed eight with his American carbine, followed closely by Major Mumford and Private Shuttlewood."

At the end of it all, well over a dozen vehicles had been destroyed. Those that had not been driven over the parapet littered the roadway in a mass of burning debris. The German survivors who were able to do so, in particular supporting infantrymen, escaped to the south side as best they could, pursued by British bullets ricocheting off the Bridge uprights. For the defenders, it was not merely a tactical victory against armoured troops of a first-rate Panzer division, but a morale booster *par excellence*. In Frost's words, it was, "the most lively action"; and he continued: "there they were, these awful Boches with their pot helmets sticking out. When we had dealt with them, their vehicles burned in front of us to the end of the battle." The fight had lasted altogether two hours.

For the rest of that morning, the main body of the Reconnaissance Squadron, having failed to find a way through to Arnhem, stayed in the area to the north-east of the Oosterbeek crossroads and kept the enemy under observation. Towards mid-day, they rendezvoused briefly at 'the Green', the broad triangle of grass across from the Hartenstein Hotel, on the west side of which Tom Collier had established his ammunition dump. Collier had been ferrying it from the dropping zone all through the morning and was not to complete his task until later in the afternoon. Despite the routine nature of the operation, his own time had not been entirely uneventful, for, on an occasion when he had stopped to speak to a sergeant from the 21st Independent Company, the conversation had been terminated abruptly with the sergeant shot dead through the head by a sniper's bullet.

Once back on watch again, east of the Oosterbeek crossroads, the A Troop men were strengthened by the addition of their own 3 Section jeeps, which had finally been hacked out of the gliders. At noon, the 2nd South Staffordshires had come through the Squadron positions and from then until about 1430 hours in the afternoon, the Reconnaissance men were concerned to deal with infiltration as well as snipers. D Troop, especially, inflicted a number of casualties on the enemy. By and large, the activity at this stage was fairly sporadic but, in retrospect, some of the smaller actions can be seen to have had certain incongruous features. On the Backerstraat, for example, during the lulls in the skirmishing, members of the Squadron were given tea, apples and beer by the householders, who gathered in little groups to talk to them. Sergeant Bill Bentall of D Troop took cover at one point in a house occupied by four elderly ladies. They were well-informed on the latest war news, proudly showed him their hidden radio and serenaded the soldiers with "Tipperary" before they left.

Another curious incident took place in the afternoon, when a most troublesome German sniper had to be dealt with. A Troop's commander, Mike Grubb, told Corporal Jim "Spud" Taylor to handle it but, since the German was hidden round the corner of a house, it was difficult to get a sighting on him. Because of this, the possibility of carrying out the task from the vantage point of another house was noted, and it was decided to try it. "I went up the path", recalls Taylor, "carrying my Bren, and knocked at the front door. When the lady opened, I asked if I might come in, in order to shoot a German. I was shown into a room in the house, with a table in the centre of the floor. I removed the cover from the table, replacing it with my camouflage face veil, so that the front metal legs of the Bren gun would not scratch the polished surface. Quietly, I opened the window and returned to the table, from which position I could see the sniper clearly in my sights. I fired and hit him, and then gathered up all the empty cartridge cases I helped the lady to put back her cloth and left the room just as it had been, but remembered afterwards that I'd forgotten to close the window."

Politeness of that kind was something that the Dutch people had long since ceased to expect, and those living in Oosterbeek today, who remember the battle, still speak of the British soldier's unaccustomed civility, by contrast with the boorish behaviour normally displayed by the representatives of the occupying power. "You were all so gentle," recollects Jo Crum-Bloemink, "and we were not used to that." Certainly, in the establishment of good public relations, courtesy paid off. Nevertheless, it could be argued that it did not always necessarily help to win wars. Thus, it has often been asserted, not least by General Urquhart himself, that one of the obstacles to rapid progress in the hours immediately subsequent to the landing was the reluctance of the British troops to damage private property. Permission was sought to enter, flower beds which stood in the way were walked around rather than trampled over and there was a degree of dalliance which inevitably slowed down progress. In this respect, John Marshall recalls his own experience during those early hours when he had lost contact temporarily with D Troop: "I called at one house and got laughed at by a Dutchman for going round to the front door to see if I could get in, instead of just kicking in the glass, as the Germans would have done. I remember he said to me, 'What a funny lot you English soldiers are!'"

Meantime, following a weather delay, the second lift had at last got under way from England. With it came the Reconnaissance Squadron gliders which had been unsuccessful in the first lift. In one of them were the A Troop jeeps of Lieutenant Galbraith's 2 Section; in another, being escorted by Lieutenant Graham Wadsworth, was Captain Allsop's HQ vehicle, together with a trailer and two motor cycles. As on the previous day, Wadsworth was accompanied by Sergeant Kay, the Wireless Sergeant of HQ Troop and Trooper Bill Cook. They were not unduly concerned about the enemy opposition, for there was confidence that they would be landing on a zone already occupied by their own troops. On this occasion, the flight began without mishap, but there was a lot of flak over the Dutch coast which rattled on the fuselage; at the time, it did not seem to the passengers that there had been any penetration of the glider, although at one point the nose gave a frightening dip. Once over the fields of Wolfheze, however, they speedily realized that their optimism about the probability of a "cushy" landing had been completely misplaced. Cook's account tells of what happened: "We felt the jerk as the tow rope was released and down went the nose as we commenced the glide in. A scattering of holes suddenly appeared in the fuselage. 'It's just small arms fire,' remarked 'Judd' in a voice that stayed casual, despite the fact that we were rapidly getting to look like a pepper pot. We hit a raised road cross on, and half-a-dozen bumps later slewed to a halt. Our expectations of the landing zone being under control were quickly shattered when, before we had time to undo the safety belts, machine-gun fire raked us from the right and 'Judd' caught a packet in his right wrist. As I sat on the floor to bandage him up, I looked at the exit door and decided that that was one way out that I would not be using. I then crawled under the trailer and jeep, getting soaked in the process from the damaged petrol tank, and at the front of the glider found that one pilot was dead and the other wounded." Cook's first impression was that the pilots had been hit during the course of the landing, but it transpired that they were victims of the flak which had hit the front of the glider whilst it was crossing the coast. Notwithstanding his wounded condition, the surviving pilot had brought them safely in to land. The outcome was that, after a short spell of taking cover by the side of the glider, Wadsworth and Cook were able to communicate with some passing Dutch cyclists, who arranged for a British medical orderly with a jeep to collect the casualties. Thereafter, loading themselves with as much ammunition as they could carry, they set off on foot to find the Squadron.

Overall, there were varying degrees of resistance to the landings of the second lift. Out at Ginkel Heath, the 7th Battalion of the King's Own Scottish Borderers had to repel the troops of Helle's SS Battalion. This they did in fine style, by means of a bayonet charge, led by the commanding officer, Lieutenant-Colonel Payton-Reid. As a result, the drop at that point was virtually unopposed. But stiff German attacks were delivered at other places, and B Company of the Border Regiment had to retreat from Renkum to Heelsum, suffering loss of transport. Subsequent German activity on the Renkum zone took the form of machine-gun fire and this accounted for the difficulties which Graham Wadsworth and his party ran into. Only at the relatively unguarded Reijerscamp area was there little opposition. For C Troop of the Squadron, this was fortunate, since it was too small in number to have taken on any sizeable German force. Nevertheless, two men of Ralph Foulkes's Section, Troopers Dodson and Garwood, were injured by shrapnel which probably came from one of the German "ack-ack" guns that opened up in the vicinity. Clearly, the enemy had been prepared for the new arrivals and casualties would certainly have been higher had it not been for the quality of the defensive role assumed by such others as Payton-Reid's Borderers. Foulkes took his two wounded men to the main dressing station at Wolfheze, and it was there that he saw other casualties coming in by the score. As he recorded at the time: "... dirty black faces denoted first arrivals, clean faces denoted second lift." C Troop remained in position until about 1800 hours, when Colonel Barlow, acting Brigade commander, ordered 1st Air Landing Brigade HQ to take up new quarters in the Bilderberg Hotel. For this move, C Troop was required to act as a rearguard for the Brigade.

On the whole, the arrival of 4th Brigade on the second wave was remarkably successful, but the main problem of getting through to the beleaguered force at the Bridge still remained to be solved. Hicks had already attempted to do something about it by sending the 2nd South Staffordshires forward as a relieving force, but at 1420 hours, just prior to the arrival of 4th Brigade, he had learned that they had run into heavy enemy opposition on Utrechtseweg, at the same point as the Squadron had "bumped" earlier in the day. As a result, he made a second major decision to redeploy part of his force and ordered that, immediately upon arrival, the remainder of the 2nd South Staffordshires, together with the 11th Parachute Battalion, should proceed with all speed in the direction of Arnhem, to try to drive a way through.

From daybreak on, in the western suburbs of Arnhem, a confused series of engagements had built up, between the troops of Harzer's 9th SS Panzer Division and the 1st and 3rd Parachute Battalions. With the enemy in occupation of Den Brink, and German armour with supporting infantry holding the ground from there to the town, the struggle had developed into a bewildering succession of separate actions. Much of the 3rd Battalion activity had taken place in the northern part, in the residential suburb just west of St Elisabeth's hospital, whilst 1st Battalion had engaged south of the Utrechtseweg. Mark IV tanks, SP guns, armoured cars and well-armed Panzer grenadiers made up the resistance which the two British battalions had to face. As the morning passed, the inter-penetration of British and German-held positions in the combat area became such that sections of both British battalions found themselves surrounded. To the west, on Den Brink, and to the east, towards the centre of Arnhem itself, the enemy held positions in strength.

In the area of the Alexanderstraat all was confusion. As 3rd Battalion casualties mounted, Urquhart and Lathbury knew that their own effectiveness as commanders was being totally neutralized by the restrictions of the position in which they now found themselves. It was vital that they should get out without further delay, and the two senior officers decided to try to make a break for it on their own. When they were ready, some of the troops gave cover with smoke bombs, and they ran quickly out of the back door of the three-storey house within which they had been sheltering. As they climbed over the garden fence, Lathbury accidentally discharged his Sten gun, and narrowly missed hitting Urquhart. Once out of the garden, they negotiated a narrow alleyway, and ran eastwards down Alexanderstraat towards St Elisabeth's Hospital, accompanied by Captain Cleminson of the 3rd Parachute Battalion and Captain Taylor of Lathbury's Brigade HQ. Suddenly, from the top of Hendrickstraat came a burst of Spandau fire which caught Lathbury in the back. Quickly the group carried him into 135 Alexanderstraat, where he was left in the care of a Dutch couple. During the short time that they were in the house, a German soldier looked in the window, and was shot through the head at point-blank range by Urquhart himself. The General and the other two officers then slipped out of the back door and ran over to Zwarteweg, a short street immediately adjacent to the west side of the hospital. At the front, the street was stiff with German troops, but they approached from the rear and were able to gain access to number 14, where the owner speedily showed them to a safe place in the attic.

To begin with, the anxious group listened with trepidation to every sound that reached their hiding place from below, half-expecting at any moment to hear the sudden shouts and the crash of enemy jackboots on the narrow wooden stairs. Slowly the uneasy minutes passed, until eventually they were able to relax, satisfied that, for a short while at least, they had avoided detection. Through the curtains of the small dormer window they could see the foliage of the poplar trees that lined the pavement edge and, immediately across the way, the imposing bulk of the St Elisabeth's Hospital. Groups of German soldiers were in evidence at various points, but what really put paid to any hope of immediate escape was the arrival in the street of a self-propelled gun. It clanked noisily up from the corner, eased clumsily around one of the poplars and drew up outside the door of number 14. There it remained, and, for those temporarily incarcerated on the upper floor, it was a demoralizing sight to have to watch the German crew standing around chatting, clearly in no great hurry to go anywhere. In the circumstances, it was hardly surprizing that General Urquhart should have felt that the situation was slipping almost completely and permanently from his grasp.

By afternoon, the strength of both 1st and 3rd Parachute Battalions had been appallingly and drastically reduced. 3rd Battalion was down from over 600 to something like 130–140 all ranks and had made no further progress eastwards. Dobie's 1st Battalion, on the other side of Utrechtseweg, had fought fiercely in the area between Klingelbeekseweg and Den Brink but, by 1830 hours, had finished up at the Onderlangs road fork, with only a hundred men left. Isolated and, in both cases, cut to less than company size, the potential effectiveness of the battalions had all but disappeared. Now, it only remained to see if the reinforcements sent off by Hicks could restore the balance sufficiently to allow for one final desperate attempt to win through to the hard-pressed defenders of Arnhem Bridge.

Back in Oosterbeek, the Reconnaissance Squadron made fresh efforts in the late afternoon to discover a gap in the enemy lines, but reached no further than the Weverstraat, having failed to penetrate even as far as the mid-day positions. Quite plainly, the Germans were achieving an increased consolidation almost by the hour. Nor did the 2nd Battalion of the South Staffordshires, with which the Squadron was in regular contact, have any greater success in progressing beyond a distance of about 500 yards east of the Oosterbeek crossroads. By then, it had become apparent that, in the face of stiffening German resistance, no further progress could be expected within the hours of daylight.

Such was the situation when, at 1800 hours, the Squadron was ordered to return to base and leave the area in which both they and the 2nd South Staffs had been stalemated. Following instructions, they withdrew to their newly-established HQ at the junction of Oranjeweg and Utrechtseweg, almost directly across from the Hartenstein Hotel into which Divisional HQ had moved only one hour earlier. There the men ate what they had of their rations and dug in for the night. Captain Hay's C Troop had, in the meantime, successfully covered the move of 1st Air Landing Brigade to the Bilderberg Hotel, of which journey Ralph Foulkes remembers the grim sights on the way down. "All the British dead had white sheets and flowers covering them, but the Germans had been left uncovered. The smell of dead bodies was terrible." Throughout a fairly quiet night, the C Troop men established a guard on the new Brigade HQ, having first dug themselves in on a defence line in the Hotel grounds. During the night, Graham Wadsworth and Bill Cook turned up and were looked after by their comrades. "I remember," says Ralph

Foulkes, "I dug Graham a hole." In the circumstances, it was the best possible demonstration of true friendship and hospitality!

That afternoon at the Bridge, the enemy retaliated for his earlier defeat with an increase in the amount and intensity of mortar and artillery barrages from the south bank. To some extent, opposing fire from the 3rd Light Battery in Oosterbeek, directed by Mumford from his attic observation post, was effective in countering this. Even so, some houses, notably 9, were badly damaged, the toll of dead and wounded rose, and the medical centre, which had been set up in the basement of Brigade HQ, began to receive a steady flow of men. With Dobie and Fitch now in his vicinity, just west of St Elisabeth's Hospital, Frost was able to make wireless contact and speak to Dobie off and on throughout the afternoon but, from what transpired, it was soon apparent that 1st Battalion was having to deal with serious problems of its own. At the Bridge, determined German infantry attacks from the south were sustained, and a new threat developed as the enemy sought to infiltrate along the river bank. The most easterly British positions found themselves very vulnerable to this, and the Brigade Defence Platoon took heavy casualties, being forced to withdraw from Houses 12 and 13, to join Briggs and Mackay in 14, 15, 16 and 17. House 10, under Lieutenant McDermont of the 2nd Battalion, caught the worst of the fighting, as did House 11 to the south. Much of it was a vicious hand-to-hand business and the high quality of German prisoner taken made it apparent that if 2nd Army did not arrive soon, such engagements were likely to become fiercer and more frequent.

Sniper fire also became a constant danger, as the Germans moved in closer and were able to pick off any British soldiers who unwittingly appeared at windows or shell-hole openings. Corporal George Dixon, who was Major Gough's wireless operator, remembers one such occasion: "Behind the main Brigade HQ and near to where we had parked our three jeeps was an outbuilding, with parts of the wall formed from wooden slats, with spaces in between. One man had the Bren trained through one of the slits, and I was on the 22 set at the back of the room, trying to raise someone. I felt I needed a cigarette, and asked the lad on observation if he could oblige. When he threw it over, it landed just a little short, so I had to crawl over to get it and, in doing so, pass one of those slits in the woodwork. As I did so, and just as I was reaching out for the cigarette, a line of machine-gun bullets ripped into the floor, not more than two inches away from where I lay."

It was from that late afternoon and evening that the Germans then started to employ a tactic which, in the end, the British could do little to combat. Using incendiary devices, including phosphorus bombs, they began to set fire to the houses, and although numerous gallant and often successful fire-fighting attempts were made by the defenders, the British had neither the apparatus nor the men available to contain and deal with all the fires that broke out, one after another. By the time darkness fell, Houses 1, 11, 9 and 17 were well and truly alight, and only the most strenuous efforts had prevented Brigade HQ from suffering the same fate. By then it was obvious that the small defensive perimeter around the north end of Arnhem Bridge was shrinking with an increasing rapidity, although, with memories of the morning's success still fresh, spirits remained reasonably high. Clearly, there was a need to conserve ammunition, but it was still plentiful, and the wireless contact with Dobie's 1st Battalion, a little over a mile away, had raised hopes that help would come soon. Everything, of course, depended upon the speedy arrival of 30 Corps, which was spearheading 2nd Army's advance from south of the river, but those who were holding out at the Bridge were not to know that, almost from the start, the main relief force had fallen behind schedule. By nightfall on the Sunday, it was still well south of Eindhoven.

Major Freddie Gough in "Theirs is the Glory" *(Rank Organisation)*

A Troop jeep and civilians: Backerstraat, Oosterbeek: Monday 18th September 1944
L–R: Tprs. V. Taylor, A. Dickson

(D. van Woerkom)

D Troop jeep and Sgt. Bentall: Backerstraat, Oosterbeek: Monday 18th September 1944

(D. van Woerkom)

"De Vergarde", Utrechtseweg: Site of early D Troop action

Twenty-four hours later, on that Monday night, the leading elements of Horrocks's force had reached no further than Zon, five miles north of Eindhoven, a mere eighteen miles from the start line and still forty-six miles from Arnhem Bridge.

And down by the suburbs of western Arnhem, the tired and battered survivors of the 1st and 3rd Parachute Battalions took up their defensive positions for the night. Fitch occupied houses only a short distance from where he had fought all day, unaware of the fact that Dobie's force, even smaller than his own, was just a few hundred yards away from him. At 2000 hours, the first half of the 2nd South Staffordshires arrived in the area and made contact with Dobie's 1st Battalion at a position west of the Onderlangs road fork. The benefits of advancing under the protection of darkness were then demonstrated when, just one hour afterwards and despite having had a very much later start, Lea's 11th Parachute Battalion joined them. By contrast with what had gone before, the 11th had had a relatively easy passage, despite some casualties suffered in a clash at dusk with some of the enemy forces.

As they made their plans for the final assault before first light, the commanders of those four battalions would have been astonished had they learned that their General was almost literally within hailing distance. So it was that as the night passed, in the attic of 14 Zwarteweg, Roy Urquhart waited for the dawn in a mood that he was later to describe as one of "reluctant contemplation." He had no picture of what was happening and was no more in touch with the strategic developments of the battle than were the Dutch civilians sheltering in their cellars from the ferocity of the holocaust that had descended without warning upon their quiet streets.

Chapter 7 TUESDAY 19th SEPTEMBER 1944

MORNING TO EARLY AFTERNOON

"Keep your bloody head down"

Despite the serious losses of the previous day in the area of St Elisabeth's Hospital, Fitch was still determined to try to force a way through with his Battalion on the last stage of the journey to the Bridge. His starting point was the Rhine Pavilion, a building just over 100 yards east of the Onderlangs fork, and situated on the route along which Frost, Gough and 1st Brigade HQ had travelled with relative ease just thirty-six hours earlier. Within that short but significant interval of time, however, the position had changed beyond recognition, with 9th SS Panzer Division interposed as an almost impenetrable barrier to the forward movement of the British troops. With his total force reduced to a mere fraction of battalion strength, Fitch could have had few illusions as he began his attack at 0300 hours on the Tuesday morning. The previous day's events had borne witness to the gradual change from a situation where it was still possible to make effective inroads into the German defence, to one in which an almost hourly growth in the strength of enemy resistance had demonstrated the vulnerability of the lightly armed airborne troops. So it was that, faced with the combined armour and infantry of the Panzer troops, 3rd Battalion could make such little progress that Fitch was soon brought to a halt and forced to draw back to his start point.

In the meantime, unknown to him, the other three British battalions in the area had also prepared a similar attack, which was to be a combined one and begin at 0400 hours. Such an offensive, planned with only one hour of darkness remaining had the slimmest chance of success. The late start was a result of several postponements due, amongst other things, to the delayed arrival of the remainder of the 2nd South Staffordshires who had come on the second lift. Whether the timing ultimately made any significant difference to the outcome is doubtful. Certainly, an early attack had not helped Fitch and, indeed, by the time the three battalions were poised and ready to begin, Fitch's 3rd Battalion on the lower road had already broken off its own attempt to penetrate the German screen.

The combined plan of attack called for Dobie's 1st Battalion to move forward from the road fork on Onderlangs – the same road as Fitch had used – whilst the 2nd South Staffordshires were to lead off on the more northerly Utrechtseweg, with 11th Parachute Battalion behind them in support. This meant that on upper and lower roads, the British attacking forces would be within virtual shouting distance of each other – at the widest point not more than 200 yards apart – as they set off in the direction of the Bridge. What followed was to be remembered as one of the bloodiest and most disastrous actions of the entire operation.

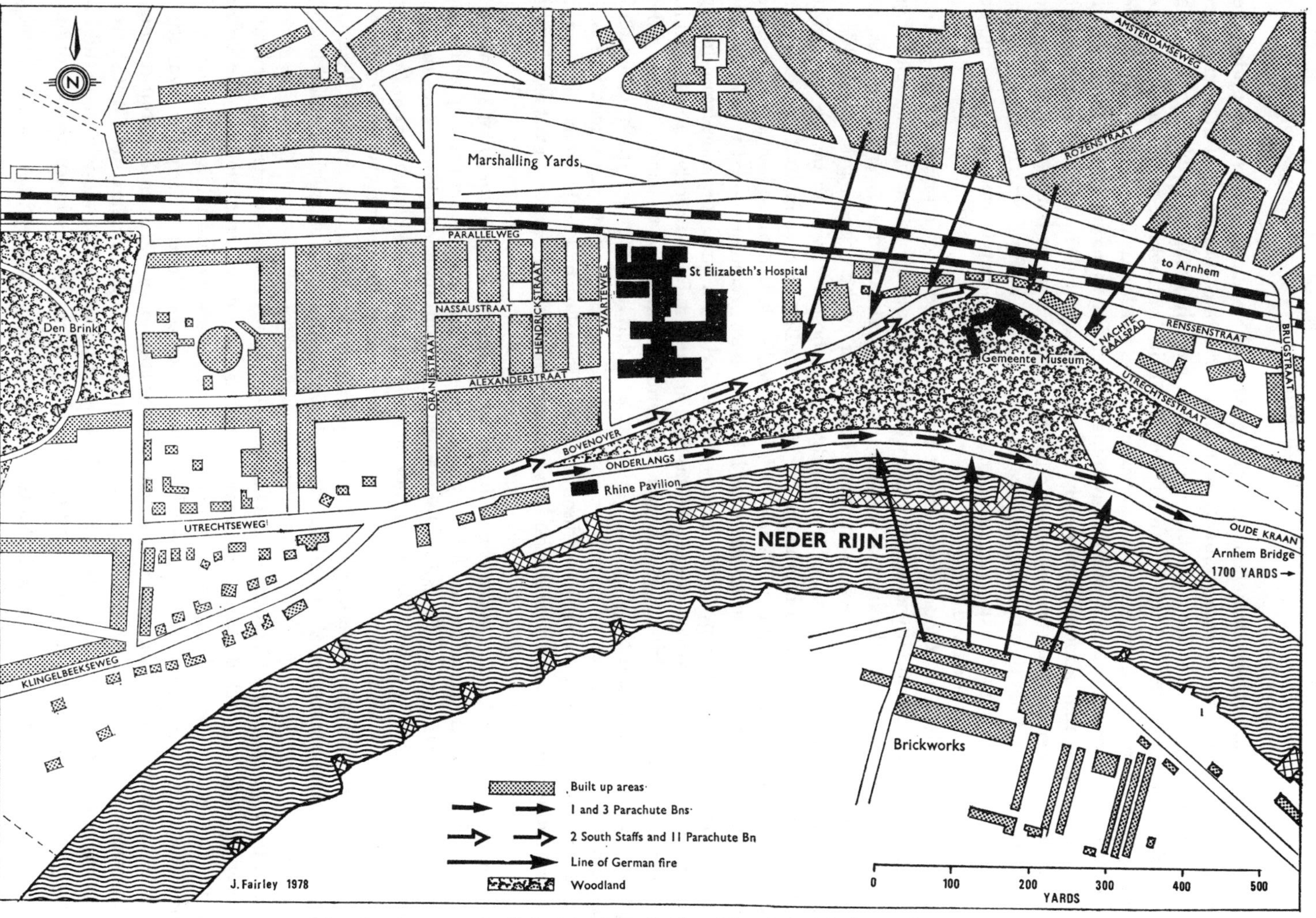

Map 8 Attempted relief of Arnhem Bridge: Tuesday 19th September 1944

At 0400 hours the attack was launched. In a strange way, the opening moves were undertaken in silence, until the enemy seemed suddenly to realize what was happening and opened fire. From then on, the struggle was fierce but highly confused, with the scene on both roads lit only by the exploding mortar shells and tracer bullets. For the British attackers, as much as for those defending the way into Arnhem, visual consciousness of the battle was fragmented and reduced to a series of successive snapshots, fleetingly revealing, yet serving to accentuate all the more, the bewildering darkness that almost immediately crowded in again to muffle and confound the senses. All around were the discordant noises characteristic of a street battle, sounds amplified by the presence of buildings that flanked the area of conflict – the swift movement of running feet, the sudden shouts, the bang of exploding shell and bomb, the ripping intrusion of machine-gun fire, the cries of men, wounded and dying.

Down beside the river, on Onderlangs, Dobie had discovered Fitch's presence just prior to launching his own attack, and it was agreed that, whilst 1st Parachute Battalion should lead, 3rd Battalion would follow on. At the start, Dobie made good progress under cover of darkness, and his leading platoons fought their way past the enemy as far as the beginnings of Oude Kraan. They were then within one mile of Arnhem Bridge. This, however, was to be the limit of the advance for, as daylight began to illuminate the scene, the British encountered significant and rapid stiffening of German resistance. Worse still, because Dobie had moved with greater speed than the two battalions on the upper road his left flank had become exposed to the defensive crossfire of German troops occupying the houses that looked down on Onderlangs from the high ground of Utrechtseweg. That was not all. As daylight advanced, from directly across the Rhine, anti-aircraft guns sited at a brickworks, began to pound out on a low trajectory, finding their targets with a merciless accuracy. On the open stretch of Onderlangs, the 1st Parachute Battalion, caught between the two sources of enemy fire and powerless to return it to any effect, was cut to pieces. By 0730 hours, when the fight was disengaged, the Battalion had been reduced to less than forty men. Dobie himself was a prisoner and his courageous unit had ceased to exist as a fighting force.

The heavy defeat of Dobie's force was followed by a similar disaster for what remained of Fitch's 3rd Battalion. Exposed to the full fury of the enemy fire that was turned upon his men following the destruction of 1st Battalion, John Fitch had again no choice but to give the order to retreat to the Rhine Pavilion. On the withdrawal, he himself was killed by a mortar bomb, and only a fraction of his force got out alive. With their going, the cry of "Woho Mohamet"* which had echoed through Onderlangs during the short, horrific action, was finally stilled. Only the dead remained amidst the dust and debris, and over it all the black smoke drifted lazily in the silence.

Up on the high road of Utrechtseweg, McCardie's 2nd South Staffordshires took the brunt of the early fighting. As on Onderlangs, some early progress was made, but at nothing like the rate at which Dobie's men had advanced. Despite that, it was of sufficient initial impetus to carry the British attacking force through and beyond the houses where General Urquhart was still in hiding. As a result, the SP gun which had remained on stationary watch throughout the night, suddenly moved off and the owner of the house ran upstairs to tell Urquhart that British troops were at the end of the street. The General seized his opportunity to leave, and within minutes was speeding by jeep back to his Divisional HQ at the Hartenstein Hotel to resume control of the

* Unofficially adopted for general use as the battle cry of the Parachute Regiment, but first used by the 3rd Battalion in the Tamara valley, two years prior to Arnhem.

battle. At that point, he did not know that the bulk of his attacking force was already in the area that he had just left.

During the period immediately prior to General Urquhart's escape, it had become increasingly obvious at Divisional HQ that things were beginning to go very badly wrong for the British. For Brigadier Hicks, however, there was an additional problem to be faced, in many ways as critical as the strategic objective of relief to the Bridge. This was nothing less than the threatened encirclement of the Division itself. What was worrying him were reports received from 1st Air Landing Brigade that indicated an encroaching movement in the area to the west of Arnhem and Oosterbeek by the various enemy units of *Generalleutnant* von Tettau. By Monday 16th September, parts of this enemy concentration were already reported to be in possession of Renkum and Heelsum, and there were mounting fears that, even with the best will in the world, such a force could not be held for long by a depleted British screen, consisting for the most part of the 1st Battalion of the Border Regiment. The advance of von Tettau's troops from the west could mean that the British, already reeling under the impact of the 9th SS Panzer Division in the east and increasingly hemmed in by the growing strength of the blocking line between Oosterbeek and Arnhem, could well be taken on from behind and find themselves holding a constricted area, within which they would be facing the enemy on both western and eastern fronts. To the south lay the Neder Rijn, so that it would only remain for the Germans to establish a linking force, in order to join those two fronts somewhere just beyond the northern extremity of the British positions. This would then secure the objective of surrounding the whole of the 1st Airborne Division, except for the small force holding out at the Bridge.

At first light on Tuesday 19th September, the acting Divisional commander had no knowledge that such an eventuality was already well on the way to becoming a reality, yet it was Bittrich's swift appreciation of the entire situation that had already led to the decision to establish Krafft's 16th SS Panzer Battalion in its new position to the north of Amsterdamseweg. Thus, Krafft, as he faced south, had his left flank resting near to the Dreijenseweg crossroads and linking up with the northernmost part of the blocking line. Further west, units of von Tettau's command, such as the *Schiffstammabteilung*, linked up with him on his right flank. In short, as one writer has effectively put it, Krafft's unit was "the lid being placed on the box."*

On Tuesday morning, whilst there was, understandably, no full information on the extent of the threat from the west, there were certainly grounds for suspicion that strong opposition might soon have to be met from that direction. It was on account of this growing unease, therefore, that the acting Divisional commander ordered the Reconnaissance Squadron to investigate and report enemy strength and movements to north and west. "At first," as David Allsop says, "with our thoughts on Arnhem Bridge, we couldn't help feeling that we were being sent in the wrong direction!" Nevertheless, it was information that had to be obtained and so, at 0630 hours, at just about the time that the 1st and 3rd Parachute Battalions were fighting themselves out of existence, A and D Troops, followed by Squadron HQ, set out in their jeeps to travel west on the Utrechtseweg. Simultaneously, Captain John Hay's depleted C Troop, which had reported back from the Bilderberg to Squadron command, was allotted the task of carrying out the more northerly reconnaissance up by Reijerscamp, as far as Amsterdamseweg, in order to report on what was happening along that particular main road. It was appropriate that C Troop should have been given this task, partly because its members were already familiar with the area and partly because it was believed that it would be the least onerous assignment, since it was antici-

* Cornelis Bauer: *The Battle of Arnhem*, p. 153.

pated that the greatest enemy opposition was most likely to be on an axis across the main Utrecht road. As matters subsequently turned out, it was evident, by nightfall, that C Troop had once more drawn the short straw!

The area of reconnaissance of A Troop was to be both sides of Utrechtseweg and, specifically, around the town of Heelsum. By 7.30 a.m., one hour after moving out from the darkness of the harbour area, Captain Mike Grubb, the Troop commander, had moved his men through the 1st Border Regiment positions and set up his headquarters, about three-quarters of a mile from Heelsum and approximately 150 yards south of the main road. It was a characteristic reconnaissance move and one which took him well beyond the main western defence points of the Division. There, he found himself in a heavily wooded area, penetrated by a criss-cross pattern of rides, with a few detached houses set in the midst of the woodland or sparsely grouped here and there to either side of the main road. Some of the gardens had marigolds in full bloom, their colourful blossoms standing out against the predominant fading greens and browns of autumnal change, the splashes of orange brilliance symbolizing as never before, the Dutch hope of liberation.

It was from the depths of the Doorwerth woods that A Troop commander then deployed his three operational sections. John Stevenson took number 1 Section on further reconnaissance westwards, beyond the cover of the woods, to the town of Heelsum itself. Reunited with his lost vehicles, which had arrived safely on the second lift, Dougie Galbraith led 2 Section to the north-west of the road beyond the relatively shallow border of trees and into the earlier dropping zone of Renkum Heath. Graham Wadsworth, seconded as 3 Section officer in place of the wounded Guthrie, had the task of reconnoitring due south on Kabeljauwallee for a mile or so through the thickest part of the wood, to link up with Koninginnelaan, a more southerly approach eastwards into Heelsum.

From the point of view of the men involved, this was an opportunity for true reconnaissance, for feeling their way carefully forward with all the caution and skill that their training had given them, in order to locate the enemy. The reconnaissance task was always identified as that of first finding the enemy and then keeping him in sight. The primary object of such a function was never to kill, yet, by operating as they so often did far beyond their own divisional fronts, the regiments of the Corps were almost inevitably brought into hard and dangerous contact with an opposing force that so often exceeded their own. Hence the need for a strength of fire power and a high mobility on the ground. Cautious probing, therefore, was the pattern of the morning's work, and all three sections noted the signs of troop movement from the west.

Exposed as it was in the open heathland, it was hardly surprizing that, at one stage, Galbraith's 2 Section should have run into some difficulty, when its outflanking and observation of the town of Heelsum was interrupted at about 0900 hours by contact with a German Mark IV tank. Although only in the "medium" range, the destructive potential of this formidable vehicle was considerable and, since Galbraith's two light jeeps were no match for such opposition, dismounted action was immediately ordered. Alex Dickson remembers that it was on this occasion that Trooper Andy Auld, who was particularly keen on tank recognition, was so carried away by the golden opportunity to display his skill that he showed an inclination to disregard certain elementary precautions. It was Auld's fellow Scot, Galbraith, who terminated the 'tank-spotting' session with the caustic admonition, "Keep your bloody head down, or you won't be spotting anything." Galbraith, of course, fully approved of Auld's efforts, for he was all too conscious that the primary task was to feed back information and not attempt what would have been a very unequal combat. But the Germans had other ideas and, despite precautionary evasive tactics, the Section was spotted and engaged. In the course of the short action that followed one man was injured in the leg by enemy fire – it was Andy Auld, the tank spotter!

South of Grubb's area of reconnaissance, John Park's D Troop was operating in a similar fashion on a front that ran approximately down the line of the heavily wooded Italiaanseweg. They made their first sighting of the enemy at about 1000 hours, just west of Breedeweg* on the Koninginnelaan. Like the others, they kept watch but did not engage, and John Marshall still recalls the unnatural stillness of those woods and how the war, which in reality was all around them, seemed for a brief spell far and remote.

By mid-day, A Troop had established an observation line along the Breedeweg, between Utrechtseweg and Van der Molenallee. It was a good defensive position, completely wooded and looking westwards down sloping ground. From there, they kept close liaison with D Troop on their left flank, and both troop commanders set themselves up in a temporary observation post on the top of a nearby water tower. It was not the most comfortable of perches, but it allowed a fairly good field of view, particularly to the west, where there were increasing indications that the enemy was on the move. Much of the results of the morning reconnaissance sorties had already been communicated back to Squadron HQ and thence to Division, and the picture that was emerging was causing growing concern. What it added up to was that the Germans had crossed the River Lek in force at Renkum and were beginning to move towards Oosterbeek, that concentrations of enemy forces were known to be in the woodland of Heelsum, Noordberg and Renkum and that already there were signs of penetration as far as Doorwerth, on the banks of the Neder Rijn. There was also evidence of an enemy presence in the Jonkershoeve area, near Wolfheze, and civilian reports had been collected regarding the movement of tanks from Apeldoorn towards Arnhem.

This whole German movement from the west was a strong threat to the position of Brigadier Hackett's 4th Brigade. After Monday's arrival by second lift, he had set off on his original objective, to reach Arnhem and the high ground to the north and west of the town. Having had 11th Parachute Battalion detached, he had been left with only two main combat regiments, the 10th Parachute Battalion under Lieutenant-Colonel Kenneth Smyth and the 156th Parachute Battalion commanded by Lieutenant-Colonel Sir W. R. de B. des Voeux. From the start, desultory enemy attacks had taken place and at dusk he had ordered his units to rest before pressing on at first light. By then, both parachute battalions were still west of Wolfheze, as were supporting troops. Initially, therefore, Hackett set up his HQ in the Buunderkamp Hotel.

Early on the Tuesday morning, 4th Brigade moved off again with the aim of reaching the high ground of Koepel, about a mile and a half from central Arnhem. Progress was made as far as the north-south line of the Dreijenseweg, where the advance was halted by heavy enemy concentration, established right along the road. This was the point at which the German blocking line linked the railway with the Amsterdamseweg to the north, so that Hackett found himself unexpectedly confronted by the combined armour and infantry of the 9th Panzer Division. As a consequence, neither the 156th Parachute Battalion, just north of the railway, nor the 10th Parachute Battalion, astride the Amsterdamseweg, could make any progress at all. In a position between the two 4th Brigade battalions was the 7th Battalion of the King's Own Scottish Borderers, ready to carry out its second designated task, which was to keep the area of Johannahoeve free for the landing, that afternoon, of the glider party of the 1st Polish Independent Parachute Brigade. In the circumstances, it was logical that, later in the morning, the Borderers should be incor-

* Now Kasteelweg.

porated in Hackett's command.* Meantime, throughout the morning, all three battalions tried in vain to penetrate the German barrier, and all the time the casualties mounted. An additional strategic danger arose from the fact that the three units were separated from the rest of the Division by the railway line and, because of the height of the embankment there were few crossing points. One of those was the Dreijenseweg itself, which ran across 4th Brigade's front by Oosterbeek station. Since this was in enemy hands, it meant that it only needed the Germans to capture the crossing at Wolfheze, just to the rear of Hackett's right flank, for his troops to find themselves cut off. Were that to happen, the Brigade would be caught in a trap, from which only a relatively small number of men might hope to extricate themselves, whilst the vehicles, would probably have to be left behind, as the embankment was too steep to permit them to be manhandled across it. It was this potential danger to 4th Brigade's position that lent significance to the reconnaissance reports that A and D Troops had been sending back from the Doorwerth woods.

Throughout this time, nothing had been heard from the Reconnaissance Squadron's C Troop, and in the course of the morning the loss of contact became a growing source of concern to the acting Squadron commander, David Allsop. In response to the original orders of the day, C Troop had moved out on Utrechtseweg, along with the rest of the Squadron. At Wolfhezerweg it had then forked off to the north-west and had not been heard of since. In the course of the morning, wireless contact between Squadron HQ and the other Troops had remained moderately good, but it was apparent that C Troop had moved out of this very limited and highly critical operating field.

From the time that it had parted company with the rest of the Squadron, C Troop had made a cautious, yet not uneventful, journey up to and beyond Wolfheze junction. Once into the Reijerscamp area, it had carried out a preliminary reconnaissance of the Wolfhezerweg to the north of the station but had again, as on the previous day, been mortared at the junction with Amsterdamseweg. Clearly, the crossroads was still a very unhealthy spot, and the decision was made to withdraw in order to seek out an alternative route. It was an awkward moment when Captain Hay's vehicle got temporarily bogged down, but the exploding mortar bombs lent impetus to the efforts to get the vehicle out in record time! Meantime the other jeeps had dispersed as rapidly as possible, each making for a new designated rendezvous at Wolfheze junction. Some used the cover of the woods; others simply took to the main road and went flat out. David Christie was one of those and recalls what happened: "We raced back the way we had come and were about 200 yards from our own positions when a group of German fighter aircraft swept down the road, machine-gunning everything in sight. We pulled into the trees at the roadside, and most of the men dashed into a nearby house for cover. I got stretched out flat under my jeep and watched the proceedings through the front wheels . . . They were never engaged by fire, even though they were sometimes flying at less than a hundred feet."

Rendezvous at Wolfheze took place without further incident and, having emerged with no casualties, the members of C Troop had reason to regard themselves as fortunate. Thereafter, they set off again on Duitsekampweg, past the spot where the victims of the Sunday night ambush had been buried on the previous day. Carefully avoiding open ground, they skirted the southern edge of the Reijerscamp zone with the intention of turning northwards by Buunderkamp, towards the area just south of Planken Wambuis. Of the enemy's imminent presence they were

* It is usually asserted that the 7th Battalion King's Own Scottish Borderers was "given" to Hackett on the Monday afternoon, as compensation for the loss of his own 11th Parachute Battalion. This assumption is not supported by the evidence.

never in doubt for, like the earlier sortie, the journey through the woods was not without incident. No opposition was encountered on the first mile, but at a farm just south-east of Buunderkamp, a group of three Germans was spotted moving along behind a wall, about 300 yards ahead. Bowles's 9 Section, having made the contact, kept them under observation and radioed back a report to the Troop commander, Captain Hay. The Section was then instructed to take the Germans prisoner for interrogation purposes. "During this time," says Christie, "they were coming towards us, unaware of our presence. I left my Bren gunner covering them and decided to crawl towards the Germans, allowing them to pass us and get between two fires. Everything went perfectly. The Huns passed us, and when they were mid-way between us and the Bren gunner, we stepped into the track behind them and shouted. They immediately stuck up their hands . . ."

There followed a search and a short questioning of the prisoners, in the course of which it emerged that their officer had earlier run off to avoid capture. Just how this came about was not clear, but the three captured men were ordered to keep their hands up and to get themselves back along the road in the direction of Captain Hay's HQ position. They went with alacrity but, as they arrived at Troop HQ, someone let off a Sten burst. Fortunately, to the relief of three petrified Germans, the firer missed the target! Following standard practice, the prisoners were then directed further back towards the British positions and the Troop continued its reconnaissance.

From that point on, the track was thickly wooded on both sides and the task of effective reconnoitring was virtually impossible. As a result, crews had to walk in pairs ahead of each vehicle, with only the driver bringing it on slowly behind. Just over a mile and a quarter was covered in this way, until eventually they encountered the unfinished road works for the new east-west highway. It was there that they got a hint that their progress might not have gone unmarked. The small disquieting episode that occurred is still vividly recalled by Jimmy Cooke: "Palmer and I were leading the Troop, and walking about a hundred yards ahead of the vehicles, when we found we had to go through a kind of culvert. It was when we got underneath that I noticed a fairly big tin, like a petrol can, sitting there with a bag on top. As I passed it, I put my hand on it and, although it was completely in shade, the sack still felt warm to the touch. I realized that someone had been sitting there only seconds before. I also wondered if whoever it was could have us under hidden observation and that I might at that very second be lined up in his sights. It was not a pleasant thought."

Despite the obvious proximity of the enemy, the Reconnaissance men passed through without mishap, investigated some abandoned workmen's huts in the immediate vicinity and finally reached the road. Once there, Lieutenant Pearson climbed a tree, from which vantage point he was able to observe that, as far as he could see, enemy armoured vehicles were moving slowly from the west in the direction of Arnhem. Behind them the woods whispered with the sound of movement and the uneasy thought arose that they had, perhaps, unwittingly walked into a trap. It looked very much as if the enemy was occupying positions to their rear and might be covering any attempted retreat back by the same route. Yet escape by the main road to the west was clearly out, on account of the armour, whilst eastwards towards the crossroads on which they had been heavily mortared earlier, the territory was unknown. In sum, their reconnaissance had been wholly successful, but its outcome looked to be a bleak one, for the Troop was probably surrounded, possibly even under enemy observation and seemed to have few options left if it were to avoid a disastrous end to the morning's work.

Whilst the various Troops of the Reconnaissance Squadron had been probing westwards, and Hackett's 4th Brigade had been meeting with a continuing lack of success in its efforts to breach the German blocking line, the attempt to relieve the Bridge defenders had reached its final stages. As the Tuesday dawn imperceptibly stripped away the cover of the night, the lightening sky soon revealed the perilous position of the remaining relief forces in the western suburbs of Arnhem. Both 1st and 3rd Parachute Battalions had been destroyed down on Onderlangs and, in the aftermath, German tanks, self-propelled guns and half-track armoured vehicles had been positioned down the side streets that intersected with Utrechtseweg. Their task was to fire at and contain the two remaining British units, the 2nd Battalion South Staffordshires and the 11th Parachute Battalion as, together, they mounted the final desperate attacks down the main line of the Utrechtseweg. From the area of the railway marshalling yards that lay to the north, well-emplaced enemy machine-gun crews, positioned in the houses overlooking the road, raked the unprotected troops below. It was the classic enfilade, guaranteed all the more effective by the manner in which the main road was kinked, at that point, into a loop, so that it threaded its way through the narrow opening between the railway and the Gemeente Museum, from the rear of which, the ground ran down in a steep slope to Onderlangs. For the Germans, it was an almost perfect defensive position, and in such circumstances it was all the more remarkable that McCardie's men should have been able to progress at all. Yet, by 0630 hours, despite serious losses sustained in the face of enemy armour and machine-guns, and against repeated attacks from mobile detachments of Panzer grenadiers, the 2nd South Staffordshires had taken the Museum.*

It was there, at about eight o'clock in the morning that the advance was brought to a halt and, for three desperate hours, a fierce static battle raged in the vicinity. Only when the PIAT ammunition had given out were McCardie's men forced into retreat. An agreed plan for Lea's 11th Parachute Battalion to come up in support of the Staffordshires' left flank never got under way for, in the breakthrough of the German armour and infantry, the leading South Staffordshire company was completely overrun and the remainder forced to fall back upon the position held by Lea's men. The resultant confusion made the enemy's job all the easier, and it was only scattered remnants of both units that succeeded in disengaging to a fresh location west of St Elisabeth's Hospital.

By the end of the morning, it was all over. Via the Nachtegaalspad and the Renssenstraat, columns of weary British prisoners-of-war were marched off to the railway station. Many were wounded, and some were helped along by comrades. On the dark red *pavé* of Onderlangs and Utrechtseweg lay the dead of four of the finest regiments in the British army. Strewn across the roads were tangles of overhead tramway wires, incongruously caught up in branches and foliage shot from the trees in the course of the battle. Prematurely disturbed, the leaves of autumn carpeted the road surfaces all around. Broken or discarded weapons and equipment, together with smashed vehicles, littered the scene. At the road fork near the Hospital, a solitary tramcar, which had failed to make it back to the depot on Sunday night, stood with smashed windows and a dead British soldier lying by its front wheels. Around the Museum, many houses were on fire; all were windowless and pock-marked by shrapnel whilst, from some, gaily striped canvas sun-blinds hung pathetically in tatters and disarray. As the lingering sounds of battle died, so did the monstrous German self-propelled guns, their tops festooned with grotesquely improvized camouflage, begin to clank their way purposefully westwards. It was then that the Dutch civilians

* Immortalized in the Regiment's history as "The Monastery".

began to emerge, one by one, from the cellars that had sheltered them from the holocaust. For them, it was time to assess the damage and destruction to their homes, and to attempt to pick up the threads of lives which thereafter would never again be quite the same.

At the Bridge, Monday night through to Tuesday morning was a period in which most of the activity took place on the eastern side. A German infantry attack was successfully repelled at about 0100 hours, but was followed just over an hour later by a much more terrifying onslaught, in which the enemy used a mobile 88 mm Pak 43 that fired a formidable 20 lb bomb. Designed essentially to penetrate the heavy armour of the new Russian tanks on the eastern front, it had a devastating effect when let off at point-blank range against the softer target of the brick and mortar buildings held by the British troops. Captain Mackay, whose engineers were defending the Van Limburg Stirum School, adjacent to the ramp approaches, later described how at the first blast, he was propelled across the room and half-buried under falling brickwork. The effect of the barrage was to blow away completely, part of the roof, together with the whole south-west corner of the school, so that Mackay was virtually reduced to defending two rooms. Casualties were extensive but, in the lull which followed, the lack of return fire from the British-held buildings appears to have been interpreted by the Germans as a sign that opposition had ceased. It was around 0300 hours when Mackay suspected this for, to his amazement, he suddenly discovered that a force of about sixty Germans were standing about quite openly chatting in little groups, not three or four yards away from the side of the building which he was occupying. For Mackay, himself already wounded in several places, it was an opportunity too good to miss. Silently, he disposed his men at all the windows, Brens and Sten guns cocked, and grenades ready with the pins already removed. At a prearranged signal, the British opened up together on the unsuspecting Germans. In Mackay's words, "The night dissolved in sound, the din was hideous, the heavy crash of the Brens mixed with the high-pitched rattle of the Stens, the cries of wounded men punctuated by the sharp explosion of grenades and, swelling above it all, the triumphant war-cry, 'Woho Mahomet'."

For Major Freddie Gough and his men, by then well integrated as part of the fighting force of 1st Parachute Brigade, it was a relatively uneventful night. Although not themselves directly involved, they had heard the firing and battle cries of Mackay's Engineers, but had been unable to find out what it was about. Around dawn came the sounds of the attempted relief from the west, but there was little opportunity for speculation on that for, at about 0700 hours, the first of the morning attacks began, with a variety of fire from mortars, flak guns, machine-guns and snipers. Once more, the brunt was taken by the defenders on the eastern side, but the enemy attack was half-hearted and easily dealt with.

The events of the night, and the signs of continued activity on the north-eastern bridge approaches, led Frost to the decision to send the remainder of 2nd Battalion's A Company over to that side to give support. With them went Trooper "Darkie" Bolton of the Squadron, who, in the actions of the two previous days had already established his reputation as an outstanding handler of the Bren gun. So devoted was he to the weapon for which he was responsible that his refusal to be parted from it became part of the folklore of the 1st British Airborne Division. "He hated the thought of anyone using it but himself," said Bernard Briggs, "and he would wake from a cat-nap at any moment, and leap to it, ready to fire." "Darkie" was a Liverpudlian of West Indian origin, who had already seen action with the Squadron in Italy, and he was held in the highest regard and affection by his comrades. Henry Venes tells a story illustrative of this: "I remember when we were in North Africa, we'd been on an exercise and had to go for a meal to an American base. We were all lined up at the counter when an enormously fat American sergeant cook came out from the back, pointed to "Darkie", and said, 'Over the other side for you boy.' We didn't like that one little bit, and I remember how 'Pedro' Booth and some others got into a right old shindig about it and were all for straightening out the cook on the spot. It was Captain Grubb who said to the Yanks, 'That man eats with us or we go,' but they wouldn't wear it, so we all walked out. They didn't like it when we told them where they could put their food!"

As the action at the Bridge intensified, and it became obvious that no immediate relief could be expected, Frost issued the order that ammunition was to be conserved and used only to repel assaults. This necessary stricture inevitably placed constraints upon British sniping action, so that the Germans were able to improve their positions with relatively lower risk than before. It meant, of course, that it became increasingly difficult for the British to move from one house to another, as the intervening roads were covered by enemy machine-gun fire. Naturally, too, certain situations arose in which the procedure to be followed was open to differing interpretations. Corporal George Dixon of the Reconnaissance Squadron was on observation in the attic of his house and was armed with a Bren gun: "I suddenly spotted a German team setting up a mortar position no more than 600 yards away and to the south-west of our building. There were four of them – sitting targets – in the middle of the road, and I fired. After I'd let off a burst, I remember how a furious parachute battalion officer turned on me and said, 'If you open up again without permission, I'll kill you' – I think he meant it too!"

At approximately the same time as the early morning attacks came in on the east side, German 20 mm and 40 mm guns sited on the south bank of the river started to destroy all the steeples on the church towers in the town. It was assumed that their reason for doing this might be a suspicion that British observation posts had been set up in them. Ironically, the Bridge defenders were profoundly relieved at this enemy action, as they also believed that some of the towers were being used for that same purpose by the Germans. At 0800 hours, the enemy then brought a 20 mm flak gun into position about 400 yards to the north of the Bridge, and within full view of the attic windows of Brigade HQ. With it, they began to attack several of the houses north of the Headquarters. In reply to this, two British Bren gunners and a sniper opened up simultaneously, and the German gun crew of three was dealt with. When a replacement crew ran out to take their places, it was similarly disposed of, following which the gun lay deserted.

Throughout the morning, the battle raged on both sides of the Bridge approaches. During that time a new German tactic was introduced into the fight, when medium tanks of the *Panzerkampfwagen III* class appeared at the eastern side to harrass the defenders. Lieutenant McDermont of the 2nd Battalion and his platoon, occupying the key position of House 10, were shelled at close quarters and had to evacuate the premises, after taking heavy casualties. In support of McDermont, Mackay's men in the school began successfully to pick off the enemy infantry, whereupon the tank fire was turned upon them, and once more shells penetrated the southern face of their building. The uneven struggle on the east side went on for five hours, with German armour and supporting infantry setting one house after another on fire. The attacking tanks seemed to be coming up in relays, and in the late morning were backed by low flying *Focke-Wulf 190*'s, attempting to bomb British-held positions.

In the face of this ferocious onslaught, the British more than held their own, and the airborne men saw to it that the enemy by no means had it all his own way. Retaliatory PIAT attacks were mounted on some of the tanks, and there was a high rate of casualties amongst the infiltrating German infantry. It is recorded that in one instance, the Germans got themselves into such difficulties that they sent out an emissary with a white flag to Captain Mackay, in order to negotiate a surrender. His uncompromizing reply was to tell them that he could take no prisoners and that they were to return to their own positions. His men reinforced the message with cries of "Bugger off!" and "Go back and fight it out, you bastards." With no other alternative, that was what the Germans did and, when they later tried to break out of the trap, all of them were eliminated.

On the west side of the Bridge approaches, attacks by the more advanced Mark IV tanks built up in the early afternoon. In addition, there was an exceptionally dangerous development when, under cover of the tank fire, an enormous 150 mm gun was unlimbered and pointed directly at Brigade HQ from a range of only 200 yards. The attic was instantly evacuated and, almost immediately afterwards, three direct hits smashed away most of the roof, in an ear-splitting crash of high explosive and falling masonry. With time running out for the defenders, frantic attempts were made to try to cope with this fearsome new threat which, in a matter of minutes, was about to reduce Brigade HQ to a pile of dusty, unrecognizable rubble. In desperation, one of the 2nd Battalion's 3-inch mortars was speedily ranged and, by a combination of skill and a little bit of luck, a direct hit was scored. It was later reported, with grim satisfaction, that, "Where the gun had been was a large crater in the road, and it is thought that the ammunition was detonated . . . certainly the gun did not worry us again."

Those engaged in the defence of the west side also found themselves, for a spell, under attack from German artillery, brought to bear from south of the river. As a result, Houses 8 and 9 were so badly hit that the top two stories were demolished, with B Company of the 2nd Battalion suffering heavy casualties. Armoured car attack also came in on the river route against House 9, and this was sporadically bothersome.

Back at Oosterbeek, by early afternoon, Major-General Urquhart had become increasingly worried about the growing danger to 4th Brigade. He was primarily concerned about the threat which was clearly developing from the west for, in the event that enemy movement were to continue, it could conceivably lead to the capture of Wolfheze and the isolation of Hackett's force. Recognizing the need for an immediate consultation with his Brigadier, Urquhart asked Allsop to lay on two Reconnaissance jeeps in order to escort him to Hackett's HQ, which was north of the railway, about a quarter-mile east of Wolfheze and near the place where C Troop of the Squadron had been ambushed on the Sunday evening. Captain Allsop himself took the position of tactical responsibility in the leading jeep and they drove up to the south side of the railway, where they parked under cover, near a Royal Artillery battery. Already it was deemed to be unwise to risk a move to the north side, either by Wolfheze level crossing itself, or by the culvert to the east of the station; because of this, the General climbed over the steep embankment on foot to get to Hackett's HQ. No sooner had he arrived than three ME 109's suddenly swooped down with machine-guns firing, and both senior officers had hurriedly to seek the cover of a nearby ditch. The escorting troops of the Squadron also came under attack for, although they had parked inside the edge of the woods, they were still visible from the air. "I can distinctly remember," says Ray Evans, "lying there on my stomach, with my hands tucked underneath me, so that they didn't show up white, whilst the bullets from these German aircraft were hitting the ground all around." It was a small incident in which, fortunately, no one was hurt, and the Squadron diary even recorded the episode with a suggestion of wry humour on the side: "Messerschmitts overhead. Planes veer from side to side. Ten come down in line ahead – bursts of cannon fire strike road near our positions. Intense barrage of Sten gun fire from RA's endangers Tac HQ more than the planes!"

General Urquhart speedily concluded his discussion with Brigadier Hackett, and they agreed upon a strategy for the possible withdrawal of 4th Brigade to the south of the railway, to be followed by a fresh line of westward advance along the main Utrecht road. The decision to carry out the move, however, was only to be contingent upon the development of further enemy pressure from the west. For the present, it was agreed that Hackett was to continue on the same line, but was to maintain a close watch on developments in the area of Wolfheze junction, the crossing point which he would have to use if the plan were to be put into operation

As his jeeps escorted the Divisional commander back to the Hartenstein, David Allsop was, understandably, much concerned to discover what had happened to the Squadron during his absence. In particular, he was anxious to try to contact his missing C Troop. Once back at base, he received up-to-date "sitreps" from A and D Troop commanders but, since nothing was known of C, he decided to set off again in the approximate direction taken by them earlier in the day. It was then a little after 2 o'clock in the afternoon, and Allsop hoped that by reducing the physical distance between his own and John Hay's HQ, it might be possible to re-establish the essential wireless contact. It was a good idea but, although he went northwards up Bredelaan, almost to the junction of Bilderberglaan, no communication was established and it was deemed to be unwise to go further.

All this time, from their positions in the Doorwerth woods, A and D Troops had become increasingly aware of the build-up of enemy pressure from the west. For all that, the sights and sounds of war were still fairly remote, but any feeling of security which might have been engendered in the uninitiated would have been totally false and misleading. Placed well out in front of the divisional positions, the men of the Reconnaissance Corps were only too well aware of the hidden dangers and unexpected hazards that could so often accompany quiet observation undertaken beyond the enemy's front line. On that Tuesday afternoon, it was a consciousness that was somehow reinforced by the very stillness of the woodland, so that there was a constant expectancy of action, and with it a feeling of perpetual uncertainty about what was likely to happen. One small, interesting incident served in part to relieve the tension, when an elderly Dutchman appeared from one of the nearby houses to ask if something could be done about one of his neighbours, whom he claimed was a notorious collaborator. Prior to the operation, the members of the 1st Airborne Division had been well briefed about this particular aspect to the background of German occupation. They had learned that, whilst the majority of those Dutch people whom they were likely to encounter would be helpful and loyal to the allied cause, there were others who were known to have been only too eager to throw in their lot with the occupying power. It seemed that for one such individual the reckoning was at hand, and Mike Grubb personally led a patrol, in order to investigate. Not surprizingly, the bird had flown the coop, and the net result was very much of an anticlimax, resolving itself into one of friendly contact with a delightful Dutch family – no more than a fleeting interlude that leavened the serious business of war.

At just a little after two in the afternoon, John Stevenson's Section made contact and engaged the enemy. For the Germans who had the misfortune to run into the A Troop men, it was, without doubt, an unlucky break. They belonged to an NCO's cadre of Panzer grenadiers which, as part of the German strategy of bringing in reinforcements from the west, had been despatched from the Hague. Their mode of transport was pedal cycle and, by the early hours of Tuesday afternoon, they had reached the eastern side of Heelsum, only two and a half miles from Oosterbeek itself. The party was of battalion strength, riding two or three abreast. About a quarter of a mile short of the A Troop positions, the Germans suddenly wheeled into the woods to the south of the main Utrecht road. Understandably, they were spaced out, but one group of five stragglers which was well behind the others failed to notice the move made by the main body. As a result, they rode on unsuspectingly, their legs rising and falling rhythmically as they propelled their bikes up the slope of the Utrechtseweg. John Stevenson remembers that they were in conversation with each other, their voices growing in volume as they approached the waiting British soldiers. To the watchers whose fingers had already taken up first pressure on the triggers, they presented the appearance of men who were not really taking the war very seriously. "I suppose looking back on it," recollects Stevenson, "we might perhaps have tried to trap them into surrender – it would certainly have made more sense. The fact is that we didn't, and as soon as they got to within fifty or sixty yards, I gave the order to fire and we let them have it with the Brens. Bicycles and bodies were flung up into the air, and to this day I can still remember how, as the sound of the firing died into silence, we could hear the loud hissing of air from the ruptured cycle tyres."

Alerted by the noise, Graham Wadsworth ran up from his own position further down the Breedeweg, bringing with him Sergeant Ray Hewer and Trooper Ken Hope. All three moved up by the ditch, automatically adopting that peculiar half-crouch that soldiers almost naturally slip into when they imagine themselves to be under fire. As they arrived, their first impression was of a confused jumble of cycles and bodies in the middle of the roadway. Hope recalls vividly how a German NCO was stretched out beneath one of the machines with one of his comrades lying groaning beside him: "The German NCO was dead, shot through the head, and already the face had assumed a waxy, ashen pallor, with the lips retracted from the teeth. The wounded man was groaning and moaning piteously 'Mutter, mutter,' and the belly of his field grey uniform was stitched across with bullet holes." The other Germans had moved into the cover of the foliage at the side of the road and had to be summoned to come out and surrender, or be instantly shot. Hope remembers how they emerged in a very nervous and agitated fashion, with hands raised: "One of the Germans had extended one arm only, and I thought, 'My God, the bastard's giving us a Nazi salute!' Then I realized that he was shot through the shoulder and upper arm." One of the remaining two had also been badly wounded in the leg, and only the fifth man of the group had escaped death or injury. From a nearby house, a tall lean man who spoke impeccable English appeared. He was a Dutch doctor come to treat the wounded and, whilst there was little that he could do for the dying German with the stomach wounds, he made use of morphine ampoules supplied by Ray Hewer in order to ease the man's suffering. That done, he responded immediately when asked about the possibility of interrogating the survivors. "I remember he walked amongst them," says John Stevenson, "and he said, 'He's no good to you, and if you want anything out of this one you'll have to get it quick. This other one here you could probably get something out of,' and so on." As it transpired, only the unwounded prisoner and one of the others were in any fit state to give information, and they were straightaway despatched under escort to Reconnaissance Squadron HQ. Later that day, another German patrol, trundling a heavy machine-gun, was almost caught at the same point. Only the premature opening up by one of the A Troop Bren gunners saved them. In the event, the Germans abandoned their gun in the middle of the road and threw stick grenades to disable it before making their escape.

In the woods to the south, D Troop was also getting increased sightings of the enemy, an ominous indication of the general picture. In the early afternoon, they experienced two fairly sharp dismounted encounters to the south of their Troop HQ and about a half-mile nearer to Heelsum. The first of those, at about 1300 hours, resulted in a quick enemy withdrawal, but an hour later a D Troop patrol suddenly met enemy troops passing on its left flank. Sergeant Bentall also recorded observing German infantry making its way through the woods on either side, and obviously heading for Oosterbeek. "Most of the time," recalls Bob Thomson, who was a member of the same Section, "we couldn't see the Germans at all, but we knew that they were there because we could hear them moving through the woods all around. They made a lot of noise."

With all this activity going on, it seemed almost inevitable that contact would be made, even although it looked as if the enemy was not expecting to encounter British troops so far to the west. As it happened, reconnaissance to the south of the Troop positions brought some near misses when, several times, patrols came close to walking into Germans not discovered until they were only a few yards away. Sergeant Jenkins of 10 Section reported watching helplessly as a group of German soldiers wheeled towards him; only a last-second change of direction by the enemy troops prevented discovery. Several close shaves of that kind took place. The only thing that could be done was to sweat it out and wait until the danger had passed before moving back as cautiously as possible.

At 1500 hours, an FW 190 air attack came in on the heathland to the right of the Squadron's advanced positions, and one of the targets was Galbraith's 2 Section. Jim Taylor remembers that there were about six aircraft in the formation and has a clear memory of the ferocity of the attack: "They *straffed* up and down the field so low that you could actually see the pilots' heads. I remember the dirt put up by the cannon shells made it impossible to see across the field." By all accounts, it was a terrifying experience, and an episode which, years later, Dougie Galbraith was to recollect as one of the two occasions during the battle when he felt very frightened: "I can still remember the vibration of bullets and cannon shells as they hit the ground around me." An hour after the air *straffe,* D Troop was discovered and came under a strong attack at the southern end of Breedeweg. This forced them to retire up Italiaanseweg to a 1st Border Regiment position just south of the main Utrecht road. It was then a little after four o'clock in the afternoon and, at that time, none of them knew that only a short distance to the north, on Amsterdamseweg, their comrades of C Troop were fighting for their lives.

Chapter 8 TUESDAY 19th SEPTEMBER 1944

LATE AFTERNOON AND EVENING

"I could have spat on the Gerries"

The predicament in which C Troop found itself at the end of the morning's reconnaissance was not an enviable one. As a result of their observations, they had been able to gauge the extent of the armoured concentration building up from the west, but it looked as if they would be unable to pass on this intelligence to anyone else, for wireless communication was non-existent and there was every sign that they were in the midst of an indeterminate but obviously large body of enemy troops. This was apparent almost as soon as they had taken up positions of observation by the side of the main Amsterdam road, in time to see a party of Germans, chatting to each other as they crossed over, only 200 yards away. "Everyone kept perfectly still," recalls Christie, "and although the Jerries kept looking in our direction, nothing apparently aroused their suspicions and they passed to our rear. Within five minutes of this, five more Germans took exactly the same course as the previous three."

In the circumstances, two alternative courses of action were open to them. One was to head off back through the woods and attempt to regain Squadron HQ by taking the approximate route by which they had come. Were they to do that, the certainty of attack was obviously high, yet there remained the outside chance that they might still reach their own lines unobserved. The bolder alternative was to seek escape by taking the jeeps in a rapid dash eastwards down the Amsterdamseweg and then south by Wolfhezerweg into the safer territory beyond. Either way, they were virtually certain to meet with unpredictable enemy resistance. The second choice presented also the frightening possibility that they might encounter road blocks or mobile artillery.

A rapid council of war was held amongst the officers and senior NCO's, in which the suicidal potential of the road dash was set against the parallel disadvantages of a relatively slow cross-country drive through woods which, they were beginning to suspect, might well be infested with Germans. It was a short debate. The sudden arrival over Landing Zone "L" of the Polish gliders at four o'clock, settled any further argument for, as the roar of the towing aircraft was heard above the trees, to the astonishment of the C Troop men, there came suddenly the distinctive "Crump-Crump-Crump" of anti-aircraft fire from all over the woods through which they had previously driven. "We must have come right through and passed by several of their positions," says David Christie, "and it left us in no doubt that to go back by the way we had come was now definitely out." Captain John Hay, the Troop commander, also recognized this, nor was he slow to appreciate the tactical advantage that had suddenly presented itself. Not only were the

Germans pre-occupied with their own ground-to-air action, but the very noise of the planes and guns might just effectively help to blanket out the sound of the jeep engines. It was a desperate choice, but the only one that he had, and so his final decision was that they should seize whatever advantage was to be had from the turn of events by immediately taking to the road and running the gauntlet of whatever enemy opposition might lie between there and the relative safety of the area south of Wolfheze.

Swiftly the group prepared itself. Brens were loaded and cocked, Sten magazines checked and the drums of Vickers "K" ammunition placed at the ready. It was decided that the jeeps would pack up tight and, from a starting point just to the east of the Planken Wambuis café, race eastwards for a mile down the Amsterdamseweg and take the right-hand turn into Wolfhezerweg. The intention was then to follow that road all the way back to Oosterbeek. The final order was, "If fired on, don't stop – keep going."

As the crews scrambled aboard, the drivers of all seven vehicles engaged gear. With revving engines and the crackling of tyres on undergrowth, the line of jeeps lurched on to the road and propelled itself with rapidly gathering speed towards whatever unknown dangers lay ahead. For the first half-mile, the way ran through heath land, with only sparse woods bordering the road and to begin with all went well. Further along, the plantations of beech trees thickened to form a continuous stretch of woodland on either side. All around were the muted browns and greens of a Gelderland autumn, the hollows by the road edges already beginning to fill with beech leaves, golden in the late afternoon sun and contrasting with the dark, menacing areas of wood that lay beyond.

In rapid succession the vehicles roared into the tunnel formed by the rows of beeches. Then almost immediately, those behind watched in dismay as the leading jeep of Captain Hay suddenly began to swerve erratically from one side of the road to the other. Clearly, the driver was attempting to take evasive action but in seconds he had lost control, for the vehicle careered off into the woods to finish smashed up hard against the trunk of one of the trees. Sergeant Fred Winder was in the second jeep and witnessed the incident: "We started off down the main road at about fifty miles an hour . . . all seemed quiet and then one of the men spotted about six of our own chaps in the wood to the side of the road. They must have been prisoners-of-war, because five or six seconds later we were under Jerry rifle and machine-gun fire. We kept going. The drivers started swerving from side to side. The buggy in front of ours turned over into the wood . . . we kept going." It was perhaps as well that they did, because it was instantly apparent to the vehicles behind that the Germans had been holding fire until the leading jeeps drew level with the beginning of the ambush position. For those who had already run into it there was no alternative, short of surrendering, but to press on. Such was their speed that most of the following vehicles were committed to do likewise, finding themselves at that same point of no return almost as soon as the occupants were able to comprehend the nature of the enemy opposition.

Most of what then happened was witnessed by the five occupants of the fifth jeep. At the wheel was its commander, Sergeant David Christie, and beside him, with responsibility for the Vickers "K" gun was Lance-Corporal Bert Palmer from Portsmouth. In the back were Troopers Cooke, McSkimmings and McCarthy. At twenty-three, Jimmy Cooke, a gardener from Basingstoke, was the oldest man in the group; he carried a Sten. McSkimmings also had a Sten, whilst McCarthy manned the Bren gun. As his own jeep approached the trouble area, David Christie recalls how the thoughts of home and family that had come into his mind only seconds before were as speedily dismissed by the reality of a bullet zipping past his head. As he was later to remark, with laconic

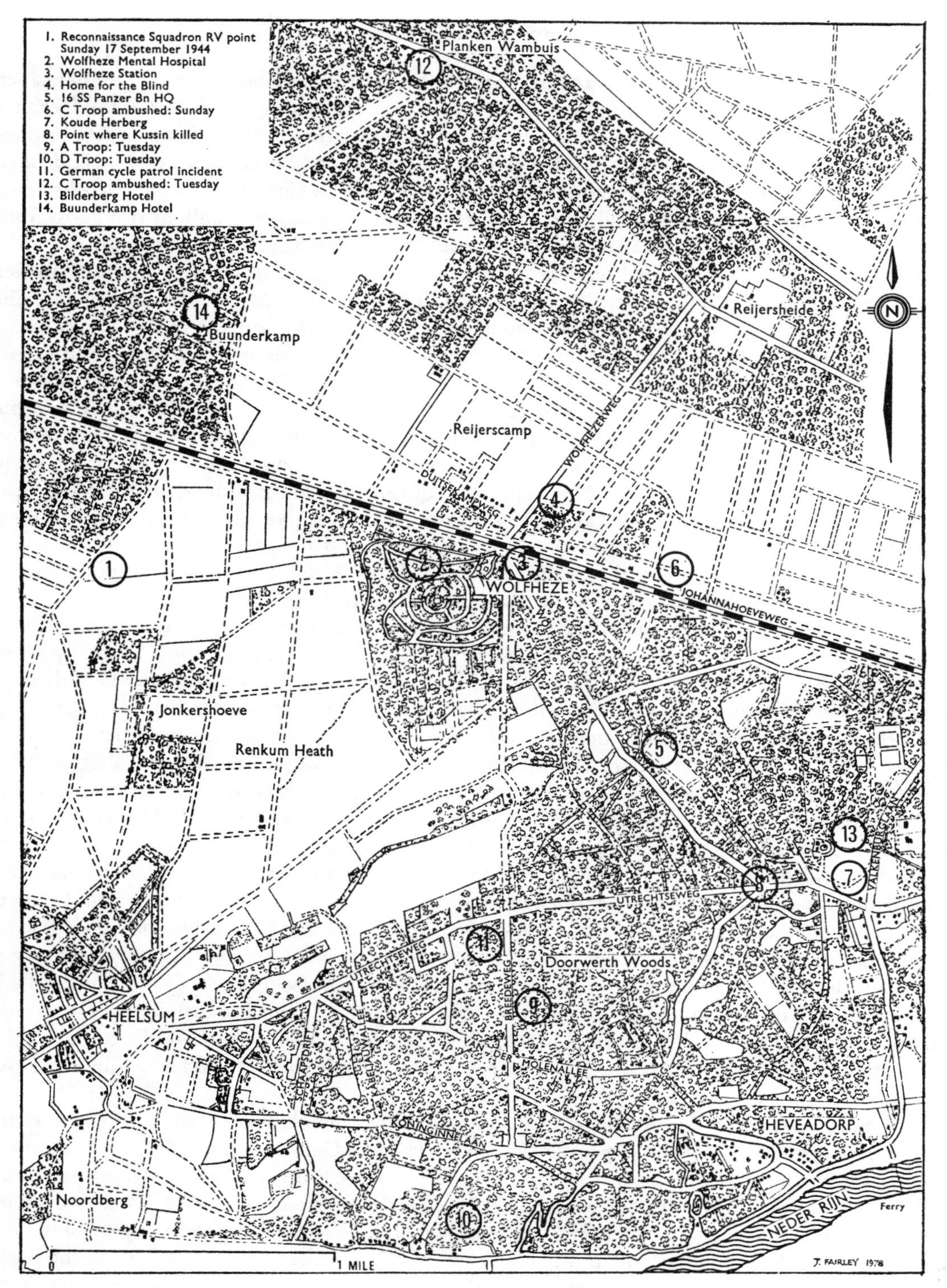

Map 9 Squadron positions in western area: Sunday 17th–Tuesday 19th September 1944

Scottish understatement, "It brought me back to the matter in hand." For a reconnaissance section, that still meant trying to fulfil the primary role of estimating the extent of the German opposition, and Christie recollects that, even as he drove into the conflict, his brain was instinctively recording enemy strength as in the region of two companies. "Hundreds of them, laid three deep on each side of the road," is how Cooke remembers it, whilst Christie adds, "I can remember the ditches at both sides of the road, and they were strung out along them about two yards from the edge, firing at point-blank range. I could have spat on the Gerries, they were so close."

Suddenly, as the convoy sped on, the third vehicle was hit. From his own position further back, Cooke saw what happened: "It was like hell let loose. I saw Mr. Pearson's jeep go right up in the air. It must have been hit by a shell, because it just blew up and bits of it landed all over the place." And accompanying those kaleidoscopic images of destruction, death and injury was the raw sense-assailing sound of the firing. The noise was deafening, as each jeep's complement in turn added its own contribution to the growing crescendo of fire. For Cooke and his comrades it reached a frightening intensity as Christie hurtled the vehicle into the thick of the fight. In the rear, Cooke and McSkimmings sat back to back, indiscriminately emptying their Sten magazines as fast as was possible into the rows of Germans lying in the dappled shadows to each side of the wooded road. McCarthy, too, was firing his Bren whilst, in front, hunched over the "K" gun, Palmer hammered away at a frenetic thousand rounds a minute, with a barely perceptible pause for changing the drums. All around, the acrid pungency of burning cordite tainted and polluted the air, as the fierce engagement mounted to its climax.

By then, the speed of the vehicles had increased to beyond sixty miles per hour, and it was only luck, together with the overall skill of the drivers that was preventing a multiple pile-up from developing. But it was at that point that some of the luck ran out. Crouched down in the driving seat, with his head ducked low behind a ration box strapped to the bonnet, Christie was steering with the left hand only. It was a position which afforded him the illusion rather than the substance of protection, but it particularly suited Palmer, who could then fire the Vickers "K" over his driver's head. Suddenly, to Christie's dismay, he realized that the jeep in front had run into trouble and begun to slow down. There was only one course which he could take. It was a split-second decision but, with the action at its most intense, there was no choice but to pull out and pass. "All the time", he recalls," I could see red, blue and green tracer flashing past my eyes. Palmer had just put on another one hundred round magazine and was firing again. I pulled closer to the left and ran level with the vehicle in front. Thank God the driver had the sense to keep it on a steady course. I was doing seventy now. My nearside wheels ran up the grass verge. I saw a little white milestone affair popping through the grass in front of me. Christ knows how I missed it, but I did. I swung into the centre of the road again, and felt a bullet snick my left elbow. A tree was lying across the road in front of me. I swung to the side where the bushy top of the tree was and never slowed down. It was now or never. Luckily the tree was fairly thin and I got through."

Sam Bowles was the officer in charge of the vehicle which Christie was forced to overtake. With him were three others, Lance-Corporal Alan Baker, Trooper Gerry Fergus and Trooper Freddie Brawn, the wireless operator. Bowles himself was driving, since Edmond, his own driver, had been killed on the Sunday at Wolfheze. He later described what happened: "There was a heavy burst of fire and a hail of bullets raked across us. One must have hit the engine or some vital part, as it died on me. Another hit me in the foot, and I was nicked on the top of my knees as well as on the back of one hand. I turned the jeep into the ditch at the side of the road, we landed with a thump and

I staggered out of the ditch into some rough scrub to take cover. Looking back briefly, I saw one man lying across the rear of the jeep, but there was no sign of any other person. I could see the Germans on the opposite side of the road, so I hobbled and ran as best I could back into a stretch of wood to seek better cover. No one came after me."

From the crew of Bowles's jeep, there was only one other survivor for, whilst Gerry Fergus was lying unconscious in the ditch by the side of the road, Alan Baker and Freddie Brawn were already dead. Fergus's last conscious recollection was of looking back and seeing Southwell, who was at the wheel of the following jeep. This, and the one at the tail of the column made up Lieutenant Ralph Foulkes's 7 Section. Having realized what was in store for them, they had taken avoiding action, and had not entered the ambush at all but, instead, headed into the woods at a point where two rather badly shot-up German ambulances had been ditched in some earlier action. At the time, Foulkes thought little more about the abandoned ambulances but, two days later, he was to have very good reason to remember them.

This evasive move by the two 7 Section vehicles was registered up ahead by Cooke, at just about the time when he realized that Raymond McSkimmings was dead: "I noticed McSkimmings had a hole in his head – a tremendous hole. He was much taller than I was, and the shot had come from my side, passed over my head and caught him." McSkimmings, only nineteen years of age, must have died instantly, for closer inspection revealed that he had received a burst of machine-gun fire, and Cooke reported finding his brains all over the map cases and on McCarthy's Bren.*

Oblivious to all this, David Christie raced on, to emerge out of the green tunnel into open country. To the right, immediately ahead, lay the junction with Wolfhezerweg and the turn to the south. "As far as I can remember," says Christie, "my accelerator foot was still hard on the floor when I swung round it, but we just made it. When I was straightening up after the bend, I heard something crash on to the road. I looked round and found only two men in the back of the jeep. 'Who was that?' I asked, 'McSkimmings, Sarge,' came the reply." There followed a swift shouted exchange between Christie and Cooke, during which time the sergeant was slowing his vehicle to a halt. On Cooke's emphatic assurances that McSkimmings was clearly dead before falling off the vehicle, Christie then depressed the accelerator again and sped off down Wolfhezerweg.

In front of Christie, one other jeep, commanded by Sergeant Fred Winder, had also emerged from the ambush; by a strange fluke, not one of its four men had suffered as much as a scratch. Once clear of the corner, the occupants of both surviving jeeps realized that as suddenly as it had begun, so had the firing stopped. What was left of C Troop had got through and, without further trouble, the seven survivors made all speed back to the Squadron base by the Hartenstein, stopping briefly at the HQ of the 1st Border Regiment. Of the thirty men who had set out on patrol just a few hours before, the majority, including the Troop commander were either dead or prisoners-of-war. Of those in the latter category, there was no saying how many had been wounded. Perhaps the unluckiest man of all was Lieutenant "Jimmy" Pearson from Cambridge. Awarded the Military Cross for the part which he had played in the previous Squadron action at Gioia del Colle, Pearson had been taken prisoner and incarcerated in a POW camp in Germany. From there, he had escaped, to make his way back to England in time for Arnhem. It was a bitter irony that he should have survived only three days of that action before meeting his death in a German ambush. He was twenty-three years of age.

Tom Collier met the two jeeploads of men as they arrived back at base in the late afternoon. As

*Des Evans, recently contacted, was himself seriously wounded and recalls that Jim Salmon was also killed.

he recalls, "They were very, very shaken, and I remember sitting them down with their backs to some iron railings and pumping rum and strong tea into them." At his HQ position by the junction of Bredelaan and Utrechtseweg, David Allsop also heard the grim news, and he realized that there was no alternative but to absorb the handful of survivors into HQ Troop. From that point on, C Troop simply ceased to exist. One very sad sequel to it all was the subsequent death of Stan Tickle. He was in Fred Winder's jeep and physically uninjured, but Stan Collishaw, who was at Squadron HQ when they arrived, still remembers how very badly shocked he was. Shortly afterwards, Tickle strayed off, and appears to have wandered about in the battle area, in a dazed condition, for days. He was later reported as having been killed.

Disastrous as all this was for the Squadron, the acting commander was only too well aware that his own losses merely mirrored what had been happening to others throughout the late afternoon in the fields and woods to the north of Wolfheze. From about 1530 hours onwards, he had watched the ambulances of 133 Parachute Field Ambulance pass by his position, along with small groups of marching men who proved to belong to the 156th Parachute Battalion. David Allsop could not have realized at the time that he was witnessing the agony of the death of 4th Brigade.

The failure of Hackett's thrust on Monday night, and the growing strength of the enemy block along the line of Dreijenseweg had highlighted a number of problems. One of them was that a supply drop was due to be carried out on Tuesday by 38 and 46 Groups of the Royal Air Force in the Lichtenbeek-Vijverberg areas. Unfortunately, because of the hold-up this location, which for command purposes had been designated as Supply Dropping Point (SDP) "V", was still in enemy hands. As a result, a signal had been sent on Monday night, requesting that the SDP be changed to the Valkenburglaan area, near the Koude Herberg café, and units had been notified accordingly. No action had been taken in respect of the proposed Polish glider landing, also due, but in the area of Johannahoeve, since Hackett's axis of advance had already passed beyond there, and the 7th Battalion of the King's Own Scottish Borderers had responsibility for protecting the Polish arrival. General Urquhart's visit to Brigadier Hackett in the early afternoon had, however, been prompted primarily by a concern for the safety of 4th Brigade itself, should the enemy look like securing a hold on Wolfheze junction. Were that to happen, the situation to the north of the railway would immediately change quite drastically for the worse. It was for that reason that Urquhart and Hackett had already agreed upon the contingency plan for possible withdrawal.

As it happened, the need to implement the plan came sooner than expected, for the General had not long left 4th Brigade HQ and recrossed the railway, when reports came to Hackett that enemy troops in growing numbers were engaged against the 1st Border Regiment's positions. This was the start of the sporadic action in which D Troop of the Squadron was also to be involved throughout the afternoon. For Hackett, the threat to his line of retreat had materialized, and he ordered 4th Brigade to immediately disengage, assigning to the 10th Parachute Battalion the particular task of holding open the Wolfheze level crossing for the withdrawal. The tactical difficulties of breaking off in the middle of an action were never so clearly demonstrated as in the events that followed. As 10th Battalion began its move back to Wolfheze crossing over the open ground, it came instantly under savage attack, made all the more deadly by the merciless cross-fire from the woods to the north and east. Through the trees was heard the sound of heavy tracked vehicles moving in for the kill and, time and again, the retreating force had to fight a costly way past well-entrenched enemy positions on the edge of the nearby woodland.

One hour after the disengaging movement had begun, and whilst the action was still at its height, twenty-eight Polish gliders began to land. It was then four o'clock in the afternoon, by which time the British front positions had already moved back, so that the Poles found themselves landing between two opposing forces. Confused by the firing all around them, the newly-arrived Poles engaged the British troops and had their fire returned. Both allied groups suffered casualties, each at the hands of the other. Despite these additional and wholly unwelcome difficulties, however, the retreat continued, but it took the 10th Battalion three hours to cover the two and a quarter miles back to the Wolfheze rail junction. On arrival they found it already partly occupied but, by 1800 hours, the 250 survivors of the Battalion had fought their way over and, by midnight, taken up a position a few hundred yards south-east of the crossing. It had been a horrific experience, and most of the battalion had been lost. In recognition of his outstanding gallantry during the course of the withdrawal, one officer, Captain Lionel Queripel, was later awarded a posthumous Victoria Cross.

The 156th Parachute Battalion suffered a similar fate, and arrived south of the railway with only 270 men; they took up a position east of 10th Battalion. Meantime, the 7th King's Own Scottish Borderers, having covered the Polish landing, sent its transport across by Wolfheze, whilst the personnel of the Battalion sought to escape south by foot over the railway. The move was a moderately successful one, and a number reached the Divisional HQ area at 1930 hours. Like the 156th, they also had about 270 men, and were directed to take up a position around the Hotel Dreyeroord on Graaf van Rechterenweg. By dusk, the Germans were in total control of the area north of the railway, having overrun all previously held British positions.

One final tragedy remained to set the seal on what was later to be termed "Black Tuesday". At 1630 hours, the supply drop came in, not on the revised area, but over the original zone. Clearly, the signal to change to the Valkenburglaan had not been received. Into flak defences of a murderous intensity flew the planes of 38 and 46 Groups, to drop their supplies straight into the hands of the enemy. Desperate attempts were made by the British troops to indicate their own positions. Yellow smoke canisters were ignited. Berets, face veils and yellow celanese triangles were waved and, one after the other, Verey lights climbed into the sky. Some men even poured petrol on the ground, and set it alight in a despairing attempt to attract the attention of the flying crews. Alas, it was to no avail, for almost all the precious cargoes were dropped on the German positions. In terms of human courage, it was all the more tragic that the resupply mission should have been a total failure, for superb feats of gallantry were performed by the soldiers and airmen manning the planes. It was on that particular operation, too, that the second posthumous Victoria Cross of the Battle of Arnhem was won by Flight Lieutenant David Lord, DFC, of 271 Squadron who, in order to let his crew escape, remained at the controls to go down with his burning plane.

The retreat and decimation of 4th Brigade, together with the earlier failure of the attempts to win through to Frost from the area of the Museum, were major setbacks that combined to end any further hope of bringing relief to the beleaguered men at the Bridge. From late afternoon, there was no longer any lingering doubt but that they were very much on their own, and all that remained was the hope that 30 Corps might still come to the rescue in time. At the Bridge itself, it was combined armour and infantry attacks that most troubled the defenders throughout the later part of the day. A major difficulty was the shortage of PIAT bombs, which meant that enemy tanks were increasingly able to fire with impunity and at point-blank range into the houses. In a number of instances, this would lead to the temporary evacuation of a house which, at a cost, would then have to be retaken from occupying German infantry. Prominent throughout such actions of the afternoon was the ebullient Major Digby Tatham-Warter of the 2nd Parachute Battalion who, with an old umbrella in his hand, led his men in spirited bayonet charges against the infiltrating enemy. As a lift to morale, the performance could not have been bettered, and Gough was later to recall how it provided both amusement and inspiration at a time when the former quality was in rather short supply and the latter was needed as never before. Nor was there any absence of comparable flamboyant behaviour amongst the men themselves. Bert Welham still has vivid recollections of how "Darkie" Bolton, on his frequent sorties with the Bren, would invariably give the Germans the "V" sign, just before dropping down into cover.

As the sustained pounding continued on the east and west sides of the Bridge approaches, the enemy increasingly resorted to the use of phosphorus shells in order to burn out the defenders. The toll of destroyed and burning buildings grew and, in the course of the afternoon, German infiltration took place into Houses 13, 14 and 15. For a time, McDermont's platoon managed to recapture House 10, but was later driven out again. Lieutenant Grayburn also tried, unsuccessfully, to rescue House 13. German pressure, obviously much stronger than on the previous day, was kept up for the whole time and, as the afternoon wore on, the battered defenders were forced out of one position after another. Blocks 8 and 10 were set ablaze and 11 was reduced to a heap of rubble. Inevitably, too, as house after house was set on fire, so also were the British forced more and more out into the open and the toll of wounded rose dramatically. Fortunately, the cellars beneath Brigade HQ were large enough to cope with both wounded and prisoners whilst, on the east side, casualties were tended in the capacious basement of the Van Limburg Stirum School. As German penetration developed, however, it became increasingly difficult for anyone to determine whether a particular house was held by British or by German troops. For the men of the 1st Airborne Division, this problem was in part resolved by using 3rd Battalion's battle cry as a means of identification, since the Germans seemed unable either to comprehend the nature of "Woho Mohamet" or to imitate it. An answering cry, delivered in the correct cadences, therefore, was a virtually foolproof way of establishing the authenticity of friendly neighbours!

In the middle of the afternoon, one small cheering incident took place, when a low-flying *Focke-Wulf 190* crashed to destruction on a church steeple, but as the day wore on there was little else of that kind to revive the flagging spirits of the defending troops, all of whom knew only too well that they had reached the stage of holding a position that was visibly shrinking in size by the hour. Early evening brought a new threat with the arrival of Mark VI tanks. Each of these fearsome dun-coloured monsters weighed fifty-four tons and, in the Tunisian campaign of the previous year, their reputation had been well established as the most formidable type of armoured vehicle till then produced in the war. Officially the tanks belonged to the class of *Panzerkampf-wagen VI*, but the British referred to them simply as "Tigers", and against their 100 mm armour and 88 mm guns, the small-arms fire of the airborne men was quite powerless.

The "Tiger" tanks came from the north, nosed their way slowly into sight, and deployed with an ungainly but sinister purpose to both sides of the ramp. Describing how the opening salvo found its mark, Mackay recalls that, from point-blank range, each shot knocked a four-foot hole through eight walls and came out on the other side! On the west too, down the Eusebiusbinnensingel, the great creaking engines of destruction dominated the scene as, repeatedly they smashed both high explosive and armour-piercing shells into Houses 1 to 6. To all of this the British response was a two-fold one, combining temporary withdrawal from whichever building happened to be under

Daily Mail — 4 A.M. EDITION

NO. 15,095 ONE PENNY FOR KING AND EMPIRE TUESDAY, SEPTEMBER 19, 1944

DEMPSEY DRIVES 16 MILES TO LINK WITH SKY-MEN

Fresh Airborne Troops Pour Into Holland All Day

THE British Second Army, sweeping forward more than 16 miles in 24 hours, has burst through the Dutch border defences and linked up with men of the First Airborne Army in the area of Eindhoven, 10 miles inside Holland. Armoured patrols of the Second Army are beyond Eindhoven, but their exact location was unknown early to-day.

Eindhoven itself has been by-passed in the rush forward, but Allied troops are to the north, west, and south. Patrols who have been into the outskirts of the town report that the Germans apparently intend to attempt a stand there.

One battle is already in progress south of Eindhoven against Second Army men advancing on the town after capturing Aalst and Valkenswaard.

As the Second Army swept forward, the Airborne Army was in many places engaged in heavy fighting with the Germans. This fighting is not general, however. In some areas the sky men have met no opposition at all.

PATRIOTS JOIN BATTLE

Dutch patriots are now fighting side by side with the British, American, and Polish troops of the Air Army, who yesterday received reinforcements and supplies by plane from England. The Luftwaffe tried in vain to stop these reinforcements, and lost at least 36 planes in the attempt. Twenty-seven Allied fighters are missing.

Allied H.Q. is still maintaining operational secrecy on the landings, but Berlin and Continental radios reported that fresh forces have been dropped a few miles north of the Hague and at Arnhem, 11 miles north of Nijmegen on the north bank of the Rhine. There is no fresh news of the forces reported by Berlin to have been dropped on Sunday at Tilburg and Nijmegen.

Opposition to the sky-army varies in every area. Some are engaged in fierce battles; some have met light resistance; others have met no opposition.

One war correspondent with the airborne forces reports that in 12 hours the troops to which he was attached captured 13 villages, four important bridges, and three road junctions.

Most of the Germans this force met were inexperienced troops, who abandoned their equipment and fled as the parachutists descended.

Another correspondent said that in his area the Germans were fighting desperately for dozens of bridges spanning the Dutch canals—bridges vital to the progress of General Dempsey's army and whose seizure was one of the objects of the air descent.

BOY SOLDIERS

In this region the Germans, many of them mere boys, are destroying bridges even if it means cutting off their own comrades.

The Airborne Army in Holland has now passed from the command of Lieut.-General Brereton, it was disclosed yesterday.

As soon as it touched ground it came under the command of Field-Marshal Montgomery, whose field commander in Holland is Lieut.-General F. A. M. Browning.

General Browning, who was second-in-command to General Brereton, landed in Holland by glider on Sunday.

As Browning and his men landed, Field-Marshal Montgomery's main forces—General Dempsey's Second Army—were sent forward in their smashing frontal assault against the Dutch border defences.

According to Berlin, 12 divisions are taking part in the onslaught.

The width of the front on which General Dempsey is making his attack is not yet clear, but his main force appears to have driven up the Eindhoven road, with a second force striking from north of Lommel.

WOOD BATTLE

His Eindhoven attack met heavy opposition. The Germans counter-attacked on his flanks, and tried also to halt him at the villages of Borkel and Valkenswaard.

At Valkenswaard the Germans let our first tanks through and then opened a cross-fire on the main force. British infantry debouched and swept into a wood where the Germans were hidden and routed them out in a fierce, close-quarter battle.

At the same time our tanks and rocket-firing Typhoons attacked the enemy armour. The Typhoons attacked in groups of eight every five minutes for the first 35 minutes of the onslaught, and then at intervals of 10 minutes until the opposition had been wiped out.

A Reuter cable describing Dempsey's attack last night said:

"This battle to break the crust of German resistance is going well.

"The crust is a defence belt several miles deep into which the Germans have crammed masses of 88's and heavy ack-ack guns. Be-

BACK PAGE—Col. TWO

Army was 'Sealed' from World

Lt.-Gen. F. A. M. Browning, D.S.O. Commands the assault.

General Browning Lost his Leave

By Daily Mail Reporter

FOR weeks before their jump over the water defences of Holland the Allied airborne forces were "sealed-off" from the world.

They completed their training in special areas under a veil of secrecy. Only Lieut.-General F. A. M. Browning—named last night as their leader in action now—and his Staff officers were allowed in and out.

And "Boy" Browning—he won his nickname for his youthful looks—never had time to go home. None of his force could bid fond farewells to their homes and families.

But every night he telephoned his wife, whom for the first time to-day he surpasses in fame.

When they were married in 1932, Daphne du Maurier had not then written "Rebecca," but she was already a successful novelist, and he was a major in the Grenadier Guards.

As the time of operations approached, their nightly telephone conversations were more and more curtailed—but they went on. Then came silence.

Waiting for News

Last night, at their home near Fowey, Cornwall, Mrs. Browning and their three children—Tessa, aged 11; Flavia, 7; and Christian, 3—were waiting for news again.

"Immediately I heard of the airborne invasion I knew my husband would be in the thick of the fighting—right at the head of his troops," she told me.

"I last saw him in May, when I went near his headquarters so that we could celebrate my birthday together."

General Browning will be 48 in December—he won the D.S.O. and Croix de Guerre in the last war—but he looks like a man in his early 30's. He went into action with his own glider troops on Sunday.

His belief that the future of airborne warfare is limitless was confirmed on Sunday and at SHAEF last night a senior staff officer declared that the First Airborne Army can jump the Siegfried Line or go anywhere else.

Fourteen missions for the airborne forces had been planned since D-Day. For various reasons they were cancelled. Sunday's "show" was originally intended for early in the morning, but fog and rain over Europe delayed operations.

Destination Unknown

None of the men knew even the name of the country they were so suddenly to attack. Not until the last few hours, when they were conveyed secretly to their assembly points, were they sure the Day had arrived.

Browning's task is to "jump" the Dutch waterbelt.

This canal-scarred area, unsuitable for tanks, meant a hard slow advance for the British Second Army. The Airborne Army was therefore sent to break in from the rear, and so disrupt the defences of the strongest gateway to Germany.

Each dropping zone was marked by Pathfinders only 15 minutes before the landing, but they were unnecessary. The weather turned out beautifully sunny in the afternoon. Every paratrooper, apart from a dozen or so, was dropped in his right zone.

More than 4,000 aircraft, carriers, and escorts, took part in the landing. Twenty-four tons of maps were dropped. Losses in men and machines were very light.

The two officers who were mainly responsible for planning the intricate details of this massive operation were Colonel John W. Oberof, 31-years-old U.S. veteran of the North Africa campaign, and, it was stated, Squadron Leader Derek Rene Wallace, 30-years-old D.F.C.

LIBERATION SNOWSTORM

This was Just One Airborne Landing

LIBERATION snowstorm descends on Holland. The Dutch landscape (above) is covered with Allied parachutes, while others can be seen still falling. There were many landings such as this.

Left: After the paratroops came the gliders, seen lying at the end of the skid-tracks they made in landing. The tails of some have already been removed for unloading. A few overshot the field.

Allies Racing to Save Dutch Key Bridges

WITH AIRBORNE FORCES, Holland, Monday.

GERMAN troops fleeing from the Allied airborne invasion of Holland last night had evacuated at least 13 Dutch hamlets and villages in this sector. These inhabited places were freed by units on the southern flank of the first operation by the Airborne Army.

The Germans, most of whom are young, inexperienced, and "bottom-of-the-barrel" troops, fled in disorder when the first parachutes blossomed overhead.

Some important bridges in this part of the country were blown up by the Germans, but at others the element of surprise was so complete that they had no chance to carry out their demolitions.

The Germans are fighting desperately over each of the dozens of bridges vital to the progress of our armoured units in this canal-wrinkled country.

Ours is a race against time to prevent their destruction.

They Held On

On the perimeter of this southern Allied-held area the enemy are still resisting with a concentration of mortars, anti-tank guns, and heavy artillery. They counter-attacked during the night against our paratroops holding one perimeter, pushing our troops back several hundred yards to the banks of a canal.

There the paratroops dug in, held their ground, and preserved the bridges.

The link between the Americans and the British advanced elements was made on the outskirts of an industrial town in which German snipers are still holding out.

From another sector came this report:

Heavy fighting continues. We expected reinforcements a little earlier than they arrived, but they did arrive. They were still coming this afternoon.

When the first gliders and showers of parachutes came in night the men clapped and cheered.—B.U.P.

CLOSE-UP of one of the gliders after the tail had been taken off so that its cargo could be unloaded. Pictures taken by an R.A.F. Reconnaissance Spitfire.

Berlin: 'We Had No Success'

FIRST German eye-witness reports on the airborne landings in Holland were given last night over the German radio by its "ace" front-line reporter, Dr. Karl Holzammer.

"At this very moment as I broadcast the Allied action still goes on," he said.

"It is clear that not a single German fighter pilot or A.A. gunner can yet speak of success. The enemy effort is approaching its climax."

Boulogne is Falling

BOULOGNE'S citadel and the fortress of Mont Lambert last night finally surrendered.

Canadian troops now are mopping-up the main section of the town, battling steadily through the streets, clearing out snipers.

The chief enemy strong-point still holding out is a gun position.

Charles Lynch, Reuter's Special Correspondent with the Canadians, reported last night that the fall of the port is imminent.

The great air assaults, he said, had reduced the elaborate Boulogne defences to a series of strong-points isolated from each other—and the Canadian troops dealt with them one by one.

GLIDER SAVED TOWN

THE pilot of an explosives-packed glider which got out of control as the second airborne force for Holland passed over Aldeburgh, Suffolk, yesterday, made an all-out effort not to crash on land when forced to cut adrift.

People saw the glider swoop over the town at house-top level and crash into the sea a few hundred yards from shore.

An R.A.F. Walrus flying-boat and the local lifeboatmen had a race to the rescue.

The Walrus won—by 55 seconds. It picked up four American glider men who were clinging to the wreckage.

The lifeboatmen rescued the fifth member of the crew, who had taken to a dinghy.

Observers on the east coast reported that there was unprecedented air activity over the coast from dawn until night.

16,000 IN CAR PAY STRIKE

Dispute on 'Peace Basis' Rates

By Daily Mail Reporter

TWO thousand workers at the Austin Motor Company's plant at Longbridge, Birmingham, who have been transferred to the production of 10-h.p. cars, are on strike over a wages dispute.

The men have been offered the peace-time wage rates for their jobs, plus a 50 per cent., and in some cases 75 per cent., increase.

This they have refused. The dispute is thus the first centring on a return to a peace-time basis for wage rates.

The strike has spread to other parts of the works, and last night between 16,000 and 17,000 employees were involved. It is a "stay-in" strike. The men are coming on duty, but do no work.

Mr. L. P. Lord, managing director of the company, told me last night: "Any suggestion that these 10-h.p. cars which are going into production are for public use is untrue.

"We are starting to make a small number, all of them ordered by Service Departments—the Ministries of Supply and War Transport.

"A suggestion that the company is making engines for private cars is also untrue.

"The men on the new job have been offered prices, in the fixing of which we have not departed from our normal practice. We have used the same method all through the war.

"The strike is unofficial. The unions have instructed the men to go back to work. When they do so the ordinary machinery for the settlement of disputes will operate."

The stoppage is stated by shop stewards to be spontaneous throughout the whole factory.

The convener of the shop stewards said that if there is an essential job to be done in the factory the men are quite prepared to go back to work.

In engineering circles in the Midlands the situation is regarded as of far-reaching importance, because it opens up the question of what shall form a fair basis for reverting to peace-time payment of labour.

U.S. PLANES HIT LUZON

Pearl Harbour, Tuesday.—Southern Luzon has been bombed during a sortie against the Philippines by a carrier task force, it was officially announced to-day. This was the first announcement that the attack has spread to Luzon, main and northernmost island in the Philippines.—A.P.

BERLIN EXPECTS SEA INVASION

Berlin radio said early to-day that Allied landings on Dutch coast are expected "at any moment."

Cologne in Chaos as Guns Draw Nearer

From CHALLINOR JAMES, Daily Mail Special Correspondent

GENEVA, Monday.

EVERY report from inside Germany reaching the Swiss border agrees that in the Rhineland round Cologne, and east of the river, the situation is tense, with transport reduced to utter chaos.

The boom of Allied guns can be plainly heard in Cologne.

Despite the congestion of roads and railways and chaotic communications caused by Allied bombing, thousands of people are trying to leave the city.

Revolts are reported among prisoners working in the Saar coal mines, and numbers of them have escaped to the Allied lines, pillaging German villages on the way.

The Nazi leaders are now trying to place the responsibility for Germany's defeat on German women. One orator declared: "If we lose the war it is the fault of the women for not being more prolific, so depriving the Fatherland of soldiers."

A Daily Mail correspondent from inside France cables:

The evacuation of the Siegfried Line now appears to be confirmed as a probability. German sources are taking measures for the withdrawal of all German units east of the Rhine.

It is thought that only rearguards will be left in the major sectors of the Siegfried Line, and that a withdrawal to Cologne and Coblenz will be organised.

Many German military critics declare roundly that the fate of Germany lies in the air, and that unless she can recover air equality she is bound to be defeated.

Germany has at long last stated officially who is the C.-in-C. in the West—Field-Marshal Model, who only two days ago was reported to have again been replaced by Field-Marshal von Rundstedt.

Broadcasting to the German forces in the West last night, the official German "Soldiers' Service" radio, Stuttgart, described Model as "incorporating the will to hold fast."

Finns Sign Peace Swedes Report

STOCKHOLM, Tuesday, morning.—Peace between Finland and Russia was signed last night in Moscow, says the Dagens Nyheter.—A.P.

EDEN IS BACK FROM QUEBEC

Report to Cabinet

Mr. Eden, Foreign Secretary, who flew to the Quebec Conference, returned to Britain by air yesterday.

Reaching London in the afternoon, he worked for some hours at the Foreign Office. Later he attended a meeting of the War Cabinet, where he gave his colleagues a report on the Quebec proceedings.

'Glass' Falling in Strait

Sea.—Practically calm.

Weather.—Overcast, with low, misty cloud after dull day and morning drizzle. Maximum temperature 66deg.; 56 deg. at 10.30 p.m. Visibility fairly good. Wind N.E., light.

Barometer.—Falling slowly.

Meantime, back at the Longbridge car works . . .

A Troop, 1st Airborne Reconnaissance Squadron, Ruskington 1944
Back row: Tpr. Spicer, L/Cpl. Gassett, Cpl. Taylor MM, L/Cpl. Southwell, Tprs. Ogden, Sylvester, Auld. *Second back row:* Tprs. Weaver, Cooper, Roberts, Brett, Bell, Pow, Fraser, Taylor, Bruce, Blackman. *Second front row:* Tprs. Houghton, Webb, ——, Langan, Palmer, Sutherby, Hazell, Dickson, Mann, Park, Willeter. *Front row:* Sgt. Hewer, Cpl. Rembridge, Sgt. Venes, Lt. Guthrie, Capt. Grubb, Lt. Galbraith, Lt. Stevenson, Sgt. Williams, L/Cpl. King [Missing: Sgt. Riches]

Burnt-out Reconnaissance jeep after Planken Wambuis ambush: Amsterdamseweg

attack, with heroic attempts, against all the odds, to take on the enemy armour, in order to inflict some kind of damage, however slight. For this purpose, PIAT and 6-pounder anti-tank guns were manhandled into position, under enemy fire, but the most astonishing feats of courage were those carried out by individual soldiers on foot and who, armed only with "gammon" bombs, formed themselves into tank-hunting parties. These bombs were ingenious devices of plastic explosive, contained within stockinet bags, which detonated on impact. In using them the aim was usually to go for the most vulnerable parts of the German tanks, either the tracks or the turret mechanism, but it was a suicidal occupation and the decision of the airborne men to take on the armoured might of the Hohenstaufen Division in this way was bravery of the highest order.

The ultimate effect of this courageous retaliation was that, whilst none of the huge tanks was knocked out, as a result of the combined British efforts, the "Tigers" eventually withdrew, at some time around 2200 hours, from the immediate area of the conflict. The sustained and terrifying attack had been very serious, with heavy casualties on the British side. Amongst many others, Chaplain Egan and Major Tatham-Warter had both been wounded and, as a result, Major Gough had to take over temporary command of the 2nd Parachute Battalion. Meantime, Houses 14 and 16 had also been set alight, and the enemy, by then in occupation of all buildings to the north and west of the Brigade HQ positions, was then able to keep the western side of the British defences under constant automatic fire. Nor were the British able to reply to this as effectively as they would have wished, because stocks of ammunition were noticeably and rapidly dwindling.

By the end of the day, it had become clear that the earlier defeats of the relief forces had set the seal on the virtual isolation of the men at the Bridge. The subsequent German encroachment and the general tightening of the ring around the constricted defence perimeter was also a logical outcome of the increasingly vulnerable British position. Nevertheless, despite the sealing up of the defenders, it still remained possible for an individual to get in and out, as was demonstrated by one of the members of the Reconnaissance Squadron. On that Tuesday evening, Trooper Arthur White, a despatch rider with HQ Troop, was asked to try to take a message through to Frost. This he succeeded in doing, by leaving the Hartenstein and detouring around northern Oosterbeek, before coming down to the Bridge through the northern suburbs of Arnhem itself. It was a courageous and audacious journey, and all the more remarkable for being successful. Nevertheless, for "Chalky" White, the delivery of the message to 1st Brigade HQ was only half of the job, for there still remained the return journey to be undertaken, and that was to depend as much upon good luck as on his own courage and skill as a despatch rider.

White remained at the Bridge for no longer than was necessary, but it was enough for him to get the impression of what he later described as a "chaotic" situation, with defenders heavily engaged and several houses burning. Right at the outset of the return journey, "Chalky's" mission was almost prematurely ended when he came close to running into a mobile German patrol. There were three of them in a Volkswagen vehicle, with an MG 34 on a front mounting, and he had to take swift evasive action by riding up a narrow alleyway that ran between adjacent buildings. There he waited briefly until the way was clear, before opening the throttle and heading west. This time, he took the more direct route by Onderlangs and near the road fork, at the junction with Utrechtseweg, he was fired at. Unscathed, he rode on but, shortly afterwards, felt his leg wet, and discovered that the German fire had punctured the petrol tank in two places. The lower part of the bike was covered in petrol and, as he ditched it, the petrol ignited and the whole thing went up in a sheet of flame. Immediately, he ran off, making for the shelter of neighbouring gardens and expecting at any moment to be shot down by an unseen German. Nothing happened and so, realizing that his move appeared to have gone undetected, he began to make progress cautiously on foot, in the direction of Divisional HQ. It was a journey which, in ordinary circumstances, would have taken not more than twenty minutes. Having to undertake it through back gardens and past German detachments meant that it took a great deal longer. At one stage, he found himself near a garden in which a German tank or SP gun was parked, with the crew, clearly visible, standing around the vehicle. Similar sightings of German groups were made all along the way but, eventually, after a great deal of stealth, he arrived back safely at the Hartenstein and delivered the reply to the original message.

That evening, both A and D Troops rendezvoused once more at Squadron HQ, to receive orders for the remaining tasks of the day. To D was assigned the job of watching the area along the south of the railway from the north end of Lebretweg eastwards to Schelmseweg. The job was primarily a reconnaissance one, but not entirely so for, although the main function was that of reporting on enemy movement, there was also concern that the Germans might try to penetrate the north-eastern suburbs of Oosterbeek. For that reason, the possibility existed that the Troop might also have to defend the area of observation, which was why a six-pounder gun was provided by way of support. To the relief of the watchers, no serious attempts were made to breach the meagre British defences, but a number of enemy probes were undertaken and, at about seven o'clock in the evening, D Troop was able to inflict some losses on the Germans in a skirmish down by Schelmseweg. Troop HQ was then established in the houses on Hilhorstweg, and standing watch was maintained for some hours. During that time, foot patrols were sent out to try to locate enemy positions, and these were found to be very close, as John Marshall recalls: "I remember, I walked through the woods on my own, near to the railway line. I rather think I might have put on gym shoes, because I was walking very quietly, when suddenly I found myself almost completely surrounded by a crowd of Jerries who were all just standing about, looking towards our positions. I stood quite still, and then did a very swift 'tippie-toes' right back to join my own chaps." Even the evening stroll of the reconnoitrer was rarely dull!

Grubb's A Troop, meantime, had been given a similar task of watching the railway to the east of Wolfheze, and its Troop HQ was set up for a time at the north end of Oranjeweg. There, the members of the Troop saw the tail end of the 4th Brigade withdrawal, a situation described by Captain Mike Grubb as one of "considerable chaos." At that stage in the day's events Jim Taylor recollects that they arrived at the restaurant just south of Wolfheze station, in time to see the 10th Battalion still fighting its rearguard action. Ken Hope, who was also there, has recorded his own recollection of the scene: "Wolfheze railway station and village was a shambles. It had been pulverized to a fire-blackened heap of rubble and twisted metal. I was standing in a shallow, sandy trench, my back to the railway crossing, with a Bren trained along the *pavé* road which bisected the woodland. A few yards away, was toppled the ruined hulk of a Panzer half-track and multi-rocket mortar. The situation was disturbing and rather unnerving. A violent battle was in progress, and yet I could not see a single German soldier. The noise was frightful, a constant hammering of machine-guns, an incessant crashing of high explosive. Even more sinister, was the persistent snapping, cracking and whispering of bullets through the woodland foliage. A platoon of 10th Parachute Battalion passed through our line of vehicles in single file. One section was led by a Scots corporal, whom I remembered as a Lance-Sergeant in the 63rd Reconnaissance Regiment. Instant recognition was mutual, and we embarked upon a brief, inconsequential chat of the 'fancy-meeting-you-here' variety. We both pretended to be oblivious to the violent sounds surging around us. It seemed a quite ludicrous situation."

It was during that period of watching and waiting by Wolfheze that the members of the Squadron had no less than two further demonstrations of the unpredictability of the Sten gun. First of all, Lieutenant Wadsworth's gun accidentally discharged, and pierced the radiator of the following jeep. No one was hurt, and a remarkably fast radiator replacement job was carried out later by the fitter Sergeant. The other incident took place not long afterwards, during an 'O' group convened by Captain Grubb, when Sergeant Henry Venes wheeled round abruptly and, in the process, struck the butt of his Sten. With the safety catch off, it was enough to activate the mechanism, the gun fired and the tyre of a nearby jeep slowly deflated in a steady hiss of sound. "Why don't we bloody well clear out of here?" cried a frustrated Venes, clearly annoyed at himself for what had happened. He was too far away to hear 'Gunner' Webb, to the very obvious enjoyment of the others, give a passable imitation of his sergeant's voice as he murmured, "How do we do that, Henry? You've just shot our f - - - - - - jeep!" Henry Venes, however, did not have long to wait, because shortly afterwards the order was given to return to Squadron HQ. Before it could be carried out, three casualties were suffered as the result of a mortar bomb.

Inevitably, during their swift dash back from the area of Wolfheze station the A Troop men were able to help some of those who had been involved in the earlier withdrawal, and Louis Hagen was one of a small number of glider pilots who were picked up. In his own account of the battle* he recollects the incident: "They (A Troop) were glad to take us as they had had some casualties and their numbers needed making up. We raced through the woods at sixty miles an hour, sitting sideways on the jeep, and covering the woods on either side with our guns. We were lucky, and got right through to the 'Recce' HQ, without meeting any of the enemy. It was getting dark, and they were already dug in for the night, so all we had to do was get some tins of food and blankets. Of course, we had nothing at all, having had to leave our rucksacks behind, but the 'Recce' blokes gave us plenty of everything and we did not have to take turns on guard. I got myself a Sten gun, plenty of filled mags and had a whole night's sleep in my slit trench."

By contrast, those members of C Troop who were on the run following the ambush, were in a much more perilous situation. Cut off from the rest of the Division by surrounding enemy troops many of whom were literally within earshot, their chances of successfully making their way back from the woods of northern Reijerscamp were obviously slim. But most felt that the chance was worth taking, and one of them was Lieutenant Sam Bowles who, despite his wounded foot, managed to work his way undetected through the woodland to the crossroads of Amsterdamseweg and Wolfhezerweg. From there he made a painful progress to the south, and eventually dragged himself into the three-storeyed home for the blind that stood just north of the railway station on the east side of the Wolfhezerweg. "There," as he recalls, "one of the nurses took me into the underground shelter where I was given some porridge which, I seem to remember, was the first thing of any substance, apart from apples, that I'd had to eat, since landing on the Sunday," It was perhaps as well that Bowles was delayed in his arrival at the home for, had he reached it any earlier, he would have found himself in the middle of the battle, as 10th Battalion retreated through Wolfheze.

Ralph Foulkes and his two jeeps, which had been last in line, had escaped the ambush by running into the woods. Now, his group was joined by a small party of paratroops from 4th Brigade. These were the men who had stood at the side of the road and shouted to the convoy

* Louis Hagen: *Arnhem Lift*, p. 25.

just before the ambush had taken place. Fred Winder had mistakenly assumed that they were prisoners-of-war, but they were stragglers, detached from their units, and their purpose in shouting had been to warn the Reconnaissance men of the presence of German troops further up the road. With something like a dozen in the party, there was much less prospect of being able to achieve anything like the progress that an individual might make. Nevertheless, Foulkes and his men did succeed in taking themselves and their two vehicles down to the railway at the southern side of Buunderkamp, and a mile and a half west of Wolfheze. By then, of course, the Germans were well established in the area, and every attempt which the small British group made to cross to the other side of the railway was frustrated by fire from German positions to the south of it. The party returned the enemy fire, and Lance-Corporal Eddie Morris courageously attempted to get one of the vehicles moved out of the firing line. Although he was wounded in the process, he managed, with Speller and Southwell, to get the jeep out. Unfortunately, in the general confusion, those three became separated from the rest of the party. Meantime, the exchange of fire continued across the railway line. Foulkes remembers the episode for a number of reasons: "While standing in the middle of the road, I started to have a private battle with a Jerry who kept popping up over the embankment. I found the Sten which I was using not very accurate, and it was most infuriating to see his damned head keep popping up, while my bullets sent up little clouds of dust on the concrete near him. Suddenly I experienced a strange, warm feeling in the stomach. I found out afterwards that a bullet had hit the tummy-plate of my bullet-proof vest, glanced off into my smock pocket and finished up inside my tobacco tin."

With no prospect of getting across, the group turned back into the woods. Having successfully negotiated the enemy-occupied area that lay to the south of the ambush point on Amsterdamseweg, only to be frustrated at the last stage, was a demoralizing experience. The whole point of adopting the course which, in the first place, had led the Troop into the ambush situation had been to avoid an alternative which looked like offering only death or capture. Now, having eluded both and achieved what must have seemed virtually impossible, Foulkes and his group found themselves balked at the very point when successful withdrawal appeared almost to have been accomplished. By then, it was getting dark and they could clearly hear the Germans beating the woods to find them. This went on for some time, and it was hardly surprizing that, in such a situation, the imagination should have played tricks upon nerves already stretched to the limit. In recalling this, Ralph Foulkes remembers how, in the middle of the night, he took a pot shot with his revolver at what he imagined was a figure creeping up on them. Fortunately, there was no response from the enemy and the remainder of the night passed uneventfully.

Not all the C Troop survivors were able to take part in the attempts to find a way back through enemy-held territory. One of those was Gerry Fergus, who had been in Sam Bowles's jeep and who, following the ambush, had lain unconscious for hours in the roadside ditch. "When I came to," he recalls, "it was pitch black, and I thought I could hear Baker shouting. Somebody was shouting, 'Don't – don't,' but I have no idea who it was. Then I drifted off into unconsciousness again, and what brought me round was a German soldier turning me over and taking my pistol from me. He obviously thought I was dead, because he went away. After a while I dragged myself across the road and into the woods on the other side. As I did so, I could hear the Germans singing nearby, and I wanted very badly to get away, but I was still so concussed that I couldn't stand up."

Back at the Divisional area, D Troop was the last of the Reconnaissance Squadron to be pulled back into harbour. It was then around midnight and, at the Squadron HQ position across from the Hartenstein, they found the rest of their comrades already dug in. Amongst them were the survivors of C Troop, by then, to some extent, recovered from their ordeal; indeed, Christie and Winder, who had collaborated in the digging of a slit trench, were already asleep in it. Tom Collier's brandy had had the desired effect. As the night sounds diminished and the firing died down, it was with a sense of foreboding that the late-comers quickly dug themselves in for the night. It had been a difficult and harrowing day, with little prospect of those to follow being any better.

Throughout the bitter struggle that made Tuesday 19th September so momentous, one thing above all else had sustained the defenders of the Bridge. In terms of the original plan, Montgomery had seen 1st Airborne Division's role as no more than a two-day holding operation. This fact was generally known throughout the 1st Airborne Division, so that Tuesday afternoon was the anticipated time for the arrival of the tanks of 30 Corps. Rumour was already rife, and the noise of the German tanks heard earlier that day was at first assumed, with misplaced optimism, to herald the arrival of the Guards Armoured Division! Understandably, therefore, it was a time of great excitement when, in the course of the morning, one of the wireless operators picked up Canadian voices on the air – the first contact with the main relieving force. Initial attempts to establish R/T* communication were unsuccessful but, at about 1000 hours, two-way contact was made. From his position in the building to the rear of Brigade HQ, George Dixon was one of those who succeeded in achieving this, and he recollects holding a short conversation with the wireless operator on the 30 Corps net: "I netted-in to their frequency without any difficulty, and they were coming through at Strength 3 or 4,† incredibly good. It was certainly easier than getting through to the rest of our own Division who, as I now realize, were just down the road." Unfortunately, Dixon's contact was only for a matter of seconds, and he remembers that, just as he turned to hand his microphone over to Major Gough, a fresh German attack came in, so that the transmission had to be broken off. "I never contacted them again," he says, but he recalls that there were others who succeeded in establishing and maintaining the tenuous link, despite the trying circumstances under which they had to work. One of those difficulties was, in particular, the periodic need to relocate the 22 sets and the two heavy "dags"‡ that constituted the power supply to each. The destruction of the upper part of Brigade HQ by the 150 mm gun had led to the shifting of the HQ sets to the square behind the building and, later in the afternoon, to the attic of an adjacent house. In the circumstances it was hardly surprizing that, under such conditions, the men developed an increasing irritation at the assurances which came through occasionally on the rear link, to the effect that Horrocks's force would be with them "soon".

Nevertheless, on such indeterminate intelligence further rumour fed, even faster than before, and expectation, falsely bolstered by a continuing faith in the anticipated arrival of 30 Corps, led men, like desert viewers of a mirage, to interpret the slightest movement on the southern bank as the long-awaited relief. They could only wait and watch and hope, not knowing that the vague promises of early rescue were belied by the realities of a situation in which the 82nd United States Airborne Division had still to capture the main Nijmegen bridge. It did not help that, from 1700 hours on, no further successful wireless communication was made between the

* R/T = Radio Telephony, i.e. communication by speech as distinct from Morse.

† The standard mode of reporting signal strength received was by reference to a five-point scale. Strength 5 was a good satisfactory signal, detectable and understood without any trouble; Strength 1 was a very weak signal comprehensible only with difficulty.

‡ Signaller slang for batteries.

Bridge and 30 Corps. Carrier pigeons were, therefore, despatched to take the detailed "sitreps" that could not be relayed by the sophisticated, yet ineffective wireless equipment.

And so it was that afternoon blended into evening and still no one came. As frustration mounted, megaphones were made from wallpaper and used to try to contact the rest of the Division, who were thought to be within possible hailing distance. "Where are you, you lazy bastards?" and similar, not entirely unfriendly injunctions brought nothing in reply, for the men at the Bridge were not to know that, by then, the last supremely courageous efforts of their comrades to assist them had already passed into history. To their repeated cries of "Woho Mohamet" there was no answering response from the west – nothing at all. Only the sizzling of light rain on burning buildings was heard, as merciful night fell on the scene of desolation and conflagration, recollected later so dramatically by John Frost: "Two great churches were flaming fiercely and for a little while the shadow of the cross which hung between two lovely towers was silhouetted against the clouds of smoke rising far into the sky. It was like daylight in the streets – a curious metallic daylight. The crackle of burning wood and strange echoes of burning buildings seemed unearthly."

Chapter 9 WEDNESDAY 20th SEPTEMBER 1944

"It's the man who goes in for funny weapons"

With the Hohenstaufen armour spread out along the line of the railway and up Dreijenseweg, it was logical to assume that the British could expect further pressure from the north. Having forced 4th Parachute Brigade to quit the area of Johannahoeve, it was unlikely that Bittrich would be content to stay behind the blocking line, but would rather wish to force home the advantage by some kind of move southwards. Reasoning from this, it was anticipated that enemy probes would probably begin at first light on Wednesday, in order to test the efficiency of British defences at the two vulnerable points of Wolfheze and Oosterbeek railway crossings. To some extent this had already begun for, on Tuesday night, some German armour had pursued the retreating 4th Brigade over Wolfheze crossing and had attacked in the woods to the south of the railway.

In view of the danger, the Reconnaissance Squadron was ordered to undertake observation near Oosterbeek station at 0630 hours. They were also asked to try to make contact with the 7th Battalion of the King's Own Scottish Borderers who were somewhere in the area between there and the positions of the 21st Independent Parachute Company a little to the west in the Ommershof estate. In response to these orders, the Squadron went up through northern Oosterbeek by jeep, and drew the vehicles into the side of the road on Mariaweg and nearby Cronjéweg. Some even sought the shelter of alleyways between the houses, reversing their vehicles so that only the snouts of the Vickers "K" guns protruded from cover. There then followed dismounted action, in which D Troop moved across to investigate some distance into the Dennenkamp woods, whilst A Troop sent out foot patrols to the north of Cronjéweg, as well as to houses on the west side of Stationsweg.

The area was highly residential, and the houses, especially in Stationsweg, were large and individually styled, each for the most part displaying the craft-based architectural fashions popular at the turn of the century. Iron balconies, coloured brick insets and elaborate wood-carved fascias abounded, and many had also been given additional ornate glass extensions, either at the side or to the front. Some had names carved permanently into the stonework. At the junction of Cronjéweg was "De Viersprong" – literally "the crossroads" – whilst further down, "Huize Liné" was a reference to the name of an original occupant. Yet another was "Slamat Tinggal", an expression of friendly greeting from the Dutch East Indies and an appropriate reminder of Oosterbeek's strong colonial connection.

Stationsweg, which was the southern extension of Dreijenseweg and linked the railway station with Oosterbeek crossroads, was the most important road to be covered, but one of the drawbacks to taking up position was that, although it sloped down towards the station and thus provided a good field of view, there was very little shelter available in the front gardens of the houses. One or two did have a profusion of trees and shrubs but, for the most part, cover was sparse. On the other hand, across the road, the thickly wooded estate of Dennenkamp was obviously better suited to observation. This was the area through which D Troop had moved on arrival, in order to take up a more easterly position. A Troop commander, therefore, ordered his number 3 Section over there as well, so that the main road could be covered from both sides. Ken Hope was one of those involved and remembers the details of what followed: "A fairly large foot patrol was assembled, and we were joined by two or three glider pilots. We were heavily armed with Brens, Stens and grenades. Someone handled a PIAT. At a command from Lieutenant Wadsworth, we bustled, hunchbacked, across the street, slipped over the railings and entered the wood. Our patrol fanned out in a wide arc. A small group would then scurry forward and fall prone into covering positions, whilst the remainder made ground. In this fashion, we penetrated some distance into the woodland."

Louis Hagen, one of the glider pilots who accompanied Wadsworth's party, recollected later* how they were rapidly made aware of the presence of the Germans in the wood by the shouting that went on. Numerous others who have reminisced on Arnhem have also commented on this. Whether it was simply "whistling in the dark", or a manifestation of some peculiarly German characteristic is difficult to say, but it did certainly happen repeatedly. "Of all my impressions of the battle," says John Stevenson, "the one that has been most lasting has been the shouting of the German NCO's. Whenever you heard this loud parade-ground shouting and the answering 'Jawohls', you knew that there was an assault of some kind about to be mounted."

For the watchers on Stationsweg, this was to be no exception, and, indeed, it was Stevenson's own Section which first sighted the enemy. To it had been assigned the task of making contact with the 7th Battalion King's Own Scottish Borderers but, as John Stevenson recalls, "We hadn't in fact gone very far, when, coming over the crest of a hill, we saw a 'Jerry' SP gun† smack in the middle of the road, sited to fire down it." At that point, Stevenson's group turned left into Graaf van Rechterenweg, and although the German gun was still to the north of the railway on Dreijenseweg, it was clearly moving towards Stationsweg and the area covered by the Reconnaissance Squadron. First contact came shortly afterwards, and it was soon apparent that the pattern of attack was to be a combined onslaught by the self-propelled gun and supporting infantry moving through the adjacent woodland.

Slowly the gun advanced southwards from the railway crossing and started to creak up the incline of Stationsweg. In an instant, the grating of the sprockets was blanketed out as it blasted off a first shot. Soon it was systematically smashing shell after shell into the houses on the west side of the road, as a result of which most buildings were badly damaged and the one next to De Viersprong was set on fire. "Explosive missiles were also falling near our position in the wood," recalls Ken Hope, "but whether these were tank HE‡ or infantry mortar bombs, I was unable to determine. The din was frightful. I flattened myself into the soft, moist earth, my cheek pressed against the butt of the LMG.§ The explosions seemed to increase in violence. The air was driven painfully from my chest. At times, I experienced momentary panic as I gasped, sucking breath

* *Arnhem Lift* op. cit. pp. 38–9.
† Self-propelled gun.
‡ High-explosive.
§ Light machine-gun, i.e. Bren gun.

into my lungs. Away to the left, I could discern the immense elongated muzzle of the armoured monster that was seeking to destroy us. Then this seemingly impregnable menace was temporarily obscured by a stab of flame, belching clouds of smoke as another shell hurtled from the barrel. Now we could hear shouting deeper in the wood. German infantry, supporting the gun was advancing toward us. Here and there, opponents were revealed as they dodged amongst trees and thickets. They did a lot of shouting. They always seemed to be shouting. It was certainly easy to locate their general dispositions, but the raucous sounds also gave the impression of greater numbers than were possibly involved. Bursts of machine-gun and rifle fire were exchanged."

Hagen reports that these small-arms exchanges were inaccurate on both sides. Nevertheless, the sustained shelling of the houses across the way more than made up for that. As well as inflicting damage in Stationsweg, some of the SP shells were also finding houses on nearby Cronjéweg, in the course of which a house was set on fire. Because of this, those in A and D Troops who were harboured there had to adopt defensive positions and, understandably, there was a growing unease on Captain Grubb's part about the safety of his vehicles.

During the action, D Troop, which was operating further east, in the Dennenkamp woods, also had some sharp encounters, in the course of which Sergeant Ernest Jenkins was completely surrounded by the enemy and cut off from the others. It was only as a result of the strenuous efforts of his fellow-sergeant, James Pyper, who went to his assistance, that Jenkins was able to extricate himself. Whilst this was taking place, the Support Troop came up and engaged with their Polsten guns. Meanwhile, a little to the west, Stevenson and Galbraith attempted to carry out the second part of the orders, which was to establish contact with 7th KOSB; neither was successful.

In a situation, therefore, where the Squadron's leading groups could probably have been overrun or, at the least, had their transport destroyed or captured, Grubb consulted Allsop by radio. His fresh instructions were to disengage and remove the vehicles from danger by returning to base, there to reorganize for foot reconnaissance. D Troop was given similar orders although it was obvious that, for them, as for Graham Wadsworth's men of A Troop, it was not going to be easily accomplished in a situation where the enemy had the line of retreat out of Dennenkamp and back across Stationsweg fully covered.

Successful withdrawal demanded swift and decisive action. Under the cover of two smoke bombs, thrown in rapid succession by Lieutenant Wadsworth, as many as possible of his Section dashed back across the road to rejoin their comrades. For those few, flesh-crawling seconds, there was not a man who did not feel his own naked vulnerability at the thought of what a burst of machine-gun fire into the grey smoke would mean. But such introspection was quite pointless, and most of them vaulted the railings to run across the road without hesitation. For whatever reason, the enemy did not fire, and the move over Stationsweg was made in safety. Many of the D Troop personnel also took the opportunity of disengaging, but there were men of both Troops still on the east side of the road as the smoke began to disperse and it was impossible for them to follow on without presenting themselves against the rising slope of the ground as clear targets for enemy fire.

For those who managed to reach the vehicles, there was no delay in getting under way. Almost simultaneously, engines roared into life and the jeeps sped off down Mariaweg, those at the tail expecting, at any moment, a farewell shot from the self-propelled gun. As it happened, it was not the gun but a sniper that opened up on the convoy, just north of the Joubertweg junction.

He got a quick despatch. Such was the temper of the men that a concentrated volley of lead was immediately poured in through the upper window from which the shot had come. As Ken Hope whimsically remarked afterwards, "I doubt whether that Jerry got an Iron Cross – I doubt whether there would be much left on which to pin it!"

Those others who were left in the Dennenkamp woods, had no choice but to try to retreat southwards out of the combat area, hiding at intervals until it was safe to make a move. The trouble was that, with the withdrawal of the main Squadron party, the place was soon alive with Germans and this increased considerably the chances of detection. Ernest Jenkins was one of those involved and, at first, along with Trooper Blacklaws worked his way down through the wooded part as far as Oosterbeek crossroads, ultimately arriving safely at the rear of Divisional HQ. Having failed, despite enquiries, to find someone who could direct him back to the Squadron, he was told to take up a defensive position in the Hartenstein grounds, and there he remained for the rest of the battle. Meantime, Blacklaws, who had become separated from him, had joined up with Cyril Simpson, a driver-operator from the HQ Section of D Troop. Simpson remembers that they did much the same thing as Jenkins and covered the ground to a point somewhere beyond the crossroads. Two days later, Simpson finished up fighting alongside the 21st Independent Parachute Company in the houses down by Pietersbergseweg.

Amongst those of A Troop who were stranded at the time of the disengagement was Trooper Willie Fraser, a young Scot from Nairn. Like the others, he also found a way down on the east side of Stationsweg and, as one of a small group of Reconnaissance and Glider Pilot Regiment men, reached the vicinity of the crossroads at about a quarter past two. It was then that the supply drop came in, with something like seventy aircraft once more having to cope with a murderous intensity of flak from German anti-aircraft batteries situated all around. During this time, Fraser and his companions took refuge in a garden shed, where they were fortunate enough to find some pears to eat. There they realized that they were at the back of the Hotel Vreewijk, one of the principal dressing stations. Enquiries made of British medical personnel at the back door revealed that the Germans were at the front of the Hotel and it was obviously advisable that they should make themselves scarce as rapidly as possible. Before they did so, the orderlies surreptitiously handed over a certain amount of Sten and Bren gun ammunition, taken from wounded men who had been newly brought in. Unfortunately, just as Fraser and the others were about to clear off, the Germans began to move round the side of the building, forcing them to seek immediate shelter in order to avoid detection. In recalling this particular episode, Fraser still has memories of a nerve-racking two hours spent in a garden trench, with enemy soldiers standing at the garden gate only a matter of yards away. "At one point," as he recalls, "a Dutchman came out of the house and walked down the garden right past us. He looked straight down at us but didn't bat an eyelid – he just walked back into the house again, with the Germans still standing there."

Eventually, when the enemy soldiers had moved off, Fraser and another man managed to slip back into the more comforting shelter of the woods. There they settled down to wait, unsure of what was going to happen, and anticipating discovery almost by the minute. He was to spend the night there, not far from the small copse where John Pow, a fellow member of A Troop, had also gone into hiding, along with three glider pilots. "We lay there all night," says Pow, "and throughout that time we could hear the Germans talking on every side of us. For a time, we could also hear the noise of the armoured vehicles, so we lay very quiet and just prayed that we would not be discovered."

All over the battle area, from Heelsum to Arnhem, situations like those were being repeated, with small wandering groups or individuals trying to find a way back to their units or, at the least, stay out of the way of the Germans. At the home for the blind at Wolfheze, Sam Bowles slept undisturbed throughout the day, sedated by morphine. Up by Planken Wambuis, Gerry Fergus had lain all Tuesday night in the ditch, seriously concussed, in a state of shock, and with badly swollen feet to add to his troubles. Around him he could hear nothing but German voices, and although he was picked up on Wednesday by a small party of Dutch, they did the only thing possible and handed him over for immediate medical care. He was lucky and still remembers with gratitude how, during the journey to St Elisabeth's Hospital, his German captors took off his wet things and gave him a dry overcoat to wear.

At first light on the Wednesday, those other C Troop men who had eluded capture after the ambush of the previous day set out once more to try to find a way back to their own lines. Ralph Foulkes had decided to take his party northwards again, with the hope of detouring around from the far side of the Amsterdamseweg. It took them all day to work their way undetected through the woodland of Reijerscamp, constantly dodging German patrols, but at last they arrived at the place where they had started out from twenty-four hours earlier. Henry Crowder remembers that what assisted them most of all was the noise made by the Germans: "They never approached quietly; they were always blowing whistles and shouting and it was that which helped us to keep out of their way." Alas, the wearisome journey proved, once more, to have been in vain, and all hopes of crossing the main road were dashed at the sight of the tanks, horse-drawn transport and bicycle patrols that occupied it. With no food and water running short, it was in a mood of bleak despair that, for the second night, they looked for somewhere to hide. All were fatigued, almost beyond endurance, and yet, sleep was not to come easily, for the discordant rattle of tracked vehicles went on for hours, overlaid by the gutteral shouts, echoing from the depths of the menacing woodland. As they listened, the dispirited men knew that, whatever the next day might bring, there was little hope left of escape.

All of this, however, was very much out of the mainstream of the action, for the important focal point was still the Bridge, where, despite the battering that the defenders had suffered, John Frost was already planning to take the war to the enemy. An aggressive soldier in the finest tradition, it was his proposal at the Tuesday night "O" group that, at first light on the Wednesday, Gough and his men in their jeeps should slip over the Bridge under the cover of smoke bombs, in order to try to reach 30 Corps. Strangely enough, Horrocks had in the meantime conceived the same idea in reverse, and Colonel Vincent Dunkerley, in command of 13th/18th Hussars, had actually briefed a "Jock Column" for a breakthrough to Frost. From Frost's point of view, his own scheme was simply a rather desperate attempt to contact an army corps whose credibility as a relief force was dwindling rapidly by the hour.* In practical terms, it was a suicidal plan for which Gough had no enthusiasm. Even if successful, the contact could have been little more than a gesture and, in the face of the almost certain loss of the Reconnaissance men, Frost eventually abandoned it. As Freddie Gough later estimated, "It was about 1000 to 1 against and might have given the Gough family its fourth VC, but posthumously and to no purpose!"†

* Contrary to what a number of writers have erroneously asserted, it had nothing at all to do with the provision of a morale-booster for the Poles, due to arrive on the third lift

† The others were General Sir Charles Gough VC, GCB and General Sir Hugh Gough VC, GCB, who were brothers serving in the Indian Army at the time of the Mutiny, and Sir John Gough VC DSO, the youngest son of Sir Charles, who won his award in Somaliland.

Wednesday was the last full day of coherent action at the Bridge, if such a term could be used of a situation that had become so disturbingly chaotic. With the approach of dawn, the rain that had begun the night before was still falling gently, and the expected early morning bombardment of both high-explosive and phosphorus bombs began again. When the darkness was dispelled, it revealed a scene of multiple devastation. The hulks of burned-out houses lay roofless to the sky, some with only one or two exterior walls still standing. All were windowless and soot-blackened and, without exception, exhibited great ragged holes from the shelling and mortaring that, in an unbelievably nightmarish period of just over forty-eight hours, had reduced a well-ordered district of dwelling houses, shops and offices to a waste land of total ruin and devastation. As the sky lightened, men who were desperately tired and hungry prepared themselves for the next instalment, which they knew with certainty would be every bit as bad as the onslaught of the previous day. 30 Corps was by then at least eighteen hours overdue but was expected at any time. Frost's men would have found it difficult to comprehend the truth, that the relief force had still not reached Nijmegen bridge.

Enemy pressure from the east began to build up rapidly, and Bernard Briggs, burned out of his positions, had to fall back on those still held by A Company of the 2nd Battalion. Those were the ruins of Houses 8 and 9, the gardens of 10 and 11 and area B under the Bridge. By then, all around the Brigade perimeter, men were digging themselves into slit trenches in the vicinity of houses which were no longer defensively tenable. Action, too, was becoming increasingly fragmented, with small groups and even individuals fighting more and more independently of each other. Of the force of just under 700 men with which Frost had begun on Sunday night, something like 150 to 200 were left on their feet. On the east side, only one building, the Van Limburg Stirum School, was still occupied by what was left of Mackay's force.

Back at his Divisional HQ, Roy Urquhart, reviewing the position, knew that his entire command had been savagely decimated to a mere fraction of its established strength and, with the almost total elimination of the brigades under him, there was little more that could be done except hope for the miracle that would bring 30 Corps to the rescue of Frost's beleaguered men. 1st Parachute Brigade was all but gone, and so was much of Hicks's 1st Air Landing Brigade. Contact with Hackett on a wireless link at 0740 hours added to his disquiet. He learned that, following the previous afternoon's disengagement over the Wolfheze crossing, what was left of the 4th Brigade was, by then, in the thick woods between Hotels Wolfheze and Bilderberg and on the rough axis of Bredelaan. Hackett was a little less than a mile away from the Divisional area, but was having to fight virtually every inch of the way to it. He reported that his force was completely engaged, and that free movement was impossible. It was a classic example of understatement, but for Urquhart it was sufficient to confirm him in the view that nothing further could be done for those about to make their last stand at the Bridge. As he was later to remark, "With the weak force now left, I could no more hope to reinforce Frost than reach Berlin."

It was at this nadir of Urquhart's fortunes, at just about eight o'clock in the morning, that the telephone rang and the caller asked to speak to him. The very fact that the telephone was being used at all was in itself grounds for suspicion, for the British had tended to disregard it, except perhaps for communication with the field hospitals. There was a very good reason for this, since the Arnhem exchange was occupied by the Germans, who had not only disconnected almost all private telephones, but were also obviously able to monitor any calls still coming through. Nevertheless, there was an additional and private telephone system, run by the Gelderland Provincial Electricity Board, and this, to a great extent, was controlled by trustworthy Dutch resistance people. By dialling a certain number on it, it was possible to obtain access to the public system at Arnhem exchange, where a few reliable Dutch girls kept three lines available for the purpose.

As he cautiously answered, General Urquhart received a very cheerful greeting of "Hello Sunray." This, of course, meant nothing. It was simply standard army nomenclature used as part of the signaller's jargon to refer to anyone in command, whether of a division or a section of men. Furthermore, it was not in any way restricted and so would have been known and understood by the Germans. "Can you give me an inkling of who you are?" said Urquhart, implying that if the call were genuine, then security should not be jeopardized for the sake of identification. There was a short pause, and the voice said, "It's the man who goes in for funny weapons." As Urquhart pondered upon a plethora of possibilities throughout the 1st Airborne Division, his mysterious caller added, with a chuckle, "You know – the man who is always late for your 'O' groups." "My goodness," responded Urquhart, with warmth, "I thought you were dead." However abstruse he might have found the oblique reference to Vickers "K" guns, for Roy Urquhart, this was proof positive that he was indeed conversing with the missing commander of the Reconnaissance Squadron. From the shambles of Arnhem Bridge, the irrepressible Gough had somehow contrived to get himself hooked into the local telephone system and straight through to the General. As a morale-lifter for GHQ, the contact could not have come at a better time. It was also the first direct communication which the General had had with the besieged men, and Gough was able to fill him in on what had been happening. He, in turn, learned that the only hope left for the men at the Bridge lay with 30 Corps. By then, of course, Gough had written 30 Corps off, but he assured the Divisional commander that, no matter what happened, they would hold out for as long as possible. It only then remained for General Urquhart to wish them all the best of luck.

That was not the end of the General's contact with the Bridge. At 1000 hours, one of the 2nd Parachute Battalion signallers, who had been "searching" with the tuning dial, finally picked up Divisional forward net, so that Frost was also able to speak to Urquhart and pass back his own official estimate of the casualties inflicted on the enemy. Conscious of the acute and growing shortages of ammunition, food, water and medical supplies, of the rising toll of dead and wounded, of the almost unbearable burden of fatigue that his men had borne, John Frost reiterated the message already passed through on his behalf by Gough, that they would hold and continue to hold for as long as was necessary. It was an affirmation of faith in his men and in himself, and the assertion of a belief that, like all well-trained troops, they could stand and suffer to the very limits of human endurance. If, in the end, Arnhem was to prove anything, it was that the men of the 1st British Airborne Division possessed the unique quality of being able to stand and suffer for just that little bit longer.

Throughout the morning, the enemy made attempt after attempt to finish them off. Those in the gardens of Houses 10 and 11 were shelled out by tanks firing at point-blank range, and the survivors who were able to do so crossed to the west side. From their school, now hardly more than a heap of rubble, Mackay's men drove off three attacks in two hours, until the enemy turned to deal with the force positioned under the Bridge and in Houses 7, 8 and 9. In beating off successive enemy attacks, Lieutenant Grayburn of the 2nd Parachute Battalion, although wounded three times, displayed a particularly unique brand of courage as he rallied and inspired his men. He was killed by a German flame thrower, and later awarded a posthumous Victoria Cross.

Back at Oosterbeek, following the order to disengage from the action on Stationsweg, the main body of the Reconnaissance Squadron had rendezvoused at Squadron HQ, across the road from the Hartenstein Hotel. It was a convenient situation, but one that carried certain attendant disadvantages, since, from the time that the Hartenstein had been established as the focal point in the British lines, so had it also become a logical target for enemy bombardment. It was this which was to account for the intensity of much of the mortar fire that periodically descended on the area. Consequently, because of the proximity of its position, Reconnaissance HQ was inevitably affected and, throughout that morning, Captain Allsop was to record acute harassment from single mortars fired in battery shoots, supplemented by two 15 cm Nebelwerfer rocket launchers, which let off every 45 minutes.

At just after 2.30 in the afternoon, the Squadron vehicles drew up on the north side of Utrechtseweg, whilst Troop commanders reported to Allsop at the Squadron HQ trench positions on Oranjeweg. Shortly afterwards, word came through that a German SP gun had appeared at Oosterbeek crossroads and appeared to be turning up Utrechtseweg in the direction of Divisional HQ. It is not certain if it was the one that had been active in the earlier action on Stationsweg, but its appearance so deep inside the British positions came as a complete surprise and, so far as the Squadron was concerned, there was immediate anxiety for the vulnerability of the jeeps, which were sitting, fully exposed, on Hartensteinlaan and at the mercy of any fire which might be brought to bear on them from the main road.

No sooner had this fear been expressed, than two Squadron vehicles were hit and each was set on fire. Whether the sudden attack came from the SP gun which was advancing from the crossroads, or from the ever-active enemy mortars, is not clear, but the initiative was immediately taken by Lieutenant John Christie, OC Support Troop, who saw an opportunity for action with one of his Polsten guns. Speedily, he collected a jeep party, which included Troopers Drinkwater, Watson and Bateman and, with the Polsten in tow, they drove out on to Utrechtseweg and turned in the direction of the crossroads. It now seems likely that Christie was probably looking for an advantageous tactical position, in order to site his gun. Whatever his intentions may have been, they were never carried out for, as the jeep drew level with the Hartenstein Hotel, it came under enemy fire. The first shot missed, and the men were able to jump off the vehicle and scatter for cover. Christie then ran back to the jeep, started it up, and began to turn it, with the gun in tow, in order to get it off the road.

Lieutenant-Colonel Charles Mackenzie, Urquhart's senior staff officer, who was standing by the side of the main road, saw what happened next: "Just then, there was a loud explosion on the vehicle. I've no idea where it came from, although it seemed to me to be a mortar bomb, rather than a shell from the SP gun. Whatever it was, it struck Christie full in the chest, and took an arm, as well as part of his shoulder and chest away. Both vehicle and Polsten gun were destroyed, but the astonishing thing was that he actually got out of the jeep, and ran for several yards along the road." Despite his terrible injuries, John Christie managed to reach the cover where his men were, and it was there that Bill Bateman sought to comfort him. Seconds later, as he died in Bateman's arms, Christie's last words were, "Oh, my God! Oh, my God!"

In the belief that the incident presaged the start of an enemy attack on the Divisional HQ itself, the others in the Squadron speedily scattered for shelter. By then, the SP gun had appeared in sight, coming up the incline that ran from Oosterbeek crossroads to the Hartenstein area. Against the background of noise and the constant exchange of fire, men then dashed out to try to turn the jeeps round, each time getting back into the shelter of the houses before the Germans had time to sight their guns and open up at the movement. Sergeant Pyper of D Troop was one of those who helped organize this highly dangerous operation, until eventually it was completed. It only then remained to make a dash for it and hope for the best. On a signal, there was a simultaneous mounting of the vehicles and the Squadron moved off at speed. As the jeeps revved away, a burst of machine-gun fire from the armoured vehicle suddenly raked across the last one. The jeep had already begun to move, but Trooper "Joe" Irala, who was in the act of jumping on, was hit. John Marshall remembers that, as they pulled him aboard, he complained about having been shot in the leg, although it was obvious to the others that it was much more serious. "When I saw what had happened to him," says Marshall, "I drove straight across to the first-aid post at the Hartenstein. We were shot at continuously on the way, but I didn't pay any attention to it. By the time we'd arrived, 'Joe' was unconscious." In fact, Irala, the boy who had come from Spain to fight for the British, had taken a machine-gun burst full in the stomach, and he died just thirty minutes later. For Marshall personally, it was a particularly tragic episode, for there was a strong bond of friendship between the two men which transcended the difference in rank. "I still remember him today," says John Marshall, "as a wonderful soldier – highly intelligent, immensely brave, and with a capacity, which the average Englishman doesn't have, for giving enormous personal loyalty." It had been a bad half hour and, with the vehicles temporarily out of harm's way, the men dug in to await a further attack. To their surprise, the gun then simply withdrew, and one more crisis had passed.

One of the consequences of the breakthrough of the German armour was the capture of the main dressing stations of the Schoonoord and Vreewijk Hotels. Only the previous evening, 133 Para Field Ambulance and part of 181 Airlanding Field Ambulance had established themselves at those points, but on Wednesday morning both medical units were taken. St Elisabeth's Hospital, in which 16th Para Field Ambulance had set up a unit, had also been captured by the Germans two days before, which meant that, not only were all three main medical units then in enemy hands but, with the removal of the majority of the medical officers and RAMC personnel as prisoners-of-war, only a small staff was allowed to remain to deal with the particularly serious cases.

The outcome was that, from 20th September, the Divisional medical services were drastically reduced in terms of both accommodation and available personnel. Understandably, because of this, it was felt to be no longer appropriate that such scarce resources as medical officers should function at unit level. As a result, at 5 o'clock in the afternoon, Douglas Swinscow received instructions to leave the Squadron lines and report to Colonel Graeme Warrack at Divisional HQ across the road. Swinscow was fit enough to do so because, by that time, the two metal fragments which he had got in the back on the Sunday night had extruded from the muscle, and the wounds showed little infection. One of his first tasks, as he recalls, was to look at some wounded German prisoners-of-war. "I was very struck," he says, "by one boy in SS uniform, aged about sixteen or seventeen, who had bullet wounds in the thigh. As I went in with one of our own guards who carried a sub-machine gun, this young fellow, despite the wound in his side, jumped up, stood to attention and said, 'Please don't shoot me.' I must say, I was a little put out at the thought that some Germans actually expected British medical officers to shoot their wounded!"

By mid-day at the Bridge positions, the British were being increasingly mortared, and high velocity guns were shooting holes through the few buildings which were still held. At the beginning of the afternoon, the whole force had come under the command of Major Gough because, shortly after his morning radio contact with General Urquhart, Frost, wounded by a mortar bomb had been forced to join the casualties in the cellar. Despite his injuries, he was still very much concerned with the progress of the battle, and Gough continued to refer all important decisions to him. At 1430 hours, news was relayed from Divisional HQ to the effect that 30 Corps had been further delayed and would not be with them "for a bit", but that it was hoped that they would make the south end of Arnhem Bridge by 1700 hours. Considering that the relief force had still to take and secure the Waal crossing, it was an astonishingly misleading piece of intelligence. Gough reported in reply, however, that all were in fine spirits and would continue to hold on for as long as was humanly possible.

As the enemy pressure on the remaining defenders was increasingly forced home, Major Gough ordered more alternative positions to be dug in the gardens. By then, the Brigade perimeter on the west side of the Bridge had shrunk to a position based largely upon the curve formed by Houses 2 to 6. In the event of those last few houses being set alight, Freddie Gough's plan was that the men should then move into the trenches. Once the fires had burned out he believed that they could reoccupy the houses and cover the Bridge through the gaps.

On the east side, things came to an end just after three in the afternoon, when a Mark VI "Tiger" tank and a 105 mm self-propelled gun destroyed completely what was left of Mackays' school. As shell upon shell crashed into it, the defenders took to the cellar, and listened to their ammunition going up, taking with it the remainder of the roof. Out of the building, which was blazing like a torch, Mackay then brought the forty-five remaining men of his force, thirty-one of whom were wounded. As he sought shelter to the north, in the face of machine-gun and mortar fire, seven more were wounded and another man was killed. Leaving the injured to surrender, Mackay's small group, by then reduced to a mere half-dozen men, headed east through burned-out houses, still hot and smoking from the previous day. They made their way over back gardens, all the time being fired at, in one instance by a tank from a range of only ten yards. Bursting out from a row of houses further east again, they suddenly came face to face with a force of fifty Germans standing beside two sand-coloured Mark III tanks. "We stood in a line," says Mackay, "with our six machine-guns firing from the hip. We pressed the triggers continuously till the ammunition ran out." With his original force reduced to four, Mackay then retreated by the way he had come, leaving each of the others to go off on his own. Ten minutes later, whilst simulating death, this brave officer had a German bayonet stuck into him, until it came to rest on his pelvic bone. Only then did he surrender, to become a prisoner-of-war for just the sixteen hours necessary for him to organize his own escape from Germany. Thirty-four hours later, Mackay was in Nijmegen, having completed the last part of the journey by small boat, down the Rhine.

Over on Gough's side, the fight went on. Nevertheless, shortage of ammunition was beginning to tell, and later in the afternoon the enemy made the first breakthrough, when four or five tanks were able to cross the Bridge from north to south. One reason for this tactical success was that, by then, the British 6-pounders were under direct small-arms fire, and so could not be manned. In the late afternoon, Houses 3, 5 and 6 were shelled from close quarters by an 88 mm gun, located just west of House 7. A counter-blast by British 3-inch mortars silenced it for a time but, at about 1930 hours, just as it was getting dark, artillery and tank attacks were resumed. This time, as sections of the outside walls were blasted away, the Germans launched phosphorus grenades into the buildings to set them alight. Fire-fighting squads did their best to contain the fires, but were themselves constantly shot at as soon as they were spotted.

At just about the time that Mackay was finally being driven out of his school, however, something very significant was taking place eleven miles to the south. From the outset, General Gavin's 82nd US Airborne Division had been given a job which, in overall terms, was beyond its capabilities. As a result, although by the Wednesday his force had taken almost all of its objectives, the great bridge over the Waal at Nijmegen was still in enemy hands. Gavin could have done with help, but the slow progress of 30 Corps coming from further south denied him this, and no such support was forthcoming until Tuesday night, when an unsuccessful attempt was made to secure the objective, by means of a combined attack of one American battalion, together with men of the Grenadier Guards. Now, at 1500 hours on the Wednesday, an incredibly courageous and successful attack was made on that last major obstacle by another joint Anglo-American force, consisting of Gavin's 504th and 505th Regiments, with elements of Adair's Guards Armoured Division in support. It was a well-executed operation, and by 1915 hours, with detonators and explosives all removed from the Nimegen Bridge, the road to Arnhem lay open.

The failure of the British relief force to press home its advantage at that point will, no doubt, be debated for years to come. In particular, the role of 30 Corps is likely to occupy a central position in any argument concerning the strategic decisions that were made at what is now known to have been a critical time in the fortunes of the entire "Market Garden" operation. Put at its simplest, Horrocks's task was to spearhead 2nd Army's advance to Arnhem and beyond, and to do so, virtually unaided. It was true that the original plan called for a degree of flank support to be supplied by 8 and 12 Corps, but this planned strategy in no way resembled anything in the nature of a three-pronged advance. Generals O'Connor and Ritchie, the respective commanders of 8 and 12 Corps, have since confirmed that neither of their formations were involved, in a primary sense, in "Market Garden". On the contrary, their function was one of broadening the base for 30 Corps whilst, at the same time, leaving Horrocks to provide the single main thrust towards the objective.

Of the magnitude of his responsibility, Horrocks himself clearly had little doubt for, at the briefing of the officers of 30 Corps in the cinema at Bourg-Léopold, on 16th September, he clarified the nature of the proposed ground advance as he saw it: "8 and 12 British Corps will be advancing on our right and left respectively but, as most of the available resources have been allotted to 30 Corps, they will not be able to advance so rapidly, and we shall be out on our own, possibly for quite a long period."

Obviously, the overall design, whilst calling for 8 and 12 Corps to strengthen Horrocks's base, made little provision for effective flank support once his advance had developed momentum. Yet, in the absence of such support, the relief force inevitably ran into difficulties from the German opposition disposed in the countryside to right and left of the route along which 30 Corps had to travel. Much of it was, in places, criss-crossed by a matrix of water obstacles which needed to be negotiated. The area from Grave to Nijmegen was especially difficult. Such terrain could not have been tackled by armour, but one wonders why infantry could not have been deployed to either side of the chosen line of advance to help deal with the numerous pockets of resistance that did so much to put an effective brake on Horrocks's progress. Indeed, by the time the British had reached the Waal, the defending Germans had, themselves, amply demonstrated that, even in the relatively difficult local conditions, infantry could still move freely. Given the opportunity, British infantry groups could, at the least, have taken on some of the German artillery or machine-gun emplacements that were making things so difficult for the advancing 30 Corps. Flank support of such kind could hardly have been other than advantageous to Horrocks who, almost from the start, found himself stretched out on an exposed road, in constant danger of having his lines of communication cut.

In the light of this evidence, the *de facto* situation appears to have been that the ground advance was not so much 2nd Army, as 30 Corps on its own. With this in mind, there remains the matter of assessing the effectiveness of its contribution as the sole relief force. In the first place, there is no denying that it had to cope with major physical difficulties on its line of advance, largely in consequence of having to travel over a flat, flooded area, in which movement inevitably had to be restricted to accessible roads. The massive difficulties of the Betuwe* were still to come, but even in the earlier stages, vehicles often had to move along dyke roads, thus presenting silhouettes as easy targets for enemy anti-tank fire. The result was a sluggish rate of advance, punctuated by frequent halts and fierce, sharp actions.

All of this is comprehensible, and it is difficult to see how any force in a similar situation could have found the going any the less difficult. What is not so easy to understand is the practice, which seems to have been fairly consistently followed, of harbouring at night, in preference to pressing on towards the objective. On the Sunday night, for example, 30 Corps halted at Valkenswaard, still six miles south of Eindhoven, and did not resume its movement forward until 0600 hours on the following morning. This pattern was repeated all the way to the Waal. One other of the least fortunate consequences of all this was that, repeatedly, under cover of darkness, the Germans could redeploy their defensive elements. Unimpeded by distraction of any kind, they were able, time after time, to regroup and take advantage of the night hours, either to fortify defensive points that were weak, or else prepare fresh ones in anticipation of the forward movement of 30 Corps. It was a situation that offered full opportunity for maximizing the harassment of the advancing British ground force.

Such, then, was the pattern of events up to the time of the Waal crossing, and it would appear to raise two vital issues. The first is that, given a situation in which the Guards Armoured Division, with infantry support, had pressed on through from the start, might they not have arrived at the Waal in time to aid Gavin in an earlier capture of Nijmegen Bridge? The second is that, notwithstanding the late securing of the river crossing at dusk on D + 3, why were Horrocks's men not then able to pull out all the stops to get up to Arnhem Bridge, which was almost within sight? Certainly, with the Waal crossing finally achieved, that was what the 82nd US Airborne Division appeared to expect, for they rapidly deployed to form a perimeter for the protection of 30 Corps which, it was assumed, would attempt a "hell-for-leather" thrust up the corridor to Arnhem. It was the British decision once more to harbour for the night that so astonished the Americans. Even a *coup de main* party was, at the very least, expected, in order to take advantage of the loophole newly provided in the German defences. Instead, the British force ground, once more, to a halt, for reasons as explicable as they were unfortunate. Of those, the principal one was not so much any lack of motivation as a consciousness of tactical weakness. This stemmed from the fact that, whilst Adair's† armour required infantry support in order to capitalize on the successful breach of the German Waal defences, the over-cautious Thomas had not even got his 43rd (Wessex) Division as far as Grave. This was the crux of the matter, for the decision hinged upon the need for the armour to await the arrival of a necessary infantry vanguard. Furthermore, it was a decision that was all the more tactically defensible when viewed in the context of the long, high dyke road

* The area between Nijmegen and Arnhem.
† Major-General Allan Adair commanded the Guards' Armoured Division.

that had still to be negotiated. It was the failure of the infantry to keep up with the armour that generated once more a course in which planning was thought of in terms of "next day". Unfortunately, for the courageous force at Arnhem Bridge, that was destined to be as late as all eternity.

For the Reconnaissance Squadron, two things were significant about the withdrawal from the action on Stationsweg. The first, was that it marked an impending change in its role, for already at Divisional HQ plans were developing for the formation of a defensive perimeter to be based on the Neder Rijn. The other was that, within the context of an increasingly tight fighting situation, it was becoming apparent that fast-moving jeeps had lost their value and perhaps even become something of an encumbrance. The action on Stationsweg had, in particular, demonstrated that the battle was ceasing to be in any sense a mobile affair with the accompanying need for swift penetrative reconnaissance to flush out the enemy. By then, everyone knew only too well where the enemy was and, in the days that followed, the problem was often one of a much more specific and personal nature, concerned not simply with determining if the Germans were in the adjacent house, but with establishing whether or not they were in the next room!

So it was that, with its vehicles harboured in the Squadron HQ area on Oranjeweg, the unit took on a defensive infantry role appropriate to the new situation. As matters developed by the end of the day, the total perimeter area to be defended emerged as one shaped rather like an elongated thumb, based on the Neder Rijn, and extending for a mere 2000 yards from south to north. At its widest point, it was not more than 1000 yards across and this was to be gradually and progressively reduced in the days that lay ahead.

As from that Wednesday afternoon, it was determined that Support Troop should rejoin Squadron HQ at base, but that the two remaining operational troops, A and D, would take up static positions a little to the north and not more than a few hundred yards from where the morning's action had taken place with the German SP gun. It was very much a built-up area, dating from the turn of the century, with streets which, appropriately enough, were named after famous politicians or generals of the Boer War period – Botha, De la Rey, Cronjé, Joubert. Here, the houses, in either fully or semi-detached style, were much less grand than those on Stationsweg and were also built closer together. Red brick predominated, and most were two-storeyed, with the top rooms windowed out on all sides of fairly steep-pitched roofs of red or black tile. Paintwork was generally cream or white, and exterior shutters to the windows were as characteristic as the net curtains that were looped behind them inside. A profusion of red roses and orange marigolds grew in many of the small front gardens, each of which was bounded by metal fencing, which consisted of either diagonal wire mesh, set within rectangular metal frames, or a succession of uprights with spiked tops, placed only three inches apart. All the fences were waist high and, under the particular conditions of the street fighting which was to follow, were to constitute a major impediment to both sides. In a number of cases, beech, laurel and privet hedge had also been grown behind the fence, and that was to add to the difficulty of negotiating them whilst encumbered with arms and equipment.

Leaving Trooper Weaver to look after the abandoned vehicles, A and D troops moved up in the late afternoon into their new positions. With their coming, so did the Dutch inhabitants go down to the cellars, taking with them what food and clothing they could. Powerless to influence events, they could now see that the prospect of liberation, which had seemed so sure only three days before, was now beginning to slip away from them. At that point, few were able to guess that to the bitter and growing hopelessness that would mark the remainder of the week, would be added the agony and frustration of watching their homes destroyed, brick by brick, before their eyes.

Grubb's A Troop, with a strength of four officers and thirty-eight other ranks, was given responsibility for covering two crossroads. One of those was the junction of Paul Krugerstraat and Mariaweg, and the other was a little to the north, at the point where Mariaweg was intersected by Joubertweg. The Troop's specific responsibility was for the two adjacent houses on the north-west corner of Paul Krugerstraat, together with the corner house on the south-west side. This last position was a private house but, on the north corner, the building was a combined house, bakery and shop owned by a family called Crum. Next door was the house and business premises of a furniture and curtain maker called Janssen. These positions were occupied by Troop HQ, together with 1 and 2 Sections. No. 3 Section, under Lieutenant Graham Wadsworth, was sent to occupy houses on the Joubertweg crossing.

D Troop's four officers and thirty-four men moved into position further west, on the north-south axis of Steijnweg, between the junctions with Paul Krugerstraat and the more northerly Bothaweg. Captain Park chose to site his Troop HQ in a corner house at the junction of Steijnweg and Paul Krugerstraat. On the side of the house nearest to the road, two tall French windows opened out on to a tiled patio with a diamond and star pattern picked out in coloured ceramics, and from there it was possible to command an unimpeded view to the north, up the curving length of Steijnweg to the next road junction. This was at Bothaweg, and it was almost a crossroads, since Joubertweg also ran into Steijnweg from the opposite direction, just a few yards to the north. It was in this area and a little to the north of it that John Marshall's 10 Section as well as 11 Section under Bill Hodge were disposed, with responsibility not only for the crossings on Steijnweg but also for the vulnerable junction of Joubertweg and Christian de Wetstraat. Between those forward positions and that of D Troop HQ, additional points were occupied by the remaining 12 Section, commanded by Alan Pascal, with Sergeant Bill Bentall as second-in-command.

As a result of those arrangements, the broad pattern of disposition was box-shaped, with A Troop covering the two corners on the east side, and D Troop assuming responsibility for the west, as well as the intersection of Christian de Wetstraat, halfway along the top edge of the box. All round the evolving perimeter, similar defensive positions were being taken up as General Urquhart strove to dispose and spread what limited force was available, in an attempt to keep the Germans out for as long as possible. At that stage, the emphasis was on the establishment of strongpoints at critical positions, which was why each of the operational Troops of the Squadron found itself assigned to road junction complexes. Later, as more men became available, so were they detailed to fill the gaps, in order to provide as full a strategic coverage as possible.

Further to the west, the attempt by 4th Brigade, under Brigadier Hackett, to win through to the Divisional area had continued throughout the morning of that day. By 0740 hours, the time of his wireless contact with Urquhart, it had already become clear to Hackett that his Brigade had "bumped" the left flank of what appeared to be a considerable enemy force moving from the west, and soon they were under intense fire from mortars and anti-tank guns. At that point, however, Hackett discovered that the enemy was weakest to the west of his own position, so straightway he altered the line of his advance in order to take advantage of this. With 10th Parachute Battalion in the lead, his Brigade then fought its way, a few yards at a time, through the dense woodland east of Bredelaan, in the course of which action, the 10th became detached from the rest and made headway on its own.

By noon, the 10th Parachute Battalion had crossed to the east side of Valkenburglaan, and was ready to make the final move south into the area of the Hartenstein. Anxious to speed up the rate of advance in order to reduce the risk of being surrounded, Hackett sent orders to them to "pull the plug out." Acting on those instructions, the men of the 10th Battalion fixed bayonets and successfully charged their way through. General Urquhart has recorded his own personal impression of their arrival: "I saw the remains of the Battalion as it turned off the main road, following the line of trees into the HQ area. The men were exhausted, filthy and bleeding; their discipline was immaculate . . . their commander, Lieutenant-Colonel Ken Smyth, his right arm bandaged where a bullet had struck, reported breathlessly, 'We have been heavily taken on, sir. I have sixty men left' . . . It was 1.30 p.m." Smyth and his men were afterwards assigned to defend a number of houses at the Oosterbeek crossroads, east of the Divisional area. There, they were to fight, virtually to the last man, and one month later Smyth himself was to die from wounds.

In the woodland to the west, the remainder of 4th Brigade continued to try to extricate itself but, as the enemy pressure increased in the course of the afternoon, disengagement was agonizingly drawn-out and the British casualties mounted. These included several of Hackett's senior officers, a number of whom were killed or wounded. In particular, the remnants of the 156th Parachute Battalion were sorely pressed on Valkenburglaan and, in the area of the sports ground, the commanding officer, Sir Richard de B. des Voeux, was killed. Early in the afternoon, there were also some spirited brushes with enemy armour, in the course of which one German tank had its track blown off by a 75 grenade.

By then, what was left of the Brigade had worked its way southwards on Valkenburglaan to a spot just about 300 yards east of the Bilderberg Hotel. There, on the west side of the road, near to its junction with Sonnenberglaan, was a crater-shaped depression in the ground, around the edge of which about thirty Germans were established in defensive positions. The general situation at that point had also become very serious, for German tanks and infantry had penetrated the British column at a number of places. Faced with this, Hackett ordered Major Powell of the 156th Parachute Battalion to clear the depression and this was done at bayonet point. Hackett then gathered the remains of his Brigade into the captured position. Out of the two thousand men whom he had led to battle on the second lift, less than one hundred were left, and it was in that simple hollow that this fraction of Hackett's original force, lacking both weapons and ammunition, held out for the remainder of the afternoon, as the enemy mounted attack after attack with infantry-supported armour.

By nightfall, the 4th Brigade defenders were still holding on, but it was clear that the enemy was determined to overrun the position before darkness. With no other choice left to him, short of surrender, Brigadier Hackett took the decision to break out and, again, this was done at bayonet point. In half a mile, with surprizingly few casualties, they ran in to the 1st Border Regiment positions on the western side of the Divisional area. At 1850 hours, Hackett reported to Urquhart and, after a brief rest, those of his men who had won through were sent to take up defensive positions in the same area as was being held by the operational Troops of the Reconnaissance Squadron. General Urquhart then brought Brigadier Hackett up to date on the overall position and, after explaining the proposed defensive plans, assigned to him the task of looking after the east side of the British perimeter.

Having moved into the houses allotted to them, the first concern of the Reconnaissance Squadron men had been to consolidate and secure the positions as much as possible before the onset of darkness. Windows had to be smashed out, and furniture dragged over to form barricades as well as provide support for firing positions. There were other more exacting duties which had also to be undertaken, for the occupation of a defensive strongpoint did not absolve the defenders from the responsibility of determining the whereabouts of the enemy. For that reason, as soon as his men had occupied their houses on the Mariaweg crossroads, Captain Grubb immediately arranged for foot patrols to be sent out. The main concern was to investigate the situation to the north and it was whilst he was engaged on that particular assignment that Lieutenant Galbraith was blown out of a house just beyond Joubertweg. It was certainly a practical way of demonstrating the presence of the enemy and provided also an indication of how near the Germans were although, at that early stage, there were few signs of the massive infiltration of British positions that was to become so frightening and unpredictable a factor in the later stages of the struggle.

With the priority tasks overtaken, there came the long-awaited opportunity to eat. Already, the men were into the habit of husbanding their meagre food resources and most of them were coping. Some, more frugal than the rest, still had left-overs from the ration packs which were to have sustained them only until the arrival of 30 Corps. Like their comrades at the Bridge, they too were conscious of the fact that 2nd Army was already long overdue but, given the optimism that had surrounded the briefings of the previous week in England, many felt that there was still hope. One thing which had cheered them all enormously was the news that Major Gough was safe and well and had been in personal contact with Divisional HQ from the Bridge itself. Few of them had been able to accept the fact that he was dead, so that the manner of his dramatic resurrection fully matched their expectations of him. As Henry Venes put it, "Phoning up from the Bridge in the middle of a battle, it had to be him. It was just bloody typical – if he'd said he was ringing up from Berlin we wouldn't have been surprised!"

At the end of that day, not everyone would have shared in the optimistic hope of a "nick-of-time" relief. John Marshall, in recalling how he had, till then, been accompanied for two days by a young Dutchman, remembers how, on that Wednesday night, the young man asked him for his opinion on the general state of things. Says Marshall, "'Officially,' I said to him, 'we're going to win – privately, dear boy, I should hop it!'" The Dutchman had the good sense to take his advice and left within the hour. Thereafter, as the false calm of night fell over the battle area, the men of A and D Troops took it in turns to keep watch from posts on the top floors of their houses, whilst others sought temporary oblivion in what little sleep they could get.

Nearer to the Hartenstein, the men of Squadron HQ were dug in on the edge of the field that lay immediately to the west of Oranjeweg. Their slit trenches were arranged in a semi-circle, facing across the field towards the line of Valkenburglaan. The fact that they were HQ personnel made no difference to the need to take up defensive positions, for everyone, up to the General himself, was in the front line, and all, as part of a defensive ring, were equally vulnerable. The mid-afternoon attack by the German SP gun had already amply demonstrated that. So too did a mortar attack on the area later in the day, when the young 19-year-old Weaver, who had been left to look after the vehicles, died as the result of a direct hit.

By nightfall, the force at the Bridge had been reduced to 140 and, as the final strongholds burned, there was mounting concern for the fate of the wounded in the cellars. Houses 3, 5 and 6 had already been fired and, just before 2000 hours, Brigade HQ at position 2 was set alight. The wounded were then evacuated to House 4, at the back, but not all could be accommodated and, during the move, the building, which had a great deal of wood on its outside face, was also set on fire. In the open, between Houses 2 and 4, wounded men lay on the ground whilst mortar bombs burst in their midst. It was a horrifying situation, but Gough had already consulted Frost, and both had agreed that no other course lay open to them but to surrender the wounded to the enemy. The alternative of risking them being roasted alive could not be contemplated. Besides, although medical officers Logan and Wright had performed feats of superlative improvization, the time had clearly come to recognize that they could do no more.

During the cease-fire which followed, the wounded were removed. Gough remembered the details vividly: "The wounded were taken out and, in claiming that they needed transport to do this, the Germans took our Reconnaissance jeeps as well, and we couldn't really stop them. It was the most astonishing situation, with those SS troops going in and out, and us just sitting behind cover or in slit trenches. Nobody said a word – there was complete silence as we watched and waited for them to complete the job so that the battle could start again."

Not long prior to this evacuation, Tony Hibbert, the Brigade Major, had returned from an investigation of some houses to the north of the defensive position. These he had found unoccupied and so, leaving a section of men to hold them, he had returned to Brigade HQ. They were thought to be a useful acquisition but, after the wounded had been taken out, they appeared even more so because it was discovered that during the ceasefire the Germans had craftily exploited the opportunity to infiltrate infantry closer to the British positions. The result was that, when the fighting began again, Gough found his force virtually surrounded on three sides, with stick grenades being lobbed round the corner of House 4 into the square. Hibbert, thereupon, suggested that they might make a quick move into those empty houses which he had found to the north. This was initiated without delay, but at a cost which included the life of Lieutenant McDermont. Unfortunately, when they arrived, they found the houses on fire, so that they had to select other positions as swiftly as possible, with some moving to L'Ecole de Ste Marie about 150 yards further on, and the rest to the Cathedral.

In pursuit of the retreating and dwindling British force, the Germans pressed home their advantage. Major Gough, having survived the previous three days without a scratch, took refuge in a shop where he suffered his first minor injury of the battle. "The whole place was smouldering inside," he said, "and I'd taken cover, with some Germans outside waiting for me to move. The trouble was that the shop seemed to be full of burning lime and hot bricks and, although I was getting badly burned on the elbows, I didn't dare move for fear of being shot. Eventually, I had to do a sort of skid towards better cover, and they fired and missed me, but it was either that or sizzling like a piece of toast."

As the members of the small force, by then fragmented into a few scattered groups, took what shelter they could, most knew that it was all over. The long-awaited oft-promised relief had not come and, indeed, it was to be almost thirty-six hours later before the leading elements of 30 Corps would appear, even fleetingly, upon the other side.* With the knowledge that they could no longer command the Bridge, Hibbert then organized a scheme whereby, moving off in small groups, the survivors would attempt to make their way under cover of darkness to try to reach the remainder of the Division in Oosterbeek. It was not a success, and almost all of them were rounded up. A subsequent attempt to scoop out shallow hiding places within the ruins of the

* It was to be a detachment, led by Captain Richard Wrottesley of the 2nd Household Cavalry, which carried out reconnaissance work for the Guards Armoured Division. Wrottesley was, himself, a former member of the 1st Airborne Reconnaissance Squadron.

burnt-out buildings was also found to be impossible, because the ashes were still unbearably hot and the men could find no refuge.

One of Freddie Gough's last actions on that night was to organize a despatch to Divisional HQ at the Hartenstein. Corporal Saul of the 2nd Parachute Battalion, together with a companion went on foot all the way and saw the message safely delivered.

Arnhem Bridge after the battle: German photograph taken on the northern ramp
(Imperial War Museum)

D Troop, 1st Airborne Reconnaissance Squadron, Ruskington 1944
Back row: ——, Tprs. Adams, Washer, Bolton, Slater, Bell. *Second back row:* ——, Tpr. Welham, ——, Tpr. McLennan, ——, Tprs. Chilton, Tuthill, Groves, Simpson. *Second front row:* Tprs. Irala, Hart, Martin, Williams, Grindrod, L/Cpl. Thomson, Tprs. Smith, Mantz, Blacklaws, Walker, ——. *Front row:* L/Cpl. Maydew, Sgts. Ritson, Pyper, Lt. Marshall, Capt. Park, Lts. Hodge, Pascal, Sgt. Storrie, Cpl. Dixon
[Missing: Sgt. Jenkins]

D Troop HQ during Perimeter phase: Steijnweg, Oosterbeek

5 De la Reyweg, Oosterbeek: A Troop HQ in final stages of the battle

Chapter 10 THURSDAY 21st SEPTEMBER 1944

"Oh! Look what you've done to my friend!"

From about 0700 hours, all Oosterbeek positions were subjected by the Germans to heavy mortaring and shelling, an experience which was to recur again and again, throughout the battle and over the entire extent of the British perimeter defences. Squadron HQ was particularly badly affected, and Captain Allsop noted that for a time that morning, no movement above ground was possible at all. By 0900 hours it had eased temporarily, and he was able to report for orders to the Hartenstein, only to learn that, despite the Waal crossing, the relief force appeared to have made no further progress on the last stage of its journey. Mortaring went on intermittently but with great intensity throughout the morning. To Allsop and the others it even seemed at one point as if a bizarre touch had been introduced, for he reported that "the Germans appear to be firing mortars to music – a definite rhythm can be heard as primary explosions take place." At just after 10 o'clock the Germans scored one major hit when the ammunition dump at Divisional HQ was set on fire. This was a severe blow to everyone, for it had been an important source of supply.

In addition to the mortaring, the morning also saw the stepping up of temporary penetration by SP guns and tanks, against which the defenders could do so little. Throughout this time, strenuous efforts were continuing all over the perimeter to plug the gaps. During the night, as a consequence of their successful breakthrough into the Divisional area, men of the 156th Parachute Battalion had been allocated to a position near that taken up by A Troop. There they occupied a large house with an overhanging chestnut tree in the front garden that stood on the other side of Mariaweg from the bakery. Diagonally opposite the bakery, a detachment of the Glider Pilot Regiment was also dug in on the open ground. With these new occupations added to those already established, it meant that the entire junction of Paul Krugerstraat and Mariaweg was held by a composite force. Nevertheless, remnants of units were not always together, for a small detachment of the 156th Battalion was also holding houses to the west of A Troop whilst, beyond that again and slightly to the north, the Reconnaissance Squadron's D Troop was based upon its allocated positions on Steijnweg. As a consequence of the new arrangements, therefore, Major Powell of the 156th Parachute Battalion was placed in overall charge of the sector, with the Squadron's A and D Troops under his command.

For A Troop, the day began with another routine patrol to the north of Paul Krugerstraat. The purpose, like that of many similar patrols undertaken in the subsequent days of the battle, was to try to assess the strength and dispositions of any enemy forces that might later be used against them. One common concern was usually to try to locate German mortar positions, with a view to their subsequent destruction, and on that particular morning the task was entrusted to John Stevenson's Section. As patrols went, it was quiet and uneventful, but not entirely lacking in incident, as Alf Webb has every reason to remember: "When we moved out, I was leading scout, and Mr Stevenson told us that we had to go about 300 yards to the north. I remember when we got up there a bit, we went all the back ways through the gardens and up over all those bloody fences. When we got to where we were going, we found nothing, so Mr Stevenson said, 'Right – let's go back,' and I reckoned that since there was nothing doing and I didn't fancy climbing all the fences again, the best way was straight down the road. Some of us did this and we got back without any bother, but just a short time afterwards, when they mounted their attack on us, hundreds of bloody Germans came pouring out of those same houses. We realized then that the bastards could have been watching us all the time going up by the gardens and down by the road, and probably held their fire so as not to give away their positions."

At just about the time that Stevenson's patrol returned, Trooper Fraser also reported in to A Troop HQ. Following the episode in the garden behind the Hotel Vreewijk and a very disturbed night in the Dennenkamp woods, he and his companions had spotted some British troops, early on Thursday morning, in the houses on the west side of Stationsweg. Yellow disc markers were used as a means of mutual identification, following which, Fraser's small party rushed across the road to join the others. Thereafter, he worked his way through back gardens to Squadron HQ and was directed from there to the Paul Krugerstraat positions.

For D Troop, in its more westerly positions, the morning had begun in much the same way, with patrols beyond the occupied houses. At about 0900 hours, Troop HQ was able to act as an observation and listening post for the Division's own light artillery, and effective wireless communication allowed for directions to be given so that fire could be brought to bear on enemy targets. This was especially useful at about eleven o'clock in the morning, when enemy tanks appeared on Steijnweg just north of D Troop HQ. When they were engaged by the artillery, they promptly disappeared.

The final mopping up at the Bridge that morning was a fight to the finish. During the activities of the night, many casualties had been sustained and, by morning, the force was down to less than sixty all ranks. Panzer grenadiers, by then openly walking the streets, hurled stick bombs through the windows of any places thought still to be providing a refuge for British troops. The Germans began this final assault at dawn, killing some, wounding others, forcing small groups, one by one, to surrender, and meeting at times the obstinacy of despair, as when a paratrooper, out of ammunition, appeared from a cellar only to come at them with his knife. Yet, even in those desperate final hours, there were those who, like Freddie Gough, could still squeeze the last vestiges of wry humour from the situation. "I remember," he said, "coming out from hiding, in the morning, to see what was happening, and I met (Major) David Clark of the RASC with some other chaps. David was wounded in both legs, but he wasn't going to surrender if he could help it, so he said, 'Look – would you take me piggy-back?' Of course, I knew I couldn't carry him, but we didn't really get around to that, because I recollect saying, 'Well, David, for a start, take you where?'" Certainly, it was more than just an academic question for, in the course of this curious conversation, Gough could both see and hear the Panzer grenadiers working their way towards them, house by house. For that reason, he wanted to find a better hiding place immediately, and then perhaps work his way to the west to join the rest of the Division. The short discussion with Clark ended, therefore, almost as soon as it had begun when, as Gough recalled, he had to say, with some regret, "Well David, you can't move but I bloody can, so I'm going to try to get back."

As it transpired, he didn't make it. As the searchers systematically worked their way through the houses, Gough tried to burrow his way beneath a pile of logs. It was a left foot sticking out from the heap that gave him away and led to his being dragged out from cover. "I remember," he said, "as I lay on the floor and looked up at those young faces, I just burst out laughing." Taken to a collecting point nearby and divested of his weapons and ammunition, he then saw something that, over the years, remained a cherished memory of the occasion. "The one thing," he said, "that made me feel terribly proud was the sight of the diminutive ammunition pile which they'd made from what they'd taken off us – a few dozen pistol rounds, some ·303 rifle bullets, a couple of PIAT bombs, and that was all. One hears of fighting to the last man and the last round and it's so often a figure of speech. In this case, that's exactly how it was."

Immediately afterwards, Gough was sent for by a young German major, with whom formal salutes were exchanged. The German officer then told him that it was their intention to gather together all the prisoners in the nearby church. "There," he said, "you will sit down with us and we will share our rations with you. They're not very good and you won't like them any more than we do, although I can tell you that we very much like the rations which you get!" It was a gesture of courtesy and respect from one soldier to another, and he concluded by saying, "Now please don't misunderstand, I'm not trying to interrogate you, but I should just like to ask about one thing, because it is obvious that the British airborne troops must have had a great deal of experience in street fighting." "Why do you say that?" interrupted Gough. "Well," said the German major, "many of us, myself included, were for a long time in Russia, where we had much practice in that kind of warfare and, although it puzzles me, I must assume from the way in which they fought, that your men have had that kind of experience as well." "Oh no," replied Major Gough, at his most urbane, "as a matter of fact, this is our first experience – none of us has ever been involved in street fighting before." Recalling the incident, over thirty years later, Gough was still able to remember the look of utter astonishment on the German officer's face and the short exchange which concluded the conversation: "There was a pause, during which time he appeared to be at a complete loss for words, until finally, with great warmth, he said, 'Well, I must congratulate you all the more – your men fought marvellously and cleanly.' 'Thank you, Major,' I replied, 'I'm glad to be able to say exactly the same thing to you.'"

By 0900 hours, it was all over. Right to the end, the Germans had continued to monitor the British wireless transmissions from the Bridge. As the final round-up was made, one last message went out for Divisional HQ. It was never received, and the report was heard only by the German interceptors at 9th SS Panzer Headquarters. It was no more than a brief intimation of the surrender, but with memorable and touching simplicity, it ended with the words, "God Save the King."

Around noon, the first German attack of the day came in on both A and D Troops of the Reconnaissance Squadron at Oosterbeek. It was preceded by a fairly stiff mortaring, in the course of which a bomb landed to the south of the bakery crossroads, on the house which was then occupied by John Stevenson's 1 Section. He, himself, was observing from the attic at the time, and reported later how the explosion took the front part of the roof off and so gave him a better view. "It was then," he continued, "that we got our first sight of Jerry infantry on the move. They were going in and out of the houses on the other side of the crossroads, towards the bakery, which was the largest house in our defensive area. As fast as they came, we knocked them down." Ken Hope of 3 Section, who was on watch in a more northerly position also saw the start of the attack: "I became aware of coal-scuttle helmets, just visible above a ditch flanking the road. Very slowly and cautiously, one German straightened up and stood at the edge of the road. I thought, 'Now, if I give him a quick burst with the Bren, the other bastards will spot the flame from the flash eliminator against the dark background of the store-room.' I preferred using the rifle, and fired two shots. The first one missed, but the second shot struck him somewhere below the waist, one leg crumpled and he fell to the ground. One of his pals then appeared to grasp him by a boot and hauled him into the ditch." Meantime, as Maurice Riches, who was Stevenson's Section Sergeant, recalls, 1 Section then moved across to reinforce the people in the bakery, for it looked as if the Germans were about to mount an attack on it.

The attack was not long delayed, and Vic Taylor* remembers what happened when the enemy reached their positions: "I was in the bakery, at the loading window on the first floor facing north, and I saw seven or eight Germans moving from east to west on the next road up (Joubertweg), so I fired a Bren burst at them. What we hadn't reckoned on was that this would cause flour dust to rise, so we came down to the store room immediately below. My next memory is of a forearm and hand, bearing a stick grenade, appearing just over the top of the window ledge. He threw it, of course, and I let a burst go. I don't know if I hit him or not, but the grenade certainly went off alright and the blast blew the Bren out of my hand. Strangely enough no one was injured but, since things got a bit hot after that, we decided it would be best to carry out a temporary evacuation, so we popped out of the back and got into the house next door." This was the Janssen house, in which Mike Grubb had set up his Troop HQ and, in the circumstances, it was the logical place to move to.

The bakery, nevertheless, was a key position, and Grubb could not simply allow it to be taken and held by the Germans. Almost immediately, therefore, he began to organize the strategy of his counter-attack and, with a part of his small force, slipped over to the south side of the street to consult with Major Powell who, by then, had set up his HQ in the damaged house immediately opposite. Jim Taylor still clearly remembers that, when all was ready, the Troop commander said, "When I blow my whistle, a PIAT will fire and hit that bakery and we will attack." At that stage, they had no certain knowledge as to whether or not the Germans had followed up their earlier success by occupying the bakery but, clearly, there was only one way to find out. The word was given to stand by, the whistle shrilled, the PIAT banged and, under the cover of bakelite smoke grenades, the group took off across the road. Jim Taylor remembers rushing over alongside Ernie Ogden, with Mike Grubb, the Troop commander, in the lead, and being acutely conscious of a considerable amount of firing suddenly breaking out on the other side of the road.

In fact, the firing was coming from their own people for, as a support to the attack, simultaneous covering fire had been arranged under the supervision of Lieutenant Dougie Galbraith, and this was principally organized from the Janssen house, next to the bakery. "The object," as Vic Taylor remembers it, "was to keep the heads of the Germans down whilst the attack was mounted," and that was why he, himself, was positioned on the east, directly facing into the side window of the bakery. As soon as the whistle and the PIAT blast went off, Vic Taylor opened up at his target, and was almost immediately hit by a piece of stick bomb shrapnel which, thanks to his body armour, caused him no injury. At the windows on the north side of Troop HQ, others

* There were two Taylors in A Troop, viz. Corporal Jim "Spud" Taylor, MM and Trooper Vic Taylor. Both were very active during this engagement.

were providing similar support, by firing bursts to prevent any nearby enemy reinforcements from coming to the aid of those who might be in occupation of the objective. "We were facing north-west," recalls Charlie King, "and we could see the Germans, and 'Gunner' (Webb) was firing a Sten out of the same window as I was. I had a rifle, so that when 'Gunner' got down to change magazines, I took over. We had to do it that way, because the window was very small, and eventually Mr Stevenson told me to go out into the back yard with a Sten. It was then that I discovered that the Germans had moved closer, and were actually standing up behind a hedge at the bottom of the garden. From what I could see, they were not more than fifteen yards away, so I opened up on them and came back in when they'd gone."

In the meantime, during this covering action, the small attacking party had completed its sprint across the Paul Krugerstraat and reached the bakery without suffering any casualties. "We arrived at the wall of the bakery with a rush," recollects Jim Taylor, "and Captain Grubb made to lob a 36 grenade through the front window. Unfortunately, when he tried to pull out the pin, the ring came away in his hand, and I'd never before heard such colourful language from him as I did then. It didn't matter, of course, because others in the party put grenades in at all the openings and, after the explosions had taken place, we all rushed in quickly and began to search. I was in the back section of the bakery and although there were no Germans inside, they were very close, because at that point a young German on the outside actually came up to the window and I shot him." Mike Grubb's recollections of this stage of the action are very similar: "I remember," he says, "after we'd put a few grenades in, I rushed upstairs to find that there were no Germans there. At the same time, I could see a couple of them dashing into the house beyond. Unfortunately, I found my Sten momentarily jammed, causing a fractional delay in the time taken to open up, so whether I hit them or not I don't know."

As the whitish-yellow smoke wafted over the buildings, the bang of grenade and the rattle of machine-gun fire built up around the area of the crossroads. Whether the Germans were occupying the bakery or not it is no longer possible to say, but the evidence would seem to indicate that they probably were and that they evacuated the building just before the attack came in, perhaps at the point of the PIAT bomb explosion. Certainly, there were many indications that the enemy was present in force, pressing constantly on the precariously held British positions for, within minutes of breaking off their previous attack, they were again coming in on the back garden of the next-door house. Jimmy Bruce clearly remembers that this was an attack of greater force than the previous one: "I was at an upstairs window with a sniper's rifle, and as they came through a hole in the back fence, I was potting them off one by one." Downstairs, Charlie King was also involved, and once more took his Sten out to the back door, under Alf Webb's covering fire. This time, he was not so lucky. "I don't remember if I fired my Sten or not," says King, "because almost right away I got a stick grenade thrown at me and was wounded in the shoulder. All I remember after that was 'Feekie' Langan and Willie Fraser running out to pull me back inside." King was then taken down to the cellar of the house, where Sergeant Riches dressed the wound and left him in the care of the Dutch people who were sheltering there.

In the next-door cellar of the bakery itself, the members of the Crum family were also finding what shelter they could from the engagement that was going on upstairs. They had moved down into the cellar on the Tuesday and, by the time of the attack, had been joined by a group of neighbours called Wildeman. The Wildeman's own cellar was largely a wooden structure and they preferred the relative safety of the bakery's basement which was of stone. Also sheltering were two old ladies and two nurses, making a total of fourteen. Jo Crum-Bloemink, married only two years before, still recalls how she felt as the British occupied her house and used what they could find to barricade the windows. "We were very pleased to welcome the British soldiers," she says, "but we were also very worried about damage, and at first we said, 'Oh – think of the furniture!' Two days later, we no longer said that – it didn't matter any more." For the small Dutch group, the war, which till then had meant only dreary and oppressive German occupation, had suddenly taken on a new dimension. But from their situation in the cellar they had no clear idea about what was happening, for overhead and outside, it was just one sustained, confused and frightening series of bomb explosions, small-arms fire and running feet, not unlike the impression of hearing the sound-track of a film without seeing the picture.

In the lull which followed, those who had reoccupied the bakery took up fresh defensive positions inside, and Jim Taylor remembers how, during that time, a German medical orderly appeared on the scene to treat an injured comrade who was lying on the Mariaweg. "He walked calmly down the road from the north," says Taylor, "came right up to the bakery window where I was and stopped. Then he first looked down at the man I'd shot, next through the window at me, and after that deliberately turned his back and went on to attend to the injured man. In the circumstances, I had to admire his coolness."

Other members of the Troop then ran into the bakery to help consolidate the position, one of whom was Jim Taylor's Section officer, Dougie Galbraith. Both he and Taylor were twenty-two years of age, Galbraith the senior by only four months, and between them a bond of mutual trust and respect had already been established over the short period of time that they had known each other. Physically, they were quite different. Taylor, the Londoner, was fair-haired and slim, whilst Galbraith, the Scot from Cambuslang, was dark and heavily built. Their personalities were also to an extent in contrast, with Taylor very much the quieter of the two, but both had many attributes in common, not the least of those being intelligence, resourcefulness and a decisive quality in action that stamped each with the mark of the natural-born soldier. An additional quality which they possessed in common was a brand of single-minded determination, although there were occasions when this could have its drawbacks. In this connection, a minor episode from the North African period was later to be remembered with considerable amusement by Freddie Gough. At the time it arose from the arrangement whereby Taylor had been detailed to act as Galbraith's batman, a situation which he did not in the least relish. The result was that when Galbraith gave Taylor his boots to clean he got an emphatic refusal. With the lieutenant's case hinging upon his privileges as an officer and the trooper's upon the somewhat flimsier philosophical basis of the dignity of man, neither would budge from his position. It was a trivial matter but, however so, the issue was still clearly one of failure to comply with an order. Taylor was, accordingly, charged with this as well as a breach of Section 49 of King's Regulations, i.e. "conduct prejudicial to good order and military discipline", tried, found guilty and sentenced. Less than forty-eight hours later came the signal for the start of the Taranto operation and the Squadron was briefed to go. Unfortunately, since Taylor was under sentence, it meant that he would have to be left behind, and yet his potential quality as a soldier made it, in Gough's view, unthinkable that this should be allowed to happen. As it transpired, in the general activity surrounding the departure for southern Italy, the commanding officer somehow managed to "lose" the papers relevant to the case. As far as the British army was concerned, this meant that not only had the trial, charge and sentence never occurred, but Taylor had never even in the first place demurred at the idea of cleaning Galbraith's boots! It was characteristic of the unorthodox Freddie Gough that he should have found such an unmilitary and Gilbertian solution to the problem of reversing one of his own decisions, and both Galbraith and Taylor were equally satisfied with such an equitable outcome. Thereafter, in an engagement against the 1st German Parachute Battalion in the south of Italy, each acquired a shared experience in battle upon which to build the lasting respect and trust which one good soldier has for another. It was in that action on a winding road by the hillside village of San Basilio that Dougie Galbraith gained a "Mentioned in Despatches" whilst, for exemplary courage in the face of the enemy, Taylor, on Galbraith's own recommendation, won the Military Medal and that rare honour of immediate promotion in the field.

As the A Troop reinforcements arrived at the bakery, Galbraith sought Taylor out, having already decided that the two of them should work together and take care of the loading window on the upper floor at the back. Galbraith was attracted to the idea, because it appeared to offer the best vantage point for dealing with the Germans should they return to the attack. As events were to prove, it was a correct judgment, and the opportunities for action which Dougie Galbraith anticipated certainly did follow. The story is perhaps best told in Jim Taylor's own words: "I remember when he'd decided what we would do, Dougie shouted, 'Up the ladder!', so I got up it with the Bren, into a room with sacks of flour all round the walls and a clear space in the centre. I'd only just set foot there but, as I turned my head for a fraction I was just in time to see a German stick grenade come through the loading window. It landed in the centre of the room and, as it was smoking, I realized that it had been pulled. I took a fast dive behind the flour sacks and I remember thinking about how most of my body was in, but my legs were still sticking out and unprotected. Seconds later, there was an almighty bang and the whole place was covered in clouds of white flour. I staggered to the opening in the floor, against which the top end of the ladder was leaning, but it was difficult to see properly on account of all the white dust, so the next thing was that I fell through it, right on top of Dougie Galbraith who immediately started to swear. I wasn't hurt, so right away he snapped out the order, 'Up again!' and this time followed close behind me. We had no sooner come out of the trap on to the floor, when the same thing happened again – in came another grenade. This time, I didn't make for the flour sacks, but back towards the hole. Dougie reached it first, got through, and once more I fell on top of him. Obviously it was getting to be a habit and, predictably, he swore again, quite colourfully. Fortunately, we both managed to get sufficiently far down the ladder before it went off. It's funny, but the thing that still sticks most vividly in my memory is the smell of that second grenade, for it wasn't the familiar cordite at all, but something much more pungent."

"By then, all I wanted to do was get after that German, because it was obvious that he was standing close to the wall, just below the loading window, throwing these things in at us. I was all set to go out of the door to fix him, and I was so flaming mad that I remember 'Gunner' had to hold me down because by then, of course, there were dozens of Germans milling about out there. As it turned out, there wasn't any need, for Dougie had a much better idea. Acting on this, we stole very carefully up the ladder again, and crept over to the window, not making a sound. Dougie then took the pin out of a grenade, grinned at me and let it sizzle in his hand for three seconds before dropping it on the German standing below. The timing was just right, for it must have gone off just as it reached the ground. I remember that he was very good at this, the idea being to reduce the time interval between the release of the bomb and the explosion. It meant that there was no chance of a smart German picking it up and throwing it back at you!"

But the despatch of one SS Panzer grenadier, spectacular as his exit must undoubtedly have been, was no end of the matter, for the enemy was still very much in strength outside. When the next onslaught came in, such was the ferocity of the attack that it came as no surprise to the men inside to realize that the bakery had caught fire. Kees Crum, too, still recalls the moment when a British soldier ran down to the cellar shouting a warning to them to get out and how, surprizingly, the firing on both sides stopped so that the civilians could leave. Whatever caused the fire is not known – incendiary bullets, grenades, mortar bombs are all possibilities – but it developed to such an extent that the A Troop defenders were again forced to withdraw to the house next door. Characteristically, Dougie Galbraith was one of the last to leave the bakery, and, together with Henry Venes, Jim Taylor and 'Gunner' Webb, organized a rearguard to allow the others to get clear before they themselves broke for cover. Webb remembers that it was at that point that there was considerable deployment of German infantry, all of which was moving towards them on the front as well as the flanks. "I was on one side of the road," he says, "and 'Spud' was on the other, and I was looking across at what was happening just beyond him. I remember shouting across to him, 'They're coming down behind you, f- - - - - - hundreds of them, and him shouting back, 'Watch your own side – they're coming round behind you too.'"

One of the strange paradoxes of urban warfare is the way in which the normal mundane activities of ordinary living can often appear strangely out of place amidst the upheaval of conflict in which an unpredictable series of events suddenly transforms the lives of those inadvertently caught up in affairs over which they have neither influence nor control. So it was that when the hazardous rearguard action was concluded and the four had joined their comrades in the Janssen house, next door to the bakery, they found a lady in the kitchen, preparing vegetables, for all the world as if her family was due home at any moment from school or work, in time for the midday meal. Jim Taylor also recalls that as she worked, a small boy kept coming round to offer sweets to the soldiers, and how concerned they were that he should stay away from the windows. In the circumstances, it was probably the most natural thing in the world for the Dutch housewife to try to make some kind of a meal for her hungry family, but for the British soldiers the incongruity of those glimpses of domesticity was all the keener by contrast with what was happening all around.

Almost simultaneously with the attack on the A Troop positions, came an assault on D Troop's area to the north-west. It also came in from the north, and was probably all of a piece with the attack on Mike Grubb's Troop. The brunt was taken by 10 and 11 Sections, who were holding the more northerly positions, and it was led by an armoured troop carrier with supporting infantry. John Marshall still remembers how it all began with an outburst of shooting from between his own house and the one held by Lieutenant Hodge. "It was obvious that they were bringing in quite a strong attack," he recalls, "for there was a great deal of noise all around us. As it developed, the shooting from Bill's house stopped and, since that was my flank, I switched myself and three other chaps round from the road to the back of the house. I remember that what seemed to be mortar fire then came down, and when that stopped I went out into the garden in order to try and make out what the hell was going on. I know that Trooper Williams was with me and two others, and as I went forward I said, 'Cover me', but the next second, something exploded – probably a hand grenade – and I saw that my hand was dangling off. I dropped the Schmeisser I was using, just as a bullet went through my other arm and something hit my face. I then crawled back into the house and got under the sink in the kitchen. What happened to the others I don't know, but there were some chaps in the house, and I said to them, 'Get to bloody hell out of it' – I can remember it to this day – and they argued, so I said, 'Don't you know an order when you get one – get the hell out of it, back to Troop HQ' – and they did."

Just how many managed this, however, is not clear, for the available evidence would seem to indicate that only one got back. Trooper Jeffrey Williams, the man whom John Marshall remembers as accompanying him out of the back door, can still recall the Germans coming over the garden wall and how he, himself, was shot in the left shoulder and back and taken prisoner with about four others. Bert Pegnall, who was one of those, recollects how Marshall, "his hand hanging by a small piece of flesh," called upon Trooper Smith to leave the house and get on the best way he could. So it would seem that the argument which Marshall had was probably with Smith, because he appears to have been the only one of the group not injured and there is evidence that he subsequently fought with considerable courage along with the remnants of D Troop at their HQ on the next crossroads south.

Marshall, meantime, waited for a time and then walked outside. By then it was all over for his own as well for Hodge's section. "I staggered out of the house," he says, "and there were some Jerries there. Bill was there too, and he said, 'Oh! Look what you've done to my friend!' and that was the exact point at which I passed out." The captured men were then taken away. Those who could walk acted as stretcher bearers for the others; using whatever they could improvize for the purpose. "They carried me on an old deck chair," recalls Pegnall, who had a bullet enter his chest and exit through the top of his shoulder. John Marshall has a similar recollection of being laid on a door in the dark. "With my own people carrying me," he says, "I remember just being conscious enough to see some Dutch people being marched off by Gestapo men and asking what it was all about, and people being rather hushed and awed." As a prisoner-of-war, Marshall was then taken to the hospital at Apeldoorn, where his right hand was finally amputated.

Elsewhere on the edges of the newly formed and precariously held British perimeter, ferocious German attacks came in throughout the day. On the west side, the 1st Battalion of the Border Regiment found itself under severe pressure from 0600 hours on, and had to have the support of the 1st Light Regiment Royal Artillery to break up the attacks. At nine o'clock in the morning, two of its companies were engaged and, whilst one successfully "brewed-up" three enemy tanks, the other was overrun and temporarily disintegrated. Losses were considerable, and it was in consequence of this that the Squadron was directed by Division to send the 3-inch mortar element of its Support Troop to help out. With the death of John Christie on the previous day, the Troop was without an officer, so the two mortars and their crews were taken to the 1st Border Regiment's positions, in the middle of the afternoon, by Sergeant McCreedie. It was quite coincidental but not inappropriate that several of the Reconnaissance men who were involved in this move notably Troopers Heyworth and Serginson, had themselves undergone previous service with the Border Regiment.

Down by Oosterbeek Laag church, what came to be called "Lonsdale Force" was also heavily engaged that day at what was probably the most critical position of all. Following the massive defeats on the Tuesday morning attempt to break through to the Bridge, Major Lonsdale, second-in-command of the 11th Parachute Battalion, had grouped the remnants of his own regiment with those of the 1st and 3rd Parachute Battalions and the 2nd Battalion of the South Staffordshires, and taken up defensive positions near the river by the church. It was an area which the Germans particularly wanted to overrun, since by doing so they would completely surround what remained of the Division and effectively cut off any line of communication across the river, either for the arrival of reinforcements or for possible British withdrawal. For that reason, it would be true to say that, in many respects, Lonsdale was the man who, perhaps more than any other, helped ultimately to save the survivors of the 1st British Airborne Division, as a consequence of the tenacity with which he and his men fought to keep open the access to the river. Indeed, it was on the previous day that, as part of Lonsdale's force, Sergeant Baskeyfield of the 2nd South Staffordshires had won a posthumous Victoria Cross for his superb courage in handling a 6-pounder gun against German armour at the foot of Acacialaan.

Lonsdale's small area of defence was almost the entire length of the perimeter away from the Reconnaissance Squadron's position yet, surprizingly, there were three Squadron members with him, Troopers Chadwick and White and Craftsman York of Mottola fame. This was because they had earlier been directed to take wounded men by jeep from the area of Oosterbeek cross-roads down to the dressing station by the church. The reason for the decision is not clear, but it was probably in some way connected with the increasing congestion in the regimental aid post at Divisional HQ, a situation later highlighted in the official ADMS report. The Reconnaissance jeep went down by Hoofdlaan and, on nearing its objective, had to run a gauntlet of German machine-gun fire from the houses opposite the church. Once arrived, they took the wounded into Mevrouw Kate A. ter Horst's house, which was being used as a dressing station and throughout which, wounded British soldiers lay in every room, corridor and landing. Having delivered their wounded safely into the hands of the medics, the three Squadron men were then absorbed into Lonsdale's force. It was a type of decision that was being increasingly made, as units were more and more fragmented and local commanders had to do their best to organize what forces were available to them.

At that point, Lonsdale was down to only 80 men and, as he was anticipating a major German attack in order to try to cut the British off from the river, he needed all the help he could get. Shortly afterwards, when he decided to address the whole of his tired and depleted force, the three Reconnaissance men had the privilege of witnessing one of the most moving and dramatic episodes in the entire Arnhem action. It took place within Oosterbeek Laag Church, itself, where Lonsdale's men were assembled. General Urquhart's own story of the battle contains perhaps the best account of the memorable scene which followed: "Lonsdale now appeared, his hands in bandages. He looked down at the strained and desperate faces as he climbed the steps to the pulpit . . . Suddenly the place was hushed as Lonsdale, his hands gripping the edge of the pulpit, began: 'You know as well as I do there are a lot of bloody Germans coming at us. Well, all we can do is to stay here and hang on in the hope that somebody catches us up. We must fight for our lives and stick together.' From the distance came the rumble of heavy guns and out-side the shattered windows the sky was lit with the pyrotechnics of battle. Above Lonsdale and beyond the damaged organ loft some rafters hung loose. The troops, wearied with fatigue, listened attentively, their blackened faces upturned. 'We've fought the Germans before – in North Africa, Sicily, Italy. They weren't good enough for us then, and they're bloody well not good enough for us now. They're up against the finest soldiers in the world. An hour from now, you will take up defensive positions north of the road outside. Make certain you dig in well and that your weapons and ammo are in good order. We are getting short of ammo so, when you shoot, you shoot to kill. Good luck to you all.'"*

At 1840 hours in the evening, the expected attack came in. It was heavy, but it was held by Lonsdale's men and the British then counter-attacked. During this action, "Chalky" White remembers that he was on the south side of the main road, in the fringe of trees to the west of the Church. It was there that, at the height of the action, he was shot. He felt his leg go numb and,

* R. E. Urquhart: Arnhem, pp. 97–8.

since he was then unable to keep up with the others, had to lie quite still in his exposed position, listening to the spiteful zipping of the nearby German machine-guns and wondering when one of the gunners was going to put a burst into him. As it happened, he was lucky to escape any further injury and lay there throughout the twilight until darkness came. Then came the slow crawl across the road and the painful agonizing journey all the way back up the hill to Divisional HQ. It was not much more than two-thirds of a mile but, in the circumstances, it felt ten times as long, and it took him several hours to get there. By then, of course, he had lost touch with York and Chadwick and never saw them again. Having reported in, White was treated for a bullet wound in the shin and shrapnel fragments in his leg and side. He refused to remain in the medical aid post, and was able to report in to Squadron HQ on the following day, where he joined Trooper Alan Samm in a slit trench in the field just west of Oranjeweg.

Immediately to the east of the Divisional HQ area, just beyond Oosterbeek crossroads, the day was also marked by hard fighting, as what was left of the 10th Parachute Battalion held off infantry and armour from the east. There, preliminary mortaring and shelling was followed by attacks of such ferocity that the positions were ultimately completely overrun, and the remaining officers of the regiment killed or wounded. Amongst them was the commanding officer, Lieutenant-Colonel Kenneth Smyth, who was mortally wounded. The astonishing sequel was that, even after all this had taken place, survivors crawled back into the wreckage and rubble of two ruined buildings on the crossroads and held out for a further forty-eight hours.

To the north, that day, fierce attacks also came in on the positions held by the 7th Battalion of the King's Own Scottish Borderers. These were particularly exposed, as they lay a few hundred yards beyond the Squadron's D Troop positions, and enemy pressure which began in the morning built up gradually throughout the day. The location of the Borderers was on the Graaf van Rechterenweg, in the garden and adjacent grounds of the Hotel Dreyeroord, a large rambling building which, because of its exterior appearance, had been simply designated as "The White House". At about 1630 hours, a heavy mortaring took place, followed by an infantry attack by SS Panzer grenadiers. Repeating the pattern that had already proved successful in the earlier defence of Ginkel Heath, Lieutenant-Colonel Payton-Reid once more ordered his men to fix bayonets and, himself leading the charge, routed the enemy from the vicinity. As he was later to remark, with a certain grim satisfaction, "They would not stand to the bayonet and made no attempt to fight us." The determination and ferocity of the Borderers' counter-attack inflicted heavy casualties on the enemy, but at a cost to its own meagre force. One result of this was that it was erroneously reported that the remnants of Payton-Reid's Battalion had finally been wiped out. In fact, it was the development of a gap of 400 yards between them and members of the 21st Independent Parachute Company that led to the rumour. At the time, however, this was not known, and, since there was no radio contact, the Reconnaissance Squadron was asked to undertake a foot "recce" in order to check on the situation.

The job was given to A Troop, and Captain Grubb detailed Lieutenant Graham Wadsworth, Sergeant Ray Hewer and Trooper Ken Hope to carry it out. Short as it undoubtedly was in terms of distance, the assignment was manifestly fraught with potential hazard, as there was no sure knowledge of the strength of the enemy, either in the intervening built-up area or at what was assumed to be the former KOSB positions. What was certain was that the perimeter had been increasingly infiltrated during the course of the day, and many of the houses between A Troop's positions at the bakery and those assigned to the Borderers were likely to contain enemy soldiers. For the three concerned, it was a disquieting thought.

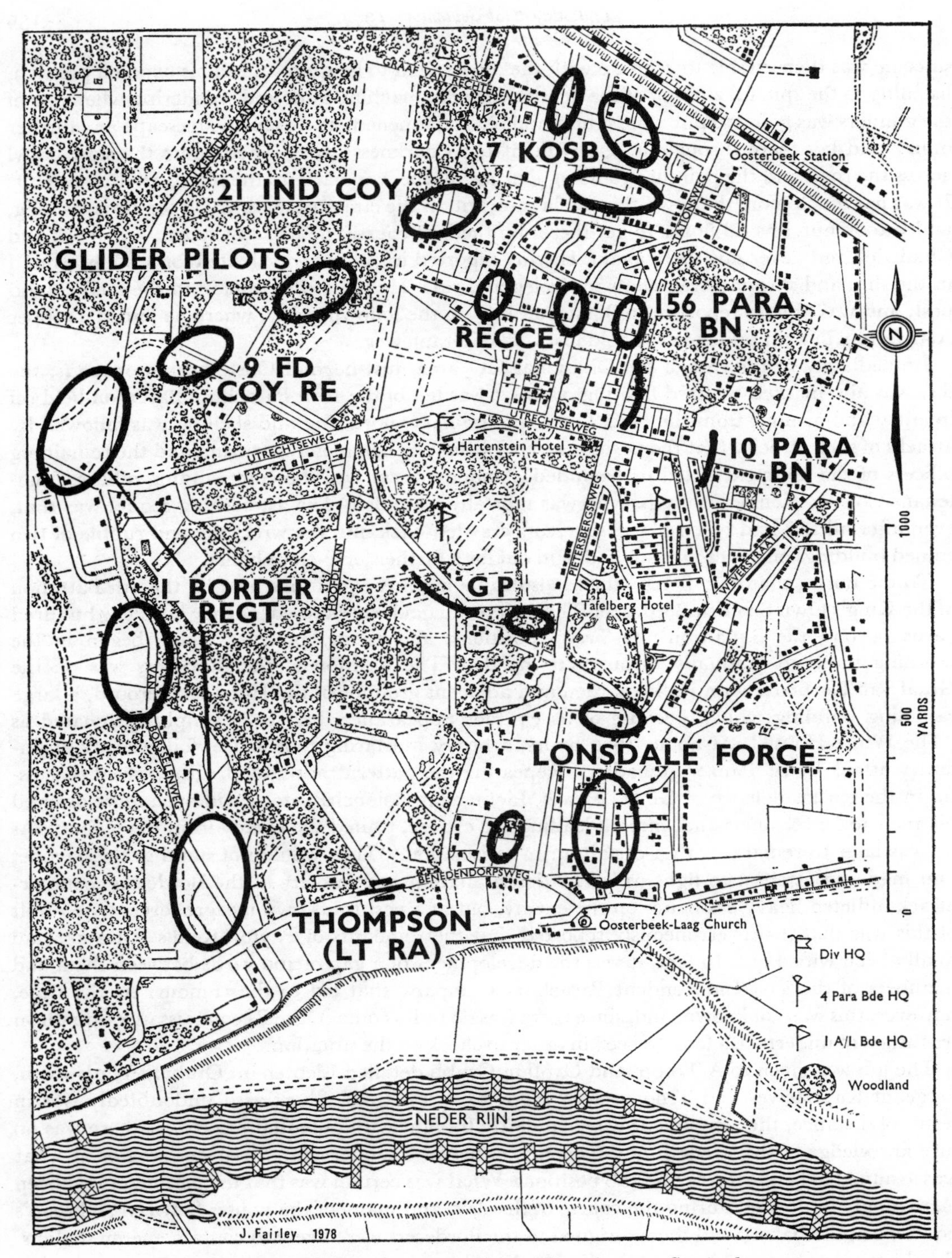

Map 10 Divisional Perimeter positions: Thursday 21st September 1944

Hope, then only 19 years of age, has recollections of that journey that are amongst the most vivid of all his memories of Arnhem. "We began our 'leap-frog' progression as we made our way from house to house, passing through gardens, orchards or vegetable patches. Sometimes the officer, then the sergeant or myself would be in the lead. At one point, we came upon the lifeless body of a powerfully-built German lying face down, the rim of his helmet pressed into the earth. Beyond him was a narrow passage-way between houses, leading to a road. I entered cautiously, reached the end wall and looked left and right, up and down the street. A few yards to my right, and abandoned in the middle of the road, was a supply container, festooned with rigging lines and parachute. Suddenly, there was the shattering of glass at the bedroom window of a house directly opposite. For a second I stood mesmerized at the sight of a grenade lying near the base of the wall. We scrambled for cover just as it exploded and the wall took the force of the blast. Lieutenant Wadsworth made a quick appreciation and rapped out an order. He and Sergeant Hewer opened fire with their Stens from the left of our cover, whilst I sprang into the mouth of the alleyway and opened fire with the Bren. For a few brief seconds, a torrent of fire poured at the upper windows from the three guns. Glass, woodwork and wood frames were splintered and shattered, and the fire was not returned. We resumed our patrol."

Eventually, the group cautiously progressed to the edge of the wooded area, which was the estate of Ommershof, and within which were the slit trenches that constituted the first perimeter positions of the 21st Independent Parachute Company. They had finished up a little too far to the west, but were guided safely to the KOSB lines by Lance-Corporal Barclay of the 21st Company. This was done to the accompaniment of the "crump" and "whump" of mortar and shell fire, because the attack on this sector, which had gone on all day, was still being sustained, and the A Troop men had arrived at a time when it had reached a considerable level of ferocity. "I remember," says Hope, "that Lieutenant Wadsworth approached Lieutenant-Colonel Payton-Reid, whilst I dropped into a fairly deep, sandy hole, closed my eyes and attempted to take a snooze. The noise was deafening, a constant clattering of machine-guns and the roar of exploding mortars and shells. 'Are you all right Hope?' asked a voice. I opened my eyes to see Lieutenant Wadsworth standing on the rim of my foxhole. 'Yes sir, I'm fine,' I replied. 'In that case, do you mind if I join you,' he said, 'it's a bit on the hot side up here?'"

The barrage continued for some time after that and, until it died down, the two sat facing each other, with their knees together, sharing what was then their most precious joint possession – the temporary lease of a little hole in the ground. At the first obvious lull, they seized the opportunity to make a move and set off back to their own unit lines. This time, with an increased awareness of the local topography, their progress was swifter than it had been on the outward journey, although it was not lacking in its diverting moments. "There was one occasion," recalls Hope, "when the three of us dived into the black earth of a vegetable garden. Clusters of mortar bombs were passing from the east into the perimeter defences. I remember looking up and watching with amazement as scores of the projectiles were simultaneously visible against the grey sky. The German supply of ammunition was inexhaustible."

Of all the reconnaissance tasks undertaken by the Squadron in the course of the operation, this was recognized as one of the most successful, for Grubb's subsequent interrogation of Wadsworth provided invaluable information for a Divisional "O" group held that evening. It was then that the decision was made to pull back on the northern tip of the perimeter, by moving the 7th Battalion King's Own Scottish Borderers towards the south-west and relocating them in the area at the west end of Bothaweg and Hartenweg, in contact with Glider Pilots at one side and D Troop of the Reconnaissance Squadron at the other. As part of this constriction, 21st Independent Parachute Company was to be placed under Brigadier Hackett's command, and take up new positions in the area from Oosterbeek crossroads, down Pietersbergseweg, to just beyond the dressing station at the Hotel Tafelberg. The Reconnaissance groups in the perimeter were also, for the first time to come under Hackett. Amongst other things, it was this particular sortie to the KOSB lines that earned Graham Wadsworth a well-merited American Bronze Star.

In the meantime, the pressure on the bakery crossroads had eased, although the Germans had withdrawn to sniping positions and there was sporadic firing from the north-west. Jim Taylor recollects how they tried to deal with this change in German tactics: "We put an old blanket round the head of a broom and held it up to try to draw, and so locate, the German firing. First of all, Ernie Ogden was clipped by a bullet in the neck, so we put up the broom again and, in return, received a burst which sprayed into the room and smashed the wardrobe mirror. At this rate, we weren't making much progress, so we sent 'Daisy' Houghton downstairs to watch from one of the lower windows, whilst we stuck the broom and blanket up again. There was another burst from outside, but no response from our look-out below, so we tried again, although by then the blanket was looking a bit the worse for wear. This time, the machine-gun burst thumped into the window brickwork, so we stopped and went downstairs to discover why we hadn't heard from 'Daisy'. We found him on the look-out, alright, but he was keeping watch out of the wrong window!"

In the course of that afternoon, resupply arrived in four waves. At the time, David Allsop recorded a number of impressions – of the pleading of men standing in the grounds of the Hartenstein, trying to signal to the planes above, of Verey lights chasing each other up into the sky, of the way in which, despite temporary relief from mortar and machine-gun fire, it brought the alternative hazard of falling "ack-ack" flak. One squadron casualty was accounted for in this way for, as he looked skywards towards the planes, Trooper Smith of HQ Troop was badly wounded in the eye by a piece of shrapnel.

The first wave came in at 1245 hours, but was badly shot up by ME 109's, so that most of the stuff landed beyond the limits of the defensive area. Fighters and anti-aircraft guns were also brought to bear upon later waves, and it is estimated that about fifty-two per cent of the force was destroyed or damaged. The last wave, which flew over the drop point just to the north of the Hartenstein, was probably the most successful of all yet, despite that, most fell into the German hands. By the Thursday, of course, success could only be measured in relative terms, since even the limited amount of supplies that did come into the British lines could no longer easily be recovered, largely owing to the gradual loss or destruction of recovery jeeps and trailers. Responsibility for the collection of dropped supplies and their centralization at Divisional HQ was still that of RASC personnel, but the struggle had taken such a turn that independent initiative had already come to be generally regarded as acceptable.

On that day, some stores did land in the gardens and streets all around the defensive area, and it is hardly surprizing that a certain amount of "foraging" was carried out by individual units. Gathering it in, could be a hazardous business as, in a number of cases, it became apparent that the Germans had the panniers under observation. Furthermore, those who risked their necks to collect found themselves in much the same position that they would have been had they been trying for the "lucky dip" at the fairground. A Troop, for example, did secure some useable ammunition in this way, but Alan Pascal's Section of D Troop was not quite so fortunate. Seeing a container bearing ammunition markings, which had landed just outside the house, one of

Pascal's men managed to crawl out to it and succeeded in attaching a length of strong string. It was then drawn in very slowly and carefully, only to be found to contain artillery shells! Perhaps, however, the greatest let-down of all was that experienced by some of the HQ personnel, of whom Ray Evans was one: "We watched this hamper land about fifty yards in front of our slit trench, in the middle of the field and, after dark, Corporal Edgington and myself crawled out and fetched it in. I remember we were so excited at the prospect that it might contain food that, instead of unbuckling the strong leather straps, we cut through them with our knives, only to discover that it was full of red berets!" Nearby, Tom Collier organized the recovery of a similar hamper which was found to contain an assortment of crowns, pips, chevrons and cap badges. Obviously both were part of the same batch of stores and, as Captain David Allsop wryly recorded afterwards in the official diary, "a sight to gladden a Quartermaster's heart!"

Stories of this kind are often told today, at airborne gatherings and, invariably, they raise a laugh. At the same time, one cannot help thinking that this one has its disquieting features, for it is incomprehensible to contemplate that there were those who knowingly risked the lives of the men in the supply planes, subjecting them to all the ferocity of German "ack-ack" fire, in order that they might deliver loads of haberdashery to the men in the Oosterbeek trenches! What is even more difficult to comprehend is why such rubbish was ever sent at all, at a stage in the battle when it must have been apparent that so much had gone wrong and that the real urgent needs were not for pips, chevrons and red berets, but for food, water and medical supplies. As a demonstration of bureaucratic inflexibility, it could hardly have been bettered. Perhaps, indeed, one of the few people to experience satisfaction with the afternoon's pickings was Kees Crum of the bakery at 23 Paul Krugerstraat. For years, after the war, the Crum family used a British airborne resupply hamper, which finished up that day in their own back garden, in order to carry the bread on delivery rounds to their customers in Oosterbeek.

Some supplies, of course, were delivered "internally" through more orthodox channels for, in the course of that afternoon, Lieutenants Lickerish and Collier from Squadron HQ took fresh stocks of ammunition up to the forward positions, together with a much-welcomed replacement 38 set. This was one of the little 13-pound infantry man-pack R/T sets, which regimental signallers, accustomed as they were to the more elaborate 22, tended to regard as a toy. Ironically, it was the 22's which so demonstrably displayed their inadequacy at Oosterbeek, and the short-range 38's which proved, by contrast, to be the more successful. Furthermore, particularly in street-fighting conditions, where close proximity to the enemy was a common occurrence, there was much to be said for the 38 set's throat microphone, which allowed for clear vocal transmission to be made, almost in a whisper.

It was, indeed, an inability to raise its northern positions further up Steijnweg, on what had till then been a perfectly reliable 38 set link, that first gave D Troop HQ an inkling that something was wrong. They had heard the firing, but it was difficult to distinguish it from the rest of the noise that was going on, and it was only after it was over that the worst fears were confirmed. For a Troop which, from the outset, had never been at full strength, it was particularly bad news. Captain Park, therefore, asked Sergeant Bentall to undertake a careful reconnaissance and report back on the situation. Bentall took Trooper Walker with him, and they crept through the gardens in the darkness up to the positions formerly occupied by the men of Marshall's and Hodge's Sections. The first house appeared to be empty but, once inside, they could hear German voices from some of the rooms, and they retreated cautiously to the outside. From there it was possible to peer into the broken top lights of the cellar and make out the forms of women and children so, without arousing alarm, they dropped in for a few minutes in order to try to discover what had happened to their comrades. The return journey was then undertaken without mishap.

About an hour later, Captain Park sent word round to all groups to the effect that a detachment of enemy armour and infantry appeared to be moving in on them from the north-west and that they had to be prepared for another attack, this time launched under the cover of darkness. "The circus," as Bentall later described it, arrived at the Steijnweg/Paul Krugerstraat crossroads at 2100 hours, and consisted of one tank, a self-propelled gun, a half-track troop carrier and something like forty supporting infantrymen. To a force of the size of John Park's, this was overwhelming opposition, and the order was given to do nothing unless the enemy attempted to enter the houses; no one was to fire, but men were to be posted in the darkness at each door and window. For a very uneasy half-hour, they waited in silence as the Germans milled around on the crossroads. "They kicked the doors and shouted," says Bentall, "but did not try to enter. Then, as a parting gesture, the self-propelled gun fired one round at our house and hit the upper part. There were no casualties." To the relief of the defenders, the Germans then withdrew, and the night ended with yet another barrage of mortaring. Clearly, the enemy had suspected the presence of the British but was either uncertain or unwilling to commit himself to a night attack against unknown odds. Bob Thomson, who was in Alan Pascal's Section, recollects quite well this oddly repeated aspect of German tactics: "They never seemed to have enough supporting infantry to press home their attacks with the self-propelled guns. As a result, the gun would come to the crossroads, fire a few shots and then retreat. If we fired back, it would move off again and perhaps try coming at us from one of the other roads in the vicinity."

By the end of the day, several houses in the D Troop area were burning, and across the back gardens, the men could also see the flames from the bakery roof at the east end of Paul Krugerstraat. Water was also becoming a problem, as there was none in the houses and, although it was still available from simple pumps situated at various points in the streets, collecting it could be a hazardous business. One of the larger pumps was in the Paul Krugerstraat, about 150 yards west of the Mariaweg junction, and Kees Crum remembers how, for about half an hour each evening, the Germans would stop shooting, in order to allow the Dutch civilians to emerge from their cellars and queue up at it for the precious water. At the same time, there was no question of the besieged British soldiers being allowed to do this, and so they had to take their chance in the darkness, with the slightest noise likely to bring a burst of enemy fire straight on to the pump. Naturally, thoughts frequently turned to ways of getting around the problem, and the story is told of how, that night, Henry Venes actually went out and queued up with the Dutch civilians during the half-hour lull. He had attired himself in some civilian clothes over the top of his uniform, and all went well until he was hurrying back along the Paul Krugerstraat with the precious cargo. Unfortunately, he had forgotten about his boots and khaki gaiters which were revealed rather prominently below the hem of the coat. As a result, he was fired on, and had to make a run for it over the last few yards. He arrived back unscathed, but with a punctured bucket from which the water soon disappeared into the ground.

As the casualties mounted, the already depleted medical services came under increasing strain. During the Thursday, there was particular concern about the congested conditions in the Divisional HQ regimental aid post, and it was felt that the wounded would have little chance of survival in the event of it catching fire. To minimize the danger, therefore, two things were done. First, safe conduct was obtained for the removal of wounded to the dressing stations then in

German hands, and, secondly, instructions were issued for an additional building to be opened up as a regimental aid post for the less badly wounded. It was agreed that this should be placed in the care of Douglas Swinscow, and be located in an imposing house of red brick with a thatched roof, situated on the west side of the Hoofdlaan at its junction with van Lennepweg. It was one of the largest houses in the vicinity, and thus provided as much space as it was possible to get in one unit. From the outset, Swinscow had little in the way of either medical equipment or supplies and, unfortunately, all of that disappeared when his jeep and trailer were stolen from outside the aid post, not long after he had set himself up. Fortunately, the house had previously had a medical unit in it, and some few supplies had been left behind, although they were not in any way sufficient to make up for the loss.

Over the next few days, he attended to those who were brought to him to receive what little aid could be given. Throughout that time, the house, situated as it was between Divisional HQ and the heavily pressed positions of the 1st Border Regiment, was particularly vulnerable, and it was hardly surprizing that it was not long before it was hit. The main impact was taken by the roof, the thatching of which remained intact, even although it was left hanging down, in a grotesque manner, into the house itself. Other hits followed, and it was in this particular aid post that Father Benson, Chaplain to 181st Airlanding Field Ambulance, was mortally wounded as a result of shell fire which badly damaged the ground floor area. It was a sad loss, and Douglas Swinscow still remembers him today as "a most charming and gallant man."

The adjacent three-storeyed house, called "Gelders Hof", located on the Utrechtseweg junction was also a medical centre, under the care of Captain Graham Jones. Shortly after his own aid post had been hit, Swinscow went there to try to get some medical supplies. Whilst engaged in this, he was, himself, wounded for a second time and, in consequence of a shell blast, suffered haemorrhaging of the lungs as well as concussion. These injuries put him out of action for something like twelve hours.

Elsewhere, throughout the day, the lost men of the Squadron had been trying to rejoin their comrades. John Pow of A Troop, who had hidden all night in the Dennenkamp woods after the Wednesday fight at Oosterbeek Station, was one of those who set out that Thursday morning to try to get back. He joined up with a small group of men from another unit, and they worked their way down through the woods to the Oosterbeek crossroads. Unfortunately, such was their degree of disorientation that, instead of striking out west as Fraser had done, they crossed straight over the junction, by-passed Divisional HQ by only a few hundred yards, and finished the day down by lower Oosterbeek, in sight of the blown railway bridge across the river.

In his hospital bed at Wolfheze, Sam Bowles had also survived the night without detection, only to be disturbed by the sudden arrival of a British paratrooper, pursued by a party of German soldiers. With the inevitable shouts and brandishing of weaponry, the Germans captured their man and then turned their attention to Bowles. As a result, he was removed from the blind home and, later in the day, taken as a prisoner-of-war to hospital in Utrecht, where subsequently he had an operation and treatment for gangrene.

Thursday was also the day on which Ralph Foulkes and his party ended their wanderings. After a second cold, miserable night, they tried a fresh route down the east side of Reijerscamp, adjacent to Wolfhezerweg. By then, all their water was gone, and mouths were so dry as to make food unpalatable. On the way down, they came across the jeep which Speller, Southwell and Morris had had at the time when they became detached from the others in the course of the Tuesday evening skirmish at the railway line; it was a burnt-out wreck. Shortly afterwards, they noted a German cycle patrol on Wolfhezerweg, and realized from the way in which the Germans seemed to be pacing them, that they had been spotted and were being kept under observation.

It was in this somewhat threatening situation that the group eventually arrived at a house near Wolfheze junction. It was the one to which the wounded men, Dodson and Garwood, had been taken by Ralph Foulkes on Monday and, with the prospect of much-needed refreshment, the members of the party made for the pump in the garden and filled their water bottles. Whilst this was happening, a German medical orderly came out of the house and stood watching them. Henry Crowder remembers that it was this, coming on top of their obvious detection by the German patrol that made a number of them, including himself, thoroughly apprehensive about what might be imminent. As a result, three of them decided to make a break for it on their own without any further delay. "After they'd all filled their water bottles," says Crowder, "most of them started to climb up the trees to collect apples. Three of us were bothered about this, especially because we knew that the Germans weren't far off, so this sergeant and another lad from one of the 4th Brigade battalions and I decided to get out of there fast. We looked to see if the road was clear and nipped into cover on the other side. We only just made it, because we'd hardly got across, when some German troops came down the road, shouting, 'Hande hoch – hande hoch', made straight for the house, and rounded all the rest of them up." As Ted Hares, who was one of those captured, now testifies, the British probably inadvertently aided in their own capture. "It was dusk," he says, "and we'd just filled our water bottles at this house. Suddenly, we heard the sound of an engine on the road, and the vehicle was identified as a 181st Field Ambulance. When they saw it, some of the lads ran out to flag it down, thinking it was British, but it was a captured one, so that was us all in the bag."

Following this, there was a degree of apprehension, when the party was lined up against a brick wall, but they were soon reassured. One of their guards made a point of telling Hares that they had nothing to fear, as he, himself, had been a prisoner-of-war twenty-five years earlier in Southampton. It was an attempt at friendly reassurance but, however illogically comforting the guarantee was for most of them, it appeared to hold less security for Lieutenant Foulkes. The trouble was that, from the outset, the German officer in charge seemed determined to regard him as having been directly involved in the shooting up of the two abandoned German ambulances on the Planken Wambuis road, and he was loudly vociferous in his assertions that Foulkes would shortly be shot for it. The hysterical tirade went on at length, and was accompanied throughout by the waving of a loaded revolver in the British officer's face. It was true that, in eluding the Tuesday ambush, Foulkes had run off the road behind those vehicles, but it was obvious at the time that they had already been knocked out prior to the action. Crowder, who was in fairly close contact with the 4th Brigade men whom they had picked up, still believes that they could probably have shed light on the affair, but the Germans clearly had the notion that Foulkes was in some measure responsible. Fortunately, they did not press the matter, and the whole thing blew over, but it was an awkward interlude, and for a short time it looked as if matters could easily have taken a disturbingly unpleasant turn. Just after that, German transport arrived to take them to Ede, where they were placed under guard by Dutch SS men, all drunk, very noisy and rather nasty. They had not long arrived when someone told them that, on the night before, four Reconnaissance Squadron men had been taken out and shot by the Germans. The story, one of those typical products of front-line rumour, was quite untrue, but they were not to know that, and so all of them immediately removed their badges and regimental signs.

At the Bridge, the Germans had kept the promise to share their food with the surviving British defenders. In the initial stages of the surrender the ordinary soldier had a few uneasy moments of wondering how he was going to be treated. "I remember when we came out," says Bert Welham, "we were being escorted by the Germans past a line of slit trenches and, up ahead, I could see this old German, with a bandage round his head, belting all the British soldiers with his rifle butt as they went past. I managed to switch sides with the German guard so that as we went past he was nearer to the old bloke. That way, I escaped getting clobbered." Welham's fears, however, were strengthened by what happened next: "I was with 'Darkie' in a small group of twelve, and they got us between some buildings, where they searched us, having first lined us up facing a wall. After that, they stepped back, and we heard what sounded like the click of rifle bolts. Not a word was spoken, till someone in the line said what we were all thinking – 'If you're going to shoot us, bloody well get on with it.' I shall always remember how the German officer laughed as he replied, in perfect English, 'Oh, we're not going to shoot you – it's given us too much trouble to take you prisoner!'"

The prisoners were really very well treated by their captors. They were given food, water and cigarettes, and spent the rest of the day and night in quarters near the Bridge. Officers were separated from men, but Bert Welham still remembers how cheered he was by the sight of Freddie Gough, under escort of two armed German guards, moving amongst the men with words of comfort for them all. As senior British officer, he had assumed responsibility for making sure that his men were being properly looked after, and he knew that this would be his last opportunity to do so.

Gough, however, had other thoughts in mind that day for, in the place to which they had been taken, there were a great number of stretchers on which dead British soldiers, covered over with blankets, had been laid. It was the presence of an additional stock of empty stretchers, as well as a pile of spare blankets, that gave him an idea for helping some of his friends to escape. "I got Digby (Tatham-Warter) and about four or five of the others to lie down, quite still, and we covered them up with blankets. As the Dutch chaps came in to remove the bodies, I pointed to those other stretchers and said that they were 'different'. The Dutch understood right away, and the result was that those chaps finished up 'by mistake' in another house, and some of them got away." Tatham-Warter, was one of them and went on to have a succession of further adventures with the Dutch underground, the highlight of which was probably an occasion on which he helped push a German staff car out of a ditch! Freddie Gough would have dearly loved to have been one of those who escaped, but his prematurely white hair had already made him so conspicuous that even a short absence would have been immediately detected.

Just after five o'clock on that same afternoon, the parachute element of the 1st Polish Independent Parachute Brigade Group dropped on the south side of the river. The original dropping zone was to have been just south of Arnhem Bridge, but circumstances had, of course, forced an alteration, so that they came in just east of Driel, opposite the site of the Heveadorp ferry. It had not, from the outset, been a successful operation, for the weather had been bad, and although 110 C 47's left Grantham, forty-one returned without dropping, thirteen went missing and three landed at Brussels. As a result, only fifty-three aircraft reached the area of the dropping zone, at which point they ran into a murderous barrage of anti-aircraft fire. Nor was there any hope that the new arrivals could achieve an immediate crossing of the Rhine for, by then, the ferry was no longer there, and there were neither rafts nor boats of any kind to take them over. With the Arnhem road bridge back in enemy hands and thus providing unimpeded access across the river, there was the additional possibility that the Poles might be attacked from the flank by German armour. With this in mind, Major-General Sosabowski ordered defensive positions to be dug on the south side. All of this meant that, for the perimeter defenders around Oosterbeek, there was to be no additional help that night.

Meantime, 30 Corps had made little progress. Massive traffic problems on the narrow road from Nijmegen to Arnhem were bedevilling the proposed advance, and a German anti-tank screen to each side of Ressen held up the movement forward of the Guards Armoured Division. By nightfall, however, the 43rd (Wessex) Infantry Division had moved up to the Nijmegen area, and the 43rd Reconnaissance Regiment had reconnoitered ahead in anticipation of a decisive move on the following day.

Thus it was that at 2144 hours on that Thursday night, General Urquhart sent the following signal to Corps:

> No knowledge elements of Div in Arnhem for 24 hours. Balance of Div in very tight perimeter. Heavy mortaring and machine-gun fire followed by local attacks. Main nuisance SP guns. Our casualties heavy. Resources stretched to utmost. Relief within 24 hours vital.

With the Bridge gone, and the last gallant efforts to relieve it long past, the enemy was clearly in a more advantageous position to be able to concentrate an increasing amount of armour and infantry on what was left of the British force in Oosterbeek. Indeed, from that night on, it became more and more apparent that the term "perimeter" was something of a misnomer, representing little more than a fluctuating line on the map. In notional terms, it delineated a British-held area, but on the ground the reality was very different and a more suitable analogy might have been that of a leaky sieve. Already the Germans were referring to the defensive area by a much more appropriate term – "Der Kessel", meaning "encircled troops", but with an alternative translation of "The Cauldron".

As midnight approached, to bring to a close the fifth day of the Battle of Arnhem, the men dug in at Reconnaissance Squadron HQ could see great fires to east and west. From their bases a little to the north, A and D Troop commanders had carried out the last task of the day, which was to tour the entire defensive area, along with Major Powell, in order to gain as clear a picture as possible of the remaining positions. These were seen to be quite meagre and very precariously held, and, in retrospect, their very inadequacy lends much point to General Urquhart's assertion, made years later,* that, with a determined and concentrated attack on that day, the Germans could hardly have failed to overwhelm his entire force.

* Urquhart: op. cit. p. 124.

Chapter 11 FRIDAY 22nd SEPTEMBER 1944

"Raise your hat . . . and buy him a drink"

Friday dawned as a fine, warm day, but spoiled by the inevitable "hate" which came down at 0730 hours. Recalling that morning, David Christie remembers how, throughout the night, he had taken it in turns with fellow-sergeant, Fred Winder, to keep guard. Their situation was one totally lacking in any kind of creature comforts, but by that time such things were purely relative. Simply that the night had remained free from shelling and mortaring, with only the occasional shot breaking the silence, was in itself something to be grateful for. Many of the single shots that would suddenly ring out are remembered by Christie as the responses of jittery sentries peering into the darkness with an intensity that soon invested every shadowy place with imaginary movement; in other instances they would be provoked to an over-hasty reaction by the stirring of their comrades in the other slit trenches. As it happened, "stand-to" was, as usual, at 0530 hours, half-an-hour before dawn, but it was the morning mortaring which followed, two hours later, that really heralded the day and continued, on and off, to take a steady toll of victims. By noon, four Squadron HQ casualties, all victims of mortar bombs, had been transported by the Adjutant to the regimental aid post. This was one duty which Geoff Costeloe made almost his own, and there are those men of the Squadron alive today, who still remember with gratitude how this very courageous officer ran his shuttle service, making regular journeys with wounded men across to the Hartenstein, under the most intense enemy fire.

The first major set-back of the day came at 0945 hours, when Sergeant McCreedie of the Support Troop reported back to Squadron HQ from the 1st Battalion Border Regiment. He brought the news that just after nine o'clock that morning, the enemy had mounted a massive mortar attack which had been particularly costly. As a result, the Border Regiment's entire transport had been reduced to two jeeps and a motor cycle, its ammunition reserve had suffered a direct hit, and the Support Troop's own two 3-inch mortars had been destroyed. Squadron casualties were also sustained, as Ray Price recalls: "Corporal Des Mason was the first, and he was killed mainly, I think, because he just didn't dig in deep enough. After that, John Serginson was hit when a piece of shrapnel caught him in the thigh. I was affected by blast. I don't really remember what happened but, apparently, I got up and walked around the trenches in the open in a daze. Some of the others then got me under cover and I was taken up to the aid post at the Hartenstein and put into the cellars. I remember one chap in there was very, very badly shell-shocked and crying all the time like a little child, so I got him in my arms to try to comfort him."

The loan of the mortars had been short-lived, but it was, perhaps, a small consolation to the Support Troop men to know that they had at least been able to engage the enemy prior to the destruction of their weapons. After that, it was simply a matter of reporting back to Squadron HQ, and Richard Heyworth recalls that before they did so, the baseplates of the two 3-inch mortars were first buried in the woods. It may well be that they are still there to this day.

On that morning, some of the wounded men from the Bridge were removed from their temporary overnight premises and taken to St Elisabeth's Hospital. Bert Welham, whose entire time at the Bridge had been spent with a broken ankle – the result of a landing accident – was one of those who spent a night there before transfer to the German field hospital at Lochem. He remembers that, as he lay on his makeshift bed at St Elisabeth's, he could hear the sounds of the fighting to the west in Oosterbeek, yet all around the hospital itself, the same area which a mere seventy-two hours earlier had witnessed the horrendous savagery of the attempted relief, was an atmosphere of relative peace and calm.

It was on that day also that the captured officers and men from the various units which had fought at the Bridge were marched to Velp, an easterly suburb of Arnhem. There, they were placed under guard in a large house called "Bene Sita", standing about twenty yards back from the road, and distinguished by two monkey-puzzle trees in the front garden. Three officers of the Squadron, Trevor McNabb, Tony Platt and Freddie Gough himself, were involved in this move and, in the course of the day, others joined them. One of those was Major Anthony Deane-Drummond, second-in-charge of Divisional signals a resourceful officer, to whom captivity was anathema and who had already made a successful escape from Italy into Switzerland in 1941. In the course of the early attempts to relieve the Bridge, he had ultimately found himself out of ammunition and in a house in western Arnhem which was suddenly occupied by the Germans. At the time, he was with a number of 2nd Parachute Battalion men so, with three of them, Deane-Drummond simply locked himself in the lavatory of the house and waited for the enemy to move on. Periodically, a German would try the door yet, surprizingly, no one made any attempt to break it open, and the four airborne men were not discovered. Only when the Germans quit the house early on Friday morning was the group able to emerge and, at about 0200 hours, each swam successfully to the other side of the river. Unfortunately, they were soon captured and brought back to Arnhem – via the Bridge!

Deane-Drummond was afterwards taken to the house in Velp, where one of the first persons he met was Major Freddie Gough. The two exchanged news, and the signals officer, having already decided to try a repeat of the method which had earlier proved successful, declared it to be his intention to escape again. Searching around in one of the large downstairs rooms into which they had been shepherded, he discovered a small cupboard, about four feet across by seven feet high and decided that it would be his chosen hiding place. It was relatively inconspicuous because the cupboard door had been papered in the same style as the walls, so that it was already effectively camouflaged. The recess, which was about twelve inches deep was taken up with shelves, but these were easily removed. The cupboard lock was also shifted to the inside to allow the door to be secured from there.

Having in mind, perhaps, the pattern of his earlier confinement, Major Deane-Drummond then suggested to Gough that they might share the hiding place together. "I remember," said Gough, "that he showed it to me and said, 'Would you like to come in here with me?', and my replying, 'Actually, if you don't mind, old boy, I'd rather not.'" It was a most gentlemanly gesture of friendship on Deane-Drummond's part, and one that was declined with comparable courtesy, but Gough knew that, were he to accept the offer, it would in all probability inhibit any chance that the other man might have of making good his escape. What space there was, was extremely limited and cramped and, although Deane-Drummond had estimated that he would have to be holed up for no more than seventy-two hours, as it turned out, he had to remain there for an agonizing thirteen days before the Germans vacated the premises. During that time, he overheard them questioning other captured British troops, and was astonished at the amount of information which a certain few individuals were only too eager to pour out. In particular, the distasteful memory of one British officer's opprobrious behaviour remained with him long after his ordeal was over. Throughout it all, he could neither sit nor lie, nor was there any light by which to see. He existed solely on water and a tin of lard until eventually, having emerged, he was looked after by the Dutch underground.

At the Oosterbeek positions, north from Squadron HQ, D Troop had also been subjected to the periodic mortaring and, in addition, experienced several minor encounters with the enemy throughout the morning. In one of those, Trooper Slater had a narrow escape from snipers, during a sortie to try to get water for the wounded men in the cellars. Unluckily, he fell into a cesspit, one of the many physical hazards which the soldiers could encounter and which, along with the high metal fences, made daylight patrol work under fire so much more difficult. At about noon, an infantry attack came in on the positions, in the course of which Bentall's house was almost overrun. Without supporting armour, the Germans did not seek to press their attack home, but Bentall remembers that a number of the more determined ones actually got as far as the back door, and he was only able to be rid of them by sticking a machine-gun out of the window and firing straight down. Following this very effective action, a German medical officer then appeared with a white flag and requested permission to deal with the wounded who were lying in the back garden of the house. As a result, a ten-minute pause was agreed upon, before the attack was taken up again.

On Paul Krugerstraat, morning for A Troop was much less eventful and, in a curious way, relatively quiet by contrast with the action of the previous day. In part, this was due to their being subjected to much less enemy pressure than D Troop, but also because Captain Grubb discouraged intermittent firing which merely tended to give away positions for no corresponding tactical gain. Today, such professional aspects of Grubb's leadership are still remembered with gratitude by those who served under him, and who recall that their troop commander would always weigh up the risks to his men before undertaking any action where calculation and planning were involved.

No change had taken place from the previous evening. A Troop still held the northern and southern sides of the Paul Krugerstraat/Mariaweg crossroads, although the burnt-out shell of the bakery was of little value as a strongpoint. Nevertheless, it remained covered from the other houses to prevent the Germans, had they been so inclined, from reoccupying it. Graham Wadsworth was also still holding on to his position on Joubertweg, with an occasional exchange of fire with passing German troops. Although the British defenders at all those points fully expected to be attacked, no attempt was made by the Germans to mount anything of the intensity of the previous day's efforts. But, quiet as that Friday morning was, there were still occasions when the action would suddenly erupt, and this, as John Stevenson has every reason to remember, applied particularly to mortar attack. Arising out of the Divisional decisions made on the previous evening, the Squadron had been moved from Hicks's command to that of Hackett's. As a result,

"Shan" Hackett went on a tour of his positions on that Friday morning in order to refine the arrangements for the defences by talking directly to those responsible. "He came up on a jeep," says Stevenson, "and there was a hell of a rumpus going on at the time, to which he paid not one blind bit of attention. It was just as if it wasn't happening. I remember he sat up on the bonnet of his vehicle, and opened out this map and proceeded to give me the most precise instructions. I cannot now remember what it was that he wanted me to do, but I do know that more than anything else I wanted to get down, because those mortar bombs were going off around us all the time that he was talking. The briefing lasted for not more than five minutes, but they were about five of the longest minutes of my life."

In this, as in other sectors, the blast of shell and the crump of mortar bomb rocked the area intermittently throughout the day. Self-propelled guns were also more in evidence as they patrolled from the north, seeking out the weak spots in the British defences. Curiously enough, although D Troop was pressed by infantry attack, nothing came in on the A Troop positions at the bakery crossroads. Clearly the enemy was concentrating his pressure elsewhere, although a new factor, particularly favourable to the British had entered into the reckoning. From as far away as Nijmegen the 64th Medium Regiment, Royal Artillery, under Lieutenant-Colonel Hunt, had settled into a highly successful supportive role, directed against German-held points in the perimeter area. From the morning of Thursday 21st September, this regiment, which was part of 30 Corps, had established radio links with the hard-pressed 1st British Airborne Division. Thereafter, from something like a distance of eleven miles, its personnel had consistently produced superlative gunnery, to be described later by Urquhart, himself as ". . . one of the most exciting and remarkable artillery shoots I had ever experienced."* Targets selected by Brigadiers Hackett and Hicks – in some cases no more than 100 yards from British positions – were methodically destroyed by the 4·5-inch guns operating from Hees, just a little to the west of Nijmegen. By the excellence of their artillery fire, the "Mediums", later supported by a "Heavy" battery of 7·2-inch guns, broke up several Panzer attacks of SP guns with supporting infantry, and thus rendered invaluable assistance to the defenders at Oosterbeek.

Jimmy Cooke, who was at the Squadron HQ positions, has personal memories of those shoots which, heartening as they were, did induce a considerable amount of fear, especially as many of the shells landed very close to the British trenches. "There was a house just over the road from us," he says, "and it must have been hit a dozen times or more, for I can remember an old car that kept being put up in the air as the shells landed. We could hear the 'wump-wump-wump-wump' in the distance, and then we'd wait in the silence for the loud whistling overhead and the crashes as they hit their targets – but, my God, they were close!" Cooke's worry, like that of all the others, was that the guns at Nijmegen only had to drop a fraction for the shells to land on top of them. "We were under those tallish trees just over from the Hartenstein," remembers Tom Collier, "and there were obviously four guns firing from south of the river. The trouble was that the fourth shot in each salvo always came down just a little bit short, so that it clipped the tops of our trees. Because of that, we used to count 'One-two-three' and then get right down into the trenches." For all the initial apprehension, however, there were no British casualties from their own guns, and the airborne men soon came to recognize that they were witness to a recurrent display of gunnery that was both skilful and dependable. It was this which evoked the General's

* So impressed was General Urquhart by the 64th's performance and help throughout the final five days of the battle that, afterwards, he suggested that they be allowed, as a battle honour, the right to wear the airborne "Pegasus" on the lower-right sleeve. Regrettably, the request was denied by the War Office.

Lt. John Christie's wrecked vehicle: Utrechtseweg, Oosterbeek. The Reconnaissance Corps "41" is discernible on the front bumper

(Bundesarchiv Koblenz)

HQ Troop, 1st Airborne Reconnaissance Squadron, Ruskington 1944

Back row: Cpl. Gates, Tprs. Crane, Jackson, Price, Bell, Collishaw, Simpson, Bellwood, Parish. *Second back row:* Tprs. Seymour, Neilson, Dowell, Smith, McIntosh, Tyler, Le Luyer, Coldicott, Toeg, Cooke, Pearce, Craftsman York MM. *Centre row:* Tprs. White, Foot, Cpls. Watson, Belcham, Edgington, Tpr. Samm, Sgts. Kay, Redfern, Haydon, Smith, Quinn, Tpr. Bailey, Cpl. Trinder, Tpr. Kerr, ——, Tprs. Evans, Silcox. *Second front row:* Tpr. Jones, Sgt. Ferguson, Lt. Lickerish, Capt. McNabb, Capt. Poole, Capt. Allsop, Major Gough MC, Capt. Costeloe, S.S.M. Meadows, Lt.-QM. Collier, Lt. Ladds, S.Q.M.S. Holderness, Tpr. Smith. *Front row:* Tprs. Clough, Outram, Hayes, ——, L/Cpl. Williams, Tprs. Chadwick, Dunn, Thomson, Spence, Cpl. Dunn, Tprs. Prescott, Mullenger own comment on the reactions of his men, when he noted that, "the tremendous confidence of the infantry was such that repeat shots were continually demanded, and the medium artillery never failed in their consistent and accurate support."

To a great extent, the success of the "Mediums" at Arnhem was undoubtedly due to the extremely close and skilful liaison between Loder-Symonds* on the ground at Oosterbeek and Hunt at Nijmegen, and, indeed, had it not been for the guns of 30 Corps, the 1st Airborne Division could not have held for as long as it did. Understandably, the increased concentration of German armour in Oosterbeek in the last days of the battle, made the supportive artillery role more difficult to sustain. Nevertheless, the help of the 64th Medium Regiment and that of 419 Heavy Battery was the only outside relief which Urquhart got, prior to the arrival of Sosabowski's Brigade.

In itself, the absence of any other form of tactical assistance, particularly logistical air support, remains one of the principal unexplained features of the entire "Market Garden" Operation. Close backing of such kind, especially in the initial stages when the Division was still mobile, would undoubtedly have been of enormous tactical value. Unfortunately, no such action took place until Typhoon rocket aircraft came in on some very successful sorties in the last days of the battle. The reasons advanced, both at the time and since then, for the general absence of tactical air support have not been convincing. In the first place, it was held that the weather conditions were bad for flying. Furthermore, there was a ruling that 83 Group of the 2nd Tactical Air Force, which was based on the continent of Europe could not, for safety reasons, be in the battle area during the resupply missions, which were controlled from Eastcote in England. Since resupply took place, for the most part, over the period from Monday to Thursday and, thereafter, on Saturday, it meant that there were considerable restrictions on any plan for air back-up. Yet it is difficult to see how those administrative drawbacks should ever have been regarded as insurmountable. The pilots of 83 Group were already, for the most part, well acquainted with the terrain and, considering the relatively short duration of each supply drop, one cannot but wonder why resupply was not slotted into a predetermined lull, during which time the strike aircraft would have remained grounded. The additional and inexplicable factor, that no signals link existed between Air-Vice Marshal Hollinghurst's HQ at Eastcote and that of 2nd Tactical Air Force across the Channel, would also suggest a major flaw in the detailed planning behind "Market Garden", particularly in relation to inter-services co-operation.

Such major strategic issues and the details of whatever shortcomings were becoming increasingly apparent in the top-level organization, were unknown to the men who continued to hold on to their shaky positions in the Oosterbeek perimeter. The question on everyone's lips was, "Where is 30 Corps?" but it was one to which not even their General could have supplied an adequate answer. In an atmosphere of mounting confusion, Montgomery's grand plan was clearly coming apart at the seams and, as the world looked on, the wonder was that the airborne men were still there at all. Like others in the units that made up the 1st British Airborne Division, the men of the Reconnaissance Squadron were more than ready for deliverance, and would no doubt have been greatly cheered had they known that their "recce" counterparts of the Guards Armoured Division, the 2nd Household Cavalry, had, that very morning at 0800 hours, made first contact with the Poles at Driel. Yet, it was perhaps just as well that hopes were not to be built on this, for it was more the product of a typical piece of reconnaissance spearheading, in no way reflecting the ponderous advance of the great cumbersome cavalcade which was still

* Lieutenant-Colonel R. G. Loder-Symonds DSO, CRA, 1st British Airborne Division.

edging forward north of Nijmegen, through the Betuwe, on a road that had already acquired for itself the appropriate name of "Hell's Highway."

For those in the battered houses and slit trenches of Oosterbeek, there was no awareness of the increasing difficulties being encountered by Horrocks's force. For them, one thing only was of significance, and it was that they had been briefed for a two-day holding operation yet, already, they had held for five. And so it was partly in a spirit of fun, but with more than a hint of gentle cynicism, that Jim Taylor of A Troop sat down at a typewriter in the Janssen house that Friday afternoon and, with the aid of numerous carbon papers, knocked out his own "field newspaper". This revealing document, the fame of which spread beyond the Reconnaissance Squadron positions, is all the more remarkable when viewed in the context in which it was produced. It was also, as far as is known, the only one of its kind to emerge from the Arnhem operation. It said much for the spirit of the perimeter defenders, and Taylor in particular, that the tone was neither bitter nor hopeless, but the expression of a successful blend of humour with hints of a growing disbelief in the arrival of the main force from the south.

DER HOLEN DER WARL, RECCE NEWSPAPER. 23rd Sept.

Incorporating the OOSTERBEEK BLOODY LIAR and the DOUBLE DUTCH TIMES.

N.B. There is very little chance of this operation being cancelled.

Oh to be in Arnhem
Now that Autumn's here
And slap a dozen Bren rounds
Into a Panzer Grenadier.

If you go down to the woods today
You're sure of a big surprise,
If you go down to the woods today,
You'd better go in disguise.
For there's an SP gun knocking about,
And he's not particular what shit he slings out . . .

There is no truth in the statement that Jack Dempsey's Army is having a succession of free days, but it wants to get a jillo on, all the same.

An intercepted report states that women parachutists were seen, six feet tall, and wearing strange frocks. This may or may not be the Glider Pilot officers.

It is stated by the girl's father, that Alfy Webb of 1 Section is making eyes at the Dutch maiden with the white socks. He asked in broken English if Alf's intentions were strictly honourable.

There will, at 1010 hrs today be a fast stick of NAAFI girls. Pat, Ethyl and Mrs. Knight will, I think, drop with four containers of tea, brandishing a bottle of gassy lemonade in the right hand, and also armed with NAAFI rock cakes, fitted with four-second fuses. They will attack the position North, with the traditional warcry of "Orderly".

> Watch out for a Recce officer named Mr. Stevenson, whose line of approach is to hop smartly up to you, and try and cadge a "Ciggy". He has a reserve of some seven or eight million hidden in the cellar that he has won in this fashion.
>
> Sgt. Venes will play anyone not on duty at pontoon or banker. Being an honest man, he will accept credit notes when he has won all the guilders in the vicinity.
>
> The porridge this morning will, in all probability, have half bricks in it.
>
> *WHAT THE STAR SHELLS FORETELL* – bags of 8 cm mortar, I presume.
>
> Save up ten used Bren rounds, and get a packet of Players when Jack Dempsey arrives.
>
> This newspaper is a front line edition, and if it's not front line, it's as near as it's bloody well going to be for a few hours.

Further over to the west, D Troop found itself in action at intervals throughout the morning. This pressure continued into the afternoon and, in the course of repulsing an attack of particular intensity, one of the Bren guns overheated to the extent that it seized up. Casualties, too, were increasing all the time, and Bob Thomson remembers how the combination of a high casualty rate and the problem of maintaining regular communication with others was undermining the notion of the Troop as a coherent fighting force. "By that time," he says, "we were really operating in groups that did not always relate to the Sections that we were supposed to be in. We had also taken to moving from house to house according to the ebb and flow of the battle, because we didn't want to find ourselves isolated or overrun. Orders still came through from time to time, but we were not always sure about where they'd come from, and some were so vague that we simply had to interpret them as best we could. For a great deal of the time, however, we moved from one house to another according to our own estimates of the situation." An almost inevitable consequence of this was interpenetration of positions which, as Thomson remembers, frequently produced the bizarre situation in which both British and Germans would be in the same house at the one time. "On a number of occasions," he recalls, "two of us would be upstairs in a house, whilst a party of Germans, using the ground floor for cover, would run in one door and out by the other. That's why we'd take it in turns to have two hours on watch and four off, so that the gardens and the road outside could be kept under observation."

By the end of the day, the sniping and skirmishing had made fresh inroads into D Troop's strength and, in Bentall's house, only Slater, Peach and himself were still on their feet. A dwindling stock of ammunition was also giving cause for concern, and it was this which prompted Captain Park to organize a patrol in order to try to get hold of additional supplies. In the course of their previous day's sortie to the houses which had been overrun, Bentall and Walker had noticed that arms and ammunition, which had been taken by the Germans from the captured 10 and 11 Section men, were stacked in a corner in one of the houses. Having in mind the possibility that it might still be there, Captain Park asked Bentall to investigate. Bentall took Slater with him, and this time found the house completely empty. As luck would have it, the arms and ammunition were still there and, as a consequence of the Thursday supply drop, the Germans had added more to the pile. The presence of the store, however, suggested that the enemy was probably near at hand – possibly not more than a house or two away and so, loading up with as much as they could reasonably carry, the two men left and slipped back as rapidly as possible to their own lines.

Daylight had gone by the time they got back, and everyone welcomed the relief afforded by the darkness and the easing of enemy pressure on the positions. Major German attacks, when they were launched, tended to come in during the hours of daylight. This meant that, whilst the need for caution remained throughout the night hours, any enemy opposition more generally took the form of small patrols. These lacked the ferocity of an all-out attack, but could still be unnerving, which was why, when Bentall heard a scratching noise outside later that evening, his first thoughts were of the possibilty of an infiltrating enemy group. "Don't fire," croaked a voice from the darkness, "it's Sergeant Venes." He had almost lost his voice, from smoking ersatz coffee wrapped in toilet paper. His mission through the perilous streets of Oosterbeek had been voluntarily undertaken to bring them some spare ammunition and a copy of Taylor's *Oosterbeek Bloody Liar* which, as Bill Bentall remarked, went a long way to cheering them up.

It was, perhaps, wholly in character that it should have been Henry Venes who was the one to risk his neck to try to bring a bit of cheer to those of his comrades who were hard-pressed in the more westerly positions. By no stretch of the imagination could it ever have been claimed that Arnhem was a joyous occasion and yet, in the face of death and the constant threat of it, there were still those who found time to explore the lighter side of the human predicament. Such a one was Henry Venes, Troop Sergeant of A Troop and a regular soldier with years of experience behind him. Like all good senior NCOs, he regarded soldiering as more than skill in tactics and weaponry. For him, the welfare of his men, both physical comfort and morale, was also a prime concern. Because of this, he was immensely respected and liked, and of all the incidents which illustrate this none, perhaps, is better than Alf Hazell's tale of an occasion at Bulford, just before the Squadron left for North Africa. After a hard night in the Sergeants' Mess, Henry Venes was in rough shape the next morning, and obviously unfit to be seen on parade. Unfortunately, a major camp inspection was scheduled and this negated possible plans for keeping him out of sight in any of the usual places. Achieving the seemingly impossible, however, the A Troop men spirited him away by making a space in the midst of a large pile of ammunition boxes that was stacked in the open outside the Squadron Stores. With shouted commands reverberating all around, there he remained, until the conclusion of the inspection brought merciful resurrection.

Loyalty of this kind could also, of course, operate in the other direction, and Venes still recalls the time when, as Orderly Sergeant, he accompanied a young, newly-commissioned officer on obligatory "rounds". All went smoothly, until at 10.30 in the morning, they came upon the recumbent form of a soldier, fully clothed, sprawled out and asleep on top of a bed in the D Troop billet. Obviously, the man was still "sleeping it off" but, by army standards, it was very late in the day, and to Venes's horror, he realized as he shook him to his feet, that the prostrate slumberer was none other than Trooper Alf Webb of his own A Troop. To the fulminations of an outraged orderly officer, the sergeant added his own little bit, following which Webb was "booked" according to the recognized army procedure of having "name and last three numbers" taken down. The officer was well satisfied that justice would be done. So too was Webb for, as Henry Venes still recalls, "I got hold of him afterwards and I said to him – 'Here – since when did you change your name to bloody Smith?'"

Such brief digressions, whilst of no direct relevance to the course of events that overtook the Squadron at Arnhem, perhaps serve to illuminate something of the quality of human relationships that existed. In those permanently horrific days of fading British hopes in the perimeter, it was hardly surprizing that Henry Venes's soldierly qualities were displayed in a number of ways, yet never more so than in the manner in which he jollied along the men of A Troop with a brand of entertainment that was robust and uniquely his own. Much of it came in musical form and, although it could never have been asserted that he had the tonal qualities of a Caruso, the repertoire was unchallengeable in variety and extent. Indeed, Taylor, spurred on to further literary effort by the success of the "Liar", next produced a spurious set of "Orders", in which prominence was given to the item: "Third Parade 1900 hours: Songs you might never have heard, by Sergeant Venes."

So it was that, during lulls in the fighting, those in the Janssen house on Paul Krugerstraat were regularly favoured with a succession of titillating and uncensored vocal gems of an earthy quality that could hardly have been better and that were colourfully appropriate to the occasion. It was true that the customary big drum accompaniment to the "Sheikh of A-ra-bee" was absent, and the intermittent "Boom-booms" had to be vocally improvized, but that was a minor drawback. Besides, there were alternative avenues of "showbiz" potential to be explored, particularly since the wardrobe of one occupied house revealed a frock coat and a very tall top hat. The clothes were emphatically not in the Fred Astaire style, being of more archaic origin, but that was all to the good. To this day, there are few of his Troop who can readily forget the sight of Henry Venes, attired in his undertaker's outfit, rendering his own unique version of the Toreador's song from *Carmen*, with the memorable opening line, "In-to the bull ring jumped the f- - - - - - bull." Thus, at Arnhem, face to face with war in all its fearsome immediacy, Sergeant Henry Venes did what professional soldiers before him have always done – he found something to laugh at, and those who fought by his side were the richer for it.

Around the time that Venes made his trip to the D Troop lines, Captain Allsop and a small party of men took PIAT bombs and wireless batteries up to the forward positions. The batteries were dry-cell replacements for 38 sets and were needed particularly by D Troop which, for some time, had been dependent on "runners" for all its communications. The bombs were in response to a request from Brigadier Hackett that defending forces should, as far as possible, make strenuous efforts to try to deal with the alarming increase of tanks and self-propelled guns that had filtered into the perimeter area and were freely and menacingly creaking their slow progress through the tight little streets and ravaged gardens of Oosterbeek.

Servicing of this kind from Squadron HQ to the more forward positions was, of course, a regular feature of life in the perimeter, and much of it was undertaken by the acting Squadron commander himself. In constant touch with Divisional HQ on the other side of the Utrechtseweg, David Allsop successfully ran his own headquarters and also kept in personal contact with both A and D Troops in the houses to the north. As liaison officer to the Squadron's forward elements, Lieutenant Bertie Lickerish was officially responsible for taking up whatever was required as and when the need arose. Nevertheless, all the HQ officers helped out in this supporting task, and Allsop was no exception. So it would happen that, having returned from attending one of the General's "O" groups at the Hartenstein, he might then personally undertake one of those practical yet very necessary chores which fulfilled the dual function of supplying the needs of his operational Troops, whilst at the same time serving to provide him with first-hand intelligence of the overall Squadron situation.

One who shared responsibility with Allsop for keeping an oversight of the Squadron's involvement was Geoff Costeloe, and he recollects how particularly hazardous were those short excursions to the more northerly positions: "David and I took turns on those patrols, and I remember on the Friday going up to the bakery area, and meeting Dougie Galbraith. When I set out back on the return journey, I decided it might be safer to return by Stationsweg but, unfortunately, at its junction with Paul Krugerstraat, I was fired on, and when I got down in the gutter, I was mortared. I lay there, quite still, until there was a break, when I managed to get myself into the basement of a house. There, to my surprise, I met two RASC men who were sitting down there eating fruit. I'm glad to say, I managed to shame them into coming out. I then made my way through gardens and over fences with them until we had worked our way back to Squadron HQ."

Others, however, had been undertaking liaison duties that day, beyond the perimeter, of greater significance to the outcome of the operation and concerned with the fate of the entire Division. In response to his message of the previous evening, General Urquhart had received a reply from 30 Corps, which read, "43 Div ordered to take all risks to effect relief today and are directed on ferry. If situation warrants, you should withdraw to or cross ferry." Despite this, he was not entirely convinced that either Horrocks or Browning fully appreciated the increasingly desperate predicament which the 1st Airborne Division was in: "The urgency of our situation," as he later remarked, "had to be driven home," and so it was decided that two senior officers from Divisional HQ should undertake this task. Those chosen were Lieutenant-Colonel Charles Mackenzie, GSO 1 (Ops), and Lieutenant-Colonel Eddie Myers, CRE.

There can be no doubt at all that the General's fears were wholly justified for, once more, there had been inexplicable delay in the relief from the south. The main plan, as worked out, was that the Guards Armoured Division should rest in its Thursday positions, whilst 43rd (Wessex) Division would press on through them and move out of the Nijmegen bridgehead in two directions. One force was to head for Arnhem Bridge, with the ultimate objective now limited to Apeldoorn instead of the Zuider Zee. Another was to flank west by Oosterhout, in an effort to link up with the 1st Polish Parachute Brigade at Driel. What actually happened was that, not only was there no attempt to move on this plan on the night of 21–22 September but, even at first light on the Friday, no benefit was sought from the early morning mist, in order to try to cover the remaining few miles. Only Wrottesley's reconnaissance troop of the Household Cavalry succeeded in exploiting this advantage, and it was this forward unit with which Lieutenant-Colonels Mackenzie and Myers made contact when they crossed the river to the Polish positions. From Captain Wrottesley's HQ, Mackenzie then sent a lengthy message to Corps headquarters, explaining as clearly and precisely as he could the position of the 1st Airborne Division.

By the time the main infantry force of 43rd (Wessex) Division got under way that morning, the mist was lifting, and already enemy tanks and artillery had been brought to a point of readiness to block the advancing British troops. As a consequence, slow progress was made and, by nightfall, 129 Infantry Brigade was halted halfway between Nijmegen and the little town of Elst. In the meantime, 130 Infantry Brigade, having been relieved of its task of guarding Nijmegen Bridge, had come up in reserve. What success was gained during that day really belonged to the remaining Brigade of 43rd Division, the 214th, commanded by Brigadier Hubert Essame. He, in particular, had felt a mounting frustration at the lack of progress and was all the more annoyed at further avoidable hold-ups, which prevented him from having an early start on the Friday morning. But, making what speed he could, and despite an agonizing six and a half hours delay at Oosterhout, he succeeded in getting one of his battalions through to the Polish positions before dark, and another to Valburg by midnight.

Those of Essame's Brigade who were successful in this link-up were the 5th Duke of Cornwall's Light Infantry, under their resourceful commanding officer, Lieutenant-Colonel George Taylor. Following the breakout at Oosterhout, Taylor was quick to seize the opportunity to make a rapid advance and, with the support of a squadron of tanks and armoured cars of the 4/7th Dragoon Guards, covered the remaining ten miles to Driel in an astonishing thirty minutes. With him, he took two amphibious vehicles (DUKW's), each loaded with supplies and ammunition. Meantime, at Sosabowski's HQ, Myers had been organizing transport to ferry the Poles across to the north side of the river. His idea was to use a string of two-man rubber dinghies, as supplied to airborne forces, together with improvized rafts. It was agreed that the ferrying would get under way from 9 p.m. on, using the small boats, and that the two DUKW's should be launched as soon as possible thereafter to expedite the operation.

To begin with, the ferrying went well, but when the Germans got wind of what was going on, the Poles were machine-gunned and mortared on the way across. Because of this, they suffered many casualties, in addition to which some were drowned and a number swept down the river into enemy hands. At 2 a.m. on Saturday morning, the two amphibious DUKW's were taken to the river for launching. It was not a success. The river bank, at that point, was steep and soggy and ran into a deep ditch. As a result, both two and a half ton vehicles slid down the slope and became hopelessly bogged. In that rather ignominious manner, the relief operation came to an end. Altogether only fifty Polish soldiers, and almost no supplies, made the crossing that night.

Until the final perimeter was formed men would frequently become detached from their units. It was a common feature of the early days of the battle, and the Reconnaissance Squadron was affected as much as any other. Few of those who were separated managed to find the way back, but either finished up with another regiment or joined the swelling numbers of prisoners-of-war. One of the exceptions was Trooper Pow, a quiet young man from the shipyard area of Glasgow. After the Wednesday morning fight on Stationsweg, he had spent two very difficult nights in the woods but had eventually reached the Divisional HQ area. There he had reported to the Hartenstein to enquire about the whereabouts of the Squadron. "I asked a captain," he says, "and he didn't know, but he told me to go down to the cellars and make enquiries there. I opened the door of one of the rooms and in the middle of it was a table with a big chair drawn up to it. General Urquhart was sitting there by himself, with his head just resting on his hands. He didn't look up and I didn't say anything. I just closed the door quietly and left." Soon afterwards, Pow reached his objective, since by then it was fairly well known that the Reconnaissance Squadron was just over the road by "the Green", and he was directed to the HQ position. There, he was put in a slit trench on Oranjeweg, but the reunion with his comrades was short lived as, not long afterwards, he was wounded in the hand by mortar shrapnel, and finished the day in the regimental aid post.

At 1005 hours that Friday night, General Urquhart had sent his "sitrep" to Browning. It ran as follows:

> Perimeter unchanged. Positions heavily shelled and mortared during day. Minor attacks defeated. Some SP guns knocked out. Assistance given by supporting artillery forward Div. Intend ferry some Poles over tonight. Small attack direction ferry first light tomorrow. Morale high.

It was astonishing that, notwithstanding the increasing strain on his depleted force, Urquhart could still report, "Perimeter unchanged . . . Morale high", and yet the will of the British defenders to resist had not in any way been weakened. "From that Friday morning on," recalls Geoff Costeloe, "it became just a slog, with chaps just sticking it out and hanging on. One did one's best to keep morale up, and it was high right to the end. By then, we'd collected people from other units – some RASC, a few glider pilots, and even an American Air Force pilot, who'd been shot down." As he implied, it had indeed become a test of sustained courage and endurance yet, as the mortaring and shelling took their toll, and ammunition became increasingly scarce, no ground was given. One of the developing problems was a growing shortage of food and water. Another was what Brigadier Hackett described as the "bolder" use of tanks and SP guns by the enemy, but there was never any question but that the soldiers of the 1st Airborne Division would hang on for as long as they were required to do so. Impressed beyond measure by the bearing and fortitude of the men with whom they were sharing these privations, the war correspondents, from their own slit trenches by the Hartenstein, drafted out their reports and radioed them back to London. Included in one of those, compiled by Alan Wood, was a passage of simple and eloquent sincerity, which ran, "If in the years to come, you meet a man who says, 'I was at Arnhem,' raise your hat to him and buy him a drink."

Chapter 12 SATURDAY 23rd SEPTEMBER 1944

"If you go down to the woods today"

Squadron HQ diary opened for Saturday 23rd September with an inauspicious entry:

> 0700: Raw and cold. Lack of food and sleep is beginning to tell. Usual hymn to the rising sun comes down in the form of mortar fire – heavier today than anything previous.

This particular form of harassment was probably the most vexatious trial which the men of Arnhem had to endure throughout the last stages of the battle. All around the perimeter, as it grew steadily in intensity from day to day, it was the repetitive, spiteful sequences of mortar fire that were most difficult to bear. Numerous survivors of Arnhem have also commented upon the methodical way in which German mortars began and ended, almost to the minute, in each day. In a later entry of that same day, David Allsop, himself, made the point:

> 1900: Evening hush. It is rather strange that we are mortared morning, midday, afternoon and evening until dusk. One could almost set a watch by it. It is so regular.

In the use of the mortar, the Germans ranked second only to the Russians as the most expert of all the combatant nations. For that reason not only did they make extensive use of captured Russian weapons, but many of their own designs were modelled on those of Russia. As a result, a wide variety of mortars was employed, most of which were of fairly high calibre, ranging from 81 to 120 mm. The 15 cm Nebelwerfer 41 was also used for firing rockets from its six barrels at two second intervals. These missiles had a quite distinctive sound in flight, which is why the British referred to them as "Moaning Minnies." Towards the end of the battle, it was the mortaring more than anything else which led to the build-up of casualties since, from high-trajectory missiles, there was no guaranteed cover. Inevitably, with the type of saturation bombing which the Germans put across towards the end of the week, there was an increased incidence of direct hits on many of the trench positions.

One extremely frightening development which accompanied it all was the use of phosphorus bombs. This was recalled by Bill Cook, who was in the line of slit trenches by Squadron HQ: "I remember how I partially covered my trench for protection against them. What made it worse was that they used to burst in the trees behind us and, since they were just twenty feet to the top, it was only because the trees were so bushy that we had any kind of protection at all against falling pieces." But, as Cook and the others found out, not even nature's cover was permanently guaranteed because, towards the end of that week, the trees themselves gradually became denuded of foliage and branches. "I had seen photographs from the 1914–18 war," says Ray Evans, who was in one of the adjacent trenches, "and of woodland completely stripped, but I never thought that I should actually see it happen. Yet over the days that we were there, the trees behind us became barer and barer, until only the stumps, without branches or leaves or anything, were left sticking up. It was quite uncanny." This same impression is also one of Bob Coldicott's most lasting memories of Arnhem: "Every tree in our area finished up," he says, "as clean as a telegraph pole."

In the midst of it there were some lucky escapes. One such instance from his own experience is remembered by Douglas Swinscow who, prior to his temporary departure, was in a slit trench near that which served David Allsop as a Squadron HQ. "The night was quiet for part of the time," he recollects, "because I do remember sleeping, but when I woke up I was astonished to find an unexploded 105 mm shell sitting tipped on the rim of my trench. It must have landed with a great bump in the night and just not gone off – perhaps because it landed on its edge instead of on the nose cone."

In the face of the bloody carnage brought about by mortar and rocket fire, it was truly astonishing that so many men managed to bear up as well as they did. As one writer* has put it, "To remain cheerful beneath it, when desperately short of water, food and ammunition needed a constant effort of will." Yet the remarkable thing was that, not only did so many put up with it day after day, some even managed to extract humour from the situation. This is particularly illustrated in a story told by Ray Evans, arising out of the British awareness that some German mortars, like the 10 cm Nebelwerfer 35 were designed to fire gas bombs. "One morning," recollects Evans, "there was a mortar explosion close at hand, accompanied by a lot of smoke. It was only smoke, but presumably someone must have thought that gas was at last being used, because he blew a whistle. We all knew that this was the official signal for gas but, immediately it sounded, right away someone piped up with the cry of 'Half-time'!"

That morning, the Germans laid down a heavier concentration than on previous days, so much so that, at the time, David Allsop was prompted to note that "it made the eardrums sore." From the early hours it was also evident that, following the relative restraint of the previous day, strong enemy attacks were being mounted around the perimeter. At the Squadron HQ positions, German voices could be heard quite clearly, and figures discerned moving about in the woods, only one field's distance away to the west.

Fears of increasing penetration by German armour were also seen to have been well justified, as various sectors of the British defensive area reported attacks. By noon, the 1st Border Regiment had been assaulted by SP guns, flame-throwing tanks and infantry, reported to be Roumanian SS. Fortunately, the "Mediums" south of the river again proved to be invaluable in support, and once more the enemy was repulsed. On the east side, at several places, similar infiltration took place, and the 21st Independent Company on Pietersbergseweg had a bad time, with self-propelled guns systematically reducing houses to rubble. Nearby, Hackett's Brigade HQ, which lay to the south-east of Oosterbeek crossroads was, for a time, overrun in the course of the early attacks.

At 0900 hours, Brigadier Hackett, whilst inspecting his area of responsibility, called on Captain Allsop at Squadron HQ on Oranjeweg. David Allsop still remembers how Hackett almost

* Hilary St J. Saunders: *The Red Beret.*

always seemed to want to ignore the battle, and talk instead about the more pleasurable aspects of life back in England. "He also," says Allsop, "seemed to have the idea that it was good for the chaps in the slit trenches to see him walking about, and so he tended to ignore the firing. When Hackett came and talked to you, it wasn't crouched down in a hole in the ground – you got out and strolled around, as if you were at Henley!"

By this time, the growing penetration of the perimeter and the mounting pressure from enemy groups east and west of Divisional HQ was pointing to the very real danger that the British positions could be cut right across. In retrospect, one cannot but conclude that the Germans could have done this at any time from Thursday onwards, and certainly with ease from Saturday. One must simply accept that, for whatever reasons they may have had, they chose not to do so. Nevertheless, the gradual shrinking of the perimeter, if it did not produce an overwhelming of the British-held positions, did lead to some incongruous situations in which it would appear that some Germans, at least, rode or walked unwittingly into difficulties. Ernest Jenkins, who, from the time of his separation from D Troop on Wednesday, had been dug in at the side of the Hartenstein, later recollected some of those. "I remember a German supply truck," he said, "coming up the main road (Utrechtseweg), and the driver seemed suddenly to realize that he was in trouble, so he accelerated and tried to get away up the road straight over from our position (Steijnweg). As he was turning, a 6-pounder fired, and killed the driver and one of the passengers – the shell went straight through both of them. We got cigars and black bread from that truck, because they brought it in with a towline. We also discovered that the front-seat passenger had had his arm and shoulder blown away, although his hand was still left in his pocket. I remember, too, that shortly after that incident, a group of Germans came up the same road in marching formation. Whether they didn't know their way around properly or not I couldn't say, but it was astonishing how everyone just waited and held their fire until the Germans could be taken on with maximum casualties. I remember the chap from Chesterfield, who was sharing my trench, opened up with his Bren, and then they were scattering in all directions, but mainly up the same road as the lorry had gone. A number of them were killed and others wounded."

Following the earlier mortaring, enemy action began to build up at the A Troop positions on Paul Krugerstraat. To meet it, artillery support was called for by Division at 0742 hours, and answered only eight minutes later. Thereafter, intermittent skirmishing went on throughout the morning and, from the increased intensity and accuracy of small-arms fire, it was obvious that the enemy was engaging from points that were closer in than those of the previous day. Later in the morning, as part of a general retrenchment, the A Troop men on Joubertweg fell back on the main Troop base at the bakery crossroads. By then, too, alternative positions had been dug by the defenders in the gardens of the houses, mainly as a consequence of the increasing activity of self-propelled guns. "Houses," as Brigadier Hackett was later to remark, "are a snare, unless you can keep the SP guns at length and round the corner." Unfortunately, the British had neither the men nor the resources to do that, which meant that, to the danger from high explosive, was added the additional hazard of falling brickwork and wood timbers. In such circumstances, a slit trench in the front garden could be a more desirable defensive position than any alternative in the solid house that lay immediately to the rear.

To understand the true nature of this new threat, one needs to bear in mind that the SP gun was a vehicle similar in nature to a tank. The main distinction was that the original tank turret had been replaced with an anti-tank gun. For that reason they were often referred to as "tank hunters". Foremost amongst the various models produced was the *Sturmgeschütz* III, which was based on the tank chassis of the PzKpfw III. The StuG III had armour up to 80 mm thick with side-skirting plates for greater protection, it weighed twenty-four tons and carried a 105 mm gun. Its firing range was something like seven miles, which meant, of course, that its destructive potential was massive when discharged – as so many of them were – at the distance of only a few feet from the side of a suburban house!

On that morning, one SP gun in particular had been roaming the area in the vicinity of Paul Krugerstraat. Occasionally it would crash a shell into one or other of the houses, and the obvious increase in this activity was giving rise to serious concern. To combat the mobile gun there was little that the British airborne men could do, for they were only lightly armed. A Troop did, however, have one anti-tank gun, a PIAT, which was designed to fire a three-pound bomb. It operated on the spigot principle, whereby the missile was launched from an open trough and was driven on the first part of its journey by a steel rod propelled into a hollow tube in the bomb's tail. The weapon itself weighed only thirty-two pounds, but it was not a particularly pleasant one to handle, and there was never any assured guarantee of success. PIAT bombs, however, could be effective against tanks and SP guns up to a distance of 100 yards, although the result could be unpredictable, for the bomb might simply glance off the armour. The main disadvantage – and it was a considerable one – was that the user had to allow the enemy vehicle to come within effective range before firing, and against a StuG III that took a very great deal of courage. Nevertheless, the decision was made to try to do something about the threat and, with only two bombs, Trooper Frank Mann, a young Scot from Coatbridge, took his PIAT out to a slit trench in the front garden just across from the burnt-out bakery, there to await the arrival of the self-propelled gun. Henry Venes can still remember how calm Mann was, for no one had any illusions about the danger and the probable outcome. It was true that he had already distinguished himself by disposing, with one PIAT shot, of a sniper in the grounds of the Hartenstein. This time, the circumstances were very different, for the advantage would lie almost certainly with the enemy. In the event that Mann should fail to register a successful hit, his chances of escaping alive would be slight.

Into the slit trench with him went 2 Section Sergeant, Gwyn Williams, a short stocky Welshman from Glamorgan, and his job was to support Mann as best he could. As Williams recalls, this turned out to be support in the truest sense of the word: "'Jock' (Mann) and I started off and reached our trench at the crossroads. It was too deep to get a firing position, so I told him to kneel on my back. We first carefully placed the PIAT in position, loaded ready for firing, I then took up a stooped position, and 'Jock' knelt on me. I remember thinking that we had only one chance, and could not afford to miss."

The SP gun was expected to follow its usual route southwards on Mariaweg which, at that point, ran down a fairly steep slope to the crossroads. John Stevenson recollects that they had to wait about half an hour before the dreaded clanking was once more heard and the StuG III gradually came into view, crawling around the bend of the road and slithering down the hill, its great steel barrel ready to stab out fire and destruction. From the partial cover of the privet hedge that bordered the garden, Frank Mann saw it appear, and whispered a cautious warning to Williams. He knew that the lumbering monster had one weak spot and had already made up his mind to concentrate on that. "I remember the gun coming down the hill," says Mann, "and how it was covered over with camouflage net and tree branches, so that it was difficult to see the outline clearly. I lined up on it, scarcely daring to move, and waited until I was sure I had it in range, then gently squeezed the trigger. I had aimed at the track, and as the bomb exploded I

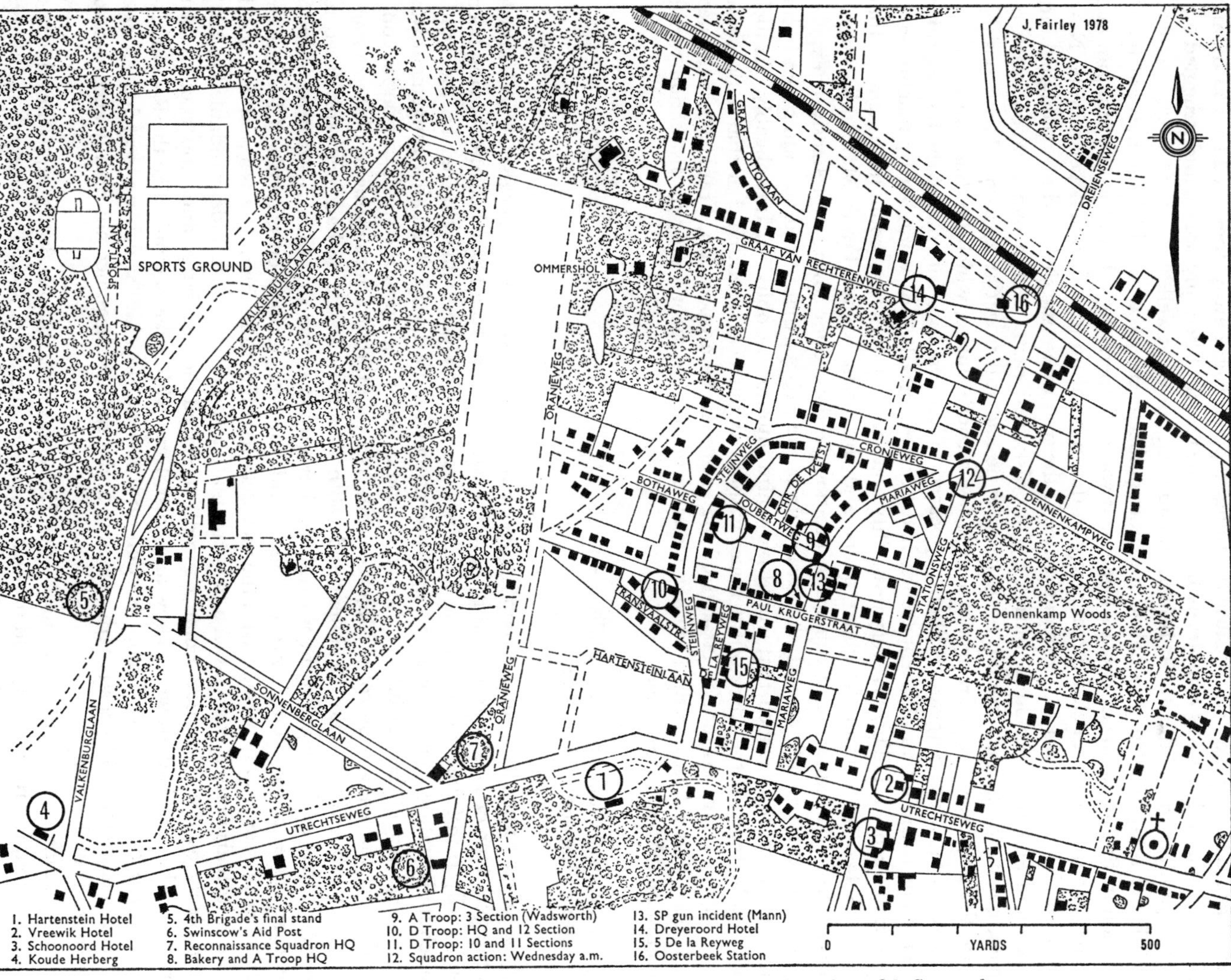

Map 11 Reconnaissance Squadron positions: Wednesday 20th–Tuesday 26th September 1944

knew that I'd hit it square on, because the thing stopped. Right away, they fired back at us, and suddenly I found that I was completely buried in the trench. I held my breath and struggled out, but I couldn't even find the PIAT, because it had been buried as well."

With the self-propelled gun halted and immobilized, the crew would later have to try to abandon it. But in the meantime, its armament was still operating – both the 105 mm gun and the associated MG 34, a belt-fed machine gun that fired at up to 900 rounds per minute. Now, in front of the trench, was an enormous crater at the spot where the shell had first ploughed into the ground and then exploded. Buried by the disturbed earth, Mann had escaped death by inches, but his problems were not over, because he had still to get away as quickly as possible before the gun crew could fire again. In the few seconds during which he dug himself out, it registered that, whilst Sergeant Williams appeared to have escaped into one of the houses, some glider pilots manning an adjacent trench had been either killed or wounded by machine-gun fire from the StuG III. There is every possibility that the crew of the gun could have assumed that the attack had come from the glider pilots, and this perhaps gave Frank Mann his chance. Breaking from the exposed and vulnerable position, he dashed for cover, apprehensively expecting to hear, at every split second, the savage zip of the MG 34 that would cut him down in his tracks or the crash of a shell that would blow him into instant oblivion. Inexplicably, his luck held, and he reached the cover of the house without as much as a scratch. For that action, one of the most courageous individual acts of the entire Arnhem operation, Frank Mann earned the United States Distinguished Service Cross, a decoration second only in distinction to the Congressional Medal of Honour.

> So David prevailed over the Philistine
> with a sling and with a stone

Most of his comrades from A Troop had been able to witness Mann's successful PIAT attack on the gun. One of those who missed it, however, was Trooper Ken Hope because, having been temporarily transferred to one of the near-by houses which was being covered by the 156th Parachute Battalion men, he was no longer operating with the Troop. Such an arrangement was one consequence of the flexibility achieved through the setting up of the small composite command under the overall control of Major Powell. As a result, the various elements of Reconnaissance Squadron, Glider Pilot Regiment and 156th Parachute Battalion had inevitably fused to the extent that *ad hoc* secondment was a logical extension of the situation. A major drawback was that moves of this kind, however logical and however justified on grounds of immediate tactical need, were rarely popular with the men detailed off to fulfil them. It was a problem as old as the British army itself, very much a personal matter and all the more understandable for that. In simple terms, it was just that a man assuredly preferred the association and support of his own comrades whom he had grown to know and trust. Even within the one unit, like the Reconnaissance Squadron, there were Troop, Section and personal loyalties which transcended all else and were characterized by a strength of feeling and a special allegiance not readily accorded to those outside of the group.

So it was that, on the Friday morning, when Hope was sent, with his Bren gun, to the adjacent 156th position, in order to help add to their fire power, the move was not entirely to his liking. They were fellow members of 1st Airborne Division and, like him, they wore the red beret – badge of brotherhood – with pride. Nor, as he recalls, was there any lack of friendly welcomings;

but they were not his comrades, nor was he theirs. United, albeit temporarily, with total strangers, he was very conscious of being the outsider. As he was to remark later, "In a tricky situation, a soldier believes he can rely on his mates and they on him." In this case, the human factor on both sides was unpredictable, so that there could be no unqualified assumptions of mutual trust. It was during that Saturday, the second day of what he describes as his "involuntary transfer", that Hope's hypothesis was put to the test. At that time, he was further along the Paul Krugerstraat, between two houses, with a pair of jeeps parked at the back of them. A short time after Mann had knocked out the SP gun, both vehicles were hit, probably by mortar fire, and each went up in a great "whoosh" of flame and exploding ammunition. "We retired hastily," says Hope, "across gardens and vegetable plots, and I remember racing for a gap in a wire fence to reach cover. As I was about to burst through it, a 156th man flung me off balance with a perfectly delivered soccer shoulder charge, and I was sent sprawling. As the 156th paratrooper entered the gap, he collapsed in a heap, shot dead through the head. One of his pals then began to rain curses upon me, implying that I was somehow responsible for his friend's death. It was then that I quietly picked up my Bren, stole away and rejoined A Troop, orders or no orders. I saw the familiar faces, no one asked questions and I felt very relieved." It is a sad story and yet, irrational as in some ways this small incident may appear, within the context of what comradeship often meant at Arnhem, it is quite comprehensible.

On Saturday morning, D Troop was still holding on Steijnweg. It had also suffered a heavy barrage by mortars, following which, intensive small-arms covering fire had been used by the Germans in order to screen a forward movement. By 0900 hours, the enemy was in occupation of a line of houses on the north side of Bothaweg, Steijnweg and Cronjéweg. At that time, Bob Thomson was in a trench in the garden of a house on the west side of Steijnweg, between Paul Krugerstraat and Bothaweg, and he recalls that the British had the backing of a Mark III 6-pounder anti-tank gun which had been sited in a shop window about 200 yards beyond the Troop HQ position.

The opening enemy attack came on Steijnweg at about 1000 hours, with a mixed force of tanks and infantry. "The German tanks came down from the north," recalls James Pyper, "and having first fired their guns they retreated, but came back twice more, with infantry spread out on either side. At first, they were engaged by the anti-tank gun, but it didn't last, for one of the tanks blew it to smithereens." Both gun and crew were destroyed, and two D Troop men who were out in support of it with Brens were wounded. One of them was Thomson, who managed to make his way back into the house unaided, despite the fact that he had been hit in three places. His companion, who had bad leg injuries, had to be helped and it was Trooper Smith who volunteered to go out and bring him in. This he did successfully, under intense fire. Recollecting his impressions just before being hit, Thomson clearly remembers engaging the tank, which had infantry sheltering behind it. There then occurred one of the German withdrawals described by Pyper, when the tank pulled back out of sight into Cronjéweg. When it suddenly reappeared, Thomson recalls that it let fly immediately and it was then that he was wounded in the back and head.

The destruction of the British anti-tank gun left the dwindling force on northern Steijnweg with little defence against any further attack of armour. Because of this, at about 1100 hours, the house occupied by Pyper and Smith was completely destroyed by shells. To the onlookers, all that could be seen was smoke and dust but, miraculously, the defenders escaped injury and withdrew across to Captain Park's house. Pyper still has chilling memories of how, in the destruction of his strongpoint, the momentum of the shells carried them straight through both the outer and inner walls of the house, just as if the structure were made of cardboard. Throughout the actions in which D Troop was to be involved that day, James Pyper, as Troop Sergeant, was a tower of strength. Married and coming up for thirty years of age, he had transferred to the newly-formed Reconnaissance Corps from the Scots Guards, the regiment which he had joined originally as a young, peace-time recruit. To his new unit he brought a sense of committed professionalism, and in recognition of the courageous part played at Arnhem, he was later to be awarded a well-merited Military Medal.

At the Squadron HQ positions on Oranjeweg, the occupants of the slit trenches were also becoming increasingly conscious of the mounting fury of the battle. In the course of the morning, they too had found small-arms fire more and more troublesome, in itself an indication that the enemy was moving in closer. One of the casualties was a young Dutch resistance worker, who had attached himself to the Squadron. Ray Evans recalls that he had made himself useful in a number of ways, particularly during the evenings when he had fetched water from nearby houses. By the Saturday, he had managed to get hold of a British uniform, but had not long put it on before he was injured. Stan Collishaw, who was there at the time, remembers that the boy's main concern, expressed as the stretcher bearers were taking him away, was that the Germans should not get hold of him whilst he was wearing it, as he was certain to be shot. In addition to the casualties, several near misses also took place, the most notable of which involved Lieutenant Ladds, the Signals officer, who came under heavy machine-gun fire whilst trying to repair a fault on the Squadron control 22 set.

All morning, there was continuous noise around the Divisional area and, as an obvious prelude to yet another attack on the British perimeter, a fresh mortar barrage came down at about 1430 hours. It was during this particular "stonk" that David Allsop was himself wounded by shrapnel, but made do with first-aid in order to stay at his post. To make matters worse, a terrifying addition to the German onslaught was introduced. "That was the day," Jimmy Cooke recalls, "when they brought the flame-thrower up, and I think it was that which frightened me more than anything else. It fired out of the wood, and those great tongues of flame, about twenty feet long, travelled over our slit trenches and landed at the back of us. We knew when it was going to be used, because they had it on a tank, and we used to listen for the tracks coming up. These things struck fear and terror into everyone, because we reckoned that they only had to dip down a little, and that would be it."

Towards mid-afternoon, the Squadron HQ men heard the sound of music coming from across the field to the west of their positions. Something similar had been audible on the previous morning, but it had been too far over on their right flank to be comprehensible. Now, it was much closer and, as their ears became attuned, they realized, to their astonishment, that it was a record of the "Teddy Bears' Picnic". Corporal "Tommy" Trinder of the Squadron's HQ Intelligence Section was in one of the trenches, and remembers the occasion as one of a number of such episodes: "It sounded as if they had some kind of loudspeaker, and they'd start out with this tune, 'If you go down to the woods today . . .' Then a voice would tell us that we had fought well, but that the 2nd Army couldn't reach us, so we were to walk out of the trenches with our hands up, and come forward to surrender. They always said that we'd be well treated." Trinder reports that the speech would then be repeated, always with an emphasis upon the fact that they were being sacrificed for nothing, but the musical repertoire would perhaps be changed to Glenn Miller or the voice of Deanna Durbin in a sugary rendering of "Home Sweet Home".

Needless to say, the German offers were not accepted, and what verbal responses there were from the British side of the field varied from the fairly innocuous "Bollocks" to more imaginative suggestions which even a contortionist, howsoever determined, could never have hoped to achieve. As for the suggestion that surrendering British troops would be well treated, David Christie recalls one reply from the Reconnaissance positions: "Come out and fight, you German bastards, and *we'll* treat *you* well!" They were brave words but, for the men who were separated from the enemy by only the width of a potato field, it could hardly have been anything other than a period of tense waiting and watching. "For us," said Bill Cook, "it eventually seemed to come down to the simple alternatives of whether 30 Corps would get through in time, or whether we would be overrun. My little world was that wood in front of me, and I don't know yet why the Germans didn't come over, because I could see nothing to stop them."

The most probable reason, of course, was that the enemy had no clear idea of the strength of the British positions around the Divisional HQ area. Certainly, they had shown no such reticence to attack elsewhere and, in the afternoon of that day, both A and D Troops suffered fresh assault. A Troop's most northerly position was, by then, the house adjacent to the bakery, and Mike Grubb recalls how, early on that Saturday afternoon, he went out into the back garden and found something quite unexpected: "I remember I walked up through the vegetable plot, just on my own, when I suddenly realized that there was a great long gun barrel, poking over the hedge at the bottom. It was either a tank or an SP gun, so I hastily withdrew. I don't know whether they saw me or not." It was, in fact, an SP gun, and Willie Fraser, who was standing looking out from the top floor remembers that the whole hedge started to sway and then came down as the gun penetrated the back garden. Almost immediately, it opened up on the house and, in a few shots, made it completely untenable. Jim Taylor, who was also upstairs at the time, remembers how a great gaping hole suddenly appeared beside him, whilst Dougie Galbraith, who had been standing nearby, simply disappeared: "I was standing at the top of a flight of stairs at the time," recollected Galbraith, "when the shell demolished a part of the wall in front of me. I was picked up by the blast, and immediately found myself at the foot of the stairs, still standing up!" It was a narrow escape for both Taylor and Galbraith and, as a result of that one incident, Galbraith was to be partially deaf for the remainder of his life.

Shortly afterwards, A Troop had to carry out a rapid withdrawal to the south side of the street. So rapid was it that Ron Spicer still has the memory of somehow getting across the road, with a rifle in one hand and a large tin of newly-made tea in the other! From there, they ran westwards across a number of the back gardens, under heavy enemy fire, to finish up in occupation of houses on both sides of the De la Reyweg, a short street which ran southwards from Paul Krugerstraat, and then angled westwards into Steijnweg. Inevitably, there were casualties, one of them Mike Grubb himself, who was hit in the foot. Maurice Riches, who was 1 Section Sergeant, has his own memories of the action: "After the attack, Lieutenant Stevenson and I went down the street with plenty of fire at us, so we cut across and ran through the gardens. Whilst we were doing this, we saw an officer from another unit go down. We took up fresh positions in houses in the next street, and it was only later in the night that this officer knocked on the door. When we opened it, he fell in." The officer was Captain Raymond Stevens of 1st Forward (Airborne) Observation Unit, Royal Artillery, and he had been badly wounded. John Stevenson remembers getting him down into the cellar and administering morphine: "He was obviously in dreadful pain," recalls Stevenson, "with a fracture in one of his arms that was so bad that the bone was sticking right out. I remember that the cellar was full of Dutch people and he lay in one corner. From the look of him, I had a feeling that his deteriorating condition was not simply due to his arm, so I undid his battledress trousers, and found all his intestines out in a great lump. I remember that one of the Dutch people said some prayers as he lay there, and how he spoke with a great effort, and said something to me about a cricket ground. I had to leave him at that point, and the Dutch people said they'd look after him as best they could." Captain Stevens died in the early hours of the following morning.

The newly-occupied houses on De la Reyweg were approximately one hundred yards west and slightly to the south of the bakery crossroads, and the first priority was to make them as defensible as possible. Fortunately, the German attack eased off, so that the men were able to do this, relatively undisturbed. In a way, this pattern was almost characteristic of perimeter action, both here and elsewhere, for it was noticed that the enemy very often failed to press home any advantage gained, with a final decisive thrust. Time and again, this served to provide the British with a welcome respite and an opportunity to consolidate.

One of the fresh positions on De la Reyweg was in the wooden loft of a brick wash-house, which abutted the rear wall of the house itself. It was there that, under Galbraith's orders, Spicer, Sutherby and Hope established themselves, with weapon slits in the timber of the loft sides, and a "mousehole" knocked through the brickwork into the house at ground level. Hope recalls that once they were set up, they could see German infantry working their way across to the front and right of their positions: "They ran full pelt between the gaps in the houses, and it was rather like a fun-fair pot-shot range, when one tries to anticipate the appearance of the target and open fire. Then, almost unbelievably, the biggest German I ever saw ran into the alley, halted, and stood there in full view. He must have been about six feet four inches tall, wearing full infantry equipment. I think I was too astonished to fire, but Stan Sutherby's reaction was quicker. He slammed off a burst, and the German fell and screamed for what seemed ages." This same incident was referred to later by Lieutenant Stevenson, principally on account of its unusual sequel. "Our chaps," he said, "couldn't get to him because of sniper fire, so they gave him a lullaby of 'Lili Marlene' through the window – the sort of mad thing that people were doing."

Not long after this, there was a period of shelling, in which Ken Hope's house was hit. The effect of this was to demolish the front wooden wall of the loft occupied by Hope and his two companions, with all three having a lucky escape. When the dust had settled, they found that they were sitting up there, completely exposed to view, and so all of them scrambled quickly down the ladder into the brick wash-house below. "It was then," says Hope, "that Lieutenant Galbraith poked his head through the 'mousehole' and demanded a 'situation report' – that's expressing it mildly! We attempted to explain that our cover was virtually non-existent, but he simply dismissed this with a curt, 'Get back up there and fix it, then!' So, we climbed rather sheepishly back into the loft, and shored up the woodwork as best we could. The fork of the apple tree was riven and lacerated by the blast, and there were jagged rents in the upper part of the woodwork. Apart from superficial scratches and being smothered in dust, none of us was harmed."

In terms of general location, the net result of A Troop's move had been to push them closer to both D Troop and Squadron HQ, and the whole action, taken together with what had been happening at the D Troop positions, was illustrative of the extent to which the perimeter had been extensively infiltrated from both sides. D Troop, in the meantime, had been enduring a battering which was, no doubt, part of the same concerted German attack. At around 1430 hours in the afternoon, a thrust came in from the east side, in the course of which shells ripped into Bentall's house and made it as untenable as Pyper's had become in the morning. It only took three shots from an SP gun to demolish and blow out the walls, with the curious result that the roof caved in, almost intact. Amidst the dust and smoke, Bentall, Slater and Peach crawled out of the rubble, dazed and groggy, but each still in one piece. All three then dashed over to the one remaining house, held by Captain Park and what was left of his men. On the way, they met with a token show of hostility from a small party of young SS men, but managed to get back safely to Troop HQ.

There then occurred one of those curious episodes which, incongruous as it would have been in normal circumstances, was additionally so in the context of the battle. From the garden outside came shrill screams, which the D Troop men at first attributed to one of the elderly Dutch ladies whose home was being used as a strongpoint. Acting on the assumption that one of them might have left the shelter of the cellar and been wounded, Sergeant Bentall crawled outside to render assistance with a morphine amphoule. To his astonishment, he then discovered that the noise was not coming from either of the ladies, but from one of the young SS men. He appeared to be not older than seventeen, and it was apparent that he had been slightly wounded. The principal cause of his distress, however, appeared to be terror at having been left behind by the others. Obviously he expected the worst to happen. Contrary to his expectations, Bentall did not shoot him, but instead took his trousers off, belted his backside and then threw him over the wall into the street. All firing stopped as the representative of the master race scampered up Steijnweg, clad only in steel helmet, boots and underwear, to the accompaniment of wolf whistles, laughter and the inevitable bawdy comment from the British defenders.

With a record of mounting success in blasting the British out of their positions on Steijnweg, it was virtually certain that the Germans would keep up the pressure and, perhaps, mount yet another attack before nightfall. It came in at 1600 hours, this time from both east and west, and two more casualties were immediately sustained due to shelling. Park's men held for half an hour, before eventually withdrawing about 150 yards south to a house at the junction of Steijnweg and Transvaalstraat. This one had escaped damage, but the growth in activity of the German self-propelled guns had demonstrated that the house itself would be vulnerable. Recognizing this, Captain Park ordered his men to dig in in the garden, but in view of the growing seriousness of his position decided also to seek advice as to future strategy. As a result, Lieutenant Alan Pascal volunteered to return to Squadron HQ to report on the situation.

It was after dark when Pascal arrived at Allsop's position on Oranjeweg. Geoff Costeloe, who was present at the time, still remembers how Alan Pascal conveyed Park's message that, with the Germans right on his doorstep and his own level of casualties extremely high, he had considerable misgivings about the ability of D Troop to hold any longer. Clearly, the infiltration of the perimeter area at that point was becoming more serious all the time, and there was every indication that the Hartenstein could very well, itself, soon become the most northerly-held position. Having listened to the report, David Allsop felt it right that General Urquhart should be informed, and Costeloe was asked to escort Pascal across to Divisional HQ. "I remember," says Costeloe, "how desperately tired Urquhart looked, but how patiently he listened as we explained the situation. He didn't interrupt at all, but when we'd finished, he turned to Pascal and said, 'I'm very sorry, my boy, but I'm afraid you must go back and hold.'" The remnants of D Troop were also requested to try if possible to retake their former position, and, as they returned to the Squadron lines, neither the adjutant nor the young subaltern had any illusions about what the outcome would probably be. Like all the others who had fought and endured, Alan Pascal would continue to find the stoicism and the courage to go on, but Geoff Costeloe has never forgotten the look of distress that was registered upon his face as he set out to rejoin his Troop. Costeloe never saw him again.

On his return, Pascal found that the dwindling group of weary survivors had taken another heavy mortar attack during his absence and there had been two further casualties. Taking advantage of the lull which followed, Park then complied with Divisional instructions by leading his men back to their previously held positions at the Steijnweg/Paul Krugerstraat junction. It was not his intention to reoccupy houses whose value as strongpoints had gone, but to dig in, in the gardens, as they had done before. To their surprise, the Germans were found to have once more withdrawn, this time to the line of Bothaweg/Joubertweg, one street further to the north. Despite this, one additional casualty was suffered on the way back into the positions, when Trooper Slater was hit by a sniper. Whilst Pyper and Bentall were dressing his wound, in the shelter of a low wall, Slater was once more shot, this time in the thigh. In the circumstances, they could do little other than get him into a cellar, making him as comfortable as possible and then continue with their task. At that stage D Troop had been reduced to two officers and ten other ranks, and it was with a sense of justifiable foreboding that, at 1830 hours, the survivors once more dug themselves in. The ammunition situation was not good but, again, the intrepid Smith volunteered to scavenge around the houses previously occupied by the Troop. This task he accomplished successfully, although again under fire. Thereafter, listening posts were kept all night.

By late afternoon, the A Troop men were well established in their new positions. One of the main strongpoints was at numbers 5 and 7 De la Reyweg, two small semi-detached houses that made up a red-brick block. Troop HQ was set up in a shed at the rear of the house, and Hope recalls how Spicer and he were given the job of digging a slit trench in the floor of the shed, with observation holes splintered out of the base of the wooden walls. Further slit trenches were then dug in the back gardens and, from an adjacent chicken coop, field telephone communication was established with the HQ position. All over the confined area at the southern end of the street, men sweated until long after midnight to get themselves well dug in before the dawn. Positions were also taken up south of this, on the east side of Steijnweg, in three other blocks of semi-detached houses. "All around us," recalls Hope, "we could hear the clink of metal against stone or brick, with the interminable orchestration of explosive, rattling machine-gun fire, and the crackle of flames."

Understandably, too, in the face of mounting enemy pressure and a deteriorating situation, the need for vigilance was all the more necessary, which meant that foot reconnaissance had to be maintained, in order to try to anticipate any possible renewal of the onslaught. Cover of night provided the best opportunity for undertaking this, and Jim Taylor who went out on several occasions with Dougie Galbraith, recalls the technique employed: "We used to walk quite openly and in step, so that the sound of our footsteps would be difficult to pinpoint. In that way, we believed that it would be less easy for the Germans to determine whether we were in the middle of the road or to one side or the other. When we walked, we did it together, and when one of us halted, the other did too."

These were also the occasions on which there were fruitful possibilities of being able to catch the odd German sniper off guard, and it was from one such sortie that Galbraith returned, triumphantly bearing an MG 42 and ammunition. This prized weapon was one of the most sophisticated all-purpose light machine-guns in the German army and had an incredible fire rate of up to 1500 rounds per minute. When it was discharged, it produced a noise like the sound of tearing linoleum. Galbraith acquired it by disposing of its two-man team.

By mid-day, it had already become clear that the stepping up of enemy activity had affected almost every other area of the defensive perimeter. Even before nine o'clock in the morning, what remained of the 10th Parachute Battalion was forced to evacuate the rubble of the houses to which it had desperately clung at Oosterbeek crossroads. Down by the river, an attack came in, towards noon, on the west side. This was the position held by two HQ platoons of the Border Regiment, together with some stragglers from their shattered B Company. There were also Poles – those who had crossed the river in the early hours – who had been added to the Border Regiment's meagre numbers. They, more than any other group, suffered a heavy toll of casualties in the pre-noon attack, and lost approximately fifty per cent of their strength, mainly because they had failed to dig in to sufficient depth.

Meantime, anxious to make personal contact with Lieutenant-General Browning, in order to spell out the details of the 1st Airborne Division's predicament, Charles Mackenzie had set off southwards on the other side of the river. There he had met up with Captain Richard Wrottesley again, and so was able to travel with a group of four Household Cavalry vehicles. On the way, his own armoured car had a brief brush with a German half-track, before becoming bogged in a ditch. After narrowly escaping capture by an enemy patrol, Mackenzie eventually got through, but did not gain much comfort at the reception given to his news. The situation, of course, was that both Browning and Horrocks had a mounting set of problems in other directions for, in the early afternoon, their own lines of communication had been cut between Veghel and Uden.

By 1300 hours on that day, most of the Polish troops, a little under 1000 all ranks, were still on the south bank of the river whilst, at the same time, steady German pressure was being maintained on the British perimeter positions to the north of it. Just about then, Brigadier Hackett was approached by a German officer carrying a Red Cross flag, who told him that unless the British troops withdrew from the vicinity of their dressing station at the Hotel Tafelberg, he would be forced to bring self-propelled guns to bear and blow it to pieces. Hackett stalled for time, then called the man's bluff by refusing to entertain the idea that the British should withdraw a single yard. In the event, the MDS was spared, and the barrage came in on more southerly positions. The fact that there were something like thirty wounded Germans in the British hospital could well have helped to influence the German decision.

At just after 4 o'clock in the afternoon, the last supply drop of all came in from England. In the conditions of the shrinking perimeter, only a very small quantity was picked up, for snipers had become a strong deterrent to any movement above ground, and this made collection extremely difficult. With almost all recovery vehicles also out of action, the few that were left could make little progress along roads blocked by fallen trees and the rubble of shattered houses. One successful piece of air transportation was, however, carried out further south when, on the orders of HQ Airborne Corps, the forty-one delayed aircraft of the 1st Polish Parachute Brigade successfully and accurately dropped the remainder of Sosabowski's force just east of Grave. It was well clear of the combat area, and the move demonstrated that already steps were being taken to avoid reinforcing failure. In the meantime, as the Guards Armoured Division continued to secure the Nijmegen bridgehead, 43rd (Wessex) Division made a determined attack to take Elst. By the end of the day, 130 Infantry Brigade, consisting of the 7th Hampshires and the 4th and 5th Dorsets was established at Driel, whilst 214 Brigade fought in Elst itself.

For Freddie Gough, Saturday ended on a note of high tragedy. Throughout the day, he and his brother officers had been kept under guard at the house in Velp, but in the afternoon it was made clear that they were to be moved to Zutphen for interrogation. Having in mind that something of this nature might occur and not wishing to have himself included in any nominal roll which might be compiled by the Germans prior to departure, Major Deane-Drummond had already disappeared into his improvized hiding place. As a last precaution, he had stuck a matching piece of wallpaper over the keyhole on the outside of the door and settled down to await developments. These came late in the afternoon, when the rest of the officers were led out under German escort and put aboard a 3-ton lorry.

It was no more than a twenty mile trip ahead of them, but some never saw the end of the journey for, in its course, there occurred a thoroughly discreditable episode which destroyed completely whatever favourable impression the captured British soldiers had built up of their adversaries. Freddie Gough, who was deeply involved, retained in his memory every detail of what happened: "We got under way for Zutphen in the lorry, and I was standing next to Tony Hibbert and Dennis Mumford. Somewhere north of Arnhem, as we were going through a village, they said to me, 'We're jumping,' and I said, 'OK, go ahead,' so right away they jumped from the left of the vehicle, which was its off side. Unfortunately, just as they were doing it, a truckload of SS appeared on the road, coming from the opposite direction. Tony and Dennis both got away, but the SS, instead of firing at them, signalled our lorry to stop, then turned their guns on us and shot straight into the back of the stationary vehicle, killing a number of our chaps as well as hitting two of their own guards."

The incident took place at the village of Brummen, and the fact that both vehicles were at rest when it occurred and that the SS quite deliberately opened fire on what they must have realized was a group of unarmed and defenceless prisoners made this a deliberate act of murder. In truth, four British officers and a war correspondent were murdered by the SS in this criminal act. The correspondent was novelist Anthony Cotterill and two of the officers, both of whom were mortally wounded, were members of Gough's own Squadron. Captain Tony Platt, OC HQ Troop, died later that night, and Captain Trevor McNabb, the Intelligence Officer died four days afterwards.

Of the immediate aftermath, Freddie Gough later remembered three things. The first was that, as they sat by the side of the road, the SS refused to allow a very heroic Dutch doctor to attend to the wounded; it was made very clear that if he persisted in trying to do so he would be shot. The second was that one of Gough's companions, John Killick, who understood German, told him that the SS men were seriously discussing when and how they ought to shoot the rest of them. Because of this, Gough felt impelled to make a very conscious effort to talk to the Germans, to distract them from further murderous intent. It was a very courageous thing to do, because he had obviously encountered one group of enemy soldiers who had little regard for human life or the rules of the game. Having tasted blood already, it was unlikely that they would shrink from further atrocities. The third thing which impressed Gough was the extreme youth of those responsible, each a fearsome product of the ideologies of the Third Reich, yet not one of them, in his estimation, much older than seventeen years. Fortunately for the British officers, they were delivered from any further savagery at the hands of the trigger-happy SS youths, because the German staff at Zutphen, concerned at the delay in their arrival, had sent down a car with a major of German intelligence. Never was Gough so pleased to see anyone for, just prior to the German officer's arrival, Killick had indicated to him that the boys had virtually made up their minds to kill them all and be done with it. As the officer stepped out of his car, Gough made the imperative demand to him: "Tell these little bastards to lay off!" The German officer's response was immediate and helpful and he very quickly established control of the situation. Unfortunately the murderers were never brought to justice. The names of two of them were known but, although considerable efforts were made to trace them after the war, they were never found. As a result, to this day, the whole unsavoury episode has remained as just another unpunished war crime. Platt and McNabb were later buried at Enschede Cemetery.

At 2015 hours that night, General Urquhart once more despatched a signal:

> Many attacks during day by small parties inf, SP guns and tanks including flamethrowers. Each attack accompanied by very heavy mortaring and shelling within Div perimeter. After many alarms and excursions the latter remains substantially unchanged. Although very thinly held. Physical contact not yet made with those on south bank of river. Resup a flop, small quantities amn only gathered in. Still no food and all ranks extremely dirty owing to shortage of water. Morale still adequate, but continued heavy mortaring and shelling is having obvious effects. We shall hold but at the same time hope for a brighter 24 hours ahead.

Two and a half hours later, Lieutenant-Colonel Mackenzie, having safely negotiated the river crossing, reported back to the Hartenstein. He had made the return journey with relative ease and, in the last stages, had opportunely seized the chance to cross in a boat which was returning after having ferried a shot-down RAF officer over to the south bank. Not far away from where Mackenzie crossed there was other river activity, for Myers was organizing twelve assault boats of 130 Brigade which were engaged in attempting to carry over supplies and more of Sosabowski's men. The limited nature of the transportation, however, and the presence of the enemy in strong harassment positions on the north bank, made the Polish crossing a dangerous business, so that considerable numbers were picked off by the Germans. Not more than two hundred officers and men reached the other side. Mackenzie, meanwhile, reported to Urquhart on a plan devised by Horrocks and Thomas for a joint effort by Thomas's 43rd Division and Sosabowski's Poles. Had he chosen to do so, Mackenzie might also have communicated his own conviction, based upon what he had seen and heard, that all hope of relief had finally gone.

Towards evening, it was obvious that conditions within the perimeter had further deteriorated. By then, as Ernest Jenkins was later to remember, "the dead were laid out in rows in the grounds of the Hartenstein, in some cases piled one on top of the other." Food was desperately short and throughout the Hotel itself, the central heating radiators had long since been drained to provide drinking water. One growing menace, that of snipers, had become especially troublesome around the Divisional HQ whilst, all over, the wreckage of war had mounted steadily, with disabled vehicles littering the area and fallen trees, their branches tangled in overhead lines, lying in profusion across the roadways. "On the faces of the men," says Major-General Urquhart, "I could see the cumulative wear of lack of sleep and food and exposure. Dirt-caked and with heavy-lidded, reddened eyes, they had not an unlimited endurance before them, but their spirit was magnificent to see."

Amidst all the trials of a clearly deteriorating military situation the weather had not helped, for it had been an unpleasantly damp day. Heavy and continuous autumn rainfall was a fairly common characteristic of Oosterbeek and, with a saturated terrain consisting largely of grass and woodland, it could so easily become a cold and inhospitable place. To men who had barely slept for a week and had virtually run out of the basic necessities of life, it was one further burden that had to be borne. Yet even in adversity there could be compensations, for all through the night, as it poured down on the slit trenches and turned the sandy soil to mud, the rain water was gratefully collected by the airborne men in their oilcloth gascapes.

The onset of darkness also brought time for reflection. On that chilling Saturday night, it was hardly surprizing that for the members of the Reconnaissance Squadron, it was difficult to believe that a mere seven days earlier, each had been leading a regular and orderly life in the peaceful atmosphere of Ruskington village. So much had happened in the interval, that events and places which only a short time before had been so readily taken for granted, now suddenly appeared unreal. Images flickered into consciousness – of the little stream in the main street, of the exuberant conviviality of happier Saturday nights in the "Shoulder of Mutton", of Sunday morning worship in the quiet village church, of Whitehouse farm and Mr and Mrs Newton and Topsy – only to be driven out almost as soon as they had begun to sharpen into focus. From all that had been so familiar and so well-loved, those men, in the short interval of seven days, had grown to feel in every sense as detached as if they had been transported to another planet. Now, the true reality was measured, not by the sights and sounds of an English autumn relatively untouched by war, but by the blast of shell, the tearing crump of mortar bomb or the savage rattle of a machine-gun burst that in an instant could bring to any one of them an end of all things on earth. Nor was there any longer the possibility that in the days to come, normality as they had known it could ever again return, for such were the traumatic effects of what they had already endured that, for many, the memories of the week that was gone would rarely be absent from their thoughts for the remainder of their lives.

Roofless bakery at 23 Paul Krugerstraat, Oosterbeek: after the battle

(*R. Guthrie*)

Lieutenant A. A. "Bertie" Lickerish, HQ Troop.
He subsequently achieved fame by arresting William Joyce ("Lord Haw-Haw")
(See footnote p. 193)

(*Associated Newspapers Ltd*)

Sorting out arms at Nijmegen: Wednesday 27th September 1944
Extreme left: Tpr. Arthur "Chalky" White, *Centre:* Tpr. J. Cooke, *Extreme right:* Tpr. R. Coldicott

(Imperial War Museum)

Campaign map of Arnhem area: 1:25000
Arnhem Bridge should be shown at point captioned "Slachthuis" (*bottom right*).
Crossing point indicated further west was the location of the former "pontoon Bridge"

Chapter 13 SUNDAY 24th SEPTEMBER 1944

"*Thank you for the party*"

As the battle moved into its final stages, so did the character of enemy attack become bolder and more unpredictable. On Sunday, the pattern of a tenuous cease fire, hitherto observed during the early morning hours, was broken when, from 0120 to 0300 hours, the Divisional HQ area was continuously mortared. At seven o'clock, the limited number of Polish troops who had successfully crossed the river during the night were placed under Brigadier Hackett's command. Having decided that the greatest need was within the sector in which A and D Troops were operating, Hackett visited Squadron HQ forty minutes later, to discuss with David Allsop the arrangements to be made for guiding the Poles into the sector. Since his command post was not far from Allsop's own base, it was arranged that the Brigadier should take one of the Squadron men as a runner, to be sent back to report as soon as the Polish troops had arrived at 4th Brigade HQ. It would then be Allsop's responsibility to have them taken up to their positions.

By the time Hackett had organized this, the shelling and mortaring had become very heavy. Undeterred, he set off, but was hit by mortar splinters in the stomach and left thigh, and his escort's leg was broken. Despite his severe wounds, Brigadier Hackett waited for the first lull, walked to the Divisional aid post, about 100 yards away, and, before seeking attention for himself, saw to the organizing of a stretcher party for the runner who had accompanied him. It was the second occasion on which Hackett had been wounded. On the Thursday, during a visit to Captain Martin's dressing station at Kate der Horst's house, his companion, Major Maddon, had been killed by a mortar bomb and he, himself, cut about the face and hands by shrapnel. Characteristically, in recording the details of the incident in his diary, Hackett later referred to Maddon and also to the wounding of his own driver, Private Ward, but made no mention of himself.

So it was that, for this brave soldier who had done so much, not only to organize the eastern part of the perimeter, but to sustain the morale of others, the Battle of Arnhem ended at that point. For the last stages of the struggle, command of Hackett's sector was taken over by Lieutenant Colonel Murray of the Glider Pilot Regiment. For a time, Brigadier Hackett's life hung in the balance, but he displayed great fortitude and, having pulled through a serious operation in which he owned his life to the skill of Lipmann-Kessel, one of the British surgeons, "Shan" Hackett, although still seriously ill, spent his post-operational period in St Elisabeth's Hospital, drawing up details of recommendations and awards for his men. At the end, he added a short postscript for Roy Urquhart. It was simple and to the point: "Thank you for the party. It didn't go quite as we hoped and got a bit rougher than we expected but, speaking for myself, I'd take it on again any time and so, I'm sure, would everyone else."

From that morning on, Lieutenant Dougie Galbraith took command of A Troop, a consequence of Mike Grubb's removal to the main dressing station at Hotel Schoonoord. Although wounded on the previous day during the retreat from Paul Krugerstraat, Grubb had remained with his Troop, but had found it increasingly difficult to carry on. He had kept his damaged boot on but, with the blood oozing out of the eyelets, it was obvious that he was in need of treatment. As he was soon to realize, he had little appreciation at the time of how final would be the outcome of his decision to seek medical attention: "I thought that I was being taken simply to get a piece of splinter removed from my ankle, and then I'd get back again. But, of course, having driven through the German lines in an RAMC jeep, under the Red Cross flag, I arrived to find that there were many more people very much worse than I was. As a result, there was nobody to take it out and, as I couldn't walk very well, I had to stay there, and so I was captured."

As dawn approached, Galbraith's force, which had suffered a number of casualties in the previous day's action, had completed the establishment and consolidation of its defensive positions. Over all, they were holding houses from the middle to the south end of De la Reyweg with the accompanying trench positions set up overnight in outhouses and back gardens. Just before dawn, the Dutch inhabitants of the Troop HQ house emerged – a little family group, consisting of father, mother and two children, a girl of about twelve and a boy, perhaps three years younger. They were carrying a few possessions wrapped in bedsheets. "The boy," says Hope, "was dressed in a Scout or Cub uniform, and he obviously regarded the sortie as something of an adventure, as he cheerily bade us 'Good morning. Long live General Montgomery!' Then the little family was swallowed up in the darkness, abandoning its home, resigned to what must happen when daylight revealed our positions." The defenders, of course, had made the best of their situation, but knew that against armour or the more powerful infantry weapons of the Germans, it was only a matter of time until they would be driven completely out of the buildings and forced to adopt a last-stand position in the trenches. That belief was reinforced by indications that German opposition was all the time growing more obvious and increasingly moving without hindrance.

On that Sunday, the mortaring, accompanied by shellfire, started at 0630 hours, half an hour earlier than usual. It was an ominous sign, as if the enemy were itching to get to it, in order to finish off what was left of the 1st Airborne Division. At about 0730 hours the all-too-familiar creak of armoured vehicle sprockets was heard on De la Reyweg, and a new intensity of enemy machine-gun and sniper fire began to build up. One very aggressive sniper seemed to be concentrating upon the wall near to the rear of numbers 5 and 7 for, all around the windows, the red brick gradually took on a pock-marked appearance, as bursts of machine-gun alternated with rifle fire. Hope remembers the way in which they were pinned down by this persistent and accurate shooting: "Ron and I had piled a considerable amount of sandy sub-soil behind our trench, and an old, dilapidated table lay partially buried in the earth. The table was struck several times, and little cascades of disturbed earth fell into the collar of my jumping smock. Several times, Ron and I peered around the rear mound to try and spot our persistent antagonist. We failed to locate him, for he could have been concealed in any of the nearby buildings, or heavily camouflaged amongst the trees. Bullets sang uncomfortably close, bare inches above our heads, and I hunched lower into the trench. There was a sudden shout of pain from the trench system in the garden. 'Doctor' Henry Venes was applying a field dressing pad to someone's arm."

Through the early hours of the morning, as the rain fell on the battered houses and trenches of Oosterbeek, the battle-exhausted survivors of D Troop also awaited the dawn, in tense apprehension of what it would bring. Any talk of the arrival of 30 Corps had become a sick joke, for it was clear that promises and rumours of last-minute relief had been little more than illusory pipe dreams. Those who were left, well knew that a determined German attack would finish them, and although the enemy had left them alone during the night, it was seen as merely the deceptive calm before the gathering storm. Any German hesitancy could only rationally be explained in terms of unwillingness to commit men against defended British positions which appeared still to have sufficient fire power to be able to repel infantry attack. It was unlikely that this would deter them for long.

At seven o'clock, a D Troop patrol, out to draw water, was driven back by heavy machine-gun fire and suffered two casualties. By then, there were several bodies around the well, a result of the Germans having a fixed line of fire on it. From then on, the enemy pressure increased, with patrols of varying strength appearing and sporadic skirmishing went on throughout the morning. In both A and D Troop positions, the growing proximity of the Germans became more and more apparent. "All morning," reported Galbraith, "the enemy seeped through, making it impossible to move."

Food shortage was also acute and, for the most part, men existed on what they could scrounge in the way of fruit and vegetables. "Compo" tea rations had long since been used up, so it was a delighted Henry Venes who discovered some tea and sugar in one of the newly-occupied houses. Better still, he found also a supply of porridge and a packet of salt. Those were true riches, beyond the wildest dreams of the hard-pressed men, and Henry was determined to make the most of them: "I got over to Major Powell, because he had a little fire for cooking on. Well, I made a brew of tea and a thick porridge cake, and, being a handy sort of man, I put sugar in the porridge and salt in the tea! When I realized what I'd done, I was flamin' mad with myself, but I was'nt the only one, I can tell you. I remember, I said to Mr Stevenson, 'I'll give it to Jimmy Bruce.' Jimmy was on look-out with the Bren at the time and he took one sip, spat it out and said, 'If the Gerries don't do us in, that bastard will!'" Despite his temporary culinary lapse, however, Henry Venes had all the ferreting instincts of the seasoned campaigner and was continuously and successfully foraging for what he could get for the Troop. One of the most amusing memories which surviving A Troop personnel have is of Galbraith and Venes, each smoking clay pipes, which Henry had found in one of the occupied houses.

For the men at Squadron HQ, conditions were no better than anywhere else. If anything, the situation was a shade worse, because they had none of the "perks" that foraging in the houses could provide for the troops elsewhere, even if the tea did happen to taste salty to the palate! "We were reduced," says Bill Mullenger, "to looking around the gardens for anything at all that could be eaten. But even when you did manage to brew up, the mortars would send earth into the foxholes to cover the lot." One depressing privation was a lack of cigarettes although, as Bill Cook remembered, there were those like Mullenger who had been sufficiently wise to anticipate the possibility and so had stocked up with plenty before leaving England. Corporal Cyril Belcham, HQ Section clerk and Trooper Alan Samm, with whom he shared his slit trench, had taken similar precautions: "We had a good supply of 'Compo' tea and cigarettes," said Belcham, "which we had packed into my jeep before take-off. These items took absolute priority over any other rations." Those who were less well provided, of course, had to make do with whatever substitute was available. Stan Collishaw still has the grim memory of being under a wet blanket, smoking German "tabak" rolled in toilet paper stuck up with jam. It was said, however, that for sheer foulness, Henry Venes's "Brazil Specials" were almost impossible to beat!

The intensity of the early morning "hate" was also felt down at Squadron HQ positions. Captain Harry Poole, who was on special liaison duties at Divisional Headquarters, noted that, "This bears no comparison with anything which has come our way previously. The ground shivers like a jelly." Not until 0930 hours was there any let-up, only for it to be renewed, three-quarters of an hour later. Most of the mortaring came from the west, and the men in the trenches could clearly hear the German fire orders from the direction of Sonnenberglaan. At intervals, too, the loudspeaker was heard again. By then, it had been discovered that it was a mobile van, which the Germans had rigged for the purpose. Once more the watchers in the slit trenches by the Oranjeweg heard the tinny, unmelodic strains of the "Teddy Bears' Picnic", although Ray Evans recalls that the musical repertoire had been extended by the addition of "Mairsy-doats", a popular song of the day. On this occasion, it was a female voice which followed with the commentary, but the British response was unchanged, and bizarre suggestions were made that ought never to have been put to a lady – at the very least, not in public! Evans noted also that the appeal had become more emotional than before: "She said that if we ever wished to see our mothers, wives or sweethearts again, then we ought to surrender because we hadn't a chance of getting out alive. I remember this went on for some time – the same thing, over and over again – and then it suddenly stopped. Later on we were told, with what truth I don't know, that someone had successfully put a PIAT bomb into the van."

In the more northerly positions occupied by A and D Troops, enemy probing patrols continued to alternate with mortar attack into the afternoon. From about 1415 hours, however, one redeeming feature was the build-up of offensive air support. It was because no supply drops were scheduled that the opportunity arose and it proved to be successful in a way that the Royal Air Force had not anticipated. The circumstances of the wooded terrain made it difficult for the ground forces to pinpoint required objectives so that, in the absence of a precise six-figure map reference, the strike aircraft of the Typhoon wings could not easily engage specific targets. The alternative, that of a general area attack, was not strongly favoured by the Royal Air Force but, in the peculiar difficulties of the Oosterbeek situation, a certain amount of this was done. The results were satisfying beyond any expectation, for the very presence of aircraft in the sky overhead made the Germans reluctant to open fire with artillery, lest their own well-concealed positions were given away. In those cases where actual pinpointing was possible, the Typhoons of 83 Group were extremely precise, and in no instances were there reports of rocket strikes being more than fifty yards wide of the designated objective.

Jim Taylor of A Troop was one of those who watched the strike aircraft come in, with a great surge of noise, to blast the roof off a nearby house, which had obviously been selected as a target. He remembers that he suffered some kind of mild blast effect: "It felt as if my head were free-wheeling." Further over, in the D Troop positions, Bill Bentall was witness to the same incident. Impressed by the frightening appearance of the planes, and the way in which they boosted morale, he was moved even more by the belief that they were from England: "We were treated to an attack by rocket-firing Typhoons . . . fearsome things, with a shark's head and teeth painted on the undernose, and rockets screaming . . . It was galling to think that they had probably come from Fairlop." In this last bare, simple comment, Bentall was putting into words the yearning for home that all of them must have felt, for there was a general belief that the Typhoons overhead had not long left their base in the south of England and would be returning there after the sortie. So it was that, as the planes banked away at the end of the action, the airborne men in their slit trenches experienced something of the emotions of storm-wrecked mariners, forced to watch helplessly, as the ship that might have rescued them slowly recedes over the horizon.

Such reflections, in truth, were self-deluding, for the planes had come from Antwerp. But for the man from Ilford, it was natural and understandable that his thoughts should have linked them with the RAF station near his home in England. What was perhaps more truly ironic, however, was that, whilst the airborne soldiers envied those in the planes, and the Typhoon pilots in turn pitied the plight of the men on the ground, such emotions could prove entirely misplaced when related to the ultimate outcome. Flight Sergeant Jimmy Darlington of 245 Squadron was one of those who, from 22nd September onwards, flew his Typhoon in attacks over the Arnhem and Oosterbeek area. Originally a Hurricane pilot, he had many combat hours behind him and, on that Sunday afternoon, as he skimmed the roof tops of Oosterbeek, there was every reasonable prospect that he would continue to add to his total until the end of the campaign. By contrast, for Bentall and those in like predicament, there seemed to be little hope left. Yet, such were the fortunes of war, that in three weeks time, Bentall would be walking down the High Street in Ilford on a day when Jim Darlington was not to return from a routine air reconnaissance over Apeldoorn.

The respite given by the air support was only a temporary lull, for, in the middle of the afternoon, the enemy drove in his main attack. Willie Fraser of A Troop was at the Troop HQ base on De la Reyweg when it began, and has good reason to recall what happened: "We'd had heavy sniping directed at us all day, and I remember I was in the house with one or two of the others. The trouble was that it was difficult to know where to go to be safe, because the Germans were firing all the time, in through the windows or any holes in the walls. I know they were using tracer bullets, because occasionally one of those would be fired into the room where we were, and at the time I thought how like firework 'sparklers' they were."

"Just before the attack began, I was sitting on top of the kitchen table, beneath which was a white goat and, as we watched, we saw one of those tracers come from somewhere and pass right under the animal. Unfortunately, we were so busy watching the goat that we didn't notice a German running past the window outside. I remember Dougie Galbraith bursting in and giving everyone hell for not shooting him, and he certainly had a point, because I believe now, it was that German who was responsible for the trouble that came to us not long afterwards. One of those in the room at the time was a gunner, who had been batman to the artillery captain who died, and just after Galbraith's visit, he went up the stairs to observe. Almost immediately, he fell down again, shot between the eyes. I don't know how it came about – possibly they got him from a sniping position in another house – but the next thing that happened was a terrific bang, and I was hit. As I lay on the floor, I could see legs running over me, so I staggered up and tried to make for the door, but it was difficult, because I couldn't see properly."

Outside, those others who were manning the trench positions saw that the shattering explosion was due to a direct hit which had blown a four-foot-wide hole in the end wall of number 5. Ken Hope also remembers how, at the time, Stan Sutherby was standing just inside the rear doorway: "A great, belching, orange-tinted cloud of dust vomited from the door. Slowly, almost languorously, Stan sank to the ground. 'Stan's had it,' Ron exclaimed. Then incredibly, Stan got to his feet again, rather dazedly, like a boxer pushing himself off the canvas, and reeled and swayed in the doorway. In the next instant, 'Jock' Fraser came hurtling towards us from the interior of the house: 'The bloody wall's down!' he cried. He had a head or face wound and appeared to have an eye hanging on his cheek. His blood was dripping on to my head and shoulders and he was trying to take refuge in the restricted space of our slit trench. I had already got one leg hoisted on the lip of the trench for a rapid exit. It was a moment of extreme panic. I remember gazing around wildly, wondering from which direction opponents in field grey would suddenly appear." It was Dougie Galbraith who brought order out of mounting chaos, and Hope still remembers how he called out, in mild affront, "Where the bloody hell do you think you're all going – now just bloody well settle down." It was a calmly delivered admonition, all the more effective for its simplicity, and the moment of crisis passed.

Part of the same attack was responsible for finishing off D Troop. The prelude was a terrifying mortar bombardment on their positions, of an intensity not previously felt, and James Pyper still remembers the succession of events that brought the long drawn-out agony to a horrific end. "During the afternoon," he recalls, "we were dug in in the garden of a house. My own trench was right beside a stone wall, and Captain Park and two others were in the next trench along. Following the first mortaring, there was an exchange of shooting, and it was then that Captain Park said, 'I'll change places with you, Sergeant.' Three times after that we beat them off, until later in the afternoon came an extra fierce mortar barrage. I remember at one point, shouting 'Down!', and when the smoke cleared, we found Captain Park, Lieutenant Pascal and Trooper Walker all still standing upright in the trench by the wall, but with their heads blown off." The bombardment was then followed by the inevitable infantry attack, which closed in in strength, and those who were left fought until their ammunition ran out.

Others, too, were feeling the effects of the shortage of ammunition, which is what David Christie remembers of the position at Squadron HQ on that Sunday afternoon: "I hadn't eaten or smoked for four days. My throat felt like a lump of dry wood. The road to the water well was infested with snipers, and no one mentioned the 2nd Army any more. From our position across from Divisional HQ, the front line was about 300 yards away. One of the glider pilots with me said, 'I've still got six 36 grenades, so that's two apiece – we'll at least take a few with us.' We also had one Bren gun and one pistol among the three of us. Ammunition for the Bren was limited to two magazines, and we had six rounds for the pistol. How I wished we had some of that training ammunition we used to fire off at odd times in England!"

Mid-afternoon also saw the resumption of mortar attack on the Squadron HQ positions. "Like a small hammer on a wooden box," was how Harry Poole described the primary explosions which presaged by only seconds the arrival of the high-explosive bombs. Then just before four o'clock, at about the time that the attacks were being mounted elsewhere, a self-propelled gun, with its supporting infantry, appeared in the woods of nearby Sonnenberglaan. It opened up, and some shells were added to the harassment of the mortaring, but when the enemy was engaged from the Squadron positions, both SP gun and Panzer infantry withdrew.

In the course of the late afternoon, the mortaring gave way to machine-gun and sniper fire, which was heavier and more persistent than anything previously encountered and was productive of casualties. It was not a new problem because, from the start of the holding operation in the perimeter, snipers had always been a menace to be reckoned with. All around the defensive area, from Lonsdale's sector in the south, to the northernmost tip, they were an ever-present danger, and many senior officers removed from their shoulders the badges of rank which so clearly marked them out in the telescopic sights as the most desirable targets. Ingenuity in dealing with the matter took a number of forms, popular amongst which was holding up a dummy in order to draw fire and thus reveal the enemy marksman. In coping with the problem, however, no one was more inventive than Dougie Galbraith, who developed his own singular technique. His success stemmed from an unorthodox use of the 2-inch mortar. This weapon, the standard type as issued to infantry platoons throughout the British army, was an unpretentious affair, only nineteen pounds in weight, and its two-pound bomb was estimated to have a maximum range of just 500 yards. With the base plate on the ground and the barrel pointing upwards at a relatively steep angle, the bomb went into the normal mortar trajectory, to fall on its target from above. Galbraith's anti-sniper tactic was simply to aim the weapon at the trunk of a tree, having first taken into account the height at which it was suspected the sniper was hidden. As the bomb hit the trunk, it fragmented, sending shrapnel pieces in all directions. From Friday onwards, throughout the remainder of the battle, Galbraith steadily increased his own personal score of 'kills' by that method, and in the reckoning of David Christie, was credited with the death of sixteen German snipers.

But the most persistent sniping was in the vicinity of Divisional HQ itself, and it was as a result of their close proximity to the Harstenstein that Reconnaissance Squadron HQ personnel were regularly troubled. Most of the activity which was directed against them came from the tall trees that bordered the eastern edge of the Sonnenberg estate, because it was only 200 yards from there, across the open field to the thin line of slit trenches on Oranjeweg. Alan de Looze still remembers with sadness one tragic episode of that particular Sunday: "My friend, Mike Gasset, a Londoner, was in a slit trench with Alf Odd from Glasgow, and he asked me if I could cheer Odd up, as he was feeling low. I went across and crouched on the parapet, talking to him. I remember that, although he didn't smoke much, he had a full tin of cigarettes, so I scrounged one from him. As I was returning to my own trench, I heard the whine of a bullet close by, but thought little of it as there was so much stuff flying about. I'd scarcely settled down, and was still smoking the cigarette, when Mike called out that 'Jock' had been shot clean through the temple and had died instantly. That was the bullet that I'd heard." Over the years that have passed since then, Alan de Looze has assumed that it was his own movement that perhaps attracted the sniper's attention, and that a bullet, possibly intended for him, killed Odd instead. On the other hand, Stan Collishaw, who was in an adjacent trench, remembers that just before he was shot, Odd was trying to spot the sniper with the aid of binoculars, and that he had just exclaimed, "I can see the bastard," before collapsing in the trench. It could be that the reflected light from the binocular lenses gave the German the perfect pinpoint guidance that he needed. He was only nineteen, and the youngest of the Squadron to die.

De Looze himself was extremely lucky to escape unscathed for, in the course of that Sunday afternoon, the perils of movement above ground became increasingly apparent: "If you left your trench at all," says David Christie, "you had to crawl for what you wanted or wait for darkness." The lesson of this was underlined later in the afternoon when the necessity arose to fetch more ammunition. It was getting on towards dusk when Lieutenant Ladds, who was using a Vickers "K" gun taken from one of the vehicles, detailed Ray Evans to fetch some from the jeep. It meant that Evans had to leave his slit trench, and negotiate a hole in the hedge, through to Oranjeweg, where the vehicles were parked. "Obviously," says Evans, "the hole must have been covered by a sniper, for I'd no sooner moved than I was cut across the back of the neck." Corporal Trinder, who was witness to it, also remembers how close Evans came to death: "As he got up there was a sudden 'zim-zim-zim', and he yelled out and fell back into the trench.

His battledress tunic had been holed at the neck, and the bullets had emerged from the cloth further down. When we examined him, we found three burns, like red pencil marks, down his back."

Meantime, not knowing the relatively mild nature of Evans's injuries, Ladds had summoned the assistance of Corporal McLean, a medical orderly, from a nearby slit trench. Unfortunately, as soon as McLean emerged, the vigilant German sniper got him too, and he fell back into his own trench, seriously wounded. Trooper Kerr was then detailed as Evans's replacement to try to fetch the ammunition, but he was also wounded at the hole in the hedge and was only pulled back into cover with great difficulty. It being obvious that any further movement before darkness would probably mean more casualties, nothing further was attempted. After dark, Evans went over to the Hartenstein to fetch two stretcher bearers for Kerr and, as they were taking him away from the slit trenches, the orderlies were given explicit instructions to come back for McLean. It was assumed – wrongly as it transpired – that this would be attended to.

On Sunday, the process of evacuating the casualties from the Oosterbeek area gathered momentum. It had begun earlier, but the constriction of the perimeter and the increased danger to the wounded men now made it imperative that the operation be speeded up. Largely through the skilful personal negotiations of Colonel Graeme Warrack, the ADMS, this was done with smooth efficiency. John Pow, who was one of the walking wounded, remembers how he was removed with a number of others from Oosterbeek to St Elisabeth's Hospital, a distance of two miles. "We had to walk all the way from the regimental aid post near the Hartenstein," he says, "and the Germans took photographs of us when we got down near the Hospital. It was crammed in there, and they had us seated in the corridors. I remember, I walked out three times that night, to try to escape, and each time, I was brought back in, till eventually they brought transport to take us to Apeldoorn."

George Adams was another in the same plight. He had seen many of his comrades die in the rubble of the battered dressing station and counted himself lucky to have survived. He can still recall, with some humour, the details of that journey from the hospital to Apeldoorn, although, he admits that it was not at all amusing at the time: "I remember, they packed us into this pantechnicon thing," he says, "but there were so many people in it that we were all lying on top of each other. I was sort of laid across Bert Pegnall's legs, and he was saying, 'Oh for Christ's sake, George! You're bloody killing me!' We were in there for about thirty-six hours and, with all those chaps breathing, the condensation was dripping down on us from the metal roof and sides."

The mid-afternoon action by the A Troop defenders on De la Reyweg was successful, not only for the repulsing of the enemy attack, but also because, in the process, heavy losses were inflicted on the Germans. Amongst other things, the defenders owed much to the effectiveness of the fortifications established on the previous night. Nevertheless, the attack had taken its toll of these and made it necessary for the Troop to draw in from the more exposed house positions in order to consolidate within a smaller area. By nightfall that day, they were still covering the southern end of the street, but such were the conditions of the shrinking perimeter, that they now found themselves mingling with surviving members of the 7th Battalion of the King's Own Scottish Borderers. In the circumstances, the principal concern was more than ever to determine exactly how individual houses were occupied. So uncertain had the situation in the area become, that one could not move from one position to the other without running the immediate risk of being shot. Fraser recalls how Galbraith's initiative was brought to bear on this problem too, and that, for a time, they moved between two adjacent houses by taking advantage of a blind spot between one attic window and another. It meant climbing over the tiles and, in a sense, was the substitution of one perilous hazard for another, but it worked, and that was all that mattered.

Access between houses could also be arranged in even less orthodox ways. Jim Taylor recalls how, on that Sunday night, he was on a patrol that took them past the end of the street. There, from one of the semi-detached blocks, they heard the sound of hammering, but did not investigate, as they knew that it was held by A Troop men. The one responsible for the noise, as they discovered later, was his namesake Vic Taylor, who was busily engaged in that peculiar Arnhem strategy known as "mouseholing". It was a universal practice which the British adopted during their time in the perimeter area, and consisted simply of choosing a spot – preferably an attic or upstairs room – in which to remove bricks from the internal dividing wall between the house in occupation and the one next door. The purpose could be either offensive or defensive, providing for either access to or escape from the enemy. Recollecting the incident, Vic Taylor says, "I was sure that the Germans knew that we were in that particular house, and that they'd come to attack under cover of darkness. With this in mind, I took out the bricks from inside a cupboard between our house and the one next door, which I knew was still empty. This took me into the next-door cupboard, and I remember looking for a dustpan and brush, so that if we did have to retreat from one house to the other, and the Germans came upstairs, they wouldn't see the traces on the floor. When we'd finished, for some reason we decided to go through into the empty house – probably because we felt it might be safer – and it was not long after that that we heard stealthy movement in the house we'd left. What we didn't know was that 'Spud' and the others, having heard us bashing away earlier, had come back to look for us. Naturally, they found the house empty, but I heard them walking about on the other side of the wall and, just in case it might be the Gerries, I lay myself quietly down behind the Bren gun and trained it on the little cupboard door. Nobody came through – perhaps it was just as well!"

The justification for all this activity was well borne out even before the "mouseholing" task was completed, for Sergeant Maurice Riches, who at one point went upstairs to check on Vic Taylor's progress, still has a clear recollection of returning back downstairs again, in time to see two Germans standing outside one of the windows. As was so often the case, nothing came of it, but it was an indication of the extent of the ever-present dangers. Indeed, at the last stage in the battle, with the enemy continually infiltrating by stealth into the houses of the perimeter area, the British soldiers became uncomfortably aware that, time and time again, only nine inches of brickwork could separate them from the Germans. Once the possibility was recognized, it was then more than ever necessary to guard against the incautious sound that would betray a precariously held position to a nearby enemy group. Because of that, men learned to move as little as possible, and only to do so quietly, with extreme care, avoiding loud conversation and the telltale noises produced by dropping objects on to the floor. Even the simple and natural act of propping a rifle against the communicating wall of one house and the next could mean all the difference between continued concealment and instant detection. Such a pattern of precautionary behaviour was being observed in all parts of the Divisional area and, by the end of that day, it had become even more apparent that there were no "lines" in the strict military sense, but merely isolated positions, in which the occupants of a house or garden fought their own individual battles, with no certainty as to whether or not the neighbouring houses in a street were inhabited by friend or foe.

A little to the north, in the D Troop positions, it was all over by 1800 hours and, with ammunition totally exhausted, the six remaining men were taken prisoner. Bentall later told of how he was first "clouted" on the head and then beckoned out of his trench by a German, who came round from the back of their house. Their weapons were taken from them and, thereafter, the little group was marched away. "We had long since accepted the fact," said Bentall, "that there was no chance of getting out alive, but now, perhaps, we would, after all, survive as prisoners." Half asleep, soaked to the skin and caked in mud, the survivors were marched up Steijnweg to a house in the German-held area. There they were put into a ground-floor room, with a sentry at the doorway to guard them. Clearly, it was a temporary arrangement, pending their transfer elsewhere to begin the journey to Germany as prisoners-of-war.

Not long after their arrival, the sentry at the door was removed and, instead, a guard patrol of three Germans was set to pace around the house. It was this changed situation that provided the opportunity for possible escape. Most British soldiers knew that the logical time to attempt it was as soon as possible after capture, rather than from inside the barbed wire of a prisoner-of-war compound. With this in mind the D Troop survivors worked out a plan by which, given the luck, they might still get away. It all hinged upon the movement of the sentries. These had been timed, and it had been discovered that, although it varied, there appeared to be an average interval of fifteen seconds between the disappearance of the first man around one corner of the house and the subsequent arrival of the second around the other. Just how long the chance to escape would last they had no means of knowing but, certainly, there seemed little prospect that there would be a better one. With this in mind, they decided that, since daylight had almost gone, they would seize the earliest opportunity to take themselves off through a gap in the house wall where a window had once been. To their captors, they must have seemed a most unpromising set of potential escapers, which, of course, could have accounted for the almost perfunctory nature of the guard.

With Pyper leading, and Bentall bringing up the rear, they waited for a clear period in the sentries' rounds before immediately exiting through the hole and sprinting across the back garden. There was one awkward moment when Bill Bentall, only ten yards from the house, got his trousers caught on a barbed wire fence and was still hanging, suspended, just as the second German sentry appeared around the corner. Those few precious seconds that he needed to extricate himself seemed like an eternity, for he fully expected to be shot in the back. With a tearing of cloth, he desperately freed himself and plunged for the shelter of the shrubbery beyond the back fence, just as the first of the shots rang out. Fortunately, they were wide of the mark, but the escapers lost no time in getting away, because the screen was only protection from observation and there was every possibility that at any moment the bushes would be sprayed from end to end with a hail of bullets.

Once clear of the immediate danger, the desire to press on through the enemy positions in order to link up with their own people was very strong. But physical and mental fatigue had taken an enormous toll and it seemed suddenly that they had no more reserves on which to draw. They had hardly progressed any distance at all, before all six realized that they were in extremely poor shape. This, together with a consciousness of the movement of Germans in the dark ness all around, made it obvious that they stood little chance of getting through to the British positions. So, having progressed not more than two houses beyond where they had been, they came to the remains of a shop which appeared to be empty. There, they took shelter in the cellar which, to their surprise, they found full of potatoes. Seated in the pitch darkness, they ate them raw, for it was the first food that some had tasted in days. The exhausted men then squeezed in on top of the pile of potatoes, and went to sleep, whilst Pyper and Bentall went upstairs to the room above, on the ground floor of the house. There, Pyper took cover behind an upturned table, whilst Bentall went under the settee. The object of all these precautions was to hide from the enemy for they were still very much inside German territory, and there was every likelihood that, although the house was temporarily empty, there could well be nocturnal visitors at any time before the dawn. As it happened, their arrangements proved to have been completely justified for, during the night, a group of Germans did come into the room where Pyper and Bentall had concealed themselves, and it was only the all-encompassing darkness that saved the British pair from detection. Bill Bentall later recorded his experience in this note: "Germans come into our room and make plenty noise. Each time one sits on my settee, my nose grinds into the floor and a spring tries to screw its way into my spine – I'll lie on my back next time. Am developing cough – stuff rag into mouth to stifle noise. Boche shares our billet all night, but leaves at daybreak."

In the case of the main relieving force, little real headway was made that day. 214 Brigade was involved in heavy fighting at Elst, and the Guards Armoured Division was held up to the south-east at Bemmel. In the course of that night, however, elements of 130 Brigade crossed the river. These were mainly three to four hundred men of the 4th Dorsets, whose landings were, unfortunately, too scattered as well as too far west to be of any direct assistance to Urquhart's force. Nevertheless, their presence on the following day allowed the airborne men to hold on for just that bit longer, and must also have greatly helped in the evacuation which was to take place on the following night.

Towards the end of the day, Divisional diary recorded as follows: "A day of very heavy shelling and mortaring and desperate fighting on all sectors. Many attacks at first achieved some penetration, but the situation was almost always restored, and by nightfall the perimeter was substantially the same. Never was darkness more eagerly awaited. Shortness of serviceable weapons, particularly PsIAT for dealing with tanks and SP guns, becoming a very serious handicap."

Chapter 14 MONDAY 25th SEPTEMBER 1944

"Operation Berlin must be tonight"

The rain continued to fall steadily throughout the night, with the result that the survivors woke to a day in which the air was chill and the saturated trees dripped moisture steadily on to the water-logged ground. At the Squadron HQ positions, the usual desultory mortaring began the day but reached a new intensity at about nine o'clock. Captain Poole once more recorded the events: "The worst mortar fire so far. 50 bombs or more to 100 square yards. If this continues very much longer, very few left. Black smoke and yellow flame everywhere." The sudden unexpected lull at just after half-past nine, however, heralded the appearance of the first Typhoon strike of the day and, in the following ten minutes, the British once more had the satisfaction of seeing their own rocket-firing aircraft engage enemy targets in the vicinity. Quite apart from the value of the strike capability, it was again noted that the very presence of Typhoons overhead was sufficient to inhibit enemy gun and mortar action. This welcome relief from the ferocity of the German shelling did much for the spirits of the men who were doubly cheered by the rising plumes of black smoke that indicated successful rocket hits on enemy targets.

It was the briefest of respites, with relief lasting only for as long as the duration of the air attack. When this was broken off, the mortaring began again but, at noon, the planes returned and the men on the ground received another break. Meantime, at the positions on Oranjeweg, advantage had been taken of the lulls to try to do something for the wounded medical orderly who had been shot on the previous day. In the course of the morning, it had been discovered that the stretcher bearers who had removed Kerr to the regimental aid post had not returned, as requested, for Corporal McLean. Unfortunately, the extent and seriousness of his injuries had been such as to leave him speechless and, from the bottom of his slit trench, he had been quite unable to communicate his plight to the others, all of whom mistakenly assumed that he had been removed to the Hartenstein. The upshot was that, during one of the breaks in the bombardment, Lieutenant Ladds managed to get him out of the trench and into one of the Reconnaissance jeeps. Like all the other vehicles harboured at Squadron HQ, its tyres were punctured with bullet holes. Despite this, Ladds successfully forced it over, under fire, to the Divisional aid post, in order to deliver the wounded man. Thereafter, the vehicle was left abandoned on the other side of the main road.

On the A Troop positions at the junction of De la Reyweg and Steijnweg the first attack came in at 7.30 in the morning, with bundled stick grenades used against them. By then, the Germans were holding adjacent houses, and their visible presence was much in evidence in the brief but regular glimpses of coal-scuttle helmets and flashes of field grey. Galbraith noted how their patrols seemed to be everywhere, always manoeuvering for greater advantage and completely dominating the situation. At nine o'clock, he ordered his men to evacuate most of the houses completely and concentrate on holding the trenches which they had dug in the gardens on the previous night. There they remained throughout the rest of the morning, awaiting the final attack which, for some reason, did not materialize. Certainly, the persistent Typhoon sorties, which were regularly sustained, did much to keep the Germans subdued, but the danger of being overwhelmed remained as a very real one, forcing the defenders to maintain a constant state of alertness and generating a growing feeling of tense expectancy. During this time, Hope recalls being posted by Galbraith, with instructions that could not have been more succinct: "Hope – I want you to make a gun position here. Don't move. You are to stay here unless you get personal orders from me to the contrary. If any of the Gerries cross the road – shoot them!" No immediate action followed, but Ken Hope remembers that, as he kept watch, he was witness to a sad episode that illuminated with great poignancy the plight of the Dutch civilians caught up in the struggle: "I heard a noise directly behind me. I whirled round, thinking that the Germans had broken in at the rear, but it was the cellar door which had been opened by an aged couple, about mid-seventies. They stood there, looking at the shambles of what had probably been their best front room. The old lady was sobbing, and tears streamed down her wrinkled face. The husband was quite immobile, with a blank dazed expression on his features. Then Henry Venes, our Troop Sergeant, appeared, patted the old lady on the shoulder and escorted them to the steps. The old man turned again, shrugged his shoulders and followed his wife down into the cellar."

Lieutenant-Colonel Myers had, in the meantime, returned from the south bank to Divisional HQ. He arrived there at 0605 hours with a letter for General Urquhart from GOC 43rd Division. It was to the effect that there would be no further attempts by 2nd Army to form an alternative bridgehead at Oosterbeek. Instead, 1st Airborne Division would, by arrangement between the two divisional commanders, withdraw to the south of the river at a date and time to be determined. The evacuation operation was to be known as "Operation Berlin", a choice of title that was, perhaps, not the best of all possible alternatives! With only a quarter of his original strength left, with acute shortages not simply of ammunition but of the barest necessities of life, with the conviction that already his gravely depleted force was very much on borrowed time and that his men had been pressed to the uttermost limit of their endurance, Urquhart did not hesitate to make the final decision. At precisely eight minutes past eight that morning, he radioed his reply in the simplest of terms to 43rd Division:

Operation Berlin must be tonight

It was a decision that officially marked the end of British hopes, but there was not a man in the 1st Airborne Division who had not already accepted the true position. From that point on, the final effort had to be put into making the withdrawal as painless as possible. Above all, security had to be tight, which was why Urquhart decided upon 2200 hours that night as the starting time for the evacuation. At his briefing of senior officers that morning, he was concerned to emphasize the importance of concealing the intention to withdraw from the enemy who might otherwise be expected to exploit the situation to the full.

Throughout the day, the action on most sectors of the perimeter was surprisingly quiet. There were a number of local attacks similar to the one which had come in at first light on the A Troop positions but, on the whole, things seemed relatively easier than they had been on the previous day. For such respite, much credit undoubtedly was due to the Typhoon attacks, which were kept up throughout the day on a scale that was more intense than before. On the other hand, what did show a steady and consistent increase was the degree of infiltration of British positions. By evening, various points around the perimeter had been deeply penetrated including the woods at the Pietersberg dressing station, just 400 yards south of the Hartenstein. Clearly, all this was the prelude to another series of attacks which could well be anticipated on the following day, if not earlier. So successful and extensive was this enemy movement inwards, that the Divisional diary noted that "most units were to some extent encircled and cut off from their neighbours." As far as the Squadron was concerned, this certainly applied to Sergeant Pyper's small, surviving group of D Troop personnel who remained under cover throughout the whole of that day, resting up and yet wondering at every minute just how long it would be before the Germans, in occupation of adjacent and neighbouring houses, would come suddenly bursting in on them.

For the Squadron, preparations for the evacuation began at 1500 hours, when A Troop was given orders, from HQ 4th Parachute Brigade, to withdraw to the junction of Utrechtseweg and Mariaweg. This was undertaken with despatch and, surprisingly, without casualties. By 1530 hours, they had regrouped in a house just to the north of Utrechtseweg. There, they occupied a large downstairs room, overlooking the main road, where they were amalgamated with a small party of men from the Glider Pilot Regiment. Shortly afterwards, they received further orders regarding the next phase of the withdrawal. Sergeant Venes was then sent to contact the remnants of 156th Parachute Battalion and, by 1900 hours, they too had reported in and joined the others. From then on, it was a question of waiting for the beginning of the move out, and Jim Taylor still remembers how, during that time, they had a look around the house. He recalls that he and Dougie Galbraith discovered some tea, which they smoked in their clay pipes.

Some time earlier at Divisional HQ, Douglas Swinscow had sought clarification about his own position. Was he to stay behind, as a number of medics had been told to do, in order to look after the wounded, or was he to return to the Squadron, pending the withdrawal of the Division? Following the injuries received on the Thursday, which had put him out of action for about twelve hours, he had eventually made his way back to his own aid post on Hoofdlaan, and had carried on treating the casualties. On Sunday, when the evacuation of the wounded was ordered, only one from his post, a man who had been shot through both thighs, was handed over. The others, less seriously wounded, were not given up, and so, by the time of the final withdrawal Swinscow still had a fair number in his care. The orders which he then received were that any wounded man who could do so was to rejoin his unit. It was at that stage, on Monday, that he went across for instructions to Divisional HQ, which was just slightly to the west of his own position. "I do remember so well," he says, "running through those destroyed, deserted and incredibly silent woods in the late afternoon, and seeing men still lying dead in slit trenches or, in some cases, standing dead in them. There was a doctor there already, who was with the Divisional HQ regimental aid post, and I was told by one of the staff officers that one of us would have to remain behind. I remember that the officer went away to ask the General for a decision on the matter and of feeling some apprehension about the outcome. Eventually he came back after what seemed a very long time, and told me that the Headquarters doctor was to stay and that I was to rejoin my own unit."

Unaware of all the activity that had begun for ultimate evacuation D Troop's remaining men had waited throughout that day for darkness to come. From the hiding-place which they had shared in the night with the enemy, they had been made well aware of the German presence all around. By late afternoon, strengthened and refreshed, they were ready to go and, after dark, Sergeant Pyper issued instructions that they would leave in two groups. He and Bentall would move first and, if no shooting was heard, the others were to assume that the way was clear to follow. What happened after that is not known, for none of the members of the second group made a successful escape. Only the two sergeants managed to avoid observation and find their way into the Divisional area. There, in another house, they met up with a number of men from various regiments, including their own, and learned of the evacuation plans which were already well under way. Pyper and Bentall were all that was left of the forty officers and men of D Troop. As they mustered with the others for the departure, each prayed that their luck might hold for a little longer.

At all such gathering points, the survivors were getting themselves ready for the final ordeal, by tying pieces of curtain material, sacking, strips of carpet or anything else available around their boots, in order to deaden the sound that they would otherwise be sure to make on the journey down to the river. It was a preparatory safeguard that was being observed throughout the perimeter. From 2000 hours onwards, the evacuation then got under way and, along with the others, the A Troop men, together with the D Troop survivors, began to slip in twos and threes across the Utrechtseweg, to make the first rendezvous at 4th Parachute Brigade HQ.

The personnel of Squadron HQ had received similar instructions. These were that, starting at 2050 hours, the slit trenches on Oranjeweg should each in turn be evacuated, with the men moving in small groups across the Utrechtseweg and so into the Hartenstein area. For the most part, all went well and, as they left the narrow holes in the ground that had been home to them for almost a week, they took only what was necessary for survival. Anything that could conceivably be of use to the enemy was first buried or destroyed. Stan Collishaw still remembers carrying away a number of the small but essential breech blocks from several Brens that had to be left. These he subsequently dropped into the Neder Rijn. Group by group, they stole quietly off in a disengagement that operated smoothly, even although "Tommy" Trinder's own personal account might seem to indicate otherwise: "I remember," he says, "that the decision was that we would leave, slit trench by slit trench, at three-minute intervals. As each lot moved off, they were to tell those in the next trench to the right that they were going. They would then know to wait three minutes, do the same and follow on. In our case, the trouble was that no one bothered to tell us. After a while, I got out to have a look around, because it was so quiet and found that there was no one there. When I told Lieutenant Lickerish, he said, 'Oh well, we'd better just stay where we are,' to which I remember replying, 'You can stay if you like – I'm off!'"

As it transpired, no one was left behind, and the last to leave the Squadron positions was David Allsop. Thrust unexpectedly, at the outset, into a position of command, he had displayed throughout the battle the qualities of steady and imperturbable leadership. It was wholly appropriate that, in the following July, his courage and determination should receive just recognition by the award of the Dutch Bronze Lion, one of the highest orders that the Netherlands could bestow.*

Considering the handicaps, "Operation Berlin" was, in general, extremely well-executed and

* David Allsop tells the interesting story of how, when he went to Holland to receive his award, he visited Oosterbeek and found the face towel which he had used during the battle, still hanging from the tree branch above his slit trench.

highly successful. The fact that it was a dark night with pouring rain helped enormously, and for once no one complained about the weather. Responsibility for aiding the evacuation lay with 43rd Division, but the task, for the most part, devolved upon 130 Infantry Brigade, with the plan that 4th Dorsets should act as a covering party from north of the river. Available water transport was meagre and consisted, initially, of fourteen storm boats with outboard motors, provided by two companies of Canadian engineers, together with some canvas assault craft laid on by two comparable British companies. British and Canadian soldiers worked in collaboration throughout, but by the conclusion of the operation almost all of the small boats had been sunk.

Strong artillery shoots from south of the river were arranged, partly to deter enemy attack on the airborne men and partly also to cover the sound of the withdrawal, especially the ferrying. There was, of course, no justification for believing that the evacuation could be concealed indefinitely from the enemy, but the more time that could be bought, the greater the prospect of keeping down the casualty figures and the better the chance of pulling it off. General Urquhart decided that two exit routes would be followed, one on the western, and the other on the eastern side of the perimeter. Since the defensive area had by then shrunk to only 700 yards, the two avenues of escape were not far apart. Each was marked by tapes laid on the ground, and men of the Glider Pilot Regiment positioned themselves at key points on the route, in order to ensure that parties did not unwittingly move into sectors held by the enemy. As an additional guide, it was arranged that the outer limits of the "safe" lanes would be indicated by red tracer fire every 30 seconds, directed from the south bank.

The stealthy progression of the small groups down to the river had about it an unreal quality. David Christie, who was with a party of eight, remembers his own experiences on the journey: "Our route took us through close, wooded country in which, aided by darkness, it was impossible to see anything more than three yards ahead. We gripped the tail of the man's smock in front in order to keep together. This incident reminded me of Christmas parties, but this was rather a different type of party." This, as it happened, was all too tragically brought home to another of the Squadron HQ groups which was under the leadership of Geoff Costeloe. They were about fifteen in number and had made good progress when, not far south of the Hartenstein, they came under German machine-gun fire from somewhere in the direction of Hotel Tafelberg. In the ensuing confusion, the party was slightly dispersed, and the rear man, SQMS George Holderness, had the job of getting them all back into line. It was whilst doing this that, in the darkness, he approached a standing figure whom he assumed was a member of the group. Unfortunately, it was a German, who shot him dead.

This sudden, instant eruption of violence was a terrifying reminder of how close the Germans were to the evacuating troops. There were other indications too, as Stan Collishaw recalls: "As we followed a path through the woods to the south of the Divisional HQ, I remember that there was a house on the left with a light in the window. By it, it was possible to see figures moving about, one of whom was clearly wearing a German helmet. There also seemed to be a group seated at a table, in the attitude of people playing cards." Douglas Swinscow also has a very similar recollection: "As we went down, we passed a little tent with a light burning inside it – a German tent. They didn't hear us, because at the time there was a tremendous artillery barrage going on from our own guns, which were firing at the limit of their range and bursting above our heads in a most alarming fashion."

Throughout, they had the German mortar barrages to contend with. These still came down at intervals and made the task of evacuation even more hazardous. In a subsequent report,

Sergeant Peter Quinn recalled how this all-too-familiar danger affected them: "About 2130 hours, a clatter of mortar bombs came down, lighting the woods and road with a queer blue light. The men scattered like demons in a pantomime. I was lifted off my feet with the blast of one bomb, and came to lying against the foot of a tree. There was no one about, so I pushed on quickly and eventually contacted two of my section. An MG was firing at us, so we dashed pretty fast across where there was a clearing on the right, until we came, more or less, under cover. Everything went all right then until we came to a T-junction. Here, we saw some figures standing in the darkness of some houses opposite and slightly to our left. Having our previous experience in our minds, we went as quickly as we could to the right, which proved to be the correct way."

Lieutenant Lickerish and Corporal Trinder were, in the meantime, bringing up the rear and, as Trinder recalls, it was a journey that was testing in more ways than one: "Mr Lickerish had a machine-gun on his shoulder and his tunic was packed full of ammunition. He'd stuffed the rest of us up with it too, so that we were all bulging out like a bunch of pregnant women. I didn't fancy carrying all that weight with me, so after we set off I started getting rid of it gradually, when he wasn't looking, and just tightened my belt. On the way down, the noise of firing was overpowering, and all around us things were exploding. I remember there was a big sewer trench which linked up with the river, and in it was about eighteen inches of water. I suggested to Mr Lickerish that we would be safer there, because the firing would then be over our heads. He wouldn't go down at first, in case he soiled his clothes, but later on he joined me when it got too hot on top. I had to hand it to him – he was a cool one all right. It was a bit dodgy at times, but we followed a guide tape and eventually we arrived at the end of the queue."*

Loss of direction and of contact with others was only too common on the way down to the river, and many men have since claimed that, throughout the journey, they saw none of the guide tapes. Some managed to stay together all the way, but others, like Jim Taylor, found themselves on their own. "I remember," says Taylor, "that at one point, a grenade fell amongst us and we scattered. Whenever that happened, it was always difficult to find your mates again because, in splitting up to take cover, we would move off in all directions in the darkness. It was this which led to me finding myself on my own, and I eventually came out by the gas works. When I got to the river bank, I started to take off my equipment, intending to swim, when I bumped into a group from the 21st Independent Parachute Company, so I tagged on at the back and reached the embarkation point."

For most of them, this was where mobility ceased, and it then became a matter of waiting, as the small overworked craft plied to and fro across the river. Something like half of the boats were lost during the first hour of the operation, and Lieutenant-Colonel Myers, who was in charge of the embarkation, was hard put to it to compensate for the losses by ensuring both efficient loading and as speedy a turnround as was possible. Down by the bank, the ground was very muddy, which added to the difficulties, since it was still raining hard. "After an hour in this position," recalls Christie, "we moved forward approximately twenty yards. Then the officer decided to go up front to see what was happening. He returned in about thirty minutes and said there were only two boats and nearly 400 men in front, all waiting like us. He estimated that we should get across at about two o'clock in the morning. It was then a quarter to twelve."

* Following a successful return to England, Bertie Lickerish was seconded to Intelligence and sent to Germany as a Field Press Censor. Subsequently, whilst walking in a wood in Germany, in the company of a fellow officer, he was approached by a civilian who was rash enough to chat to them. Lickerish, recognizing the voice as that of William Joyce, the Irishman, better known as "Lord Haw-Haw", promptly arrested him. Later, in 1946, Joyce was executed in the Tower of London.

With all this activity, it was hardly surprising that the Germans should have tumbled ultimately to the fact that something was happening. They reacted accordingly. Christie remembers this as manifesting itself at about fifteen minutes after midnight: "A heavy mortar barrage was laid down around our area, and then the field was swept with machine-gun fire from the east and west. We had no foxholes now, but if ever I burrowed into the ground, I did then. I could see the flight of tracer bullets whining over my head by about four feet. I managed to place the source of the fire as the corner of what appeared to be a wood about 300 yards away. It was rather an uncertain position to be in and, as we were unable to return the fire, it made everyone nervous and jumpy."

Through midnight, and into the small hours of Tuesday, the little boats travelled back and forward across the river. Many of those who arrived at the loading point came supporting wounded comrades whom they had been reluctant to leave behind. Not a few gave up their places in the boats to the wounded. Some were men who had been injured in the fighting, others during the journey down through the woods to the river bank. One of the latter was David Allsop, who was hit in the left thigh by mortar fire, when only 200 yards from the river. With one leg totally disabled, he had to be helped along by Sergeant Quinn who saw him safely into one of the boats. Not that the danger of last minute injury was ended once the river had been reached. Like sitting ducks on the water, those who set out in the boats were fully exposed during the crossing to the full ferocity of the enemy barrage. To the flying fragments of mortar and shell was added the greater danger of machine-gun fire, which raked across the surface of the river with deadly effect. From both sides of the water, the flickering illumination of fires invested the whole scene with an inferno-like quality, and the cries of wounded men mingled horrifically with the crump of exploding shells and the staccato rip of machine-guns. Crossing time was only a few minutes but, for the defenceless men, pitilessly exposed to the sporadic enemy fire, it seemed like an eternity. It was perhaps inevitable, too, that the overworked rescue boats should at times have developed the occasional minor malfunction. "When we got into the boat," recollects John Stevenson," the Canadian engineer pulled at the lanyard to start the outboard motor, but nothing happened. I remember we were stuck there at half-past three in the morning, wondering if we'd still be there when daylight came. All the time he was pulling away, he kept saying, 'The bastard – the bastard – the bastard,' when suddenly it 'phutt-phutted' into life and we were away and off to the opposite bank."

There was also the very real fear of drowning accidents, for almost every craft left overloaded on each of its journeys. "Normally," says Stevenson, "you'd expect a sizeable clearance between the water and the gunwales, but it was only about a half-inch, so that the slightest bit of rocking was dangerous." In the circumstances, it was hardly surprising that the excessive loading should ultimately have had fatal consequences. David Christie can still recall how, during a lull in the bombardment, a loud scream suddenly rang out, which they were told was the death cry of a drowning man, tipped out of a capsized boat. There was sympathy from the waiting line but, equally, concern lest the sound should have drawn the attention of the Germans, and someone in the queue was moved to say, "If he has to die, why the hell should he make such a bastard noise about it?" It was an unworthy sentiment, in no way characteristic of men who had, in general, displayed conduct that was not only heroic but also honourable and charitable. Exceptional as it was, however, it indicated in some measure how the stress and tension of the nine-day hell had taken their toll, leaving in many cases only a primitive desire for personal survival. With this tragic incident, too, there was every possibility that David Christie had heard the voice of one of his own Squadron comrades, for it was in such circumstances that Leo Cairns of the Support Troop was drowned by the capsizing of an overloaded boat at the embarkation point.

As was subsequently revealed, many men, in a variety of circumstances, were drowned that night in the course of the withdrawal south of the river. Most of those were lost in trying to swim across. For a swimmer of moderate ability, the river was no great obstacle, but many made the mistake of attempting it without first removing clothing, arms and equipment. Weighed down by their heavy army issue boots and thick, water-sodden battledress uniforms, they stood little chance. Captain Ogilvie of the Glider Pilot Regiment, who had come to battle in his kilt, was tragically drowned whilst attempting to cope with the heavy weight of the saturated garment. On the other hand, those who, like Trooper Mike Gassett took off all their clothes, found the effort of the crossing relatively light.

Once on the other side, there were any number of willing hands ready to help. Again, there were white tapes to follow, but first, a muddy uphill slope to be negotiated and a steep drop down on the other side, which many of the men managed by sliding on their backs. As he climbed the river bank on the south side, David Christie felt a surge of exhilaration. Thereafter, ignoring the cold and the pouring rain, he lit up the cigar given to him by one of the Canadians and set off to walk to Nijmegen. For John Langan, the scramble up the bank brought an unexpected reunion for, by a strange coincidence, the two who helped hoist him over were men of the 43rd Reconnaissance Regiment, who had previously served with the Squadron.

In terms of simple human relationships, perhaps one of the most remarkable and impressive aspects of the whole evacuation was the way in which the men queued up to leave and did so with no regard for rank. It seems to have been universally acknowledged that the only priorities should be those accorded to wounded men. As for the rest, commissioned officers and other ranks alike took their turn in the line. It was tacitly assumed that it should be so, but it was also a situation which could have interesting consequences, as Stan Collishaw discovered: "I was in company with a chap from another regiment and, having helped each other in the scramble up over the high slippery embankment, we set off together on the road to Driel. I remember we were still under shell fire but feeling marvellous, and on the journey we were both of us very free with the expletives. After we had gone about a mile, we knew that we really were with 30 Corps, when we met a soldier in a wide-brimmed steel helmet and gas cape. He directed us to a barn where they were serving hot soup. It was only then, in the light, that I realized that my companion was a major, and I apologized for my language. 'Don't talk bloody rubbish,' he replied, 'we're all the same here. I'll tell you something – I was at Dunkirk, but this lot's a f- - - - - - sight worse!'"

There was little of humour in this grim final phase yet, perhaps predictably, some funny things did happen. Had there been a prize for ingenuity, it must assuredly have gone to the pair who, on landing safely on the far side of the river, scrounged around for something to protect them from the disagreeable downpouring of rain. Being both men of some resource, they found a supply hamper which they commandeered and inverted, so that it covered both of their heads and shoulders. It was still possible to see out through the basketry at the front and, providing the man in the rear kept in step with the one in front, progress could be made. It was in this way, looking for all the world like a wickerwork pantomime horse, that Dougie Galbraith and Henry Venes set off to march down the Nijmegen road!

Perhaps, however, one of the most moving stories of the evacuation is that told by John Stevenson, who recollects that one of the first persons whom he saw after clearing the river bank and getting under way on his walk south, was a lady of the Salvation Army, serving tea from a mobile canteen: "It was not more than a few miles from the river, and there was a grey-haired woman pouring out from behind the counter." When one considers the precariously held corridor through which the little van must have passed, to bring comfort to the men of Arnhem, its presence on the south side of the Neder Rijn must surely stand as an outstanding example of true practising Christianity.

All through the night, the evacuation proceeded. Rearguard parties, many composed of wounded men being left behind, kept up the pretence of a continued British presence by firing indiscriminately into the darkness in the direction of the enemy. Some, with knowledge of radio procedure, kept the 22 sets going with make-believe transmissions designed to deceive the monitoring sets of German Intelligence. At the POW "cage" in the Hartenstein tennis courts, a group of volunteers from the Corps of Military Police kept the German prisoners under continued surveillance until 0130 hours, before themselves stealing quietly away. And as the night wore on, the supply of boats gradually dwindled as more and more were put out of action. With the coming of the first sign of dawn, the last ferry left from the north bank. The time was then 0550 hours, and something like 300 men were left behind. For them, there were assurances that the boats would return for survivors on the following night, but no one really believed that that was anything other than an impossibly forlorn hope.

Initially, those who crossed the river rendezvoused at Driel, a village about three-quarters of a mile south of the Neder Rijn and still remembered by John Stevenson as "the most miserable place on God's earth." Thereafter, they walked or were transported to Nijmegen, where all were assembled in a red-brick school. There, the various units of the Division had an opportunity to check personnel, clean up, sort out what arms and equipment they had and catch up on some of the many hours of lost sleep. Some men flopped out in their sodden clothes and fell off immediately, yet even this longed-for rest was to be interrupted, for the building was set on fire by an enemy shell and had to be rapidly evacuated. It was at Nijmegen too, that the Squadron's survivors linked up with their seaborne party under Captain Russell Clark; the particular advantage of that was that most men received their large packs each of which contained a complete change of clothing.

By Wednesday 27th September, units had sorted themselves out and at 1700 hours on that day they paraded for an address by Lieutenant-General Browning, who thanked them for what they had done and promised one more job – the victory parade! On 28th September, the Squadron moved to Louvain, where the night was spent in a monastery, about four miles from the city, on the Brussels road. Now, like the gradual easing of a great weight, the pressures and tensions of their short but intensely disturbing experiences were at last beginning to lift. Already life was taking on a routine normality, with the return to regular meals, clean beds and an orderly and predictable progression of daily events. All of those were things which had once been taken so much for granted, but without which life in the latter stages of the battle had become so difficult to bear. Now also, there was time for reflection and, in particular, for thinking of those who would never return from Oosterbeek – Bucknall, McGregor, Weaver, Odd, Holderness and the other twenty three members of the Squadron – a sizeable percentage of the total strength – who had given their lives in the battle. Very many more than that had been wounded, a great number taken prisoner, whilst others, like Grubb, Bowles and Gough himself, were still posted as missing.

On Friday, 29th September, the 1st Airborne Reconnaissance Squadron, together with other units, flew from Brussels to England and landed in Lincolnshire at 7.30 in the evening. Wilfred Saint, who was one of the members of the reception party later remembered how some of them got out of the planes and kissed the ground at their feet. Several were also overheard to remark that England had never looked so good as at that moment. There followed a hot meal and then the dispersal of individual airborne units to their various bases.

It was late that night when the Squadron returned to Ruskington. A mere twelve days before, on a bright Sunday morning, it had taken ten lorries to transport the parachute party to Barkston Heath. Now, what was left of the entire Squadron came back in two vehicles. As the lorries drew to a halt outside the orderly room, and the shaded headlights illuminated the darkness of the silent village, the men jumped from the tailboards and stood uncertainly for a few minutes looking at the street that many had come to believe they would never see again. Already before they had finished getting down from the vehicles, a small group of villagers had gathered, each seeking someone special. As the last one alighted, the combined assembly moved off, almost by unspoken consent, to the "Shoulder of Mutton". Just who knocked up the landlord is not clear, but it seemed the logical thing to do. As they crowded into the place which for years to come would trigger off memories of those who had not returned, the dimmed lights of the houses began to go on all over the village. Soon the hurrying footsteps of others were heard, as the word was swiftly passed from one to the next that the Squadron had returned from Arnhem. "I remember, too," says John Stevenson, "how, when we got inside the "Shoulder of Mutton", people would ask about this one and that one and how those who knew often couldn't tell or daren't tell – it was all very sad and very, very moving."

On the Sunday immediately following the return, the personal involvement of the villagers with the airborne men was never so clearly demonstrated as in the gathering which filled the church for the special service of thanksgiving. It was only two weeks to the day since the Squadron had left – an impossibly short time – yet one into which most had packed the experiences of a lifetime. What made the service unique on that particular Sunday was that the people of the village came not only to worship God, but to do honour to those who had gone forth and had in truth traversed the valley of the shadow. In itself, the united act of worship on that calm English Sunday was somehow symbolic, enshrining in an act of simple dignity a common belief in the abiding values for which the airborne men had fought, and in the course of which some had not returned. Like all the epic battles of centuries past, Arnhem had already passed into history yet, when the memorial was subsequently unveiled in that same church in Ruskington, it was appropriate that its valedictory inscription should have highlighted so effectively the close bonds of warmth and friendship that had developed and, in many cases, become cemented for life within that quiet corner of Lincolnshire. Composed by Lord David Cecil, it was both moving and eloquent:

> From this place where it had found a home during its last months in England, the Squadron flew to the Battle of Arnhem.

Chapter 15 SEPTEMBER 1944–MAY 1945

"It was always bloody fünfs"

A total of 2398 men was successful in getting across the river on the night of the evacuation. The number included 160 Poles and 75 Dorsets, so that the 1st Airborne Division could claim 2163 as its own figure. At the time, something like 550 men were listed as killed in action, but the true figure was much greater, for 1500 of those posted as missing never returned. Of those who survived, most were in German hands, over half of them wounded and, in confirmation of this, a German OKW signal of 27th September reported the taking of 6450 prisoners. In addition to this, something over 300 men remained at large, being hidden by friendly Dutch or, in a few cases, fending for themselves.

In the immediate aftermath of the battle, those in hospital were reasonably well looked after, although the conditions under which the German medical staffs had to work were extremely difficult. Sam Bowles recalls the scene at Utrecht as one in which overworked doctors carried on, day and night, amputating and patching up the casualties from both sides as best they could: "My turn," he recalls, "came after two or three days and, after a whiff of anaesthetic, which was not sufficient to put me out, the German surgeon skilfully prised out the offending piece of shrapnel from my foot and dressed the wound with a plaster. After a few weeks, and suffering from gangrene, I was moved from Utrecht, by rail, to a hospital in Munster where I recovered fairly rapidly."

Much of this makeshift treatment was due to the inevitable confusion consequent upon sudden pressure being brought to bear on very limited resources. In time, as things settled down, hospital conditions improved, and reports of subsequent experiences are, in general, favourable. Ralph Foulkes, wounded in an allied air *straffe* during his period of captivity, speaks most highly of the work of the German hospital staff and attests to the first-class nature of the treatment received. He has particular praise for Sister Anna, a Bavarian nurse, whose sole interest, quite irrespective of nationality, was always the well-being of her patients.

Men who could not be moved initially remained for a time in Holland. One of those was Bert Welham, who was kept for some weeks in the hospital at Lochem. Like Foulkes, he also has favourable memories, some of them even spiced with a certain recognizable brand of Teutonic humour: "When the German doctor used to come round in the morning, he'd say, 'Show us your wounds,' and he always used to think it was very funny that four or five of the blokes had to show their backsides because they'd caught shrapnel there. He used to roll about with laughter at that. Still, they did look after us well – as well as they looked after their own chaps. At one time, as a matter of fact, they were feeding us on thick Advocaat to build us up."

Welham was eventually shifted to a prisoner-of-war camp in Germany, but there were those others who were too ill to be moved, and whose treatment continued in Holland. Dickie Minns was one who remained, having been shifted north to the Willem III Barracks at Apeldoorn. Three blocks of the complex had been converted into a hospital, and he remained there until the end of hostilities. Minns had been on McGregor's jeep during the Sunday night ambush at Wolfheze, and had been seriously wounded in the stomach, hip and thigh. He recalls that, from a medical point of view, they were well treated, and remembers also, with gratitude, the reassurance and comfort which so many of the badly wounded men received from Padre Buchanan,* who had remained behind. Boredom, however, was one of the chief enemies, and Minns still recollects how delighted he was when one of the friendlier German orderlies gave him a book written in English: "I can't remember much about it now," he says, "but it did a great deal to lift my spirits up. One thing which does come back to me is that it had a lot in it about the 'Peckham Moochers', but whoever or whatever they were, I've no idea."

Unfortunately, kindness of this sort could not always be guaranteed, and Minns has good reason to remember that not all his German captors were disposed to behave in such a civilized manner: "As well as the medical staff who took care of us," he says, "there were guards posted to prevent us from escaping. Not that we would have done, because most of us could not even have got out of bed, never mind take off. Almost all the guards were older men – some even had the old-fashioned helmets with the spike in the centre. They didn't bother us at all but, from time to time, two young SS men would appear, and they'd go around the ward, hitting at bandaged legs and obviously trying to hurt people. I had a pin in one leg, and it was up on a pulley with a weight on the end. If anyone touched the weight, the pain used to go right up my leg. Those two used to make a point of knocking it and pulling it quite deliberately, and I'd feel it right up to my head. Fortunately, they didn't come round often but, when they did, we always knew we were in for a little touch."

As for the rest, those whose wounds were considered to be less serious or who were regarded as able to travel, were despatched as swiftly as possible to prisoner-of-war camps in Germany. The process invariably began with a rail journey, undertaken in cattle trucks, in which there was a great deal of overcrowding, little proper feeding and no sanitary provision. George Adams was one of those who was moved from Apeldoorn to Germany in this way. "I cannot remember how many there were in each of those trucks," he says, "but I do remember that from time to time the guards would throw in so many loaves of bread, and it was never anything like enough. All the time, there were blokes wanting to go to the lavatory, but they wouldn't open the doors for us."

Not everyone, of course, was wholly committed to the idea of completing the journey into the Fatherland. When it was discovered that each truck had a small opening in the roof, through which it might be possible to squeeze, a number of the prisoners took the opportunity to plan their escape. It was a difficult feat, and meant scrambling up, using arms, legs and elbows but, for the most agile, it was a possibility, and Sergeant Kay, who had been wounded on arrival with the second lift, was one of the Squadron men who escaped in this way. He was later picked up and looked after by a Dutch family, before successfully escaping across the river. Despite his wound,

*Later Archbishop of Dublin, but at that time Chaplain to the 2nd Battalion of the South Staffordshire Regiment.

Kay had fought throughout the battle with another unit and received a well-merited MID for his courage.*

Once arrived at the various camps, the men settled in to the wearisome survival routine which characterized the life of a British prisoner-of-war. Astonishingly, in one or two places, there were unexpected and emotional reunions, as Jimmy Pearce remembers of his own arrival at Stalag IVB. There, they were greeted by members of the old B Troop, who had been captured in the Italian campaign. "I remember their tears," says Pearce, "both of joy and sadness at finding us there, and how Sammy Burgoyne, a Birmingham lad, was just completely overwhelmed at meeting members of the Squadron again."

Reception by their captors was generally a straightforward affair, with little in the way of intensive interrogation. Some prisoners had been apprehensive about possible brutalities, but Arthur Barlow, who eventually arrived at Stalag XIIB, testifies to the fact that fears of this kind speedily proved to have been unfounded. There were exceptional incidents, of course, as George Adams recounts in recollecting the circumstances of his own entry into Stalag XIB at Fallingbostel, the place to which most captured members of the Squadron appear, at first, to have been taken. "When we got off the train at the camp," he says, "they lined us up five deep and marched us up the road and, because we were singing, they said we were arrogant. Once inside, we found ourselves in a large compound, as big as a playing-field, around which they marched us, still in fives – with the Germans it was always bloody 'funfs' – until they had everyone in through the gates. At any rate, as we were wheeling round like that, one of the blokes spotted a mate of his further over, and broke away to join him. At that, one of the guards caught hold of him and pushed him to the ground. The British lad then got his fists up and threw the guard off one, whereupon they all lammed into him with rifle butts."

Stalag XIB was not the most popular of camps. By contrast with conditions reported elsewhere, life seems to have been distinctly unpleasant. One of the major problems, as John Serginson and George Adams both recall, was that the huts were infested with lice. All of those who were there also seem to agree that the food was abominable and that living was only made bearable by the receipt of one and a half Red Cross parcels per man, each seven weeks. Sleeping conditions were also primitive – three-tier bunks with four 9-inch bed boards per man, and one blanket apiece – and men would team up in pairs in order to make things easier for themselves, by having enough boards to lie on as well as a blanket on top and one below.

Many of those incarcerated at Fallingbostel were also wounded, and a proportion of them had still to be operated on. Thereafter, they received only the most rudimentary treatment. George Adams remembers having his wound dressed with a paper bandage just once in every four days, and this meant that, with a lack of sulpha drugs, there was a constant danger of gangrene. Once they had recovered sufficiently, however, the Germans removed many of the prisoners to work camps elsewhere, in Germany as well as in occupied territory. Such were the conditions in Fallingbostel that most were only too relieved to go. As a consequence of this, Jeffrey Williams went to work in a sugar beet factory at Hildesheim, whilst John Serginson was taken to Celle, about 25 miles north-east of Hanover, to work on the railway. Several Squadron men – Alf Hazell, George Adams, Bert Pegnall – went to *Arbeitskommando* 7001 at Brunswick, and worked near the Hermann Goering steel works.

Despite his captivity, however, the British soldier could display a measure of resilience which

* Tragically, he survived Arnhem, only to die in a road accident, whilst serving in Norway, just after the end of the war.

Return to the Bakery: September 1974
L–R: Jim Taylor, Henry Venes, Charlie King, Vic Taylor

Squadron reunion, Union Jack Club, October 1977
Standing L–R: G. Williams, G. Adams, H. Tillyer (2nd Para), A. White, C. Roberts, J. Taylor, A. Hazell, J. Stevenson, A. Webb, J. Marshall, J. Pearce, W. Bateman, M. Grubb, W. Chandler, R. Nabarro, R. Price, H. Venes, D. Holt (7th KOSB), V. Taylor. *Kneeling, L–R:* R. Minns, T. Godfrey, E. Hares, R. Miles, Author

(*J. Watson*)

Airborne Cemetery, Oosterbeek

(H. A. Duin

IN·MEMORY·OF·THE·OFFICERS·AND·MEN·OF·THE
1ST·AIRBORNE·RECONNAISSANCE·SQUADRON
WHO·GAVE·THEIR·LIVES·IN·THE·WAR·1939–1945

A. C. BAKER
F. BRAWN
R. BRUMWELL
P. L. BUCKNALL
L. CAIRNS
F. W. CHILTON
J. A. CHRISTIE
W. M. EDMOND
D. GILES
E. J. GORRINGE
L. P. GOULDING
G. E. HOLDERNESS
N. R. ILLINGWORTH
J. M. IRALA
R. W. JAKEMAN
G. KAY
R. MC GLEW
T. MC GREGOR
T. V. P. MC NABB
R. MC SKIMMINGS
D. H. K. MASON
L. MUMFORD
T. MURPHY
A. H. ODD
J. R. C. R. PARK
A. F. PASCAL
H. E. PEARSON
H. A. PLATT
R. POTTS
D. F. POWELL
T. J. QUINCE
P. S. REID
W. B. REW
J. G. SALMON
W. G. SLOPER
J. G. SMART
P. J. SOUTHWELL
W. C. STACEY
S. TICKLE
T. A. W. WALKER
A. J. WATERMAN
M. J. WEAVER
H. J. WOOD

From this place, where it had found a home during its last months in England, the Squadron flew to the Battle of Arnhem

1st Airborne Reconnaissance Squadron Memorial, Ruskington church

was wholly admirable. Even when working as a coal heaver in Czechoslovakia, Jimmy Pearce contrived to turn the situation to the disadvantage of his captors. "For a time," he says, "we were at it all day, unloading coal waggons at the railway station. After a while, we did so well that we got promoted to weighing out the coal, and that was when we could get a bit of our own back. The system was that people would come down to the yard with permits for coal, and we had to let them have the amount on the permit. Some of those who came were forced-labour people, and we used to give them their coal, then slip the permits back to them so that they could use them again to get more. The Germans used to come too, but we never gave them theirs back – these were the ones that we always tore up, so they never got any extra. Just the same, we had to be very careful not to be found out, because the Austrian civilian in charge of us, Wolff by name, was very unfriendly and a dedicated Nazi."

Certain survival techniques also came naturally, as is evident from another of Pearce's recollections: "One day, they sent us out with a horse and cart to a warehouse, to load up with crates and take them to the railway station. The way it was, we had to drop them out of a loading window to be put on to the cart. When we discovered that the crates were for the Gerries on the Russian Front and that some had chocolates and cigarettes and stuff like that in them, we took to dropping them on their edges. That way, they got a real good bashing and some of the stuff fell out, making it easier for us to pinch it. What put paid to that was that, in our hurry to heave the crates out of the window, we didn't notice a German sergeant standing in the way, and we almost clobbered him – if we had, we'd have put him six feet into the ground!"

For others, there were fewer opportunities for exploiting the weaknesses of the system. Arthur Barlow was also sent to Czechoslovakia, but to a town called Grasseth. There he joined an American working party (*Arbeitskommando* A2), working down coal mines in very bad conditions. In March 1945, he was admitted into hospital in nearby Falkeneau suffering from diphtheria, a consequence of drinking stagnant water down in the mine workings. Barlow survived, but still recalls the occasion with clarity: "I was put to bed in an isolation ward and, with a shrug of her shoulders, the elderly nurse said that I would be dead by morning. Nevertheless, with the usual German thoroughness, my clothes were taken away and the door locked to prevent my escaping!" He was still there when hostilities ceased, and in his small notebook he made the following entry: "On 7th May 1945 at 7.20 a.m., the American 9th Armoured Division entered Falkeneau, where I was in hospital with diphtheria. Felt rather sick and didn't fully appreciate I was no longer a P.O.W. At 11.30 a.m., the last tank went by. Happy day."

Some men were luckier in that they were ultimately sent to an Offlag, to look after imprisoned British officers. Conditions in such camps were infinitely better than in the Stalags and, as far as POW postings were concerned, a move to one of those places was considered to be the best that an 'other rank' could get. Two such fortunate individuals were Charlie King and Bill Chandler, who ultimately arrived at Offlag 79. Chandler kept a diary during his time there which reveals that, although his living conditions were tolerable, they did nothing to alleviate the boredom and the yearning to be liberated. He expressed this in a short poem:

This forced existence,
This created home,
Monotony of life
Which eats to the bone,
Decaying the soul

Eats up all emotions.
My God! To be Free.

As the allied advance rolled on, so did a fresh danger present itself, that of being at the receiving end of an attack by one's own side. It was a time when the 1000 bomber raids were being mounted by the RAF, and Sam Bowles has recollections of a memorable night in the marshalling yards at Stuttgart, when the German guards simply locked the prisoners into the carriages and themselves departed for the shelters. Alf Hazell, too, has horrific memories of being caught up in a similar situation during a spell in Brunswick hospital, to which he had been removed with a perforated duodenal ulcer. He was recuperating from his operation, when an incendiary bomb from a British plane crashed into his room. He owes his life to the bravery of the British medical orderly who carried him out and thus saved him from being roasted alive.

Predictably, of course, it was inevitable that Freddie Gough should attempt to escape at the first opportunity, although there were reasons why this was a long time in coming. In the first place, as officer in charge of the section of the camp occupied by the Australian and New Zealand officers, it was much less easy for him to disappear than it would have been had he simply been one of the crowd. There was also the handicap of his prematurely grey hair which guaranteed that any absence from "appel" was almost always certain to be detected. The chance came towards the end when, in response to the threat of the advancing allied armies, the Germans began to move prisoners-of-war from camps likely to be overrun. His camp was at Eichstatt in Bavaria and, in the early part of April, word came round that it was to be evacuated and the prisoners marched off – destination unknown. By arrangement with the Senior British Officer, Gough ensured that his own party would bring up the rear of the column, a position likely to offer the most favourable opportunities for escape. The guess was that they were being taken to Munich, over forty miles away, and it was estimated that, although it was a relatively short distance, such was their condition, it was likely to take some time to get there.

Early in the morning of 14th April, the move began, on what was to become a day of tragedy. Ralph Foulkes was one of those involved and recorded what happened in his diary: "We staggered on parade at 0500 hours and were counted several times – several people missing already. We moved out of the camp, and it was the funniest sight – home-made barrows dropping to bits, wheels dropping off before we were through the gates. The slow straggling column idled about half a mile before falling out. Two US Mustangs came to have a look at us, dived low over the road, wagged wings and went off. Jim fixed up a pram at the next village. The Mustangs returned together with several groups of Thunderbolts and started to shoot up the main road and railway over the valley. Then the great mistake came – they started on us, with cannons and MG. I was in a ditch just off the road, with Jim, Colonel Taylor and Major Morley. After about the second attack I was hit by cannon in the leg." Colonel Gough afterwards confirmed that the attack caused many similar casualties and that a number of men died as a result.

By the second night out, Gough had made the break and was on his own. His later recollections of what happened afterwards were fairly concise but sufficiently adequate to show that the months in captivity had in no measure affected his natural ebullience: "I was about twelve days on the run and, in that time, had some very interesting adventures. I joined company with two US Sergeant Pilots, Ed and Frank, and we took refuge with about sixty French O.Rank POW's in a village called Geisenfeld, at that time held by a Hungarian SS Division. When they withdrew in the face of our advancing allies, the Mayor, who apparently knew of our whereabouts, came to our hovel and formally surrendered Geisenfeld to me. Ed and Frank then promptly renamed it Goughenfeld! Shortly afterwards, the Black Hawk Division of General Patton's army came in, and a good time was had by all."

Not everyone who was left behind in the Arnhem area, after the battle, remained as a prisoner. Such a one was Henry Crowder from County Durham. As a member of the small C Troop group which had been wandering about for two days after the ambush on the Amsterdam road, he had eluded capture at the time when the others were taken prisoner on Thursday, at Wolfheze. With his two companions from 4th Brigade, Crowder had then worked his way westwards in the direction of Ede, spending a very cold Thursday night in the open. "The following night," he recalls, "we found a farm, and there was a Dutch nurse there, with a lot of kids who shouted and cried when they saw us, because we were very dirty. The nurse told us to go out into the woods, and there we found two more paratroopers and an RAF air gunner. When it was dark, the Dutch brought out food and left it for us to collect." Considering the nature of the German reprisals already being carried out against the civilian population who had assisted the British, it was help of a most courageous kind. Thereafter, the group got hold of civilian clothes which they put on over the top of their uniforms. "After that," says Crowder, "we walked past Germans and sometimes even alongside them. I had a feeling that, although the Germans didn't suspect, some of the Dutch people knew who we were all right."

There followed a succession of hiding places, as the Dutch underground took over responsibility for their safety and kept shifting them from one location to another. For most of the time, this was a tedious business with one move indistinguishable from the next, but Henry Crowder remembers, in particular, a series of events which began when they arrived at one farm north-west of Ginkel: "They chased the hens out and put us in the hutch, and we'd only been there about an hour when they turned us out as well, because the Germans were searching the village. That night, we were moved once more to another place where we were accommodated for two days in a barn. Half of the barn had more of our lads in it, and quite a number of them were field ambulance men. The other half was given over to Dutch SS, who were being kept under guard. I remember the Dutch underground men having a discussion and we were told that they had decided to execute the Dutch SS men, which they did, right there in the barn. One was only a kid about sixteen. Another was a big, arrogant bloke and he fainted, so they shot him right there as he lay on the floor. Five of them were executed that night, and one of the men from the field ambulance group pronounced them to be dead. We then buried them just outside the barn – three in one place and two in another."

In considering the background to this episode, one has to avoid making over-facile judgments as to the morality of it all. It would be naïve to infer that those responsible were not in any sense motivated by simple revenge – the ethical crudity of an eye for an eye. At the same time, it needs, perhaps, to be borne in mind that, such were the predictable patterns of behaviour of the occupying force, no other decision could have been made. From the moment that they saw the British troops being looked after, the fate of the Dutch SS men was sealed, for there was no alternative which could have secured the safety of the farmer and his family from the inevitable German reprisals. Never was rough justice so rough nor so just.

There were about 150 soldiers of the 1st British Airborne Division in hiding in the Ede area alone, and another 100 or so east towards Arnhem. Naturally the Germans were suspicious, and Crowder still remembers how this would constantly produce a crisis situation in which they had to be passed from one hiding place to another. Sometimes they would travel as a group on bicycles, with a Dutch helper in front and another behind, and one day they heard that some of those brave guides had been caught and shot out of hand by the Gestapo. Eventually, on 22nd October, armed and clad in his full British army uniform, Henry Crowder escaped across the river to freedom. In the same party went Sergeant "Judd' Kay, also of the Squadron. The escape had been a well-planned affair, to a great extent organized by the Dutch resistance and aided by the HQ of 101st US Airborne Division, but owing much to the personal initiative of such men as David Dobie, Digby Tatham-Warter and Tony Hibbert. Over 120 men crossed safely, including Anthony Deane-Drummond and Gerald Lathbury, the commander of 1st Parachute Brigade.

Lieutenant Bob Guthrie, who had been incapacitated just after landing as the result of a Sten gun accident, was another who spent some time with the Dutch resistance. Taken initially to the dressing station at the Vreewijk Hotel, he had lain listening to the sound of the battle raging outside. By the end of the week, he had been removed with the rest of the wounded to Apeldoorn, and placed in a cattle truck to be taken to Germany. Prior to the departure of the train, he had managed to tamper with the lock on the door of the waggon, and soon after the train was under way he had jumped out, along with some others. They were fired on but the train did not stop. Having made his move early on, he was still in Holland and obviously in a better position to obtain help than would have been the case had he delayed until the train had passed over into Germany. He found himself in sight of two farms, and it was a question of which to approach. He learned afterwards that his unwitting choice was the correct one, as the other was owned by a collaborator who would probably have betrayed him. At first, Guthrie's pattern of life was very similar to that of Crowder's, in that he was passed from one hiding place to another by the Dutch underground. Like Crowder, Guthrie too became involved in their activities, but he went much further and, having discarded his uniform but for the battledress jacket, became something of a full-time participant, taking part in night-time forays, like helping to collect after an arms drop from England.

For six months, Bob Guthrie was transferred from place to place, always with the threat of exposure, capture and possible execution hanging over him. For a time, he lived in a brushwood hideout in the woods, with underground workers, Dutch Jews and other British service personnel. Movement from one area to another was often particularly nerve-racking, as the party with which he was travelling would often have to pass over bridges, manned as checkpoints by German troops. Inevitably, there were a number of narrow escapes, some of which he still remembers: "We were with the Lieverdink family in Eibergen, who were marvellous to us, and were downstairs at the time, when some troops came into the room. Fortunately, they didn't speak to us but, shortly afterwards, we had to shift when one of the children inadvertently gave us away to the milkman. He'd asked how many people were in the house and twigged that there were too many." Because of that the party had to move and it was just afterwards that they had their closest shave. Sheltered in the roof space of another farm, they heard the Germans arrive. "They obviously suspected," says Guthrie, "that there was someone in the place, because they ransacked the building quite thoroughly. They never found us, but they took the family outside, and I remember being up in the roof, looking down through cracks in the tiles and seeing the children being beaten up by the Germans to try to get them to say where we were. They didn't say, and the Germans didn't find us, but the family was finally taken away and the eight of us were eventually moved out again by the underground." Guthrie remained with the Dutch until after the Rhine crossing, when he was picked up by a unit of the Guards Armoured Division and spent a few days fighting with them prior to repatriation.

In all their relationships with the British airborne men who remained at large after the battle, the courageous Dutch people always risked certain death from the Germans, in the event of detection. Faced with such a situation, the astonishing thing is that the majority of the civil population was still willing to help – with food, clothing, shelter and, where available, medical care. Yet all over Gelderland, the Gestapo was busy, ferreting out, questioning and taking away anyone suspected of having offered direct assistance to the British during the battle. Nor were the reprisals confined solely to action against individuals. Already, in the course of the war, in other places and at other times, there had been directives from Berlin instigating mass reprisals against communities suspected of underground activity against the Reich. Orders of that kind had invariably been carried out with an unrestrained and unquestioning thoroughness, tinged with little of humanity. So it was, that by the time it came to deal with the civilian populations of Arnhem and Oosterbeek, the German SS already had behind it a wealth of experience in reprisal techniques, and these were put into operation even before the final shots were fired. What happened is not generally known outside of Holland, for accounts of the Battle of Arnhem have, in the main, concerned themselves with the struggle itself. For the people of Arnhem and Oosterbeek, however, the events that took place in the immediate aftermath have passed into folk memory and are unlikely ever to be forgotten. There are those today in Oosterbeek who cannot bear even to hear the German language spoken without experiencing feelings of revulsion.

The collective reprisals followed a two-stage pattern which could be loosely termed as "banishment" and "destruction". It all began on 23rd September, when an order came from SS Headquarters in Arnhem. Whatever else it may have lacked, it was unequivocally clear in its import, which was that the entire civilian population of Arnhem and Oosterbeek was to quit the towns and was to be given just a little over twenty-four hours to do so. It was not, as it has often been wrongly described, an evacuation. Had it been so, it would have implied help and assistance being rendered to those involved. No such responsibility was assumed by the Germans, because the 100,000 people were simply ordered to get out. As to where they were to go and how they were to travel, it was made quite clear that that was no concern of the occupying power. To questions like, "What of the old and the sick?" the response was one of total indifference. The order was to get out – or face the consequences. So it was that the pitiful processions began to leave the towns. Some had wheelbarrows piled high with bedding, others carried what few possessions they were able to take on the handlebars of tyreless bicycles, or over their shoulders, wrapped in improvized knapsacks. The entire age-range of humanity was involved in this senseless and brutal operation, from newly-born babies to those whose time had almost run its course. Some sought shelter with relatives or friends in other villages and towns. Many were accommodated in this way, although in some cases the welcome was cooler than had been anticipated. Others less fortunate simply took to the woods, where the cold damp nights of late autumn took a savage toll of the sick and elderly. It is estimated that ultimately something like 3000 civilians died as a direct consequence of the German SS action in banishing them from their homes at the onset of winter.

As for the homes that were left, these were then systematically looted by the German troops. But it was not the indiscriminate and indisciplined savagery of an army on the loose, for the plundering was a directed operation that was centrally organized. Into the towns came army lorries, which simply moved from house to house, street by street, and removed all the portable household possessions. These were then driven to nearby Rhineland towns like Essen, Cologne, Dusseldorf and Dortmund, to be distributed to German families bombed out of their homes by the nightly attacks of the Royal Air Force. What was subsequently revealed, however, was that anything which could not be removed or which was not required, was simply destroyed inside the house. Numerous accounts tell of families returning after the war, to find personal possessions heaped up in a pile and despoiled in the centre of the room. Ben Jansen of Oosterbeek, who was then a thirteen-year-old, still remembers coming back with his father to their home in Van Dedemweg to find that all their personal things had been treated in this way. Nothing was retrievable, so they simply set to and shovelled everything out of the window preparatory to cleaning the house up again. In all such circumstances, one of the most remarkable features of the aftermath was the manner in which those long-suffering Dutch people set about erasing the odious signs of German occupation and the resolute way in which all of them collectively embraced the opportunities to rebuild on the promise of a brighter future in the years ahead.

Meantime, back in England, throughout the last winter of the war, the 1st British Airborne Division was slowly built up again by the influx of fresh personnel. In the process, its composition was significantly altered, for the fact that the 10th, 11th and 156th Parachute Battalions had been left with so few men led to the decision not to reconstitute 4th Brigade. As a result, by April 1945, Roy Urquhart's force consisted of 1st Parachute Brigade, 1st Air Landing Brigade and the 1st Polish Independent Parachute Brigade. The surviving elements of 4th Brigade were simply absorbed into 1st Brigade.

Like the other reconstituted regiments, 1st Airborne Reconnaissance Squadron received an infusion of fresh blood yet, understandably, it was never again a force that was united in anything other than a formal sense. Jimmy Muir, who went as a young subaltern, was sensitive to this: "I felt that although the newcomers were made welcome, there was always something short of full acceptance. There were those who had been at Arnhem and those who hadn't and because of that there was a barrier that could never be breached."

It is no part of this story to undertake anything in the nature of a detailed post-mortem on the Battle of Arnhem. To do so would be to go over ground that has already been well-trodden. Many such analyses have been made, some based upon creditable scholarship, others, perhaps, upon flimsier foundations. Not a few have also been over-preoccupied with issues unlikely to have affected the ultimate outcome in any significant sense, and some in seeking to apportion blame for failure have been less than just.

Perhaps, however, in terms of historical causation, it is possible to identify three broad issues as significant in contributing towards the end result. The first of these relates to the nature of the advanced strategic planning and, in particular, to the fact that there was insufficient time available for it to be undertaken effectively. Instead, a massive and complicated operation was launched in just one week, with all that this implied in respect of individual unit preparedness as well as liaison at all levels, both within and outside of the divisional arms involved. Thus, whilst it was true that 1st Airborne Division was very much in a state of general readiness, each operation carried its own unique problems which required time and detailed consideration to be accorded to them, in a number of instances beyond divisional level.

With this in mind, in examining what happened in the days prior to 17th September, one has to ask oneself a number of key questions about the higher planning. Specifically, one might, perhaps, consider why there was not fuller and lengthier discussion, at the highest level, about the relationship of ground objectives to the various delivery and landing plans, about the acceptability or otherwise of proposed dropping and landing zones, or about the basic nature of inter-services co-operation, such as the vitally necessary logistical air support. In all of this, the significant and common feature was clearly the time factor, and it is this which goes far towards explaining why certain vital decisions were either never made or never reconsidered. By contrast, only three months earlier, Operation "Overlord" had been carried out. As an example of forward planning, it was a superbly successful affair, organized in meticulous detail over a period of months. Yet, for all that, the fickleness of the English Channel in June had hardly been foreseen; nor, despite the minutiae of preparation, was "Overlord" in any sense an operation of guaranteed success, as the struggle on Omaha beach alone was to testify. Nevertheless, forward planning had been extensive and much which, on top of these unaccountable set-backs, could well have negated the success of the Normandy landings, was thereby anticipated.

Those who bore responsibility for the planning of "Market Garden" enjoyed no such generous time allocation for the implementation of their schemes. Nor was the fact that sixteen major operations were prepared prior to "Market Garden", of any significance in relation to a growth of planning expertise. Each one of those was as hastily organized as the last, and effectiveness was never put to the test. Each in turn had to be abandoned when its strategic objectives were achieved through the rapidity of advance of the ground forces. Indeed, to some extent, this may in part account for the haste with which the final operation was cobbled together, in order to ensure that the highly trained British force might justify its creation by successfully undertaking at least one major airborne operation. The fact that the end of the war was seen to be imminent must have made this appear all the more desirable and, perhaps, serves to explain the easy and uncritical acceptance of a bad plan, which just might have worked and in the furtherance of which one, at least, of the grand designs could be got up and away.

It is true that in respect of advanced preparation one cannot but give credit for the vast amount of work that was still crammed into the preparatory week. Yet here again, it is possible to isolate issues of fine detail which needed time to sort out and which could and should have been resolved long before that point was ever reached. Why, for example, were the difficulties of wireless communication not anticipated prior to the operation? In practical terms, it raises the question as to the extent to which the relatively new 22 set, which first appeared in 1943, had been effectively tested under a variety of operational conditions before being issued to airborne forces. Like the heavier but more dependable 19 set, the 22 was officially credited with a standard R/T performance of up to ten miles and the two sets were basically similar in the nature of their operating controls. In the event, theory and practice were found to be totally divorced from each other for, even in the more open country of the Nijmegen area, the ground-wave reliability of the weak-powered 22 set was not substantially more than five miles in any direction. In the thickly wooded terrain of Oosterbeek, even such an absurdly poor figure was drastically reduced by the screening, making nonsense of attempts to maintain communication by standard procedures. The other set in regular use was the WS 76, operating on the principle of pre-selected fixed-crystal frequencies. It too was of low power and equally ineffective.

The interesting corollary to all this is that 1st Airborne Division did have sets of greater potential than either WS 22 or WS 76. but there were only four of them. Two SCR 193's, intended for use with the air support parties were knocked out on D+3, but the other two, which were 19 sets with HP (High Power) units attached, were used with greater success. One provided the link to the 64th Medium Regiment, and the other to a FOO attached by the Division to 30 Corps. The indications are, therefore, that whilst the 22 set proved to be a failure, the heavier 19 set with the additional bulk of a HP unit would probably have worked. It would, of course, have been impractical to have attempted to man all stations with such a cumbersome combination, but the inclusion of 19 HP sets at critical control points throughout the Divisional net might well have made all the difference between reasonable success and total failure. Unfortunately, in the determination of what was appropriate for airborne forces, this consideration does not seem to have been given anything like sufficient weight.* The fact that 22's were much lighter seems to have been regarded as of prime importance, very much related to glider loading capacity, and yet, once on the ground at Arnhem, they proved to be, for the most part, just so much junk.

But if the wireless sets were bad, the maps were worse. Many, including Freddie Gough, who tried to use them, found them disturbingly inaccurate and unreliable. Roads marked as throughways turned out to be either dead ends or overgrown tracks. On the other hand, in numerous instances, routes which were perfectly reasonable and open, and which could have been taken into account in the planning of unit movement, were simply not recorded at all. Worse still, and almost unbelievably, the primary objective of Arnhem Bridge was also missing from all the maps!

Ironically, time and again, those who have commented on the shortcomings of the maps with which they were issued have often added an element of qualification and self-doubt. One typical observation by a former Reconnaissance Squadron officer was, "I don't think the maps were completely accurate, but then, maybe it was my own map reading that was at fault." In truth, all the evidence would seem to indicate that, notwithstanding reflections of this kind, nothing like the amount of work necessary had been done, in order to ensure that the maps which were ultimately given to the airborne men were as accurate as it was possible to make them.

For this particular aspect of the pre-Arnhem preparation, the 1st Airborne Division bore no responsibility. That clearly lay with those whose job it was to supply the maps – the Ordnance Survey branch of the Royal Engineers and the US Army Map Service. It may be that responsibility for the deficiencies has to be shared with others, for there is always the possibility that the map-makers were never in full possession of the facts. Such a supposition, however, loses credibility, when set alongside the explanatory notes printed on the face of the maps. Those referring to "revisions" are especially inexplicable. For example, GSGS 2541 (1:100000) Sheet 5 was the small scale map which included the Arnhem-Oosterbeek area. Beneath the identification number appeared the following:

> Published by War Office 1913. 3rd Edition 1943
>
> Partly revised from Dutch maps of 1936–39
> Communication revised from GSGS 4183, 4238
> Autokart van Nederland
> Intelligence reports up to 1942

The dates are significant, for they were intended to indicate that, although the map was pre-1914, standard revisionary procedures had been carried out on several occasions up to 1942. The very inclusion in red print of a cautious disclaimer about the guaranteed accuracy of the

* This is not to imply that the 19 set would have been the ideal alternative. Its great disadvantage was the weight of the batteries required to power it. Nevertheless, since the more efficient and lighter WS 62 was not to become available until 1945, the 19 set was all that they had, and its over-riding merit, on HP especially, was that it worked!

road classifications seemed almost to lend implicit weight to the belief that, at least, everything else essential had been included. Nothing could have been further from the truth, for Arnhem Bridge, opened in July 1934, the great iron span which sat athwart the Neder Rijn had been consistently omitted from whatever revisionary work had been carried out in the eight years subsequent to its opening.

The deficiencies of GSGS 2541 would not, perhaps, have mattered so much, had the larger-scale maps shown a compensatory accuracy. But such was not the case. GSGS 4427 Arnhem (1:25000) Sheet 6 NW was probably of even greater relevance to the 1st British Airborne Division than was the small-scale map of the whole area, yet it was even more inaccurate. Prepared by the US Army Map Service, it also had numerous revisions attested to, but Arnhem Bridge was missing from it as well! In this case, there were additional grave errors, mainly in respect of the most important road classifications. Of the two routes leading northwards out of Elden the main road to the place where the Bridge should have been indicated was shown, erroneously, as a minor secondary track, petering out at the river bank. On the other hand, the very minor road to the west was shown on the map in red, highlighted as the principal route from Elden to Praets and shown bridging the river at a point over a mile to the north-west of the real crossing point. What the map showed was a former bridging point, that of the so-called "pontoon" bridge, which featured in the Orders for "Market Garden" but which had long been out of use and, indeed, was no longer in existence at the time of the drop!

The inescapable evidence, therefore, would seem to be that a British Airborne Division was sent off, all the way to Holland, to capture something which was not depicted in any way, on the maps with which it was issued. One can only speculate about the degree of possible misunderstanding that might have taken place as a result of the wholly inaccurate cartography. "Fortunately," as Brigadier Charles Mackenzie has since pointed out, "we had good aerial photographs taken just a week prior to the operation, so we knew where the Bridge was all right." Nevertheless, it does seem remarkable that for the identification of a major topographical feature, built over ten years previously, a whole operational division of the British Army should not have been able to depend upon its maps, the more especially so when its capture was the central purpose of the operation. Furthermore, an examination of the aerial photographs shows that, although the primary objective was shown, the subsequent over-inking of gun positions and roads perpetuated the mistaken identification of the main route from the south as running to the pontoon bridge's former position, with the actual main route from Elden to the main road bridge still depicted as little more than a track.

The second issue of fundamental importance was undoubtedly the total failure of 30 Corps to achieve its strategic objectives. To say, as do so many accounts that the Battle of Arnhem was a defeat for the 1st British Airborne Division is an over-simplistic judgment. The task was to seize and hold the road bridge for two days. The failure of the British airborne troops was in respect of the south end of the Bridge, which they did not secure. Nevertheless, the success of the gallant 700, who fought under Frost and Gough at the north side and held it from Sunday night through to Thursday morning, prevented the full strength of the 10th SS (Frundsberg) Division from reaching Nijmegen and beyond. As it was, 30 Corps undoubtedly had enormous difficulties to overcome, not the least of which were vulnerability to attack and inability to deploy effectively in awkward terrain. The reduced capability of Horrocks's force must also have been in considerable measure attributable to the total lack of protection offered to his flanks, for the necessary strategic support – both air and ground – was never forthcoming, except at the start of the operation. But, one cannot but speculate that, in the initial stages of the advance, the 43rd Division might perhaps have achieved a higher momentum, in order to secure an earlier link up with Gavin at the Waal. Night harbouring also wasted much time and offered gratuitous opportunities to the enemy to strengthen and prepare his defences in the hours of darkness. If one is to talk of failure to achieve, it has to be in terms of what happened to the south as much as to the north of the Neder Rijn.

From the point of view of 1st British Airborne Division, what lack of success there was, was only partial and confined to the initial stages of the operation. In the context of the original orders, the Division maintained its hold on Arnhem Bridge for almost twice as long as it had been anticipated would be necessary. Thereafter, by establishing a firm bridgehead, based on the Rijn at Oosterbeek, it sustained for a further five days a viable alternative for 2nd Army. In this respect, Urquhart has been criticized for not establishing his final perimeter further to the west, on the dominating heights of Westerbouwing, the argument hinging on the view that this would have provided a better defensive position. All such reasoning, however, is quite unhistorical, for it takes no regard of planned objectives. In the early stages of the battle, Westerbouwing was of no significance at all, for the effort was being expended on consolidating, extending and reinforcing the position at Arnhem Bridge. By the time an alternative bridgehead became of significance in the later stages, it was no longer possible to think in terms of attempting to move, consolidate and maintain a whole new set of British positions on Westerbouwing. As part of the evolving perimeter, some of the 1st Border Regiment men did hold positions on it for a time until overrun on the Thursday morning. But by then, Urquhart had neither the men nor the resources to remedy even this, let alone, as some have suggested, alter the whole basis of his defensive plan. There must, in any case, be considerable doubts about whether Westerbouwing ever possessed obvious features of overwhelming strategic superiority. Certainly it was high, but it was also thickly wooded and already well-penetrated by the enemy. In attempting to take it, Urquhart would have been committing a tired and battle-weary force to fight for the establishment of positions in an area where the possibilities for future enemy infiltration were likely to be more fully exploited than in suburban Oosterbeek. Even had the gamble paid off and he had been able to establish himself on the high ground, there was little prospect that he could have held it for long with such a depleted force. As it was, the perimeter which evolved in response to the practical nature of the battle in the latter days was, in the circumstances, the best that could be devised. The fact that the improvized bridgehead, thus provided, was never effectively exploited by a relieving force was an entirely different matter and one for which 1st British Airborne Division bore no responsibility.

The third factor of significance was an uncomplicated one – a fact of life which no army of the time could ignore. In simple terms, it was that infantry could not fight armour, and especially not in the strength in which it was present in the Arnhem area. The wonder is that, armed as the majority were with little beyond PIAT missiles and "gammon" bombs, the men of the 1st British Airborne Division were able to make any impression at all on enemy troops of such first-class quality. It was true that the quiet heroism of Frank Mann was mirrored every day in all sectors of the battlefield, but in such conditions heroism was not enough.

In the final analysis, however, perhaps the one feature which stands out clearest of all is the high quality of leadership displayed by Major-General Roy Urquhart. Saddled from the outset with a plan which, for all its imaginative intent, was burdened with drawbacks and illogicalities, it is difficult to imagine how he could have done more than he did. On any rational basis, the wisdom of the critical decisions which were made on the ground at Arnhem is defensible although, time and again, basic assumptions are seen to have been negated by deficiencies of higher planning, an over-optimistic view of support capability, a fundamental lack of effective intelligence information prior to the operation and – a lesson of "Overlord" – an almost total absence of contingency planning in case of need. Assessment of the handling of the battle at divisional level ought properly to take all this into account. As it happened, the 1st British Airborne Division was fortunate in having at its head a man whose soldierly qualities were already well-proven, who possessed the ability to inspire those under his command and to transmit to them something of his own tenacity and determination, and whose competence to plan in detail and with skill was more than sufficient for the massive problems which faced him. It was bitterly ironic that a battle which produced such effective leadership and stood witness to such remarkable feats of individual heroism should ultimately have had such an unhappy outcome, yet how much worse might it have been had the direction been in less capable hands than those of Urquhart.

It is not possible to say to what extent the events at Arnhem and Oosterbeek in September 1944 affected the course of the war. It is doubtful if they had any direct influence on it at all beyond, perhaps, helping to facilitate the capture of the Waal crossing at Nijmegen. One of the curious postscripts to the whole thing was, indeed, the set of three congratulatory messages received immediately after the battle by Urquhart, from Horrocks, Browning and Dempsey. Each in turn, by implication, virtually asserted that such had been the function of the 1st British Airborne Division. In the context of the original design of "Market Garden" as it emerged from 21st Army Group HQ, such an argument was little more than sophistry, not unlike the comforting irrationalities that one might, perhaps, use on the occasion of a bereavement. But the hard facts were that tactical success in one direction was no substitute for strategic failure in another. Furthermore, it could have been of little consolation to Urquhart, who knew that his men had fought to a standstill for an objective, in relation to which the Waal crossing was only a means and not an end.

As it transpired, the town of Arnhem was not liberated until 14th April 1945, when it was taken, not from the south at all, but from the north-east side of the river. But the significance of the struggle that took place throughout those unforgettable nine days can no longer be interpreted merely in terms of failure to achieve strategic objectives, however much they might have been designed to help bring about earlier victory in the West. There is no doubt that success for the western alliance before the end of that year could well have had momentous effects upon the post-war map of Europe, but it was not to be. Speculation on such a basis, therefore, is likely to be unproductive, and judgments made in the light of "what-might-have-been" would be hypothetical, probably naïve and, by their nature, unhistorical.

What matters about Arnhem and what deserves to be cherished is something much more fundamental than the success or failure of military strategy, for it is intangible and related in a unique way to the quality of human experience. For as long as man has striven to defend the freedom to live his life as he chooses, there have been those who have consistently opposed that fundamental right. In undertaking his valiant stand at Thermopylae, Leonidas faced certain defeat, but set an example to sustain and fortify the will and resolve of successive generations of his people:

> Go tell the Spartans, you who read:
> We took their orders and are dead

The words of Simonides were registered for posterity at the narrow Pass where the Spartan leader and his men gave all that they had to give. In other conflicts, in other places, at other times, down through the centuries, the legend of Thermopylae has been reborn, time and again, in comparable re-affirmations of human courage against impossible odds. Yet, in our own time, nowhere in its unique blend of comradeship, bravery and honour, has that indomitable unity of spirit emerged more than in the green woods and neat suburban villas of Arnhem and Oosterbeek. Therein must surely abide the message of Arnhem, one not of failure and defeat, but of hope that in whatever direction humanity may move in the years that lie ahead, men may still find personal enrichment and sustenance in the example of those who once fought with such unsurpassed valour. It was in recognition of this that the official account of the battle* ended with the following passage:

> In attack most daring, in defence most cunning, in endurance most steadfast, they performed a feat of arms which will be remembered and recounted as long as the virtues of courage and resolution have power to move the hearts of men.

* *By Air to Battle: The Official Account of the British First and Sixth Airborne Divisions* (H.M.S.O. London 1945).

EPILOGUE

One of the strangest paradoxes of the war-time army was the way in which the totality of involvement was as inescapable and complete for the "duration" man as for the time-serving "professional". So was it with those who fought at Arnhem and yet, with the coming of peace, there was a sudden transition and equal commitment to the goals of civilian life. Today, the men of Arnhem are indistinguishable from similar groups of middle-aged or elderly civilians, and the corporate unity of regiment, squadron, battalion or platoon is a cherished but faded memory.

In this respect, the men of 1st Airborne Reconnaissance Squadron were no different from those of any other war-time unit, although there were some who opted to continue with the soldiering as a peace-time career. Such a one was Dougie Galbraith, who took a regular commission and served for over twenty-five years after Arnhem. On retirement, with the rank of Lieutenant-Colonel, he opened a tourist motel in Leeton, New South Wales. After the war, Mike Grubb, who was the only regular officer serving with the Squadron at the time of the battle, also followed a military career, by returning to his own peace-time unit, The Border Regiment. Now, as a representative for suppliers of agricultural machinery, he lives in a quiet village in Somerset, but once a year attends the Smithfield Show at Earls Court. There he meets those with whom he shares common business interests, but there is also one with whom the bond is uniquely different, for Henry Venes of the Corps of Commissionaires is always "on parade" to welcome him and there is often talk of how it was those many years ago.

Bill Bateman, from Putney, was another who continued as a soldier. He saw service with the Royal Artillery in Korea and Malaya, where he was "mentioned in despatches". Since leaving the army in 1968, he has worked as a security officer. Bert Welham is also not long retired from the army, and is now a school caretaker in Bath. He finished as a Squadron Sergeant-Major, and tells, with some amusement, of how successive commanding officers would always make a point of introducing him to visiting generals as, "one of the chaps who fought at Arnhem Bridge." Other ex-members of the Squadron live in the west country, amongst them being George Adams, who is transport manager for a local firm. George is also kept busy as a retained Sub-officer with the Dorset Fire Service, a part-time post which he has held for over thirty years.

Henry Venes, who has lived for many years in Bethnal Green, also sees to it that former members of the Squadron in the London area meet from time to time for what he describes as "a natter and a pint." At these local reunions, there are something like seven or eight "regulars", and they include Alf "Gunner" Webb, who is a fitter with British Rail, Vic Taylor, a craftsman in fine art restoration, Alf Hazell, a painter and decorator, Bill Chandler, an engineer and Jim "Spud" Taylor MM, a chief administrative officer with local government. They have recently been joined by Dick Minns, who owns a hairdressing salon in Dulwich, and by Ron "Midge" Miles from Harlow, neither of whom had been in touch with any of the others until Minns returned to Arnhem for the first time in 1976, to discover that the standard bearer at the memorial service was Henry Venes! Being very active in all ex-airborne affairs, from formal parades to "Woho Mahomet" Dinners, it is hardly surprizing that Henry should also have contact with former Squadron members elsewhere. One of the most regular of those is with "Chalky" White who lives at Southend. He is an aircraft mechanic, and one of the organizers of the South-East Essex branch of the Parachute Regimental Association.

Another in the London area is John Marshall, who holds the post of House Governor and Secretary to a group of London hospitals. Arising out of his professional contacts, he sometimes meets Douglas Swinscow, who works at Tavistock Square, where he has responsibility for the production of the British Medical Journal. Graham Wadsworth is also London-based and is Head of Programme Contracts at the BBC.

Others in the south-east are Arthur Barlow who, having survived his premature "demise", is a building maintenance surveyor at Wokingham, and Ray Evans from Reading, who is in the travel business. Not far away in Oxford is "Tommy" Trinder, the comrade with whom Evans shared a slit trench in the perimeter. "Tommy" has recently retired from running his own painting and decorating firm in the town. At nearby Abingdon, Sam Bowles has built up an extensive business, at home and abroad, in the supply of quality light fittings. Quite recently, he purchased a boat and, on taking possession, was astonished to discover from the documents that the previous owner was a certain Ralph Foulkes of Colwyn Bay. Enquiries revealed that it was, indeed, his former colleague of C Troop, who is a well-known practising architect in that part of north Wales. Ralph Foulkes also has the occasional professional contact with his fellow-architect, Bob Guthrie, who lives at Tunbridge Wells and is also a boating enthusiast.

Two at least of the former members of the Squadron work on the land, for Tom Collier farms in Sussex, as does Bob Coldicott at Stratford-on-Avon. In nearby Melton Mowbray, Stan Collishaw, who retired a short time ago from the local police force, is now a chief security officer. Another police connection is also to be found further north, for John Stevenson, whose home is in Wolverhampton, retired from the Staffordshire force a few years back in the rank of Chief Superintendent. Ken Lapper also lives in Wolverhampton, where he holds the post of Chief Building Inspector. From time to time, he sees Ray Price who also lives locally and is an electrical engineer with the British Steel Corporation. Over in Leicester is Maurice Riches, recently retired from a job with Imperial Typewriters. He has the occasional contact with George Dixon who is a production engineer with General Electric of Coventry. George, in turn, is on regular visiting terms with Charlie King, who gardens for the local council at Littleborough in Lancashire.

Others in the north of England are James Pyper, who has a responsible post with the parks department at Gosforth, and Henry Crowder who lives at Peterlee and was at one time a process foreman with ICI. At Stamford Bridge in Yorkshire, Bill Mullenger is an AA patrolman whilst, on the west coast, John Serginson and Dick Heyworth live respectively in Maryport and Morecambe.

Still further north in Scotland, are more representatives of the Squadron. Gerry Fergus, a casting foreman in an iron foundry, lives in Coatbridge, as does Frank Mann, who has a job with an engineering works in the town. Bob Thomson, based on Edinburgh, is Hotels Manager for a prominent brewing firm, and, in Glasgow, John Pow helps to make cranes for the shipyards of the Clyde. Over the Kincardineshire hills in Banchory, David Christie is a company director in a firm of civil engineers and, between times, plays to a very respectable golf handicap whilst, further north in Nairn, Willie Fraser is a stalwart of the local branch of the Royal British Legion. Recently, on a visit to Oosterbeek, the author had the pleasure of meeting Mrs H. Tulp-Roelfsema, who is 88 years of age. She lives at 5 De la Reyweg, and for 35 years has told the story of the British soldier who lost his eye during the fighting around her house. She was astonished and delighted to learn that, thanks to the skill of a Polish surgeon in a prisoner-of-war camp, Willie Fraser's eye was replaced and he suffered no subsequent loss of vision.

By others of the Squadron, all of those just mentioned are still habitually and indiscriminately referred to as "Jock", a stereotyped form of address once common throughout the British army as applicable to all Scotsmen, and in line with the practice of dubbing all Millers as "Dusty" and all Smiths as "Smudger". But as well as the "Jocks" of Scotland, there are the 'Taffys" of Wales. Gwyn Williams, who runs his frozen food shop at Pontycymmer, is one of those, and so too is Eddie Morris, who is a schoolmaster near Wrexham.

Some others of the Squadron remained to settle down in the Ruskington area after the war. Jimmy Pearce from Helpringham is a line repair man with British Rail, and Cyril Simpson runs a shop in the main street of Sleaford. Like most English towns of any size, Sleaford has its traffic problems, but these are not great and two traffic wardens are sufficient to cope. One of them is Jimmy Cooke, who lives in Ruskington itself.

At the other extreme, there are those who have settled abroad. Geoff Costeloe emigrated to Canada after the war, where he subsequently joined the Canadian army. Recently retired, he now works in a civilian capacity and lives in a quiet village on the edge of the Black Forest in Germany. Very recently, Ken Hope, who finished the war with a commission in the South Staffordshires, moved from a teaching post in Zambia to one in Adelaide, Australia. Jimmy Bruce is another who left his native Scotland some years ago to settle in Toronto, but he makes return visits from time to time and on a recent trip made a personal contribution to the present research.

It only remains to make special mention of one other survivor of the 1st Airborne Reconnaissance Squadron. On the sea coast of Dorset in the attractive town of Canford Cliffs, David Allsop has his business in the main street. Much of it, especially in the summer, is passing trade yet few of those who come into the shop are likely to know that there was a time when this quiet unassuming man had effective command of a unit in the nine day epic Battle of Arnhem.

Finally, it was sad to find that, at the time when this book was initiated, a number had already died – Leslie Blackman, Eddie Park, John Blacklaws, Fred Winder, Bill Watson, "Darkie" Bolton and Bertie Lickerish, to name just a few. Others with whom contact was successfully established have passed on quite recently, and these include Cyril Belcham, Bill Bentall, Ernest Jenkins, Wilfred Saint and Dougie Galbraith. In September 1977, Freddie Gough went on a family holiday to Sorrento in Italy. There it was that he died thirty-three years to the day from the time that he helped fight off Grabner's attack at Arnhem Bridge. He was a man for whom there were never sufficient hours in the day and who lived life to the full. In the hearts of those who had the privilege of serving under him there will long remain the most profound affection and respect for his memory. Perhaps it is altogether appropriate that Freddie should have found his final resting place not far from where his own lads have lain buried since the actions of Mottola and Gioia del Colle.

Life has long since returned to normal in that quiet corner of Dutch Gelderland. Arnhem Bridge, fought over so fiercely only to be destroyed by the Germans after the battle, has been restored to its former state and is now officially named after its famous defender, John Frost. All around the north end of the Bridge, modern functional architecture has risen upon the ground that, in a mere four days, was once reduced to a waste land of desolation. Running off the northern ramp, the Nijmeegseweg passes hard by Airborne Plein, a sunken roundabout on to which underpasses for cyclists converge. In the centre, stands a fragment of pillar from the old Palace of Justice, on which is engraved the simple inscription, 17 September 1944.

Several miles to the west, at Wolfheze, the nineteenth-century station house still stands, and the railway operates as before, except that the trains now run faster. Half a mile nearer to Arnhem, a new motorway marches on concrete stilts, at right-angles to the line, just beyond the point where Peter Bucknall and his men died. At the bottom of the dip, where McGregor's jeep was halted, some of the trees have been cut down, but just off the road it is possible to detect a clearly defined circle of grass-covered hollows in the ground at the place where Douglas Swinscow was mortared as he tried to administer to the wounded.

Further out, the great landing and dropping zones, with their dotted farms and narrow trackways, remain virtually unchanged, and it is easy to identify the corner of the wood at which the Reconnaissance Squadron assembled for the *coup de main* attempt on that eventful Sunday afternoon. Annually, the spring ploughing still brings up and pushes to the sides of the fields of Renkum, Ginkel or Johannahoeve, the debris of battle – shrapnel fragments, pieces of glider, spent bullet cases, decayed wireless batteries and the occasional weapon. Now, as one stands by the cluster of trees, with the vast empty expanse stretched out towards the south, there comes again the pulsating throb of the immense air armada, and once more against the background of broken cumulus the great parachute army descends from the skies. Yet, swiftly as the transient impression is born, so does it disappear, for it is no more than a trick of imagination, dispelled as the roar of the Utrecht express reaches its crescendo, leaving behind an autumn stillness broken only by the shrill call of a blackbird and the faint whirring of a tractor over by Boshoeve farm.

A little to the north, at the end of Dreijenseweg stands a restaurant of inviting appearance, called De Leeren Doedel. In the woods just to its rear, the trenches of 10th Battalion are still clearly discernible at the place where Queripel won his VC. Nearby, the broad double carriageway of the Amsterdamseweg sweeps through open country, before plunging into a tunnel of dark woodland not more than a mile to the west. At the far end of the tunnel stands the café of Planken Wambuis, past which the cars speed in both directions, their drivers unaware of the drama to which the tall trees were witness on a Tuesday afternoon so many years ago.

Towards the south, at the junction of Wolfhezerweg and Utrechtseweg, a road bollard and a trim "Keep Right" sign are all that mark the spot where *Generalmajor* Kussin met his savage and unexpected end at the outset of the battle. Over beyond Hotel Bilderberg, by the football pavilion on Sportlaan, one comes to the place where the rearguard action of the 156th Parachute Battalion mounted to a horrifying climax that left it at little more than platoon strength. It was an afternoon dominated by the increasing pressure of German armour on the lightly armed airborne troops and, at the junction of nearby Valkenburglaan, it is still possible to find the crater-shaped depression in the ground, where all that was left of 4th Brigade made its desperate last stand under Hackett. Further down Valkenburglaan, by the corner of Utrechtseweg is the Koude Herberg café and just fifty yards from there, towards the east, in a little copse set on the edge of the main road, one discovers the outline of the slit trenches which the Reconnaissance Squadron's Support Troop dug for itself on the Tuesday night of the battle.

Peace has also returned to suburban Oosterbeek. By Stationsweg and Steijnweg, the humming swish of the trolley-bus has long since replaced the dreaded clank of tank or SP gun. On the Bothaweg junction of Steijnweg, where D Troop had its HQ, two young housewives, neither of them even born at the time of the battle, stop to chat. Down Paul Krugerstraat, the late-afternoon sun shines on the clean, rose-coloured brickwork and on the trim front gardens, with their profusion of autumn marigolds. The children play with tricycles on the pavement by the Mariaweg corner, and from the back of the bakery comes the delicious smell of newly made bread. There, by the side, it is still possible to see the loading window, with its protruding hoisting beam and hook, just as it was on the day when the A Troop men fought their short, sharp action, by the end of which the building was a burned-out shell. Only a few years ago, Kees Crum sold his business and retired, but it still functions as before and it remains one of the best bakeshops in Oosterbeek. In this, as in so many other ways, there is a sense of continuity about this part of the town, for so little of its appearance has altered with the passage of the years.

As afternoon begins to fade, the lights go on in the houses, showing scenes of quiet domesticity. So normal is it, that it is hard to relate the peace of an early evening stroll along Paul Krugerstraat to the hideous intrusion of the self-propelled guns or the crashing of the mortar bombs. Yet, in silent contemplation, one can, perhaps, spirit up the sounds of the running feet, the cries, the shouts and the rattle of the machine-guns that once reverberated throughout the street and echoed strangely around the red-brick walls of the ravaged houses. Halfway along is the intersection of a quiet, narrow road, where all is still and one meets little of either vehicles or pedestrians. Here too, in De la Reyweg, there are ghosts – the faint footsteps of two men walking in step, the pick-pick-picking of a hammer on brickwork, the sudden sharp whine of a rifle shot – but in a fleeting second it is gone, as the real world once more intrudes, and there is only the muted murmur of traffic on nearby Utrechtseweg and the barking of a dog from a distant garden.

Already the bustle of the day has gone and the evening hush is settling upon this small Dutch town. Passing through the still greenery of Oranjeweg, it is difficult to reconcile the quiet, commonplace nature of the street with the knowledge that where the white saloon car now stands parked, the vehicles of the Reconnaissance Squadron were battered to destruction by German mortar shells. Alongside the car was where Squadron HQ was sited, and through the little gap in the hedge, just beyond the bus stop, was Trinder's slit trench, one of a number, the faint outlines of which can still be located in the corner of the field by Oranjeweg. It was at the gap that Evans and Kerr were shot and a few yards beyond is the spot where young Alf Odd was killed by a sniper's bullet. Today, it is as incongruous to imagine snipers hidden in the trees across the width of the potato field as it is inconceivable that a mere fifty yards to the left, by the neat conifers of a spacious front garden, John Christie should have been so brutally killed on that horrific Wednesday afternoon.

The dignified mansions on Hartensteinlaan have long been restored, and the Squadron HQ trenches have filled up over the years with the fallen leaves of successive autumns. As the street lamps come on in the early evening, and one stands by the corner of the green sward that borders Utrechtseweg, it is possible to look over at the elegant grace of Hotel Hartenstein, now, appropriately, the new location for the Airborne Museum. Already, in late-September, the chestnuts have fallen from the great trees that line its driveway, and it takes an effort of will to comprehend that this dignified yet unpretentious building was once the place that stood at the heart of it all. A short distance away, the cream-coloured facade of the Vreewijk looks out on the crossing, just as it did in the days when the ambulance jeeps plied on their incessant journeys to and from its front door. Today, the scene at Oosterbeek crossroads seems indistinguishable from that of comparable Dutch towns, and the passing stranger would assuredly be unlikely to associate the normality of it all with the shambles that it once was.

But normality is a relative thing. Throughout the perimeter area of Oosterbeek, the observer who looks closely may still find much to indicate that there was a time when everything was so very different. During the fighting, the garages tended to escape the more serious damage suffered by the houses, because it was in the houses that the soldiers sought cover. As a result, whilst a fair number of pre-war garages survived, there was not a house in Oosterbeek that escaped some form of damage or destruction. A number were completely flattened and had to be totally rebuilt. In those cases, care was taken to do so in the same style as the surviving buildings, so that the pleasing harmony of the town's appearance might be preserved. Most houses were saved, although extensive repair work had to be carried out, and today one can identify those that have been re-roofed or partially re-tiled or that have betraying areas of brickwork, imperceptibly lighter than the rest. There are also the sudden discoveries, as at 5 De la Reyweg, of buildings which have weathered over the years, but whose walls still show the concentrated pock-marking of rifle and machine-gun fire around the windows.

Yet the surviving evidence of battle is by no means confined simply to the buildings of Oosterbeek, for there are curious scars that still deface many of the great tree trunks that stand within the area which acquired for itself the name of "The Cauldron". Many show extensive bark damage, either the evenly spaced perforations of the machine-gun or the deeper ravages of the flame thrower. Embedded within others are the fragments of mortar shells but, whilst some still weep the life sap from their unhealed wounds, nature has carried out her repairs well, for each year the beech leaves appear in the spring and, in an eloquent and mute symbolism, fall to the ground in late September.

Today, in the centre of the green triangle that lies across the main road from the Hartenstein, stands the Airborne Memorial, erected by the people of Oosterbeek as a permanent monument to the courage of the British airborne troops. Upon its four faces, the symbolically carved figures tell the story of the battle. Beside it, are two teak benches, on each of which there is a simple inscription:

> Here in September 1944, the 1st British Airborne Reconnaissance Squadron fought to its end. Rest here and enjoy the peace for which they fought and died.

Now it is all a place of memories. The nightmare has long since passed, although the green park upon which the Memorial stands is a place that is held in respect by the people of Oosterbeek who, out of regard for the men who came from the sky on that September afternoon in 1944, prefer to walk around rather than across it. For them the monument and its green surrounds are daily reminders of events that have now and forever become a part of their heritage.

And finally, a short distance away, just beyond Oosterbeek station, the Airborne Cemetery stands in still woodland. At the end of an autumn day, as the birds in the surrounding beech woods sing their evening chorus and the passing rays of the setting sun cast a yellow warmth upon the rows of white headstones, it is a calm and tranquil place. In this quiet corner of Oosterbeek lie 1500 men of the 1st British Airborne Division, together with others of the Glider Pilot Regiment, the 4th Dorset Regiment, the 1st Polish Independent Parachute Brigade Group and the Royal Air Force. Most, although not all, of the Squadron dead are buried here, for no fewer than twenty-one stones bear the spear and lightning of the Reconnaissance Corps.

Like all such places, the Cemetery has been lovingly tended and cared for over the years but, for the first-time visitor, it almost always comes as a shock to scan the inscriptions and to realize the extreme youth of most of those with whose lives our own freedom was so dearly bought: Lieutenant Alan Pascal, 20 years of age, Lance-Corporal Alan Baker, 20 years of age, Trooper Frederick Brawn, 21 years of age, and so on along the headstones, on each of which is recorded the name, rank and unit of the soldier. In many cases, too, relatives have requested the addition of some simple thought, of which one in particular for a lost son stands poignantly expressive of a debt that can never be repaid:

Into the mosaic of victory
Was laid this precious piece

Faithfully, over the years, a dedicated group of old comrades has kept alive the memories of those who died, by an act of annual pilgrimage. Each anniversary, within the quiet place, the Dutch and British stand informally together on the grass that grows between the graves. There, linked in a spiritual unity of undiminished strength, they join together in a simple service of remembrance, at the conclusion of which the mellow plaintiveness of the Last Post steals gently through the adjacent woodland that once shook with the din and ferocity of war. It is then that thoughts reach back into the past and, as the last sad notes fade lingeringly away, there comes the silence and the recollection of friends from far-off days.

Regularly they return – Henry Venes, "Chalky" White, "Tommy" Trinder, – along with comrades, like Doug Holt, from other regiments that were there, to pay their simple tributes. There is a sense that each time there are, perhaps, fewer red berets than before, yet, as Binyon's immortal words are read, the dim flickering images once more take shape and brighten upon the screen of memory and they remember the young men who, unlike them, were denied the chance to enjoy a life that, in so many cases, had scarce begun:

> They shall grow not old . . . *only nineteen young Odd was* . . . as we that are left grow old . . . *and when you think of them you only see the young faces – just lads, that's all they were, really* . . . Age shall not weary them . . . *Some caught it, some didn't – it was just your luck* . . . nor the years condemn . . . *Monty once said that in years to come it would be a great thing for a man to be able to say, "I fought at Arnhem." Just the same, it was a bastard – a right bastard* . . . At the going down of the sun and in the morning . . . *and you try maybe sometimes to explain what it was like, but words aren't any good really – you had to be there, you had to go through it to understand* . . . we will remember them . . . *and it's something that stays with you for the rest of your life, for you never forget it – never.*

AWARDS AND DECORATIONS
GAINED BY MEMBERS OF THE
1ST AIRBORNE RECONNAISSANCE SQUADRON
DURING THE COURSE OF THE SECOND WORLD WAR

British

Major C. F. H. Gough: Military Cross
Mentioned in Despatches
Captain T. J. Firbank: Military Cross
Lieutenant D. Galbraith: Military Cross
Mentioned in Despatches
Lieutenant F. W. Ladds: Mentioned in Despatches
Lieutenant T. V. P. McNabb: Mentioned in Despatches
Lieutenant J. W. Marshall: Mentioned in Despatches
Lieutenant H. E. Pearson: Military Cross
Sergeant S. J. Haydon: Mentioned in Despatches
Sergeant G. E. Holderness: Mentioned in Despatches
Sergeant G. Kay: Mentioned in Despatches
Sergeant K. O. Lapper: British Empire Medal
Sergeant J. Pyper: Military Medal
Sergeant G. Storrie: Mentioned in Despatches
Sergeant H. Venes: British Empire Medal
Corporal J. G. Taylor: Military Medal
Trooper C. M. Simpson: Mentioned in Despatches
Trooper J. D. Wilkes: Mentioned in Despatches
Craftsman G. York: Military Medal

American

Lieutenant J. G. H. Wadsworth: Bronze Star
Trooper F. Mann: Distinguished Service Cross

Dutch

Captain D. Allsop: Bronze Lion
Captain T. D. V. Swinscow: Bronze Cross
Trooper C. C. Bolton: Bronze Cross

BIBLIOGRAPHY

UNPUBLISHED SOURCES

Report on Operations "Market" and "Garden" by Headquarters British Airborne Corps (21st Army Group) Parts I–IV

1 Airborne Division Report on Operation "Market"
Part I – General Outline of Operations
Part II – Administrative Aspects of the Operation
Part III – The Lessons of the Operation

1 Airborne Division Report on Operation "Market": Part IV Annexures:
Order of Battle 1st Airborne Division
Directive from Commander, British Airborne Corps to Divisional Commander
Operation Instructions 1st Airborne Division
Operation Instructions 1st Parachute Brigade
Operation Instructions 4th Parachute Brigade
Operation Instructions 1st Air Landing Brigade
Operation Instructions 1st Polish Independent Parachute Brigade Group
Operation Instructions Royal Artillery, 1st Airborne Division
Operation Instructions Royal Engineers, 1st Airborne Division
Operation Instructions 1st Airborne Divisional Signals
Operation Instructions Medical Services, 1st Airborne Division
War Diary: HQ 1st Airborne Division
War Diary: 1st Parachute Brigade
War Diary: 4th Parachute Brigade
War Diary: 1st Air Landing Brigade
Copies of important letters and messages

1 Airborne Division Report on Operation "Market": Part V Annexures
Report by G(Int), 1st Airborne Division
Report by CRA, 1st Airborne Division
Report by CRE, 1st Airborne Division

Report by OC, 1st Airborne Divisional Signals
Report by ADMS, 1st Airborne Division

Operation "Market": Diary of Events: 1st Parachute Brigade HQ
War Diary 1st Airborne Reconnaissance Squadron
War Diary 1st Parachute Battalion
War Diary 2nd Parachute Battalion
War Diary 3rd Parachute Battalion
War Diary 10th Parachute Battalion
War Diary 11th Parachute Battalion
War Diary 156th Parachute Battalion
War Diary 7th Battalion King's Own Scottish Borderers
War Diary 2nd Battalion South Staffordshire Regiment
War Diary 21st Independent Parachute Company
War Diary No. 1 Wing Glider Pilot Regiment
War Diary No. 2 Wing Glider Pilot Regiment
War Diary Guards Armoured Division
War Diary 43rd Infantry Division
Pilot's Flying Log: Flight Sergeant J. Darlington, 245 Squadron, 83 Group Royal Air Force
Personal Diaries and Papers of members of 1st Airborne Reconnaissance Squadron, viz. A. Barlow, W. Bentall, S. Bowles, W. Chandler, D. Christie, C. W. Cook, R. Foulkes, M. Grubb, J. Taylor MM
War Diary: The Battle at Arnhem 17th September–7th October 1944 by *SS Sturmbannführer* Sepp Krafft, SS Panzer Grenadier Depot and Reserve Battalion 16: prepared for Heinrich Himmler
Gough, C. F. H., *Some Principles of Training, 1st Air Landing Squadron, Reconnaissance Corps*

PUBLISHED BOOKS

Angus, Tom, *Men at Arnhem*, Cooper 1976
Arnhem September 1944, Gemeentearchief, Arnhem 1969
Bauer, Cornelis, *The Battle of Arnhem*, Stein and Day 1967
The Battle of Arnhem, Municipality of Arnhem 1945
Brammall, R. *The Tenth*, London 1965
By Air to Battle: The Official Account of the British First and Sixth Airborne Divisions, London HMSO 1945
Davies, Howard P., *British Parachute Forces 1940–45*, Arms and Armour Press 1974
Deane-Drummond, Anthony, *Return Ticket*, Collins 1953
Farrar-Hockley, Anthony, *Airborne Carpet – Operation Market Garden*, Macdonald 1970
Firbank, Thomas, *I Bought A Star*, White Lion 1973
Gibson, Ronald, *Nine Days*, A. H. Stockwell 1956
Gregory, Barry, *British Airborne Troops*, Macdonald and Jane's 1974
Hackett, John *I was a Stranger*, Chatto and Windus 1977
Hagen, Louis, *Arnhem Lift*, Hammond and Co. 1945
Hibbert, Christopher, *The Battle of Arnhem*, Batsford 1962
History of the 2nd Battalion The Parachute Regiment, Wellington Press Aldershot 1946

Horrocks, Brian, *A Full Life*, Collins 1960
Horrocks, Brian, *Corps Commander*, Sidgwick and Jackson 1977
Lewin, Ronald, *Montgomery as Military Commander*, Batsford 1971
Macdonald, Charles, *By Air to Battle*, Macdonald 1969
Mackenzie, Charles B., *It Was Like This*, 10th ed. Linders-Adremo, Oosterbeek 1973
Norton, Geoffrey G., *The Red Devils*, Cooper 1971
Packe, Michael, *First Airborne*, Secker and Warburg 1948
Peelen, Th. and Van Vlist, A. L. J., *Zwevend Naar de Dood*, Velp 1976
Ryan, Cornelius, *A Bridge Too Far*, Hamish Hamilton 1974
Saunders, Hilary St G., *The Red Beret*, Michael Joseph 1950
Taylor, Jeremy, *This Band of Brothers*, White Swan Press 1947
Ter Horst, Kate A. *Cloud Over Arnhem*, Allan Wingate 1959
Tugwell, Maurice, *Airborne to Battle: A History of Airborne Warfare 1918–1971*. Kimber 1971
Tugwell, Maurice, *Arnhem: A Case Study*, Thornton Cox 1975
Urquhart, Roy, *Arnhem*, Cassell 1958
Weeks, John, *Infantry Weapons*, Ballantine Books 1971
White, B. J., *Tanks and Other Armoured Fighting Vehicles* 1942–45, Blandford Press 1975

ARTICLES

"The Battle of Oosterbeek", *The Gunner*, Vol. 27, No. 5, August 1945
Best, C. E., "The Mediums at Arnhem", *The Gunner*, Vol. 33, No. 1, January 1951
Breeze, C. F. O., "The Airborne Operations in Holland – September 1944", *The Border Magazine*, Vol. 1, No. 3, September 1948 (Part 1) and Vol. 1, No. 4, March 1949 (Part 2)
Bryant, Arthur, "A Tribute to the Corps", *The Reconnaissance Journal*, Vol. 3, No. 4, July–September 1947
Bryant, Arthur, "Commemoration of the Brave", *The Reconnaissance Journal* 1950
Cousens, H. S., "Arnhem 17th–26th September 1944", *Sprig of Shellelagh*, Vol. 28, No. 322, Spring–Summer 1948
"Do You Remember ...?" (2) *Pegasus* Vol. 1, No. 2, July 1946
"Do You Remember ...?" (3) *Pegasus* Vol. 1, No. 3, October 1946
"The K.O.S.B. at Arnhem", *Borderers' Chronicle*, Vol. 19, No. 4
Mackay, E., ("Parachute Sapper") "The Battle of Arnhem Bridge", *Blackwood's Magazine*, Edinburgh, October 1945
"Pegasus and the Wyvern", *Royal Engineers' Journal*, Vol. 60, March 1946
Ramsey, Winston G., "Arnhem", *After the Battle*, No. 2, Battle of Britain Prints International 1973
"Recce Corps", *War*, Army Bureau of Current Affairs 1944
Stevenson, John, "Arnhem Diary", *The Reconnaissance Journal*, Vol. 4, No. 1, Autumn 1947
Watkins, E., "Arnhem: 1. The Landing and the Bridge", *War*, Army Bureau of Current Affairs 1944
Watkins, E. "Arnhem: 2. Inside the Perimeter", *War*, Army Bureau of Current Affairs 1944
Wilmot, Chester, "What Really Happened at Arnhem", *Stand-to*, Vol. 1 No. 8, October–November 1950
Winder, Fred, "Postscript", *The Reconnaissance Journal*, Vol. 4, No. 1, Autumn 1947
Wood, Alan, "How Arnhem was Reported", *Pegasus*, Vol. 1, No. 3, October 1946

Fiction

Windrow, M. *and* Wilkinson, F., *editors*, *The Universal Soldier* Guiness Superlatives 1971
Zeno, *The Cauldron*, Macmillan 1966

Bibliographies

s.d. Aalbers, P. G., *Slag Om Arnhem, bibliografie van gedrukte werken*, Bibliotheek Arnhem/De Walburg Pers, Zutphen

Maps and Guides

GSGS 4458, 1:7000, Arnhem: Town Plan, War Office, 1st Edition 1944
GSGS 2541, 1:100000, Sheet 2 Utrecht and Sheet 5 'S Hertogenbosch, War Office, 3rd Edition 1943
AMS M831 (GSGS 4427), 1:25000, Sheet 387 Ede 1st Edition 1943
Sheet 388 Ginkel 1st Edition 1943
Sheet 5 NE Renen 1st Edition 1943
Sheet 6 NW Arnhem 1st Edition 1944
Army Map Service (GE), US Army, Washington DC 1943
Gids voor Arnhem en Omstreken, VVV Arnhem 14de Druk 1930
Plattegrond van Arnhem met Alpabetische Stratenlijst VVV Arnhem 2de Druk 1930
Plattegrond van Oosterbeek, G. Romin n.d.
Gids voor Oosterbeek en Omstreken n.d.
Erkens, H. J. C., *Oosterbeek in Oude Ansichten*, Europese Bibliotheek- Zaltbommel 1975
Demoed, E. J., *De Westelijke Veluweroom in Oude Ansichten*, Europese Bibliotheek 1968
Stempher, A. S., *Nog's Sjouwen Door Oud Arnhem*, Gysbers and Van Loon, Arnhem 1969
Kaart van de Zuidelijke Veluwe, C. V. Adremo, Oosterbeek 1958
Oosterbeek 1:6250, Int. Branch, HQ 1st Airborne Division 1944
Stadsplattegrond van Arnhem, NV Falkplan/CIB, Den Haag, 9e Druk 1973
Plattegrond van de Gemeente Renkum, NV Falkplan/CIB, Den Haag, 1973

Cemetery Records

The War Dead of the British Commonwealth and Empire; the register of the names of those who fell in the 1939–1945 war and are buried in cemeteries in the Netherlands, London Imperial War Graves Commission 1957

Supplementary Bibliography

Frost, Major-General John, *A Drop Too Many*, Buchan and Enright 1982
Maassen, G. H., *Oosterbeek Destroyed 1944–45*, Meyer and Siegers, Oosterbeek 1981
Powell, Geoffrey, *The Devil's Birthday*, Buchan and Enright 1984
Sims, James, *Arnhem Spearhead*, Imperial War Museum 1978
Sosabowski, Major-General Stanislaw, *Freely I Served*, Kimber 1960
Verhoeff, Wim and Vroemen, Paul, *Arnhem Voorjaar 1945*, Fotohandel Kramer, Arnhem 1989

ACKNOWLEDGEMENTS

Thanks are due to the following:

Major-General R. E. Urquhart, CB, DSO
Colonel C. F. H. Gough, MC, TD
Major-General J. D. Frost, DSO, MC
Brigadier C. B. Mackenzie, DSO, OBE
General Sir Neil M. Ritchie, GBE, KCB, DSO, MC
General Sir Richard N. O'Connor, KT, GCB, DSO, MC

Former Members of 1st Airborne Reconnaissance Squadron
G. Adams, D. Allsop, N. Askins, A. Barlow, W. Bateman C. Belcham W. J. Bentall, C. Bolton, L. Booth, S. Bowles, J. Bruce, R. W. Burton, W. Chandler, D. Christie, R. G. Coldicott, T. Collier, S. G. Collishaw, C. W. Cooke, J. E. Cooke, G. Costeloe, H. R. Crowder, G. Dearden, A. De Looze, A. Dickson, G. Dixon, S. W. Drinkwater, R. J. Evans, G. Fergus, R. C. Foulkes, T. J. Firbank, W. Fraser, D. Galbraith, M. O. A. Gasset, H. Gelder, C. F. H. Gough, H. J. Grimes, M. W. Grubb, R. Guthrie, E. Hares, R. Hayes, A. Hazell, R. Hewer, R. Heyworth, K. Hope, J. Jellis, E. J. Jenkins, J. Keay, C. D. King, J. Langan, K. O. Lapper, F. Mann, J. W. Marshall, D. Maydew, E. Metcalf, R. Miles, R. Minns, A Morris, E. Morris, J. G. Muir, T. W. Mullenger, R. Nabarro, J. Pearce, H. W. Pegnall, J. Pow, S. H. R. Price, J. Pyper, M. Riches, W. E. Saint, F. Sharp, J. Serginson, C. Simpson, J. C. Smith, R. A. Spicer, J. S. Stephenson, J. Stevenson, G. Storrie, T. D. V. Swinscow, J. G. Taylor, V. J. Taylor, R. Thomson, E. A. Trinder, P. R. Tyler, H. Venes, G. Wadsworth, K. Washer, J. Watson, A. Webb, H. E. Welham, A. G. White, G. Williams, J. A. Williams, F. C. Winder

Former members of other regiments
A. Burns: 1st Airborne Light Artillery
D. Holt: 7th Battalion King's Own Scottish Borderers
R. Peatling: 2nd Parachute Battalion
E. Read: 2nd Special Air Service

Depot The Parachute Regiment and Airborne Forces
Colonel G. O. Mullins
Colonel E. S. Lough, MBE
Lt.-Colonel S. C. A. N. Bishop, OBE
Major D. Ince
Major G. Norton
Major N. Nichols
Major H. M. McRitchie, MC
T. H. Fitch, Esq.

15th (Scottish Volunteer) Battalion
Colonel J. H. Graham, MBE, TD

Staff College, Camberley
K. M. White, Esq., ALA

Dutch contacts
Kees M. Crum, 58 Mariaweg, Oosterbeek
Mrs Jo Crum-Bloemink, 58 Mariaweg, Oosterbeek
Adrian Groeneweg, Director, Arnhem Bibliotheek
Ben Jansen, 34 Paul Krugerstraat, Oosterbeek
Piet Maasen, 21 Acacialaan, Oosterbeek
Mrs Tulp-Roelfsema, 5 De la Reyweg, Oosterbeek
Mrs N. Veldhuizen, VVV Oosterbeek
Jan Voskuil, 183 Weverstraat, Oosterbeek
Robert Voskuil, 183 Weverstraat, Oosterbeek
D. van Woerkom, Backerstraat, Oosterbeek

Newspapers
Birmingham Post; Blackburn Times; Blairgowrie Advertiser; Bucks Advertiser and Aylesbury News; Burnley Express and News; Bury Times; Cheadle and Tean Times; Chingford and Waltham Forest Guardian and Independent; Daily Express; Daily Mail; Durham Advertiser; East Kent Gazette; Evening Despatch (Durham); Evening Gazette (Teesside) Evening News (Bolton); Evening Times (Glasgow); Evening Standard (London); Glamorgan Gazette; Guernsey Evening Press; Halifax Evening Courier; Heanor Observer and Langley Mill Chronicle; Holyhead and Anglesey Mail; Huddersfield Daily Examiner; Inverurie and District Advertiser; Jersey Evening Post; Lancashire Evening Post; Leicester Mercury; Lincolnshire Free Press and Spalding Guardian; Luton Evening Post; Manchester Evening News; Mansfield and North Nottinghamshire Chronicle-Advertiser; Montrose Review; Morpeth Herald and Reporter; Nairnshire Telegraph; North Devon Journal-Herald; North Somerset Mercury; Nottingham Evening Post; Rutherglen Reformer; Shipley Times and Express; Shrewsbury Chronicle; Sidmouth Herald; Southern Evening Echo; Stirling Observer; Stratford-upon-Avon Herald; Strathearn Herald; Sunderland Echo; Tottenham Weekly Herald; West Oxfordshire Standard.

Libraries, Museums and Government Departments
Public Record Office

National Library of Scotland
Arnhem Bibliotheek
Army Central Library
Bundesarchiv, Koblenz
Imperial War Museum
Airborne Forces Museum, Aldershot
Royal Armoured Corps Tank Museum, Bovington
Royal Signals Museum, Blandford Forum
Hartenstein Museum, Oosterbeek
Directorate of Military Survey, Feltham, Middlesex
Map Research and Library Group MCE RE Tolworth
Ordnance Survey, Maybush, Southampton

Jordanhill College of Education
Principal and Governors for the grant of sabbatical leave in Session 1975–1976

Others who helped
J. S. Bailey, R. Barclay, W. Boyle, H. Buckley, J. Butchart, Mrs B. Chapman, P. Clarke, Mrs N. Cook, Mrs R. Darlington, H. De Looze, Mrs J. Deaton, Mrs N. E. Dyer, P. Farrar, J. Finlayson, F. O. Finzel (Fallschirmjäger), A. W. Gill, Mrs I. Grant, Mrs R. Haley, C. K. Hood, G. Johnstone, M. King, D. McGregor, Mrs E. Mercer, Mrs E. Morris, T. Neilon, G. Park, S. Parsons, A. Pearson, Mrs A. Peers, J. Pyper, W. G. Ramsey, M. Roberts, Mrs E. Sergeant, T. Shorrock, Miss M. Smith, W. Welding, and Mrs G. Wright.

For reading proofs and offering helpful comment, I am greatly indebted to Kenneth White, David Allsop, Roy Urquhart and the late Freddie Gough. I should also like to thank Sir Arthur Bryant for his encouragement, and Mrs Jeanne Hutchison for teaching me the rudiments of the Dutch language. Thanks are also due to the staff of Bell and Bain for all the care and attention given to the production of the book.

In a research project of this kind, where the time and expertise of so many people have been drawn upon, one hesitates to single out individuals for particular mention. Nevertheless, I should like to do this in four cases. First, I would wish to acknowledge all the assistance and sustained encouragement received from Henry Venes, former Troop Sergeant of the 1st Airborne Reconnaissance Squadron. I should also like to thank Robert Voskuil for giving so much of his time to assist with the preparation of photographs, and Adrian Groeneweg, whose encyclopaedic knowledge of the Battle was stimulating and indispensable and whose enthusiasm for going over the ground with me was never flagging. Finally, to my wife, Marjorie, I should like to record a rather special word of thanks. Her commitment has, I feel, equalled my own and she has, throughout, been more of a partner than an assistant in the enterprise.

J. F.

INDEX

Numbers of maps are shown in bold type